Observing the User Experience

A Practitioner's Guide to User Research

Observing the User Experience

A Practitioner's Guide to User Research

Elizabeth Goodman
Mike Kuniavsky
Andrea Moed

ELSEVIER

AMSTERDAM • BOSTON • HEIDELBERG • LONDON • NEW YORK • OXFORD
PARIS • SAN DIEGO • SAN FRANCISCO • SINGAPORE • SYDNEY • TOKYO

Morgan Kaufmann is an imprint of Elsevier

Acquiring Editor: Meg Dunkerley
Development Editor: Heather Scherer
Project Manager: Andre Cuello
Designer: Joanne Blank

Morgan Kaufmann is an imprint of Elsevier
225 Wyman Street, Waltham, MA 02451, USA

Library of Congress Cataloging-in-Publication Data
Kuniavsky, Mike.
  Observing the user experience : a practitioner's guide to user research / Mike Kuniavsky, Elizabeth Goodman, Andrea Moed. -- 2nd ed.
  p. cm.
  Includes bibliographical references and index.
  ISBN 978-0-12-384869-7 (pbk.)
1. User-centered system design. 2. Observation (Scientific method) I. Goodman, Elizabeth, 1976- II. Moed, Andrea. III. Title.
  TA166.K86 2012
  004.2'1--dc23
                    2012014674

British Library Cataloguing-in-Publication Data
A catalogue record for this book is available from the British Library.

ISBN: 978-0-12-384869-7

For information on all MK publications
visit our website at http://store.elsevier.com

Printed in China
12 13 14 10 9 8 7 6 5 4 3 2 1

Biographies

Mike Kuniavsky is a user experience designer, researcher, and author. A 20-year veteran of digital product development, Mike is a consultant and the co-founder of several user experience-centered companies: ThingM manufactures products for ubiquitous computing and the Internet of Things; Adaptive Path is a well-known design consultancy. He is also the founder and organizer of Sketching in Hardware, an annual summit on the future of tools for digital product user experience design for leading technology developers, designers, and educators. Mike frequently writes and speaks on digital product and service design and works with product development groups in both large companies and startups. His most recent book is *Smart Things: Ubiquitous Computing User Experience Design*.

Andrea Moed believes that research is essential in designing to support human relationships. She has been a design researcher and strategist for over 15 years, observing users of websites, phones and other mobile devices, museums, retail environments, and educational and business software. She is currently the Staff User Researcher at Inflection, a technology company working to democratize access to public records. Andrea has master's degrees from the Interactive Telecommunications Program at New York University and the UC Berkeley School of Information and has taught at the Parsons School of Design in New York. Her writing on design and technology has appeared in a variety of publications.

Elizabeth Goodman's writing, design, and research focus on interaction design for mobile and ubiquitous computing. Elizabeth has taught user experience research at the University of California, Berkeley and site-specific art practice at the San Francisco Art Institute. As well, she has worked with exploratory user experience research teams at Intel, Fuji-Xerox, and Yahoo! Elizabeth speaks widely on the design of mobile and pervasive computing systems at conferences, schools, and businesses. She has a master's degree in interaction design from the Interactive Telecommunications Program at New York University. Her scholarly research on interaction design practice has been supported by a National Science Foundation Graduate Fellowship and an Intel Ph.D. Fellowship.

Contents

Preface

Why This Book?

Many people in digital product and service development never do user research. We often hear people say things like: "Putting a product in front of consumers will be expensive—and besides, we need to ship next month!" Or: "Usability research limits design creativity." And: "It's not even necessary because the developers are themselves part of the community of users and thus instinctively empathetic to what those other users find useful or usable." Finally: "And besides, [insert the name of famous company here] doesn't do it!"

You, clearly, think otherwise. You think it's important to know who is using the products you're making. And, you know, you're right. Finding out who your customers are, what they want, and what they need is the start of figuring out how to give it to them. Your customers are not you. They don't look like you, they don't think like you, they don't do the things that you do, they don't share your expectations, assumptions, and aspirations. If they did, they wouldn't be your customers; they'd be your competitors.

This book is designed to help you bridge the gap between what you think you know about your users and who they really are. It's not an academic treatise. It's a toolbox of concepts to understand how people experience products and services. The techniques—taken from the worlds of human-computer interaction, marketing, and many of the social sciences—help you know who your users are, to walk in their shoes for a bit.

In addition, the book is about the *business* of creating usable products. It acknowledges that product development exists within the complexities of a business venture, where the push and pull of real-world constraints do not always allow for an ideal solution. User research is a dirty business, full of complexities, uncertainties, and politics. This book will, if it serves its purpose, help you tame some of that chaos. It will help you gain some clarity and insight into how to make the world a little better by making products and services more thoughtfully.

Who Are You?

This book was written for people who are responsible, in some way, for their products' user experience. In today's digital product and service development world, this could be any number of people in the trenches. In fact, the responsibility may shift from person to person as a project progresses. Basically, if you've ever found yourself in a position where you are answering for how the end users are going to see the thing you're making, or how they're going to interact with it—or even what they're supposed to do with it—this book is for you.

This means that you could be:

- A program manager who wants to know how to prioritize a team's efforts
- A designer who needs to create and refine new ways to interact with and through digital information
- A marketing manager who wants to know what people find most valuable in your products
- An information architect who needs to pick an organizational scheme
- A programmer creating a user interface, trying to interpret an ambiguous spec
- A consultant trying to make your clients' products better
- An inventor who wants to make a product people will love

Regardless of your title, you're someone who wants to know how the people who use the product you're making perceive it, what they expect from it, what they need from it, and whether they can use what you've made for them.

What's in This Book?

This book is divided into three major sections. The first section (Chapters 1 through 4) describes why end user research is good, how business tensions tug at the user experience, and presents a philosophy for creating useful, desirable, usable, and successful products.

It also contains a short chapter on a technique that will teach you in 15 minutes everything you need to know to start doing usability research tomorrow. Really.

The second section (Chapters 5 through 16) is a cookbook with a dozen techniques for understanding people's needs, desires, and abilities. We have thoroughly updated this section for the second edition, adding new chapters and revising existing ones to reflect current best practices in 2012. Some of the chapters are completely self-contained, such as the chapters on surveys and usability tests. Others describe supplementary activities, such as collage and map making, to use in conjunction with other techniques. We don't expect you to read these chapters in one sitting, in order. Far from it! We assume that you will pick up the book when you need it, reading chapters to answer specific questions.

The third section (Chapters 17 through 19) describes how to take your results and use them to change how your company works. It gives you ideas about how to sell your company and how user-centered design can make your company run better and more profitably.

Best practices in research change quickly, as do preferred tools. We have moved much of the reference material in the previous edition to the book's website. Visit www.mkp.com/ observing-the-user-experience for the most up-to-date information on tools and tips, as well as template consent forms, checklists, reports, and other documents.

What's Not in This Book?

This book is, first and foremost, about defining problems. All the techniques are geared toward getting a better understanding of people and their problems. It's not about how to solve those problems. Sure, sometimes a good problem definition makes the solution obvious, but that's not the primary goal of this text.

We strongly believe that there are no hard and fast rules about what is right and what is wrong when designing experiences. Every product exists within a different context that defines what is "right" for it. A toy for preschoolers has a different set of constraints than a stock portfolio management application. Attempting to apply the same rules to both of them is absurd. That is why there are no guides for how to solve the problems that these techniques help you to define. There are no "top-10" lists, there are no "laws," and there are no universally reliable heuristics. Many excellent books have good ideas about how to solve interaction problems and astute compilations of solutions that are right much of the time, but this book isn't one of them.

Acknowledgments

We'd like to thank the companies who provided material, some previously unpublished, for case studies: Adaptive Path, Food on the Table, Get Satisfaction, Gotomedia, Lextant, MENA Design Research, PayPal, Portigal Consulting, User Insight, and Users Know. We would especially like to thank our reviewers: Todd Harple, Cyd Harrell, Tikva Morowati, and Wendy Owen. We'd also like to thank the people who have generously given us advice and help, including Elizabeth Churchill and Steve Portigal.

And, of course, our families, who put up with us throughout the very long writing and revision process.

PART I
Why Research Is Good and How It Fits into Product Development

CHAPTER 1

Introduction

User research is the process of figuring out how people interpret and use products and services. It is used everywhere from websites, to mobile phones, to consumer electronics, to medical equipment, to banking services, and beyond. Interviews, usability evaluations, surveys, and other forms of user research conducted before and during design can make the difference between a product or service that is useful, usable, and successful and one that's an unprofitable exercise in frustration for everyone involved. After a product hits the market, user research is a good way to figure out how to improve it, to build something new—or to transform the market altogether.

It may seem obvious that companies should ensure that people will use their products or services. But even industry giants can lose sight of this common-sense proposition. In a cross-industry study of 630 U.S. and UK executives by the consulting firm Accenture, 57% of the executives reported that "inability to meet customer needs" had resulted in failures of new products or services. Fifty percent further blamed the "lack of a new or unique customer-perceived value proposition."

As these executives learned the hard way, being first to market with a new product or service isn't enough. Companies need products that people desire, that fulfill human needs, and that people can actually use. After a product or service fails, getting a company back on track can take significant effort to reconnect with one's audience and integrate those understandings back into standard business processes. That means user research, as the iconic Danish toymaker LEGO discovered.

Learning from LEGO

In the 1980s and 1990s, the LEGO Group expanded in all directions. It introduced products, such as computer games, action figures, and television shows, that veered away from its famous core business of pop-together plastic pieces. It opened amusement parks and licensed its name to other companies. And it encouraged unfettered creativity in designer teams. One result was the futuristic restyling of its classic flagship, the LEGO City product line, and the creation of many complex new lines with specialized pieces.

Yet by the early 2000s, the LEGO Group was struggling. Recessions in major markets had hurt overall sales. It also didn't help that competitors had taken advantage of the LEGO Group's recently expired patents. But one of the company's biggest problems was that kids simply didn't like the new designs. Notably, some redesigned lines had crashed more than others. The City product line, for example, had generated about 13% of the company's *entire revenue* in 1999. Only a few years later, it accounted for only 3%. The line's profitability had "literally almost evaporated," an executive vice-president told business reporter Jay Greene. At the same time, manufacturing costs had skyrocketed. Instead of doing more with the components they already had, the new product lines had multiplied the number of expensive new components. With sales down and production costs up, the company was hemorrhaging money. The LEGO Group was losing almost $1 million every day. It was more than a crisis; it looked like a death knell for a beloved institution.

In 2004, a new CEO, Jørgen Vig Knudstorp, took a "back to basics" approach. He abandoned some of the new products—the amusement parks in particular—and returned to the core product: the plastic brick. Further, he demanded that designers cut the number of specialized components. But he also directed the company to pay more attention to its core constituency: kids. Knudstorp told *Businessweek*, "At first I actually said, let's not talk about strategy, let's talk about an action plan, to address the debt, to get the cash flow. But after that we did spend a lot of time on strategy, finding out what is LEGO's true identity. Things like, why do you exist? What makes you unique?"

To find out what made LEGO unique, Knudstorp turned to user research. Over the course of a year, LEGO sent user researchers— who they called "anthros"—to observe families around the world. These anthros focused on culture: the meanings that kids found in favorite possessions; how, where, and why they played; and differences in parenting and play styles across the regions where LEGO did most of its business: Asia, Europe, and the United States. They went to kids' homes and interviewed them, and then watched them play—not just with LEGO products, but with all kinds of objects.

Through its research, LEGO arrived at a renewed understanding of the meaning of play to children. Insights from the anthros' visits had emphasized the way that toys fit into kids' storytelling. Fire trucks didn't need to look outlandishly cool to be loved; they needed to fit into kids' existing stories about firefighters. Research also led to an enhanced appreciation of cultural differences in play. Japanese families, for example, tended to strictly separate education and play; selling LEGO products as "educational" blurred that difference for parents, making them unsuitable either as toys or as teaching devices. Boys in the United States, by contrast, were highly supervised most of the time. For them, playing with LEGO bricks was one of the few parent-approved activities that allowed unstructured time alone.

Most importantly, the LEGO design team re-evaluated the importance of difficulty. "You could say," wrote *Businessweek* reporter Brad Wieners, "a worn-out sneaker saved LEGO." In the early 2000s, the company had attributed its failures partially to the popularity of electronic games. But what did kids see in these games? For years, the company had believed that kids wanted a "plug and play" experience: easier roads to speedy success. So they simplified their models. The anthros came back from time spent with kids telling a different story.

The head of LEGO Concept Lab told *Businessweek*, "We asked an 11-year-old German boy, 'What is your favorite possession?' And he pointed to his shoes. But it wasn't the brand of shoe that made them special. When we asked him why these were so important to him, he showed us how they were worn on the side and bottom, and explained that his friends could tell from how they were worn down that he had mastered a certain style of skateboarding, even a specific trick." The boys they had met, like the German skater, were interested in experiences of "mastery": learning skills and, as with the worn-down sneaker, demonstrating that mastery to others. Through observing kids play and talking to them about their lives, LEGO designers realized that they had misunderstood what computer games *meant*.

In response, the designers went back to the drawing board. While obeying the mandate to reduce the number of different pieces, designers also worked with researchers to support experiences of mastery. Models might use fewer specialized components, but they could still be satisfyingly challenging. Instead of aiming for immediate gratification, the LEGO designers drew from notions of progression built into computer games: winning points, leveling up, and entering rankings. Designers also completely reworked their LEGO City line. Out with the futuristic styling, in with fire trucks that looked like, well, fire trucks.

But that's not the whole story, though it's a big part. At the same time, LEGO also turned its attention to a large group of devoted customers who hadn't strayed: adults. Each individual adult enthusiast spent far more on LEGO products in a year than most kids would ever spend in a lifetime. However, the company's revenue overall overwhelmingly came from kids—boys ages 7 to 12, to be exact. So most LEGO execs didn't see any reason to cultivate older customers (not to mention girls, but that's a different story). In fact, the company had notoriously kept adult fans at arms-length. Communicating with older fans could inspire new product ideas… and then invite lawsuits over the profits from those ideas. But the problem with adult fans for LEGO management wasn't just lawsuits. "The impression," Jake McKee, a former LEGO Group community manager, bluntly told a conference audience in 2009, "was that these guys are weird."

"And yes," McKee continued, "some of them *were* weird." But their exuberant love for LEGO kits, he pointed out, was bringing the struggling company a lot of positive attention. On their own initiative, adult fans built massive LEGO installations in shopping malls, attracting attention from tens of thousands of kids. Their efforts brought them stories on television and in newspapers. And on the Internet, grown-up, big-spending fans had built a thriving ecosystem of fan forums and marketplaces.

At first, the websites had taken the company aback. Tormod Askildsen, Head of Community Development at LEGO, told *Ericsson Business Review*, at first, "we didn't really like it and we were a bit concerned." McKee and other members of LEGO's community relations group decided to change that attitude. McKee and his group started by meeting adult fans where they were most comfortable: on online forums, at meetings, even at bars. They started with no budget and no permission, doing "the smallest thing we could get away with." Over time, they built a pilot program, developing long-term relationships with a few "LEGO Ambassadors" as eyes into the adult fan community. By 2005, they had come far enough to post requests for product suggestions on popular fan websites. In 2009, Askildsen said, "People from my team communicate with this group more or less on a daily basis, discussing different themes, ideas or to brainstorm." In the end, LEGO even hired adult fans as designers.

While championing a "back to basics" approach for kids, LEGO managers had learned enough from the adult fan community to add special products for them. First came the $500 Star Wars Millennium Falcon kit, which became extremely popular. In 2006, the company added the Modular Buildings line, a set of complex kits with sophisticated architectural details. Most importantly, LEGO began to take their adult fans seriously as a source of ideas and inspiration. "They realized they could use adults to influence kid fans, and kids to excite adult fans," said McKee. Today, the company even launches entirely fan-designed lines.

Besides controlling manufacturing costs, this strategy turned sales around. After the redesign, LEGO the City line was responsible for 20% of the company's revenue in 2008—regaining its original place and even exceeding it. The executive vice-president told Greene, "It has refound its identity." Between 2006 and 2010, company revenue increased 105%, growing even in downturns. "The fourth quarter of 2008 was a horror show for most companies," an industry analyst told *Time* magazine. "And LEGO sailed through like it was no problem." Revenue continued to grow in 2009 and 2010. In 2011, LEGO made $1 billion in the United States for the first time ever.

As the LEGO Group thrived, so did its commitment to user research. As well as integrating desk research, field visits, and expert interviews into their idea generation process for existing lines, the company sent out the anthros again for another project—this time, to develop new products for an audience the company had long ignored: girls.

By carefully observing and engaging with its users, the LEGO Group discovered ways to overcome its most daunting problems. User research showed the company how to redesign its products to delight its core audience of kids; how to build strong relationships with adult fans and make use of those relationships in marketing and product development; and how to control production costs even as it introduced new products. The most expert toymaker or management consultant in the world could not have told LEGO designers how to do these things. They had to learn it from their customers.

LEGO Lessons

The problems you and your company need to address might not be as all-encompassing as those faced by the LEGO Group, but the toymaker's story includes some important lessons for user experience research that we want to emphasize. The obvious lesson, of course, is that knowing your customers is important, and that it takes work! That shouldn't surprise anyone who's gotten this far into this book. But there are other, less obvious, points.

Don't Take Your Core Audience for Granted

Neither the LEGO Group's storied reputation as a children's toymaker nor a knowledge of child development theory could guarantee success with kids. Instead, the company had to re-engage with kids directly in order to revitalize its design strategy.

Look Beyond Your Mainstream or "Average" Users

The company gained inspiration from adult fans' creativity and enthusiasm. Moreover, they found new profits when they designed for the specific tastes of their adult fans, an audience they had previously ignored.

Research and Design Innovation Are Perfectly Compatible

There are some persistent myths about user research: that it stifles creativity; that it's only good for incremental improvements; that real advances only happen when technical innovation drives product development. In the case of the LEGO Group, none of that was true. After an investment into user research and outreach, LEGO didn't stop making new products—in fact, it continues to launch new "brick" product lines and new digital products based on research. The toymaker just systematically, and strategically, redirected its design efforts.

Research Insights Are Most Transformative When They Are Constructive

According to business reporter Brad Wieners, the company's research "shattered many of the assumptions" it had about kids' desire for easy success—but also replaced it with a new paradigm, that of "mastery." Instead of leaving their corporate clients empty-handed, the anthros introduced a new model of play to replace the one they discredited.

User Research Can Have Systemic Consequences

As Wieners writes, "So while it didn't take a genius or months of research to realize it might be a good idea to bring back the police station or fire engine that are at the heart of LEGO's most popular product line (LEGO City), the 'anthros' informed how the hook-and-ladder or motorcycle cop should be designed, packaged, and rolled out." Then, to make sure that they stayed connected to their customers, the company integrated early user research into their Innovation Model, a company-wide sequence of activities guiding new product development. User research typically drives nuts and bolts decisions about the object being made. But you get the most value from user research when all parts of the company take part in interpreting it, so that it impacts not just the design of the product, but also the design of the business itself.

And finally:

Research Needs Supporters

LEGO management didn't just send out researchers once; they integrated research activities into everyday business processes. The fate of research insights isn't under the control of researchers; it takes collaborative relationships across companies, and support from management, to influence product development.

In Conclusion

This book is about the knowledge that will help you create and sustain great product and service experiences. It will help you avoid situations like that faced by the LEGO Group while retaining and cultivating the creativity that leads to innovative, exciting, unique, and profitable products and services. It provides a collection of user experience research tools to help you explore how products and services can engage with people's desires and abilities.

Our philosophy is not about following strict procedures to predictable solutions. It's about defining (and redefining) specific problems and opportunities—and then creatively responding to them. The ultimate goal of these tools is not merely to make people happy; it's to make *successful products and services* by making people happy. With a set of tools to help figure out how people view the world, you are much more likely to create things that help people solve problems they really care about, in ways that delight and gratify them.

CHAPTER 2

Do a Usability Test *Now!*

Basic user research is easy, fast, and highly effective. Some forms can be done with any product. The question is whether you want to do it yourself. And there's only one way to find that out: try it. In this chapter, you will learn a fast and easy user research technique by doing a usability test with your friends and family. After 15 minutes of reading and a couple hours of listening, you will have a much better understanding of your customers and which parts of your product are difficult to use.

The *usability test* will tell you whether your audience can use what you've made. It helps identify problems people have with a specific interface and reveals difficult-to-complete tasks and confusing language. Normally, usability tests are done as part of a larger research project and involve extensive preparation and analysis. That's what Chapters 4 through 16 of this book are about. However, in the interest of presenting something that's quick and that provides good bang for the buck, here are two versions of a *friends and family usability test*. It's designed to let you get almost immediate feedback on an interface with minimal overhead. If you're reading this chapter in the morning, you could be talking to people by the end of the workday and rethinking some functionality by tomorrow. But give yourself a day or two to prepare if this is your first time conducting user research.

You will need some representation of an interface to take advantage of this technique. A working product or a semifunctional prototype will be easiest at this stage, but you can also ask people to evaluate a paper sketch.

If you don't have any interface representation handy, then it's a bit too early for you to try this out. You should use one of the research techniques that will help you start designing, such as interviews or a site visit. These are discussed in Chapters 6 and 9 of the book, respectively.

But if you just want to try out this technique and don't need it to apply to your own work immediately, you can use any interface that's already familiar to you—whether a website, a kiosk, or an appliance.

A Nano-usability Test

Here's the nano-size version of a guerrilla usability test. This summary will get you started in less than a minute, not counting the time you spend reading this paragraph. Yes, you'll get closer to a "real" usability evaluation with the 15-minute model. But follow these five steps to get an immediate taste of user research:

1. Find *one* person who cares about your product. It doesn't matter who.
2. Arrange to watch them use that product. Go to their house; meet at a café; use screen sharing. It doesn't really matter, as long as you can clearly see what they're doing.
3. Ask them to use the product to do something they care about: contact a friend; cook dinner; buy something. Whatever.
4. Final step: watch them do it. Don't ask questions. Don't tell them what to do. Don't say anything. Just watch.
5. Ask yourself: what did you learn?

    And…you're done!

You may be wondering: that's it? That's all there is to usability? Why do consultancies charge so much money for it, then? Actually, no. There's a lot more science, craft, and art to usability than we can get across in under a minute. But usability isn't brain surgery, and it's important to realize that anyone can start practicing the basics in under a minute.

A Micro-usability Test

The micro-usability test, which we'll explain below, is closer to what a full-fledged usability evaluation would look like. Try this after trying the nano-usability test, or if you've got some more time to spare. It'll still take you less than 15 minutes to figure it out.

There are four major steps in the process of conducting a usability test.

1. Define the audience and their goals.
2. Create tasks that address those goals.

3. Get the right people.
4. Watch them try to perform the tasks.

Define the Audience and Their Goals

An evaluation always proceeds from 'why does this thing exist?'
Dave Hendry, Associate Professor, University of Washington Information School

You are making something for some reason. You have decided that some people in the world can make their lives better with your idea. Maybe it helps them buy something cheaper. Maybe it's to get them information they wouldn't have otherwise. Maybe it helps them connect with other people. Maybe it entertains them.

Regardless, you are making something that you feel a specific group of people will find valuable. For them to get that value, there's something they have to do. Usually, it's several things. For a website selling something, it can be "Find the widget, buy it, and subscribe to the newsletter." For a matchmaking site, it can be "Find someone interesting, write him a note, and send it."

So the first thing you should do in a usability test is to figure out whom the site is for. What nouns and adjectives describe the people who you expect will use it most often? What differentiates them from everyone else? Is it their age, their interests, their problems? It's probably all of the above, and more.

For example, say that you want to examine the usability of the browsing and purchasing user experience of an online cutlery store. You can quickly create an audience definition for the site's audience.

People who want to buy cutlery.

But this isn't very specific. My grandmother regularly buys plastic forks for family picnics, but she's not going to be doing it through a website. So the definition should have a little more detail.

The target user audience are people who
•   Want to buy high-end cutlery
•   Are value conscious

- Want a broad selection
- Shop online
- Are not professional cutlery buyers

Next, figure out what the key product features are. Write down what your product is about. Why are people going to use it? Why is it valuable to its users? If you were at a loud party and had 30 seconds to describe your site to someone who had never heard of it, what you would tell them? Write it down.

> forkopolis.com enables people all over North America to buy cutlery from one of the largest ranges available, featuring all the major luxury brands and the best designers. It allows for easy location of specific styles and pieces so that buyers can quickly and cheaply replace a single damaged teaspoon or buy a whole restaurant's worth of silverware.

Create Tasks That Address Those Goals

Now write down the five most important functions of the site. What should people be able to do above all else? In a sales site, they should obviously be able to purchase things. But they should also be able to find them, whether or not they know exactly what they're trying to buy. Furthermore, they should probably be able to find what's on sale and what's an especially good value. Make a list, describing each function with a sentence or two.

> Find specific items by style.
> Buy by single item.
> Buy by whole setting.
> Find special offers.
> Find information on returning merchandise.

In a couple of sentences describe a situation where someone would perform that function, written from his or her perspective. Call this a *task*. If "Find specific items by style" is one of the functions, a task for it would be the following:

> You decided that you want to buy a set of Louis XIV forks from forkopolis.com. Starting from the homepage of forkopolis, find a set of Louis XIV forks.

Finally, order the tasks from the easiest to the hardest. Starting with an easy task makes people comfortable with the product and the process.

Get the Right People

Now, find some people who fit the profile you created in step 1. When doing a quick exercise like this, you can get a decent idea of the kinds of problems and misunderstandings that occur with real users by bringing in five or six people who resemble the people you expect will be interested in your product. The fastest way to get such people is through the people you already know. If you're in a large company, this could be co-workers from departments that have nothing to do with your product. If you're in a small company, this can be your friends and family and your co-workers' friends and families. It can be people from the office down the hall. It can be people off the street. As long as they're somewhat like the people you expect to visit your site, it can be anybody who is unfamiliar with the product and unbiased toward it (so a doting grandmother and the CEO of your biggest competitor are probably excluded). Unless your product is designed for developers, avoid people who design or market digital products and services for a living: they know too much.

Contact these people, telling them that you'd like to have them help you evaluate the effectiveness of a product you're working on. Don't tell them any more about it than the short description you wrote at the top of the task list. Tell them that no preparation is needed, that they should just come in. Schedule them a day or two in advance for half-hour individual interviews, leaving 15 minutes in between each interview.

Watch Them Try to Perform the Tasks

First, write a script that you and your invited evaluators will follow. Put your short site description at the top of the page. This will be all that the evaluators will be told about your product. Don't tell them anything else. In the real world, a short description and a link are often all that someone will know. On separate pages, write down your tasks, one per page. Don't include any information that users wouldn't have if they had just started using the service.

Now find a quiet place where you and the evaluators can talk about the product without being distracted. Small, out-of-the-way conference rooms often work well. Make sure that there is nothing related to the product around, so as not to distract the evaluators or provide information that could be confusing. Thus, no notes, no company propaganda posters, no whiteboard leftovers, and no tradeshow mouse pads.

Set up whatever device you're using for the tasks. For example, if you're using a web browser, set it up in the most generic configuration possible, removing custom toolbars, custom colors, display options, and extraneous bookmarks. Bookmark or otherwise mark the initial pages or locations evaluators are going to need for each of the scenarios you've written. You might even want to create a new user account for the test so that your own settings don't confuse the participant. If you're using paper sketches, make sure they're well-organized.

When each participant arrives, prepare him or her for what's going to happen. Make the participants feel comfortable. Introduce the process by saying something like:

- You've been invited to help us understand which parts of the product work for you and which are confusing.
- Even though we're calling this activity a usability test, you're not being tested. The product is. There's *nothing* you can do wrong. It's not your fault if you can't get something to work, and you won't hurt anyone's feelings if you say something bad about the product.
- It's really important that you speak all of your thoughts aloud. Think of it like a "play-by-play" description of what you're doing and why you're doing it.
- I'll stay in the same room and quietly take notes, but you should ignore me. Just focus on describing what you're doing.

You'll probably want to write a script that has all these points in it, but don't stick to the script when you're talking with participants. You'll sound stiff and uncomfortable. Instead, practice it ahead of time so that you feel—and sound—conversational and friendly.

Once the participants are comfortable and you've given them the initial instructions, read the product description and the sheets with the task descriptions. Tell them to do the tasks in the best way they can, but if they can't figure one out in a couple of minutes, they should feel free to move on to the next task. Reinforce that they should be speaking aloud the whole time.

Then, let them talk. Sit back and watch, quietly taking notes. If they get stuck, don't tell them where to click or what to look at. No matter what, don't tell them how to do something. If they seem to be particularly frustrated, tell them that it's not their fault if something seems impossible, and they should move on to the next task. You may have to remind them to keep talking.

Once all the tasks have been completed, or the half hour is over, it's time to stop. Ask the participants to tell you their general impression and whether they would use the site in "real life." Then give them a present for their time (a gift certificate to a local restaurant or a bookstore, a coupon for lunch at the company cafeteria, a tank of gas—whatever seems appropriate for your audience), thank them, and send them on their way. Your co-workers probably don't need anything but a promise to help them out later.

Finally, reset the device for the next participant. If you're using a web browser, be sure to clear the cache and history and set it to a blank page.

What Did You Learn?

As soon as the usability test is over, ask yourself the following questions:

- What worked well? What didn't?
- Did the users consistently misunderstand anything? If so, what?
- Were there any consistent mistakes? If so, what?
- Did they do what you expected them to do? If not, what did they do?
- Did they do things in the order in which you had expected? If not, what order did they do them in?
- What did they find interesting?

- What did you expect them to find interesting that they did not find interesting? And vice versa: what did you expect them to ignore that they found fascinating?
- Did they know what the product was for? Did they miss any big ideas?
- How many of the tasks were they able to do? Which ones gave them trouble?
- When did they look frustrated? Confused? What were they doing?
- Did the site meet their expectations? If not, where did it fail them?
- Do you know what their expectations were?

At this point, you should have some ideas of where your product has problems. You've probably seen several things come up again and again. Maybe people don't understand the name you've given to a certain function. Maybe they don't see a critical idea. Maybe they aren't interested in what's being offered. Maybe they love it and it fulfills everything they want. All these things are good to know, since they tell you where you are having problems and, equally important, where you're not.

Now that you have a sense of how outsiders view your product, you can begin to think about what that data means for your relationships inside your organization.

- Did you confirm the existence of a problem you suspected? What do you need to do to fix the problem?
- Did something you learned contradict your beliefs about the product? Is anyone in your organization making decisions based on those same beliefs? Do you need to communicate that new learning to other people? How might you investigate that belief further, and what resources would you need?
- Did something puzzle you? Who can you work with to figure out what's going on and how to respond to it?

Friends and family usability testing is fast, easy, and convenient, but it's only a quick and dirty technique. Your friends and family may give you a general idea of the problems with your product, but (more often than not) they're not representatives of your *actual* user audience. Whenever possible, use participants who are more representative of your audience.

What to Do Next

With a first usability test completed, you probably have an idea of what the technique is good for and how it's useful to you. If you read Chapters 3 and 4, you should be able to put together a research plan for your product, incorporating discount usability testing (which the friends and family usability test is an example of) and a number of other techniques. The in-depth techniques described in Chapters 5 through 16 will tell you how to go far beyond this basic test. Finally, Chapters 17 through 19 will help you present your findings in a way that convinces development teams, clients, and other stakeholders to make the changes that will make your product or service really work for your audience, and to keep directing it toward users' activities, values, and aspirations well into the future.

CHAPTER 3

Balancing Needs through Iterative Development

In a perfect world, product development processes would only be about making the user happy. All software (and hardware, and music players, and cars and pretty much anything with a human interface) would focus on helping people lead more satisfying lives.

But the world is far from ideal. Finding a single perfect way of doing any task is unlikely. Even ideal user solutions do not always make ideal products. Moreover, products are generally not created solely for the benefit of their users: They are created by companies in order to make money. (Nonprofits are, of course, not primarily interested in making money. But even nonprofits need to stay financially viable and meet their other organizational goals that are not purely altruistic.) Making money and satisfying people's needs are two very different goals; they can be made to work together, but they will always be distinct. Adding communal goals, such as supporting environmental sustainability, doing political advocacy, or promoting public health, can lead to a "double bottom line" for the company and hence another tension.

This book focuses on understanding the user experience and will not dwell too much on either corporate profitability or communal goods. Nevertheless, it is critical to keep this and other tugs of war in mind and to consider how your organization has resolved them in the past.

Later in this chapter we present a method for resolving these tensions, but first it's useful to look at what makes a product a success when examined from the perspective of each group.

Success for End Users Is...

A product's end-user experience is the cornerstone to its success. A good user experience doesn't guarantee success, but a bad one nearly always leads quickly to failure. Experience quality is not binary—total malfunction is rare. But, surprisingly, mediocrity in user experience can actually be worse than complete failure. When something doesn't work at all, at least it's obvious where the problem lies. Intermittent problems—a shopping cart with a high dropout rate or a search engine that finds what you're looking for only 40% of the time—can make a product underperform even if the rest is perfectly designed. Worst, a mediocre user experience can go unnoticed and yet be the most serious problem in the whole business venture.

What makes a good experience varies from person to person, product to product, and task to task, but a good starting point is "usability." Something is usable if it's functional, efficient, and desirable to its intended audience.

Don Norman has some beautiful examples of unusable products in his book The Design of Everyday Things. *His examples illustrate that although we may not always know what makes a product usable, we can really tell when it's not.*

...Functionality

A product—or a portion of a product—is functional if the people using it consider it useful. Users expect each product to do a set of things. To be considered useful, it needs to be able to do them. This is a simple idea, but often forgotten. For example, as of this book's publication, Microsoft's Outlook Express email program does not have built-in spell check functionality. Not unreasonably, many people see Outlook Express as essentially a word processor. This absence of a standard word processing feature—and the effort of doing tech support for an external spell checker—can come as an unpleasant surprise.

More commonly, the complexity or incomprehensibility of the interface conceals key features. The classic example is programmable video recorders before the advent of screen-based interfaces: The functionality was so difficult to access that it may as well have not been included in the product at all.

...Efficiency

It's hard to capture what creates the surprise and satisfaction that comes from using something that works well, but it's definitely part of the best product designs. People—on the whole—value their time, and so speed and ease of operation are important. The traditional perspective measures how quickly someone can perform a task in a given situation with the smallest number of errors. Efficiency might not always be the most appropriate metric—consider games, toys, or other ways to have fun—but in general, your job is to help people spend more time on things they enjoy, and less on what they don't.

...Desirability

Although long recognized by marketers, usability specialists, and designers, desirability is the least tangible aspect of a good user experience. Desire—imagined pleasure and happiness in using a product—is an emotional response to an interaction of multiple factors: the product's "look and feel," the messages put out by marketers, and the cultural web of meanings in which material qualities and marketing messages come to "make sense" to us. Learning to navigate that web is an important step toward making desirable products.

Usability and Design

Ultimately, usability is good design. That's not to say that all good design is usable, since there are things that are well designed from one facet (identity, technology, value, etc.) that are not usable. For example, a lot of expensive designer furniture is beautiful and instantly identifiable, but often you can't put many books on the bookshelves or sit comfortably in the chairs. Similarly, the Unix operating system is incredibly elegant and powerful, but requires years of practice and memorization before any but the most basic functions are usable. In the end, despite all marketing efforts, products that are hard to use are likely to not get used—except by those incentivized to make the effort required for expertise. People faced with an unusable product will most likely be unable to do what they need to do, unable to do it quickly enough, or unhappy as they do it.

There are, of course, exceptions. Occasionally, a product will be unique (like Unix), and people will excuse usability problems for the sake of functionality. Medical records systems are a good example: They can be incredibly hard to use, but they need to maintain high standards of reliability, security, and robustness.

Moreover, the clinicians who use them are legally obligated to avoid careless mistakes. However, those situations are few and far between. In almost all other cases, the usability of a product is critical to its success.

Success for the Company Is...

With few exceptions, companies don't invest in product development to lose money or to remain anonymous. Two primary ways that companies measure the success of a product is through profit or promotion for the company. A third, social good, is increasingly in play.

...Profit

Though sometimes forgotten for a while in the heat of enthusiasm, the fundamental purpose when creating a product, whether it's a website or a fork, is to make money. Maybe it won't make money immediately, but few things are designed to lose money. Unfortunately, the desires of users and the business model don't always harmonize. And in those cases, user research must often mediate a compromise. When buying a product or subscribing to a service, that conflict only involves the company and the user. The user either pays once to own a thing or pays periodically to renew a subscription. But advertising-based businesses introduce another important actor: the advertiser.

Success for Advertisers Is...

Many products and services don't rely on advertising for revenue. Still, it would be naïve to deny that ads—and, therefore, advertisers—pervade our lives. However, until the web they were a minor part of our experience with software. Word processors in the 1980s didn't have commercials. Spreadsheets weren't co-sponsored. Killing a monster in Zork didn't get you frequent flier points on United. Today, ads are everywhere on the desktop and mobile web, from splashy multimedia on big websites to "sponsored tweets" in a Twitter feed, to location-based ads in mobile apps (Figure 3.1).

Not only are there endless numbers of advertising formats, but there are also many technologies for customizing the advertising

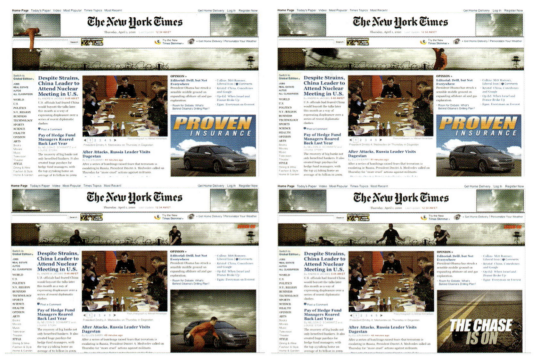

Figure 3.1 A multiposition "takeover" ad with video. Here, in the Visionaire Group's ad for *The Fugitive* on *The New York Times*' website, a coordinated video sequence of a man in an orange suit climbing from the banner ad on top to the square one in the lower right hand corner eventually plays on every advertising spot on the screen. Advertising online can be as noticeable as anything on TV (or as subtle as a few words of text).

See Chapter 16 for more on analyzing automatically collected data about online user behavior.

to its surrounding context and to the user. To make these work, software routinely collects information on users to serve them ads by demographics, geography, or even their previous activity in the system. The user is supposed to notice ads, act on them, and remember them. While tracking software and ads are also parts of the user experience, they largely serve the needs of advertisers.

Advertising revenue creates another business relationship that permeates the development process. In the end, advertisers primarily care about the effectiveness of their advertising for their chosen market. They may be willing to wait for an ad campaign's popularity to grow, or interested in how good end-user experience could positively affect people's perceptions of the product or company, but ultimately advertisers want to know how much revenue a given ad deal will drive.

...Promotion

Commodity products like nails or garden hoses don't usually carry a lot of corporate branding, while in designer clothing, professional sports, and yes, almost all websites, the company's identity is prominent and ever-present. As online experiences expand beyond the desktop web to mobile devices, Internet appliances, and environments, branding and promotion follow and become normal in each new context. For example, until recently, smart phone applications did not showcase companies other than the cellular service provider. Branded "apps" on the Apple iPhone changed that; many Android apps carry advertising of their own, adding more layers of branding and promotion.

Regardless of context, a product must do several things to survive: It needs to be different, recognizable, and memorable, and it needs to communicate its function. Designing purely for these things will result in a product that is all surface glitter with no substance, but ignoring them is equally dangerous.

Individuality is important for products. It's important to differentiate a product from competitors by features, layout, size, color, editorial tone, or something else important (even usability!). The photo-sharing service Flickr (Figure 3.2) wanted no extraneous

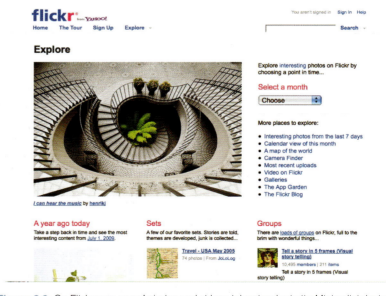

Figure 3.2 On Flickr.com, users' photos and videos take visual priority. Minimalist design, distinctive logotypes, and header colors convey the site's identity.

visuals to distract from the photos. It became known for a clean design with little branding save a logotype and iconic cyan and magenta colors. The Flip HD camera uploaded movies to a PC using a flip-up USB connector instead of an easily lost cable. The TiVo digital video recorder made an unusual but strangely appropriate sound during fast-forwarding. All these made these products easy to remember and quickly recognize.

Finally, there's *tone,* the "spirit" of the product. *The New York Times* website doesn't look exactly like a newspaper (it's not as big, it doesn't have ink smudges, the headlines are placed differently, there are ads in the corners), but it communicates enough "newspaperness" through layout and typeface to be almost instantly recognizable as such. Similarly, skateboarding sites look much more like skateboarding magazines than newspapers. For a long time, Google's simple web page defined the look of a search engine, so that now users can easily recognize search engines embedded in browser toolbars, mobile applications, and other software interfaces, leading them to do more searches (Figure 3.3).

Self-promotion does little to the immediate measurable bottom-line profitability of the product and the company, but it is still a key element in what makes a successful product.

Open-Source Product Development

The Internet has enabled people to collaborate in doing all sorts of things, and one of them is product development. Linux, Wikipedia, and the Firefox web browser are all examples of widely used products that were created by self-organized, loosely connected teams of developers, often working without pay, who made their product and its underlying code freely available. Unlike companies, these organizations often create products primarily for reasons beyond profit or promotion.

In many cases, open-source teams build products that they themselves would like to use, but that they have been unable to find in the marketplace. Iterative development can be highly beneficial in these cases, but user research is often not included in the early stages of these projects because the users are the creators

Figure 3.3 Google's interface, circa 2001 (a) … and circa 2010 (b). Samsung Nexus S image courtesy of Samsung.

themselves, and they may have a sufficiently good sense of their own needs and wishes to build at least an initial version of the product. (Indeed, if any of them desire something different, they are free to modify the product themselves.)

If the product becomes successful, however, it is likely to attract users who are different from its initial developers—in their technical expertise, in their applications of the product, or in the amount of time they are willing to spend tinkering with it. When this occurs, user research becomes necessary for the product's continued growth. More centrally organized projects can use any funding they have to hire user researchers (see the Wikipedia case study in Chapter 11) and implement the results.

The problem for many open-source projects is that that there is no central organizing body to guarantee that research results will influence development. Since open-source development is often volunteer, and user researchers often don't write code, recommendations languish because none of the volunteers are interested in working on them. There may even be resentment of what researcher Rashmi Sinha has called "drive-by" volunteering: researchers who do a quick study and then disappear, leaving developers with a long to-do list and no support.

There are no automatic solutions to these challenges. Open-source projects require both initiative and long-term commitment. If you're an open-source developer, one way to change this situation is to learn more about user research and start doing it yourself. If you're a user researcher and think open-source projects should be easier to use, find a project and get involved.

A System of Balance: Iterative Development

When listed, the complexity of interaction between these elements can be daunting. Compared to the quick and easy usability test in Chapter 2, it can seem like suddenly going from making ice cubes to trying to catch all the snowflakes in a blizzard. What's needed is a systematic way of integrating the process of finding the problems and creating solutions, focusing on individual elements without losing sight of the whole. That's where iterative development comes in.

Iterative development works by continual refinement through trial and error. Rather than trying to create a perfect vision from the beginning, iterative development hones in on the target, refining its focus and improving the product until it has reached its goal. Each cycle consists of the same basic steps, and each cycle infuses the process with richer information. Solutions are created, examined, and recreated until the business and user needs are met in a consistent and regular way.

How Iterative Development *Doesn't* Work

Before planned iterative development grew in popularity, the popular development styles (which many companies still use) were corporate edict and the waterfall method.

Corporate edict is where someone, or some group, decides what's going to be done and then the rest of the company builds it. No questions asked. The method suffers because the people issuing the proclamations aren't omniscient. If the chief architect (or whoever is giving orders) doesn't know everything about the business climate, the users, the needs of business partners, and the capabilities of the technology, the product is likely to miss its mark, sometimes spectacularly.

A real-life example: The CEO of a popular digital greeting card company had a favorite card that he liked to send to his friends. After a complete redesign of the site, he had a hard time finding the card. Thinking that this would be a problem for many of the system's users, he insisted that the development team create a search engine for the service. The company spent several months developing a full-featured search engine for the site, which allowed the CEO to find his favorite card quickly and in a number of different ways. Unfortunately, the search engine hardly got any use. After some research, it turned out that many people didn't feel the need to find and re-use a favorite card. They were happy browsing a general category of similar cards. Restructuring the information architecture to match people's expectations for greeting cards resulted in a much larger increase in the use of the site (and ad revenue) than did the search engine. It required fewer resources and much less time as well. In creating the feature by edict, the company misunderstood their core strength and lost several months of developer time in the process.

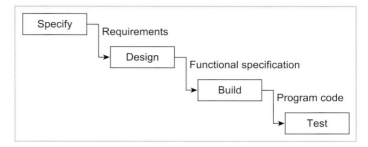

Figure 3.4 The waterfall method.

The waterfall method (Figure 3.4), although less arbitrary, has its own problems. Working as an assembly line, practitioners first create an extensive requirements document that specifies every detail of the final product. Maybe the requirements are based on the target audience's real needs and capabilities, but there's a good chance they are a collection of the document authors' gut-level guesses and closed-door debate. What if those assumptions are wrong? Or what if the company's needs change? Even with built-in feedback, the rigid waterfall method allows little backtracking, just as a waterfall rarely allows water to flow up. When backtracking becomes necessary—as almost always happens—the rigidity of the model almost guarantees that it'll be expensive.

Both of these methods share an Achilles' heel: They lack built-in sanity-checking steps that modify assumptions to match the reality of the environment. They depend on correct assumptions and complete data. If the initial ideas are even a bit off, then the end product is at risk of providing the wrong solution to the wrong people at the wrong time.

The Iterative Spiral

Iterative development methods have existed for years in large-scale software and manufacturing sectors. They carry many names: rapid application development, rational unified process, total quality management, joint application development, and the evolutionary life cycle, to name a few. Although the specific details of these methods vary quite a bit, they share the underlying idea of

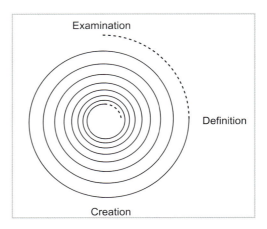

Figure 3.5 Iterative development: The final product is at the center, and the development orbits it, adjusting as it goes along.

progressive refinement through cyclical data-driven development, and although they may describe the iteration with five or more steps, the core ideas behind them can be summarized in three basic stages (Figure 3.5).

1. *Examination.* This step attempts to define the problems and whom they affect. Questions are raised, needs are analyzed, information is collected, research is conducted, and potential solutions are evaluated. Strengths and weaknesses are enumerated and prioritized. Customers' needs and their capabilities are studied, and existing products or prototypes are evaluated. For example, maybe the company extranet is bringing in new customers, but the support mailbox is always full of messages from people who can't seem to find what they're looking for. Maybe there's a usability issue in the interface, but it could also be that a fundamental service is missing or that the user population isn't the one that had been expected.

2. *Definition.* Solutions are specified. Maybe the extranet's support mail is pointing to a fundamental feature that's missing from the product. At this stage, changes in the product are mapped out with ever-greater detail as additional

information about the real needs and capabilities of the target audience is uncovered.

3. *Creation*. Solution plans are carried out. Since it's the most expensive and time-consuming phase (taking as much as half of the development time), if the work done in the creation stage is not backed by data collected during the examination phase and by careful planning in the definition phase, much of it could be wasted.

So far, this resembles the waterfall method, but what makes iterative development different from that assembly line is that creation is immediately followed by another cycle, beginning with examination. Each cycle—and there may be many cycles between initial examination and launch—isn't expected to produce a complete product, but add to the quality of understanding and to flesh out the feature set. Thus, the project adapts with every iteration, making the process thorough and responsive to new information and to changes in the business environment. This, in theory, minimizes unnecessary development while making products that are more in tune with what people need.

These ideas are indebted to Barry Boehm's "Spiral Development" method, which he introduced in the May 1988 issue of Computer magazine.

Benefits of Iterative Development

Flexibility

All the constraints on a project are never known at the beginning. The process of development uncovers the needs of the audience and the company, as well as the capacities and limitations of the technology. Dependent on their initial conditions, edict and waterfall processes are brittle and susceptible to breakage when conditions change.

Iterative methods can put flexibility where it's most needed, leaving room for change at the beginning of the project by locking in only the things known to be reasonable solutions. Initially, the product is rough, but there are lots of things that can be changed, and there are still many fundamental questions that need to be answered. As the process continues, the questions get answered, the details get filled in, the prototypes start looking more like the completed product, and the flexibility of the process goes down.

Adaptability

Every design is a trade-off. Or, more accurately, the design and production of any complicated product involve making a lot of trade-offs. Big, fast cars can't be as fuel efficient as smaller, less powerful ones. If this book had larger type, it would have to have more pages. Some choices move the product in a direction where it will be more usable by a certain group of people, some choices move it in a direction that will bring in more money, some choices will make it more desirable. The ideal choice moves it in all three directions at once, but that's not always possible.

Knowing how to make the right trade-offs is difficult. Like a new organism evolving on an island, an idea isolated in a company is exposed to certain environmental conditions. It only has to face a certain number of predators, deal with a certain kind of climate, adapt to certain kinds of diseases. The only way to know whether an idea will survive outside its sheltered world is to expose it to the environment in which it will ultimately have to live. However, rather than the shock of the waterfall method—where the final product is pushed out into the big bad world and left to fend for itself—iterative development attempts to understand the environment and predict how the idea needs to adapt in order to flourish before it is released into the wild.

Shared Vision

In addition to creating good products, iterative development can focus the whole company on continually improving the user's experience and company profitability. The focus is no longer on creating a series of single, one-off products; it's about evolving a set of tools and techniques to respond to the needs of your clients and your company, no matter what those needs are or how they change. Later in this book, we'll discuss how tools such as personas—realistic representations of fictional potential users—and scenarios of future use can unify teams behind a shared vision.

Iteration can easily apply to marketing the product, designing its identity, developing its business objectives, or creating a support system for it. For greatest effect, everyone who has responsibility for

Throughout this book, we use the term development team. By this, we mean the group of people who are responsible for creating and maintaining a product.

Depending on company structure, this group could include representatives from many different disciplines. In the case of open-source software development, no one on the team may have management-defined roles.

Some development teams are actually product teams, responsible for all aspects of the product. Such groups could include visual designers, business strategists, market researchers, quality assurance engineers, and so on.

From our perspective, these are all development teams, even if the majority of the staff don't write code or design screen layouts.

the product—engineering, marketing, information architecture, design, business development, customer support—should be part of a single iterative development process. Everyone needs to iterate through the process along with the core development team, sharing information and improving the product with every turn. For example, after the initial market has been determined, marketing can be researching the size and composition of market segments in conjunction with the development teams' research into the nature of the work and the audience's work habits. These two sets of information can be combined to produce a set of desired features, which can be used by business development to look for potential partners to provide or enhance those features, or for large clients who would be especially interested in those features.

Not only can the whole company develop the product identity together, but using the same research methods reduces the need to alter plans after the product launch by taking into account the changing needs of all facets of the organization. In treating the product as a system of solutions developed over time, rather than as a single release, the business uses its resources strategically, planning for the long term while reacting to short-term developments.

Iterative development is especially appropriate for Internet-based products since prototypes can be made and evaluated quickly. Sculpturally, it's like working with plaster, clay, or wax. Changes can be put into effect rapidly, and release cycles can be arbitrarily tight. In the interest of rapid response, one search engine goes through a full iteration every week. Unlike traditional software, the immediate user experience presented by an online product is critical. The threat of instant abandonment doesn't hang over every moment a desktop application is in use. Since the user (or the company) has paid for the software in order to use it for extended periods of time, there is an incentive to make the software work. Such stability and loyalty are luxuries few online products enjoy. For the rest, the user experience needs to be right from the start.

Iterative Development Problems

Despite its benefits, iterative development isn't perfect. It creates a lot of uncertainty throughout the process, which can be frustrating to a development team that wants to be able to delve deeply into feature development. It requires discipline and dedicated project management because it can be a complex process that requires every iteration to focus on a subset of the product, when other glaring problems may be screaming for attention. It can require backtracking to review earlier assumptions, which may extend development time. Mostly, though, the biggest difficulty in implementing iterative development is creating a company culture—from the CEO to marketing to customer service—that understands the process and integrates it into the way the company works.

Where User Research Fits In

Iterative Development

User experience research need not be a part of iterative development. Iterative development can happen without any user research (for example, Agile and Extreme Programming processes are highly iterative, but don't explicitly make a place for research). But the two work especially well together, where the results of one research project can answer questions asked by the ones before it and guide those that come after.

User research provides a consistent, rapid, controlled, and thorough method of examining the users' perspective. It appears at every rotation through the development spiral, with different techniques appropriate at different times in a product's development. Figure 3.6 depicts how specific user research techniques might fit into an iterative development spiral (the specific techniques will be discussed later in the book).

Waterfall Development

Obviously, we favor iterative development processes. However, if your company uses a waterfall method, there's no reason you can't use the techniques outlined in this book. In a waterfall process, user research typically happens at the beginning and end—before the requirements are written, and then after some code is written. The

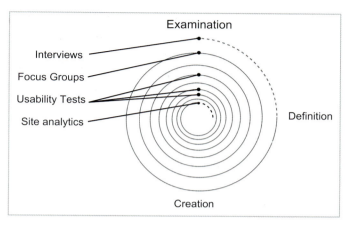

Figure 3.6 A sample research program in an iterative development process.

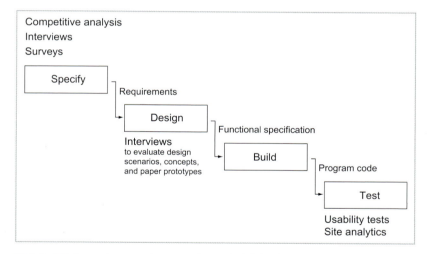

Figure 3.7 A sample research program in a waterfall development process.

first rounds of user research inform the requirements, and the last evaluate either a working prototype or a finished product.

Because so much depends on getting the requirements right, waterfall processes should include more early research activities (see Figure 3.7). One way to make the process a little more iterative is to schedule interviews or focus groups during the design stage to discuss design scenarios, concepts, or even paper proto-types. Since implementation has not begun, you may be able to get development teams to make changes based on feedback from engagement with potential users.

Example: A Scheduling Service

Here is a simplified and idealized example of how an iterative development process could work, based on a hypothetical product. In most cases, things never go this smoothly, but it's useful to see how things could be.

Suppose your company wanted to make a web-based appointment-scheduling product because some easily adaptable backend technology had been developed.

Cycle 1

Examination

Your initial assumption is that the target audience will be people who are very busy and who travel a lot, so they need a sophisticated sched-uling package that's easily accessible. Revenue will come from ads sold on the service and a subscription service for advanced features.

In your first round of research, you visit a number of busy people and observe them as they manage their schedules (a form of observational research, as described in Chapter 9). You discover that busy people are fairly comfortable with existing technologies (Microsoft Outlook, paper calendars, etc.) for scheduling their work lives, and they're generally unwilling to change to a new technology unless it's much more useful than what they currently use. They would rather not be the early adopters of a new technol-ogy unless they knew it was worthwhile and would be adopted by their colleagues. They seem apprehensive about the reliability of the service, and the Internet as a whole, saying that a down connec-tion on a busy day could be disastrous.

Put bluntly, this means that your target market isn't interested in your product unless it blows away what's there already. This limits its appeal to a segment of the market that will be unlikely to bring in enough revenue to offset development costs. One option is to look for a larger market for the product (maybe students), but let's say you decide to follow the original market but with a different tack. Several people you spoke with expressed interest in scheduling solutions for their personal life rather than their work life (which seems to be already covered). Your results reveal that, for this audience:

- Their personal schedules are almost as complicated as their work schedules.
- They need to share their personal schedules with friends and family.
- They can't use their office software because it isn't available outside the firewall, and their family and friends aren't likely to have access to it.
- They see existing scheduling software as entirely focused on business scheduling tasks.

Definition

Realizing this, you decide to stay with your target audience of busy execs, but you modify your idea to better fit their lifestyles. You change the focus of the functionality to personal shared schedules, rewriting the product description with goals that all focus on helping people share schedules in a way that's significantly better than their current methods. The description defines in detail the problems that the software needs to solve and explicitly lists problems that are outside its purpose (or scope, using the project management term). Simultaneously, you redirect the marketing and identity efforts to concentrate on the personal nature of the service.

Creation

Using the new problem definition, you rewrite the product description to reflect the new purpose for the scheduling application and the new knowledge you have of the audience's needs. The bulk of this phase is spent creating a detailed listing of the features that the product provides and the benefits it offers. You vet this list with the engineering team, making sure that the features proposed are within the capabilities of the software. In addition, you create a tentative research plan, outlining the questions that need to be answered, the markets that need to be investigated, and the areas that need to be focused on in the next round of research.

Cycle 2

Examination

Taking the product description to several focus groups (described in Chapter 7) of busy executives, you discover that although they like the idea of web-based shared schedules a lot, they're worried about security. In addition, they consider the most important part of such a system to be rapid information entry and easy sharing. One person says that he should be able to do everything he needs with a shared schedule in five minutes a day. Other features he mentions include the ability to separate the schedules of friends and colleagues from those of his family and to get the schedules of special events (such as sports) automatically.

Definition

This shows that although the core idea is solid, several key functional requirements need to be addressed for the system to be successful. You add security, entry speed, and schedule organization to the software goals and pass them on to the group working on marketing the product.

Creation

Taking these ideas into account, you redefine the solution as a scheduling system with "layers" that people can overlay onto their regular schedule. Some of the layers can come from family schedules, others can come from shared business schedules, and still others can be promotional content for TV and sports, which would not only capitalize on the personal nature of the schedules but also add a potential revenue stream.

You modify the system description to include this functionality and to address the concerns voiced in the focus groups.

Cycle 3

Examination

You are worried about the "five minutes per day" requirement. Informal usability testing (Chapter 11) shows that it's hard to do all daily scheduling stuff in five minutes a day, but if that's what most people want, it's important to be able to meet it. You decide to do more research to see how long people really spend on personal schedules and if there are common trends in schedule management. Watching (using observational methods) a half dozen people maintain their schedules, you uncover that they spend an average of 20 minutes a day—not five—dealing with their personal schedule and that their biggest scheduling headaches in practice are not knowing the whole family's schedule and not getting confirmations from invited participants to upcoming events. Further, you learn that they check their schedules anywhere from three to ten times a day on average, which gives you some parameters for how many ad impressions they're likely to generate. Through several users' comments you also uncover that there may be two other potential markets for the product: teenagers and doctors. Teenagers have complicated schedules that involve many people (most of whom have web access)—yet are fiercely protective of their privacy. Doctors' offices spend a lot of time scheduling, confirming schedules, and reminding people of appointments—and they also have privacy concerns as well.

You also do field survey (Chapter 12) of your primary target audience to discover their exact technological capabilities and desires, as well as what associated products and media they use. You discover that they often have several fast, late-model computers at home that are shared by the family, but only one family member is ever on the Internet at a time. You decide that this means there needs to be an easy way for all the family members to use the service without stepping on each other's schedules (and to maintain privacy).

Definition and Creation

As in the two previous rounds, you refine your product goals. You add goals that focus on sharing schedules, family scheduling issues, and confirmation. Finally, you create the general outlines of a system that fulfills all these goals and then write a detailed description of it.

Cycle 4

Examination

Your survey also showed that the households you're interested in have at least one mobile phone per person that are used a lot, that they're interested in sports, and that they watch a lot of television. So you decide to run another round of focus groups to investigate whether people are interested in mobile interfaces for the service and whether they want to get schedule "overlays" for sports team and television schedules (both potential targets for lucrative advertising markets).

The focus groups tells you that schedule sharing and confirmation are the most highly desired by the target audience, whereas the family scheduling and special events features are considered desirable and cool, but not as important. Mobile web interfaces are considered interesting, but the majority of people have never used the web browser on their phones—they do everything with apps—and are somewhat worried that it will be awkward and confusing, and you don't have the resources to develop a standalone app. You discover that teenagers think that a shared personal scheduler is a great idea, especially if they can schedule instant messaging reminders and chats with it and if they can get to it with their cell phones. Doctors—an audience suggested by the last round of research and desired by the business development and advertising staff because of their buying power—don't seem to be interested in the scheduler. Although useful in theory, they figure that not enough of their patients will use the system to warrant training their staff.

Definition

Using the new information, you define two fundamentally different audiences: busy executives (your original audience) and highly social teenagers. These two groups have wildly divergent needs in terms of how the product needs to be presented, even if the underlying scheduling functionality is shared between them. Although realizing that you may not have the resources to pursue both groups, you split the product in two, defining the audience needs and product goals for each group.

Creation

You create new descriptions of the product for each of the new audiences. Although the teenagers' needs are not as well studied as those of business people, you feel that you know enough about the groups' problems and their solutions to begin expressing the solution descriptions in paper prototype form. You create paper prototypes for both the web- and telephone-based interfaces based on the description. At the same time, you direct the marketing group to focus the upcoming campaign on the sharing and invitation capabilities when presenting it to the primary markets and the easy-to-use telephone interface and TV schedule overlays when talking to the teenage market.

Cycles 5, 6, and 7

Now, having determined the target audiences for your product, the features they need, the features they want, the priority they want them in, and, roughly, how to present it to them, you build it. You run it through multiple rounds of usability testing, and you test the marketing with focus groups. With each round, you uncover more about how to align the scheduler with the identity of your other products while making it more understandable and efficient and presenting the sponsored content so that it's noticed but not considered intrusive.

In addition, you create a management system so that your staff and your sponsors can add and manage content, testing it with them at the same time as you're testing it with the consumers.

When you're done with cycle 7, you release the product.

Cycle 8

You immediately begin a survey of the user base, the first in a series of regular surveys to observe how your user base is changing and what direction it's changing in. This will let you target sponsorship and capitalize on the special needs of new groups of users as they appear.

You also begin a program of extensive site analytics and customer feedback analysis (Chapter 16) to help you understand whether people are using the system as you had expected and what kinds of problems they're having.

In addition, you continue the program of field research to investigate other related needs. One of the common scheduling tasks is bill payment. Ironically, mobile plan overruns and paying bills are a big source of contention in families. You begin thinking of your product as not only a scheduler, but also a family bill-paying service and, maybe in the future, a complete suite of family management tools.

Of course, this is a highly simplified and rather idealized version of a production cycle. Its main focus is to show how user research interacts with product development, but it's not supposed to be an exhaustive description of a development cycle that may have lasted six months. At the same time that what's described here is happening, so are all the usual project management tasks. Resources are scheduled, budgets are created, software is written and tested, and so on. Research forms part of the process, but it is not necessarily the most time-consuming or even the main driving component. This description is designed to highlight how studying a product's users at all times reveals new markets, needs, desires, and capabilities, constantly making the product a better part of people's lives.

PART II
User Experience Research Techniques

CHAPTER 4
Research Planning

Never research in a vacuum. Every piece of user research is part of the ongoing project of understanding your users, whether they are longtime customers or mysterious strangers who have never heard of your product. Making a research plan supports that project in several ways: It spells out the goals, sets up a schedule that helps you deliver results when they're needed most, and lets you avoid unnecessary, redundant, or hurried research. It can help you communicate about the research and make it easier for colleagues to participate and to act on the results. It also helps defeat the most frequent objection to doing user research: "We just don't have the time or budget." But even if you don't show your plan to anyone, it will help you figure out *what* to research *when*. You should start working on a research plan as soon as you've decided to do any research at all, even if it's only a tiny usability test or some client visits.

A research plan consists of three major parts: why you're doing the research (the *goals*), what you're doing and when you're doing it (the *schedule*), and how much it's going to cost (the *budget*). These are in turn broken up into practical chunks such as report formats and timetables. To get the most out of research the soonest, you should integrate the research plan with the product development plan. Sometimes, however, this is the most difficult part.

Make a Research Plan—*Now!*

The rest of this chapter will explain a thorough process for establishing your questions and identifying ways to solve them. But essentially, all your plan has to do is cover five areas:

1. The questions that you are trying to answer
2. Why it's important to answer them

3.   The techniques that you will use to answer each question
4.   The resources (time, money, people, equipment) you will need. (If you do not have any of these resources guaranteed, you may also need to include an argument about why you should be granted them, or where you will find them.)
5.   When and where the research activity will take place, and who will do it

And that's all. In the last part of this chapter, we'll give you a very detailed example plan that you are free to adapt as you see fit. But you can scrawl your research plan on the back of a napkin, if that works for you and the clients for your research.

Setting Goals for Research

Before writing a research plan, you need to know two things: why you're doing the research and how your results will be acted upon. Together, you use these two things to figure out which questions to ask, in what order, to have the most impact on the product.

The first involves determining business priorities and setting research goals that can meet them. The second involves an understanding of the development process so that the research can make the greatest impact on the final product.

There are many reasons why you could be initiating research. Maybe your company has a product that could be performing better, maybe it's developing something new and you want to see if the concept is appealing before investing the resources to code or build it, or maybe you are trying to figure out what product or service you should create. Wherever you are at the outset, you should begin your research with the people it needs to inform and with their definitions of success.

Every department in your company has a different method of measuring its success. Development could measure success as meeting the schedule or the number of bugs per thousand lines of code. Marketing could look for the number of positive reviews and increased site traffic. Identity design might care about the ease with which the product is integrated into the corporate brand.

Customer support might want to decrease the number of questions they have to field. Sales wants to bring in more revenue. Each of these represents a different perspective on the final product, and each demands something different from the user experience.

Research can go on in any direction. To get the most benefit, it needs to target the most important features of the product. But a product's "features" include much more than just its form factor or screen layout. Its most important features are those that affect the business goals of the company. Thus, the first step is to make a list of issues or ways in which the product's user experience impacts the company. Each issue represents a goal for the research program; it focuses the research plan and helps uncover how the product can be improved for the greatest benefit to the company. Collected and organized from the perspective of the company, these issues will not (and *should not*) focus solely on the user's ability to efficiently use the product. There may be goals for advertising effectiveness, customer support load, brand recognition, and so forth.

In other words, since the user experience affects every facet of the product, you should consider every facet. The process consists of three steps.

1. Collecting issues and presenting them as goals
2. Prioritizing the goals
3. Rewriting the goals as questions to be answered

Collect Issues and Present Them as Goals

The process of determining the important issues can be a research project in itself. Sometimes one person requesting the research will claim to know all the issues it should address, but wherever possible you should take your own inventory.

Begin by identifying the stakeholders. Every department will own some piece of every product, but some will own more than others (or will care more). The product manager—who is probably the most important person to talk to, anyway—can help start the list since he or she will know which groups and individuals have the biggest stake in the project. These will almost certainly consist of engineering, design, marketing, and sales, but it can include any other department that has a stake, or say, in the product's success. There could also be a significant managerial presence in a product if it's a major moneymaker (or loser) or if it's brand new.

Sample Sport-I.com Stakeholder List

Alison, VP of Product Development
Erik, Interaction Design
Michel, Marketing
Sun, Front-End Development
Janet, Sales
Ed, Customer Support
Leif, QA
Joan, Identity Design
Maya, Rob, frequent users

If there is no single person who's responsible for the product in a given department, find the person who dealt with it most recently. Odds are that this person regularly deals with it or can tell you who does. Once you have your list of stakeholders, find out what they consider to be the most important issues. You can do this either by getting all the stakeholders together to spend an afternoon setting companywide priorities for the product, or by speaking to each person independently (often a necessity with executives and other busy people). The latter is often a good idea if there are strong disagreements and you want to make sure that everyone's viewpoint is heard.

The key questions each person (or department) should answer are as follows:

- In terms of what you do on a day-to-day basis, what are the goals of the product?
- Are there ways that it's not meeting those goals? If so, what are they?
- Are there questions you want to have answered about it? If so, what are they?

Once you've talked to all the departmental representatives, make a list of the goals and issues.

User Experience Goals and Questions for Sport-I.com

Who	Goals and Questions
Allison, VP Product Development	Better conversion of viewers to shoppers More stickiness: people coming back more often
Erik, Interaction Design	To help people better use the product recommendations and convince them to write recommendations Why are so many people starting and then abandoning the shopping cart?
Michel, Marketing	For people to invite their sports-fan friends to the site
Sun, Front-End Development	Are the 360-degree product views useful enough to wait for the viewer to load?
Janet, Sales	Increase revenue 30% by fiscal year end
Ed, Customer Support	Reduce support queries about expired promotions Shift more support from email to the site's FAQs

What if stakeholders have conflicting goals? An advertising sales manager may want to increase revenue by introducing additional ad units at the same time that the vice president of content wants to add more news stories to the home page. Since there's a limited amount of real estate on the interface, these goals may appear to be at odds with each other. At this stage, it's too early to attempt to resolve them, but investigating the relationship between them may be an important near-term goal for the project.

After you've talked to everyone in-house, you should talk to a couple of users for their perspective. That may seem like a catch-22: Why research the user's needs before you even have a plan to research their needs? Because getting their voice into the research plan gets the research focused on them early and sets a precedent that can prove important in selling your research efforts within the company. See Chapter 6 for some hints on how to find users to talk to. Add this information to the list.

Maya, Rob, frequent users	Would like Sport-i.com to remember what brands they prefer for each sport they're interested in Want to know what the best values are based on the performance of the items

As part of this process, you should try to collect the other user experience knowledge that may be floating around the company, answering research questions without doing any original research. This can include surveys done by marketing, customer support feedback summaries, interviews by the development group, and unused reports from usability consultants. The user experience researcher can play the role of information collector and integrator, and, becoming the repository of all user-related information, spread information about the value of user experience research, and build

Goals for Sport-i.com Rewritten as Research Questions–*cont'd*

Issues	Research Questions
For people to invite their sports-fan friends to the site	What services do people value? What makes them committed users of the site? Are they aware of the social features of the site? Are these features appealing?
Are the 360-degree product views useful enough to wait for the viewer to load?	How do people evaluate products on the site? What information do they need before deciding to buy something?
...	
Would like Sport-i.com to remember what brands they prefer for each sport they're interested in	How important is customization? Which things are most useful to customize?
Want to know what the best values are based on the performance of the items	How do people shop with Sport-i.com? Is it based on sport, brand, tools, price, or something else?

Expand General Questions with Specific Ones

In the final step, flesh the larger, more abstract questions into specific ones that can be answered by research.

General Question	Specific Questions
Why are so many people abandoning the shopping cart?	What is the ratio of people who abandon the shopping cart to those who complete a transaction? On what pages do people abandon it? What pages do people open a shopping cart from most frequently? Do people understand the instructions on the cart pages? Do they know they're abandoning the cart? Under what circumstances do they open the cart? How do they use the cart? How do they shop on the site?

Tips

Never go into user research to prove a point, and never create goals that seek to justify a position or reinforce a perspective. The process should aim to uncover what people really want and how they really are, not whether an opinion (whether yours or a stakeholder's) is correct

The mantra for determining which questions to ask is simple. Test what's testable. Don't ask questions whose answers won't be actionable or test things that you can't change. For example, it's generally of little use to inquire about the identity design of a product before the feature set has been determined since the feature set will greatly shape the product's identity. Likewise, it's fairly useless to be researching feature desirability after you've already committed to an interaction design since the design assumes that people want what it's showing them.

Of course, not all these questions can be answered in a single research project or by a single technique, but having a big list of questions from which to draw can help you when you're putting together your research schedule. Moreover, the process of making the list often helps define the boundaries for the larger issues, reveals relationships between the larger issues, and sometimes reveals new questions and assumptions.

Learn the product thoroughly. Research goals can be framed more precisely if you can understand how the software currently works. Do what you can to become a user: Read the documentation, take a training course, and talk with tech support.

Be prepared to deal with fundamental questions about the product. If a question comes up during research—even if it's "should we be in this business at all?"—then there should be a way to deal with it and create research that will answer it (or at least escalate it to a senior stakeholder who can address it).

Integrating Research and Action

Now you know what your objectives are in doing research, and what you aim to find out. The other critical input you need is how your research will be used. Are your findings expected to inform product development? Product marketing? Customer support or policy? Are the questions you answer going to shape the next release of the product? The next few years of releases?

Just as every part of the business has their own goals that lead to different questions, they all may operate on different schedules, with which research may need to coordinate. You can never predict exactly how and to whom your research will be useful—if you could, it wouldn't be research. On the other hand, it pays to deliver research findings when stakeholders need them most. For example, if you want to know how your prototype fared in usability tests before developers start to implement the new design, you need to build that timing into your research plan.

To gather these schedule requirements, start by talking to the person immediately in charge of the product. Go through your list of questions. For each question, find out if there are key milestones or deadlines for acting upon the answers. You may need to follow up with other team members to get the detail you need. Once you know the critical dates on the product's road map, you can work backward from those dates to determine how much time you have to do the relevant research. Based on this information, your priorities, and your available budget, you can then select the research techniques you will use and the sequence of research projects.

Don't assume that if time is short, you should forego research until after the product is released. If you can argue that the findings from research will increase the product's chances of success, you may be able to change the schedule to allow for it. See Chapter 19 for more ways of integrating user experience research into your corporate culture.

Agile Software Development and User Research

In 2001, 17 developers published the Agile Manifesto, advocating a new way to build software. In their words, this approach values "individuals and interactions over processes and tools; working software over comprehensive documentation; customer collaboration over contract negotiation; responding to change over following a plan." (The complete statement is posted at agilemanifesto.org.) Agile and similar "lightweight" methodologies have steadily gained popularity among engineers and have been adopted by large and small software companies. When user research is involved in their efforts, researchers must also "work Agile," planning research projects to inform short, frequent release cycles. This typically affects the research plan in several ways:

- Research that gathers general product requirements is completed before any development starts.
- Prototype and product testing is done in many short rounds; each round is focused on a small set of features to be built in the next development cycle.
- Research reports are brief and are often delivered to the team orally rather than in documents.
- Since customer requirements can change on short notice, research plans have to be updated frequently.

A further evolution of this thinking is the Lean Startup movement, first described by software entrepreneur Eric Ries on his blog startuplessonslearned. com. Addressing the specific case of new product development, Ries argued in

2009 that innovating at low cost requires a "continuous cycle of customer interaction" featuring "rapid hypothesis testing about market, pricing and customers," along with continuous software releases. This philosophy has broad implications for research planning in a startup environment. Agile release cycles drive usability cycles in which recruiting, testing, and analysis take less than two weeks, rather than the three or more weeks that have been more typical of the industry.

The output of every research technique not only provides information on how to improve the product, but also can focus subsequent research. Surveys describe the current audience so that you know whom to recruit for interviews. Field visits and interviews outline their problems, which can motivate the development of features. In turn, usability tests evaluate the features. Every piece of information that research provides helps you know who your users are or what they want.

Thus your schedule of research projects, although constrained by immediate priorities and the development schedule, should still be organized so that one project informs and reinforces subsequent projects. In practice, this means that procedures that gather general information fall before those that collect information about specific preferences and behaviors.

Starting Research in the Beginning

For a new product or an existing product in an early phase of redesign, the following order of research projects makes sense. Realistically, you will probably only have time for a few of these projects given the usual schedules of product releases and new product development. This is where it helps to have prioritized your research questions; the techniques you choose will depend on what types of questions are most critical.

Early Design and Requirement Gathering

- *Internal discovery* to identify the business requirements and constraints.
- A *survey* to determine demographic segmentation and technology use of the existing or proposed user base. (Surveys are described in Chapter 12.)

- *Usage data analysis* of their current behavior if such data exist. (Usage data analysis is described in Chapter 16.)
- *Usability testing* of the existing product to uncover interaction problems. And competitive usability tests to determine strong and weak points in the competitors' products. (Usability testing is described in Chapter 11.)
- *Observational field visits* (Chapter 9) and *diary studies* (Chapter 10) to uncover current experiences (both with the product and with the task it's supposed to aid), and to specify how they solve them right now.
- Two to three rounds of *focus groups* (Chapter 7) or interviews (Chapter 6) to determine whether people feel the proposed solutions will actually help them and which features are of highest value. And *competitive focus groups* to determine what users of the competition's products find most valuable and where those products fail them.

Development and Design

- *Usability tests* of prototypes that implement the solutions and test their efficacy. And *field usability visits*, in which users test the prototypes in an environment similar to those in which the product will be used.

After Release

- *Surveys* and usage data *analysis* to compare changes in the product to past behavior.
- *Diaries* (Chapter 10) to track long-term behavior changes.
- *Observational field visits* (Chapter 9) to study how people are actually using it.

Starting in the Middle

A user research plan often may have to begin in the middle of a development cycle. Decisions have already been made about who the users are, what their problems are, and what solutions to use. These cannot be revised—at least until the next development cycle. In such cases, the research plan should begin with procedures that will give immediate benefit to the product before release and plan for more fundamental research to take place during the next development cycle. The following order may make sense for such a project:

Design and Development

- Rapid iterated *usability testing* and *competitive usability testing* until release. (Competitive research techniques are described in Chapter 5.)

After Release

- *Usage data analysis* before and after release in order to know how customers' behavior changed.
- A *survey* to determine the makeup of the user population.

Requirement Gathering

- *Observational research* with the existing population to determine outstanding issues for the next release.

After this, the plan can continue as the first plan.

Organize Research Questions into Projects

Let's go back to the example. In the list of research questions, it appears that there are some quantitative questions about people's current behavior (the ratio of abandonees to those who complete a transaction, the page where the abandonment happens, etc.), and there are questions about their motivation and understanding of the site. The first set of questions can be answered through log analysis, and the second set can largely be accomplished through usability testing. There's one question, "How do they shop on the site?" that's probably too abstract to be easily answered through usability testing. It's one of those fundamental questions that will probably need to be researched over an extended period of time and with several different techniques. It can begin with a round of observational research.

Visit this book's website at www.mkp.com/ observing-the-user-experience for more research planning resources.

Choosing among the Techniques

Picking the right techniques and grouping them can be difficult. The more experience you have with the methods, the better you will know which techniques best address which questions. If you don't have any experience with any of these techniques, start with the descriptions in this book, and pick one that seems right. Try it out. If it doesn't help you answer your question, note what kinds of information it was able to gather well and try a different technique.

Here is a table of the techniques with some trade-offs. It provides a basic overview of the techniques, but it's certainly not comprehensive.

Name	Stage in Development	Duration	Cycle Time
Personas Chapter 17	Beginning of development process	Two to five days' work over two weeks	Once per major design, or when new user markets are defined
	Description: Developers turn user research into fictional characters in order to understand the needs of different users. Benefits: Low-cost method that creates good communication tools for the product team. Focuses on needs of specific groups rather than a monolithic "user." Pitfalls: Quality of personas will depend on the freshness and accuracy of the available user research.		
Field visits Chapter 9	Initial problem definition	Two to four weeks, not including recruiting	Once per major set of features
	Description: Observe people as they solve problems to create a mental model that defines users' current understanding and behavior. Benefits: Creates a comprehensive understanding of the problem that's being addressed. Pitfalls: Labor intensive.		
Focus groups Chapter 7	Early development feature definition	Two to four weeks, not including recruiting	Once per major set specification, then after every feature cluster
	Description: Structured group interviews of 6–12 target audience representatives. Benefits: Uncovers people's priorities and desires, collects anecdotes, and investigates group reactions to ideas. Pitfalls: Subject to groupthink among participants; desires can be easily misinterpreted as needs.		
Usability testing Chapter 11	Throughout design and development	One to three weeks, including recruiting	Frequently
	Description: Structured one-on-one interviews with users as they try specific tasks with product prototypes. Benefits: Low-cost technique that uncovers interaction problems. Pitfalls: Doesn't address underlying needs, just abilities to perform actions.		

Name	Stage in Development	Duration	Cycle Time
Surveys Chapter 12	Beginning of development, after launch and before redesign	Two to six weeks	Once before major redesign, regularly thereafter
	Description: Randomly selected representatives of the audience are asked to fill out questionnaires; quantitative summaries of the responses are then tabulated. Benefits: Quantitatively describes the audience, segments them into subpopulations, investigates their perceptions and priorities. Pitfalls: Doesn't address the reasons why people have the perceptions they hold or what their actual needs are. Subject to selection bias.		
Diary studies Chapter 10	After launch and before redesign	Four to six weeks	Once before a major redesign, then after the release of new features
	Description: Long-term studies of users; done through diaries that users keep over days or weeks. Benefits: Investigates processes and activities over time, and how users' views and use patterns change with experience. Pitfalls: Labor intensive. Requires long-term participation.		
Usage data and customer feedback Chapter 16	Beginning of development, after launch and before redesign	Varies	Regularly after release
	Description: Quantitatively analyze site usage data and customer support comments. Benefits: Doesn't require additional data gathering. Reveals actual behavior and perceived problems. Pitfalls: May not provide any information about reasons for behavior or problems.		

Based on what you know about the company priorities, group the questions into clusters by technique, and make a rough schedule. Usage data analysis starts immediately, whereas the usability testing will take several weeks to prepare and recruit. The site visits can start at just about any time. However, in this hypothetical situation, there are not enough resources to do a complete study. So, a small round begins immediately with the assumption that more will take place later.

What	When	Questions
Usage data analysis	Immediately	What is the ratio of people who abandon the shopping cart to those who complete a transaction?
		On what page do people abandon it?
		What pages do people open a shopping cart from most frequently?

What	When	Questions
Usability testing	Immediately (recruit now, test in two to four weeks)	Do people understand the instructions on the cart pages?
		Do they know they're opening the cart? When they abandon it, do they realize that they're abandoning it?
		Under what circumstances do they open the cart?
		How do they use the cart?
Observational research	Immediately (recruit now, interview people in one to two weeks) and ongoing	How do they shop on the site? How do they shop for these things outside the site?

Continue through your issue list in order of priority, expanding all the items this way. As you're expanding them, look for similarities in the questions and places that research can be combined to simultaneously address a number of issues. In addition, look for places where competitive analysis can produce an interesting perspective. You can also start with the list of techniques and use that to generate further questions and research ideas. So, for example, you could start by saying, "What can we learn with observational research? Will that address any of the research goals?" and work your way through the other techniques.

A single entry from the final list could look something like this.

What	Usability Testing
When	Plan immediately, test in two to four weeks
Questions	*Shopping cart questions* Do people understand the instructions on the cart pages? Do they know they're opening the cart? When they abandon it, do they realize that they're abandoning it? Under what circumstances do they open the cart? How do they use the cart? How long does it take to make a purchase? *Navigation questions* How do people find specific items? (What tools do they use? How do they use them?) How do people move from one major section to another? (What tools? How do they use them?) *Promo section questions* In what order do people look at the items on the front page? Do people understand the information in the promo section?

Consider this entry as a single unit for the purposes of scheduling. It's a block that can be put into a scheduling or project management program. The specifics of what is tested may change later, but a list of techniques and questions will allow you to put together a good idea of what is to be tested, and when.

Asking Questions across Multiple Projects

Most product development schedules are fast paced, so the plan should concentrate on the short term. However, it should not short-change the long term. It's always tempting to focus on the goals for the next release and leave fundamental questions about a product and its users to long-term projects. But deeper answers are precisely what can make or break a product over the long run. Don't put off answering these questions because they seem too general or difficult to answer. In fact, they should be investigated as soon as possible. The earlier they produce results, the sooner that planning, design, and implementation of core product changes can be made.

However, only focusing on deep questions when there's an upcoming release is rarely a wise plan, from the perspective of either the product or the researcher's success within a company. Thus, the research plan should be structured as a set of parallel projects, with long-term goals cutting across several projects. Each project addresses whatever short-term questions need to be answered but also asks a couple of key questions to nudge knowledge about the fundamental questions forward, too.

This can be represented as a grid. Each fundamental question is in a column, while research projects label the rows. Thus it's possible to keep track of which projects are asking questions about which fundamental goals they're addressing. This keeps long-term goals from being neglected by the research process. The following table shows one such representation, with the colored cells representing which project gathers information investigating which goal (with project 4 an in-depth investigation of issues studied in projects 2 and 3).

Tracking Goal Information Collection across Research Projects

	Search Engine Results	Comprehensibility of Navigation	Shopping Cart Abandonment
Usability testing 1	■		
Focus group 1	■	■	■
Usage data analysis			■
Usability testing 2		■	■
Etc.			

The research plan should be updated frequently: in between every round of research, with every major change to the product and, in general, with every addition to the knowledge of the user experience and whenever company priorities change. It would not be unusual for there to be updates every week or two. Versioning every update helps keep track of all the changes.

Of course, not all projects are going to provide data for every goal, but keeping this structure in mind will allow you to keep the long-term needs in perspective while still getting the short-term work done.

The Format of the Plan

Until this point, we have intentionally avoided presenting a specific structure or style for the research plan since those will vary based on your needs and resources. A plan should be flexible and adapted to your environment. If you use project management or scheduling software, a lot of the plan can be represented in it. If you plan to show it to management on a regular basis, it can be in a more formal written form that can be folded into the product development plan. If your company culture prefers to communicate using a wiki, it can be a set of wiki pages. Whatever. It should fit a style that is useful and comfortable for you, but that can be shared and integrated with the larger product plan. The plan is a document that you are going to use to communicate the structure of your research and to sell the value of your work to your product team and your company as a whole.

There are some things every research plan should do.

- *Set expectations.* The people conducting the research and the recipients of the results should know what research is being done, how it's being done, and what results they can expect. Don't overload expectations for any single round of testing. A round of testing will not validate or condemn the entire project, and it should not be expected to. A research plan should also communicate that it is a flexible and ever-changing document. This can be done through version numbers or even expiration dates ("This research plan is valid until 2/2/2013").

- *Set schedules and responsibilities.* Who is going to do what when? How the research schedule integrates into the larger development process. This should be specific in the short term, but it can be more general in the long term, except for research that's directly tied to the larger schedule.
- *Specify goals.* Every research project and the research plan as a whole should have specific goals associated with them. The goals collected at the beginning of the process drive the specifics of the research. It should be clear what they are.
- *Specify outputs.* There should be outputs for every research project based on the needs of the stakeholders, specifying the information that's going to be presented. Ideally, the actual deliverables (report, presentation, workshop, set of personas, etc.) should be described.

Budgets

The budget will be based on the cost of resources available to you, but it'll probably come in four big chunks.

1. People's time (including your time and the research team's time)
2. Recruiting and incentive costs
3. Equipment costs
4. Travel costs

In our experience, useful times for calculating the duration of a qualitative user research project such as a usability test (including project management time and typical inefficiencies) are roughly as follows:

Task	Time
Preparation for a single research project (for just about anything other than repeated research)	Ten hours
Recruiting and scheduling	Two to three hours per person recruited

Task	Time
Conducting research	Five hours per person
Observational research	Three hours per group
Focus groups	Three hours per participant
Usability tests	
Analyzing results	Five hours per person
Observational research	Four hours per group
Focus groups	Two hours per person
Usability tests	
Preparing a report for online delivery	Twelve hours
Preparing one-hour presentation based on report	Six hours

Quantitative research, such as surveys and log analysis, will vary greatly in effort based on the complexity of the task and the tools and expertise available. What a good statistician can do in a couple of hours can take days for someone with less training.

Incentive costs are described in detail in Chapter 6, but (as of spring 2012 in San Francisco) they tend to fall around $150 per person per 90-minute session for most research.

Likewise, equipment costs will vary based on how ambitious your research is in terms of documentation, how demanding it is in terms of space, and where you're located. As of the time of writing, the cost of software for analyzing and recording usability tests ranges from free to around $1500. Renting a full lab, complete with software, can cost anywhere from $1200 to $1800 per day. And installing a permanent, high-end lab into your own offices will cost you about $30,000. However, you can also do an absolutely professional (albeit less highly documented) job for free: just take over an empty conference room and borrow a video camera.

Example: Research Plan for Company X

This is an excerpt of a research plan prepared with Indi Young, a user experience research consultant, for presentation to the development team of a consumer product comparison website. It presents an extensive research program designed to get a broad understanding of problems and users prior to a major redesign. Since it's designed for presentation, it includes more process explanation than an internal document and fewer details than would be used for internal delivery (which would include tables like all the ones described earlier), but it gives a good outline of how such a research plan can look when fully expanded. (For the sake of this example, this plan is confined to the research, but in reality, it would probably reference production milestones.)

Summary

This research plan outlines the needs and goals of company X in order to conduct rapid user research on company X's and the competitors' products, and presents a schedule designed to meet this goal. It includes plans for five rounds of usability testing, four focus groups, and the beginning of an ongoing site visit process. A schedule of all research through the week of July 8 is included, and an estimated budget is proposed.

This research plan is valid between 5/22/2011 and 6/26/2011, at which point an updated plan will be submitted.

Research Issues

Based on conversations with representatives of design, information architecture, product development, marketing, and customer service, we have identified five large-scale issues that our research will attempt to shed light on.

- While many people use the core product comparison service, less than 1% (based on analysis of tracking cookies) ever purchase anything from the online shop.
- While the top levels of the content tree get a fair amount of use, the deeper levels, especially the product-specific sections, do not.
- The competitors' design is a lot less polished and much more chaotic, yet they get twice as much traffic with a similar amount of advertising.
- Other than knowing that they're comparing one product against another, there's little information about the circumstances under which people use the service.
- People often complain about being unable to find a specific product again after they've found it once.

Research Structure

The research will be broken into two parallel segments: interaction research and a profile of the existing user population.

Immediate User Research

In order to provide actionable results in time for the next release, we will immediately begin a testing process to evaluate the existing site interfaces. This will determine which elements of the design work best, which are most usable, and which features are most compelling, while finding out what doesn't work and shedding light on how users prioritize the feature set as a whole. There will be some competitive analysis included to uncover the strengths and weaknesses of the user experiences provided by competitors' products.

The techniques used will include four rounds of usability testing and, potentially, some focus group research.

Usability Testing

We will conduct four sets of one-on-one structured, task-oriented interviews with five to eight users apiece from company X's primary target audience, for a total of 20 to 32 interviews. The interviews will last about an hour apiece and will focus on how well people understand the elements of the interface, their expectations for structure and functionality, and how they perform key tasks. Video recordings of the interviews will then be analyzed for feature use trends and feature preference. There will be one round per week from 6/5 until 6/26. For each round, a report summarizing findings will be prepared within two to four business days of the completed research and presented to appropriate parties within company X. Each round will use the most recent prototype and will concentrate on the most pressing user experience issues at the time as determined by company stakeholders and previous research.

A fifth set of tests will be of the same format with the same tasks, but will be conducted with the services provided by Company Y and Company Z.

Focus Groups

If no additional usability testing is needed before launch, we will conduct a series of three focus groups with six to eight users apiece from two key segments of the user base, member researchers, and shoppers (as defined in the market segmentation studies obtained from marketing). These groups will concentrate on uncovering what the users consider to be the most valuable parts of the service and where the service performs below their needs and expectations.

In addition, a competitive focus group will be conducted with users familiar with Company Y's product discussing that company's product.

Existing User Profiling

In addition, we will begin a program to create a profile of the existing user base and to better understand how they comparison shop. This will (we hope) uncover opportunities for the service to expand into and provide a closer fit to people's lives, further encouraging its use.

The technique used will be site visits with one to two team members.

Site Visits

We will visit the homes or offices of three to five people representing a couple of the primary target audiences. We will schedule the visits for times when they expect to be comparison shopping for a specific item, and then we will observe and document (with video recording and handwritten notes) how they go about this task. We will create a model of the process they use to comparison shop based on analyzing the video and notes, enumerating what tools and techniques they use, what problems they face, and how they solve them.

Schedule

The following schedule lays out the planned research. Most work is done in parallel between several different tests in order to get the most research in the available time. The usability tests all involve about the same amount of preparation and recruiting, which can happen simultaneously for one test as the next test is being conducted and analyzed.

Focus groups involve a fair amount of preparation, but since the groups themselves are relatively short (two hours apiece), they can all be conducted in the same week (although the schedule allows for a week's slippage for the last of the regular focus groups). There's also a competitive focus group, which has its own deliverable.

The site visits are not slated to be completed in this time period because it was determined that although understanding the use of the product in context is very important, understanding immediate usability needs is a higher priority. Thus, the schedule displays preparation for it, but lists no deliverables.

	Research Dates (preparation weeks are shaded the Green color; test and analysis weeks are shaded the Red color)										
	5/20	6/5	6/12	6/19	6/26	7/3	7/10	7/17	7/24	7/31	8/7
Usability test 1	Green	Green	Red								
Usability test 2		Green	Green	Red							
Usability test 3			Green	Green	Red						
Usability test 4				Green	Green	Red					
Competitive usability test					Green	Green	Red				
Focus group 1								Green	Red		
Focus group 2								Green	Red		
Focus group 3									Green	Green	
Competitive focus group									Green	Green	Green
Site visits									Green	Green	Green

Budget

These are the projected budgets, broken out by total estimated time and total estimated costs. These are approximate figures based on experience, and they will be adjusted in future research plans to reflect actual amounts as the research progresses.

Five Usability Tests

Preparation	10 hours
Recruiting and scheduling (assuming 40 participants—32 regular and 8 competitive)	80 hours
Conducting tests	120 hours
Analyzing tests	80 hours
Writing report and presenting results	15 hours
Integrating with development (meetings, presentations, etc.)	10 hours
Total time	**315 hours**
Recruiting incentive (25–40 people)	$2500–4000
Supplies (food, videotape, etc.)	$500
Total cost (not counting salary)	**$3000–4500**

Focus Groups

Preparation	10 hours
Recruiting and scheduling	40 hours
Conducting and analyzing groups	20 hours
Writing report and presenting results	15 hours
Integrating with development	5 hours
Total time	**90 hours**
Recruiting incentive	$2400
Supplies (food, videotape, etc.)	$400
Total cost	**$2800**

Deliverables

The results of each usability test will be sent in an email as they are completed. Each email will include an outline of the procedures, a profile of the people involved, a summary of all trends observed in their behavior (as they apply to the initial research goals), problems they encountered, and a series of supporting quotations. A presentation of the results of each test will be scheduled for everyone affected. The presentation will allow the analyst to answer questions about the results and give further explanations of the proceedings of the test.

The results of all the regular focus groups will be collected into a single report, which will be sent by email as soon as it is complete. In addition to outlining the procedures used and providing a summary of the trends as they apply to the research goals, it will analyze any differences observed between various market segments. There will be a separate report from the final focus group that will compare the values and reactions of users of Company Y's services to those observed with Company X's.

Maintenance

It's important to revise the research plan every time new knowledge comes in. Everything is subject to change as your team and the company's understanding of the user's experience grows. Re-evaluate, refine, and rewrite research goals to take every piece of additional knowledge into account. During particularly fast-moving periods in your company's or product's evolution, you may need to plan in detail for the short term, but keep long-term research planning more open-ended.

Since every piece of research is likely to affect your understanding of a number of different research goals, all knowledge about the user experience should be consolidated whenever possible. A good way to do this is to create a wiki site that contains all the reports and goals and that links each goal to the information that applies to it, and to enter all problems into the development group's bug-tracking software.

Eventually, you should have a set of interlinked documents that, together, make up a more-or-less complete picture of your user population.

CHAPTER 5
Competitive Research

Products don't exist in a vacuum. For any given service or consumer niche, there is a whole ecology of competing products. Each takes a different approach in attending to users' needs and desires. But which differences matter? Small differences in functionality, presentation, or identity can sometimes make a big difference in how people perceive a product. And sometimes they don't matter at all.

Understanding which of your competitors' strategies work and which don't is critical to understanding what will work with your product—and thus where to focus your energy.

Business development groups or independent auditors perform traditional competitive analyses. Traditionally, a competitive analysis assesses a company's offerings from a financial or marketing perspective. By examining public documents and doing field research, researchers can understand how much competitors' products cost, who buys them, where customers live, and what aspects advertising emphasizes. This valuable information helps executives make strategic decisions affecting the general direction of the company and its products. However, it's not all that helpful in understanding which parts of a product people actually use, what they like about it, or what keeps them coming back. That's the realm of competitive *user experience* research.

Most of the techniques discussed in this book can be applied to your competitors' work as well as to your own. They can reveal your competition's strengths and weaknesses and help you identify opportunities and threats. While it can feel good and raise morale to identify problems in competitor's products, the real goal of competitive user experience research is to figure out how to creatively differentiate your product from the competition—not just fix other people's mistakes. As Michael Hawley of Mad*Pow, a design studio, writes in "A Visual Approach to Competitive Reviews." "Simply identifying usability problems in other designs did little to help me understand unique opportunities for differentiation." His goal: "Enough understanding of competitors' offerings to recognize opportunities to set my designs apart, yet minimize the influence of competitors' designs on my thinking."

In some sense, competitive research is the purest user research you can do. It ignores the assumptions or constraints under which the other products were constructed and concentrates purely on the user's perspective. This makes it some of the most useful research of all.

When Competitive Research Is Effective

[Competitive research] is one of the first things you should do. It can define your world for you and make your life a whole lot easier.
Technology strategist John Shiple

Competitive research can be done at any point in your product development cycle. Whether previewing the landscape at the beginning or comparing your finished product to others, it always provides useful information. Picking the perfect moment to do competitive research is less important than doing it regularly and thoroughly. For the most benefit, you should check on your competition repeatedly throughout the lifetime of your product. Whenever you're not testing your own work, you should be researching your competitors'. Even when you have a full testing plan for your product, it makes sense to occasionally put your work aside and investigate your competition.

That said, there are several points where competitive research is more significant within the development process.

- *When producing requirements.* Research into what the competition's customers find useful, what they find attractive, and where those products fail can guide selection and prioritization of features for your own product.

- *Before you redesign.* As your product develops and evolves, competitive research can answer questions about design directions. Competitive products can be treated as functional prototypes of some of your own ideas.
- *When your competitors make major changes.* Researching the reasons for those changes and how they affect people's perceptions and behavior helps you decide how to react. Analyzing the results of those changes can keep you from blindly imitating decisions that may not be improvements.

Competitive Research Methods

Competitive user experience research focuses on how people use and perceive a product or service. Unlike traditional competitive analysis, it does not address the relative popularity, business model, or revenue stream. Business competitive analysis or brand analysis tries to understand what makes companies successful by looking at their revenue and other "fundamentals." Aside from the occasional feature grid or brand perception study, such analyses rarely address the consumer's or user's view. User experience research can work in concert with more traditional competitive analysis, of course, but its focus is from the bottom up rather than from the top down.

Apart from this fundamental difference, the process is quite similar to traditional competitive analysis. In both cases, the analyst must determine who the competitors are, what aspects should be compared, and how to compare them. The general sequence of steps resembles those that a financial analyst would follow when surveying the market landscape—but will take a lot less time and cost a lot less money.

The process we outline here draws from our own experience, from Kelly Goto and Barbara Cotler's Web Redesign 2.0: Workflow That Works, *and from Michael Hawley's white paper, "A Visual Approach to Competitive Reviews."*

- Identify and profile the competition.
- Define a set of key dimensions for comparison.
- Compare competitors to each other (and to your product).
- Use the comparisons to create recommendations for action.

Identify the Competition

This may seem obvious, but you need to know who your competitors are before you can start to analyze them. If you are working for a client, in many cases your client will identify all the main competitors for you. However, sometimes you may need to start from scratch. Or you may suspect that your clients have missed some crucial competition. Unfortunately, making sure you've identified all your main competitors is harder than it may first appear. While some competitive products and services may seem obvious—even unavoidable—your own biases and assumptions about what your product does may cloud your ability to spot others. Part of the work of identifying the competition is getting over your own beliefs about what other people will think your product does.

The easiest way to start looking for potential competitors is by searching the Internet. Make a list of three things your company or product does. For example, take a service that helps compatible people meet to form new relationships. Usually, that's called "online dating," "matchmaking," or maybe even "meeting new people." Try searching for all of those phrases. You'll probably find that different searches return different companies. Make a note of all the companies and how you discovered them. Next, check to see if the companies you have just found use phrases that are new to you to describe the competitor's benefits or function. For example, when Elizabeth started researching online dating, she didn't know that a common word for matchmaking in India is "matrimonials." She discovered that through a series of searches.

Keep searching using any unfamiliar terms you have just discovered. As before, keep track of which search terms bring up which potential competitors. That will help you keep track of how your competitors promote themselves. You can stop looking after repeated searches stop revealing unfamiliar products and services.

However, online searches may only reveal that part of the competitive landscape which is most immediately obvious to you. There may be other competitors you haven't considered. A bicycle touring site's competition (at least for someone's leisure time) is not just other bicycling information sites, but bicycling itself, since the site user's end goal is not just to find out information about bicycles, but to go out and ride. Likewise, although Barnes and Noble is an obvious competitor to Amazon, so is the corner bookshop. What does the corner bookshop have that Amazon doesn't have? How is the bookshop's user experience better or worse than Amazon's? Take into account what other things people could be doing instead of using your product. Start with what you get from online searches, then have friends or colleagues help brainstorm ones from other platforms and other situations.

Keep a running list of your competitors as you go. There are many ways to organize your list. It's easy to start by writing names on index cards or Post-it notes, but a long list might be most easily organized and updated by using a spreadsheet (Figure 5.1).

Then prioritize your list. You can prioritize any way you want, of course, but the following is a system that we find useful:

- *Tier 1 competitors* are your most direct rivals. They will be the primary targets of your analysis. The Barnes and Noble Nook e-reader competes directly with Amazon's Kindle device; Android mobile phones compete with the Apple iPhone. Tier 1 competitors try to capture the same audiences in the same way as your produce does, offering the same (or a very similar) service. Your list should contain no more than five of these. Of course, in reality, there may be more than five (for example, there are a lot of booksellers). However, five is probably enough to give you a good idea of the competitive landscape. If you don't believe you have any Tier 1 competitors, look again. Even if you believe your product is completely new and innovative, it's still battling something for your audience's attention. That something is the competition. Cars and horse-drawn buggies look and work differently, but were Tier 1

Services	Audience	Activity	Social focus	Platform
OkCupid	middling	wide	network	web
Eharmony	middling	focused	individual	web
Y! Personals	broad	focused	individual	web
Match.com	broad	focused	individual	web
Proxidating	broad	focused	individual	mobile
J Date	niche	focused	individual	web

Figure 5.1 Screenshot of spreadsheet from online dating service competitive analysis prepared for Yahoo! Research.

competition for each other in the early 20th century. Today, the library might also be a useful Tier 1 competitor for the Nook and Kindle.

- *Tier 2 competitors* are products from the same category as the Tier 1 competitors. Either they are not as directly competitive or they are largely identical to a Tier 1 exemplar. Remember—you're not aiming for ultimate completeness, but rather a useful sample of competitors that will help you map out a landscape within which you'll make design decisions. You should look quickly at Tier 2 competitors to check your conclusions about the Tier 1 list. However, in-depth analysis of Tier 2 competitors is not as critical. There shouldn't be more than five or ten of these. A Tier 2 competitor for the Nook and Kindle might be any one of a variety of tablets and PDAs on which people now read books in electronic form.

- *Niche competitors* compete directly with part of your product, but not the whole thing. In the 1880s, horses and trains competed on long-distance travel but not in terms of local transport. Today, Powells.com and Alibris.com sell e-books, just like Amazon and Barnes and Noble. But they do not sell integrated e-reading devices. They may be Tier 1 competitors for each other, but they're not really direct competitors to the Nook and Kindle.

Profile the Competition

To focus your competitive research, you need to know something about whom you are dealing with. A complete competitive analysis doesn't just name competitors; it includes *competitive profiles* of all the Tier 1 competitors. These consist of two elements: a description of the product and a profile of its audience.

Product Description

A product description should not just be a list of features. It should be a statement from the users' perspective of the value it brings them. Product descriptions should not be more than a few sentences long. How would a typical user describe your product or service at a cocktail party to someone who had never heard of it? For example, take the original Kindle:

> The Kindle is a portable electronic reading device that can store thousands of books. With a cellular wireless connection, it allows users to easily buy books and magazines from Amazon's online store anywhere they go. Its black-and-white e-ink screen delivers crisp text that is readable even in direct sunlight, although it does not perfectly render photographs. It has a long battery life so that readers can take it with them on long trips without recharging.

Audience Profile

What kinds of people use your competitors' products? You probably won't be able to get detailed statistics—that's the sort of information that many companies keep close to their chests. But with a little research, you can make some good guesses. First, check out newspaper stories and industry publications about them (see Chapter 14 for more instructions). Then, do an Internet search for who's talking about them. User forums, blogs, and review sites will all give you some data on your competitors' audiences.

The way you characterize the audience will depend on the product or service. What categories seem most relevant to outside analysts? How do people seem to identify themselves on forums and blogs? Demographic factors—those traditional measurable values like age, gender, and income—may not be as important as job title or experience in using the product. In the case of the online dating project, demographic factors were very important—different sites might cater to people of different religions and languages. Certain kinds of entertainment preferences were also important (yes, Star Trek fans have their own dating service). But the audience profile of a mobile phone might look very different.

Then you write the profile. Like the product profile, all you need is a few words or sentences. Highlight the differences between these people and your audiences. If they're direct competitors, the profiles could be quite similar to yours, but each of them will have at least one key element: the reason why they're using someone else's product. Why? What makes the competition's user market different from yours? You may need to create separate profiles when you feel that the product serves multiple audiences.

Define a Set of Key Dimensions for Comparison

The most important step in analyzing your competition is creating a set of dimensions—a framework within which you can compare your competitors. In defining a set of dimensions, you are most importantly *limiting* the scope of the competitive analysis. You are limiting it first to what your users may consider important, and you are limiting it secondly to those dimensions relevant to the research questions you need to answer. There are an almost infinite number of attributes that could be used to compare products. Trying to include them all will only waste your time and confuse yourself when you are trying to move to actionable intelligence.

Dimensions are categories drawn from specific types of attributes. They can come from specific features (e.g., "wireless connectivity") or more abstract qualities (e.g., "tone of voice"). Dimensions, then, include a range of potential values. The dimension of "tone of voice" could include descriptive adjectives such as "casual," "clinical," or "witty." On the other hand, the dimension of "responsiveness" could include values such as "very fast" or "very slow."

Dimension identification should come from the user's perspective. Your product may run on state-of-the-art hardware in a climate-controlled data center, whereas your competitors' runs out of a dusty closet. Either way, your users probably don't care. They care about things like getting their work done quickly, finding what they're looking for, and having fun.

There are two ways to define dimensions: by asking users and by looking for yourself. You should do a combination of both. The users' perception of what constitutes an attribute may be different from yours, so you may want to start by doing some light interviews or a small focus group series. Identify what people consider the key qualities of your service and what they consider the important functionality. These may be as complex as "I like the way the features are integrated so that my phone numbers carry over from one section to another," or as simple as "I like that I can choose different colors for the case."

In addition, do your own *feature audit*. Sit down and make a list of the prominent features of your product. From a user's perspective, what does your product do? What are the prominent functions? What are its attributes? Then look at each of your competitors' products and check which ones have the same or similar features (but, again, measure similarity from the perspective of the user, not how you know the site works). As you run into new attributes of your competition, add them to the list. You can also look at product reviews to see which features reviewers highlight and what they have to say about them.

A feature list for a search engine could include:

- Fast response
- Provides category and specific site matches
- Corrects simple spelling errors
- Sorts results by relevancy

Next, combine the two lists and *prioritize the features* into two groups: one higher priority, one lower. Prioritization is important when concentrating your research. Prioritize based on the areas that mean the most to the product's functionality, to the company's success, or to the users' satisfaction. You will probably want to discuss the competitive research plan with management since they may have questions of their own that your process can answer.

While you are collecting features, you should also be collecting the important *attributes* of the competitive products. Attributes aren't necessarily related to functionality; they make a product memorable, likable, or interesting. They are the adjectives that people use to describe the product to friends or co-workers. Although not as important to the usability of a product as the actual features, attributes describe the feeling and environment of a user experience. A product's vibe can change the way people experience and use it; it should not be ignored. For example, the user experience of a product that is perceived as "bland" and "boring" will certainly be affected by people's opinion even if they are not directly related to how well it works. Form may follow function, but it shouldn't be ruled by it.

Competitive Analysis Techniques

The same techniques that provide insight into your product—usability tests, interviews, focus groups, surveys, and the like—work as well when applied to your competitors. The major difference in approach is the amount of focus you place on creating a balanced perspective. When researching your own products, it's common to focus on the problems that the product is having—after all, those are more immediately actionable than knowing where change is unnecessary—but in competitive research it's as important to understand what your competitors have done right as it is to know where they've faltered. In addition to knowing where their failings are, which parts of their product do users have *no* problems with? What aspects do they *like*?

Doing Competitive Analysis Quickly

Competitive analysis can expand to fill all the time you have, and then some. Depending on the length of the project, you can spend anywhere from a few hours to multiple months.

If you have less than a week, the following section will not be very useful to you. Concentrate on getting the most out of existing sources: industry analysis, whitepapers, newspapers, blogs, user forums, etc. Use comments from real users to drive your lists of features and attributes.

If you have more than a week, consider using some of the techniques discussed here. You don't have to use all or even most of them. If you already have research activities, you can add questions about competitors in order to get started more quickly. If you have no research activities planned, you will need to add the few days required to list your Tier 1 and 2 competitors to the time required to plan your preferred research technique.

Recruiting

Just as you should recruit real users (or potential users) when trying to understand how people perceive your product, you need to recruit real users when working competitively.

The process of recruiting is the same as that described in Chapter 6, but with the additional consideration of the target audience's experience with your competitors' products. Whether such experience is important depends on the kind of research you plan on doing. If you're usability testing advanced features, you'll probably have to find people who have experience with the more common features, so it's not necessary to familiarize the participants with basic functionality. Likewise, focus groups of current users can tell you a lot about what attracts them to the product. However, research with inexperienced users—with people who have no experience with your product or your competitors'—often provides some of the most valuable competitive information because the first experience with a product determines a lot about users' future relationship to it and understanding of it.

The logistics of recruiting people who match a competitive recruiting profile is no different from the process described in Chapter 6, but how do you find your competition's users?

One method is to do a broad public invitation and include in your screener for it a list of products that includes both your product and your competitors, but does not reveal that you (or the recruiter) represent one of them. The list should contain your product, your competition's product, and several others. Invite those who use your competition's products but don't use yours.

Keeping the identity of your company anonymous is important when competitively recruiting. People will almost certainly behave differently if they know that the research is for the purpose of comparison. Some feel defensive about their choices; others will use the test as an opportunity to vent their frustrations. Both situations create an inaccurate, exaggerated portrait of user experience and should be avoided.

Competitive Product Interviews and Observation

One-on-one interviews with users of a competitive product can reveal much about what makes that product functional and where it fails. Watching people use your competition's product reveals usage patterns that your product can emulate or avoid.

For example, while watching people reading news online for a technology news competitive analysis, a researcher observed that frequent news readers would first go to CNN or CNBC and read a couple of stories, then they would jump to a smaller news site. When questioned, they consistently said that they use the major news sources for general headlines, and the specialized news site for a comprehensive view of the topics that most interested them. The specialized sites provided better views of their favorite topics, whereas the general news sites were better for "hurricanes and stuff." The technology news site was planning to carry general news content from a news wire, but seeing this they decided that a wire feed was unlikely to compete with CNN on the "hurricanes and stuff" front, so they decided to highlight breaking technology news instead.

Focus Groups

Inviting the users of a competitive product to participate in a focus group can reveal *why* they use it and which aspects of it attract and repel them. Such groups can also reveal people's views of the brand and the identity of the product, and the qualities they assign those brands. Anecdotes collected during the focus group can be analyzed to see what the initial impetus for using product B (the leading brand) versus product A (your product) was.

For example, several focus groups with the users of a furniture sales site invited participants to talk about how they buy furniture online and offline. The goal was to understand what information they found most valuable and what presentation most compelling. It became quickly very clear that most participants would only buy certain classes of furniture from a trusted source. Unfamiliar with most manufacturer brands and unable to touch the furniture, they needed the assurance of a reputable seller. They complained about the quality of the navigation and pictures on the site, but the trust they placed in the name overrode their apprehension.

More than one product can be discussed in a competitive focus group. Introducing several products and actively comparing them with a group helps further reveal what people value and find interesting. These groups can be made up of people who have experience with one of the products or with people who have no experience with any of them (though it's probably not a good idea to mix the two groups). When presenting multiple products, the order in which they're discussed should be varied so as to minimize the bias that can come from having the same product shown first every time or having the same two products appear in the same order every time.

Usability Tests

Competitive usability tests are one of the more useful competitive research techniques. Watching people use your competition's product can show you where its functionality differs from yours (something that's not always apparent when examining the interface), where it succeeds, and where it fails.

The features you concentrate on will drive the development of the script and the tasks. Focus on the features that most differentiate your competition's product from yours and isolate the features that will best describe whole classes of functionality. For example, it may be more valuable to investigate how well your competitor's navigation tabs work than whether people understand the icons used in the shopping cart. Even though the icons may be a flashy differentiator, the tabs are more likely to affect more people's experiences with the site.

The tasks you create will likely differ little from those you use when testing your own products. In fact, you can use the same tasks. In addition to being less work, this lets you compare how different interface organizations can create different usage patterns.

An occasional problem occurs when you don't have access to your competitor's product. For publicly available sites and apps, it's easy to just point a browser at them or pay the nominal registration fee for an account or two. But testing products that you don't have access to or which cost more than your available budget can be challenging. In such situations, many questions can be answered by prototypes that you build or, in the case of software, demo versions (which are often freely downloadable, though you should carefully read the demo's user agreement to make sure that competitive analysis is an appropriate use of the product).

It's also possible to test multiple products at the same time. Compare approaches by giving evaluators the same task on several different interfaces (but only if the tasks are actually doable on all the interfaces). Again, you can reduce bias by changing the order in which you present the competing products and not recruiting users who have experience with any of the products under examination.

For example, a general-purpose web directory wanted to understand what worked in its competition's interfaces. Many of the category-based directories were based on Yahoo! and that site had already been studied, so it was decided to choose two of the lesser known directories. LookSmart and snap.com were chosen because they offered similar services to similar audiences (at the

Bias easily creeps into the testing process. A subconscious nod toward a preferred solution or a moderator's slip of the tongue can skew a participant's perceptions. Although this can happen in any research situation, it's more likely to happen when the moderator has strong allegiances. Focusing on behavior and current usage, rather than opinion, reduces the chances that an opinionated moderator will skew the results.

Bias is also the reason third-party consultants are particularly useful when doing third-party analysis.

time). People who had not used either site were asked to search for similar things with both services. Localization features (by specifying either a zip code or a region) were considered to be of highest importance and were the primary focus of the usability test. Most of the participants said these features were interesting, and everyone understood the two sites' different methods of communicating this functionality (in snap's case, it was an "Enter Zip Code" field, in LookSmart's, a "My Town" navigation tab). However, the ability to use the two sites' implementations of the features was different. LookSmart's "My Town" tab attempted to anticipate people's local needs, almost always incorrectly, whereas snap's option dropped people into a different directory, which was treated by the users as a separate service and understood as well as they understood the general snap interface. The web directory decided to go with a snap-like model.

Surveys

Before you run special competitive surveys, look at the customer and user research you already have. Useful competitive information can often be extracted from surveys not specifically designed for it. You can filter responses to pull out users of competitors' products and tabulate the responses of just those responses, treating them as a subset of the whole survey population. Although the results will likely not be significant relative to the general user population, analyzing them may be able tell you something about what differentiates your users from your competitors'.

The process of writing a survey specifically to understand your competition follows the same steps as for a regular survey. Create reasonable objectives about what your survey is to accomplish, focus most of the questions on the higher priority issues, and present the features in a neutral way. From the respondent's perspective, the questions should read as if an impartial third-party wrote them.

Some popular topics of competitive investigation in surveys include the following:

- *Other products your users use.* This question allows you to estimate the popularity of your competitors and, using published third-party audience numbers, can give you a ballpark figure for the total size of your market.

- *How much they use the products.* If you are using survey software, leverage any capabilities for customized follow-up questions to ask in-depth rating questions about any competitors that survey participants say they use. How often do people use their product? For how long do they use it? When did they start using it? Have they ever switched between competing products? How often? Why?

- *Their loyalty to the competition.* What attracted your respondents to your competitor in the first place? How satisfied are they? You can create a rating grid of rating scales that lets the respondents quickly fill out their views about specific features and attributes of the products (see Chapter 12 for more information on designing questions with scales).

- *The features they use.* These questions can be generated from a database of known competitor features, or it can be free text, letting people discuss how the product is useful to them. It can also include a feature satisfaction component.

Surveying just your competitors' users is difficult. You don't even necessarily know who they are. Unlike surveying the users who come to your door, you have to actively find your competition's. You can either field the survey to your own users and filter out those who use competitive products or you can field it to a broad range of users (say, through a sponsored search ad or a site that you feel will attract a lot of competitive users) and hope that you recruit enough competitive users to justify the cost. Of course, the best way to get a representative survey is to do a random telephone survey, but those are cost prohibitive in most cases.

Like other kinds of competitive research, surveys can be easily biased if they're revealed to be competitive. The knowledge that they're discussing one product for the benefit of another can change the way that people respond to questions, especially satisfaction and preference questions. It's probably okay to reveal your identity at the end of the survey (or at the end of any of these procedures), after they've submitted their responses, but it's generally better to do the whole thing through a third party.

Analyzing Competitive Research

The goal of traditional competitive analysis is to create a side-by-side, feature-for-feature comparison grid. The assumption in creating such a matrix is that point-by-point matching of features is important for competitiveness. This isn't always the case from the user's perspective. There is usually a core set of functionality that needs to be similar for two products to be considered competitive, but beyond that the actual feature set can vary broadly and two products can still compete. Many online companies compete directly with brick-and-mortar companies, for example, though the actual user experiences are drastically different.

Competitive user experience research should reveal the fundamental strengths and weaknesses of the competition, not create a scoreboard.

The comparison begins with the research reports you produced in the data collection phase. Taking the report, enumerate the *advantages* that the competition's product gives their users and the *hindrances* it places in their way. Again, these should be from the users' perspective. Even though it may be in your best interest to have people stay on your site longer, a site that lets people get in and out quickly may be preferable. Similarly, although new daily content may be positioned as an advantage of one product, it may make little difference to users, and, in fact, a frequently changing page may be seen as a hindrance if it requires them to relearn the navigation.

Looking at the results more closely, what do they say about the company and its development process? Where does it provide consistently strong experiences? What are the characteristics of those experiences? How does it regularly falter? Business analysts call the collection of a company's strengths their *portfolio of core competencies*. Likewise, it may be useful to maintain a *portfolio of frequent foibles* that lists consistent weak points in the competition's approach to creating experiences.

CNET, for example, had a mastered of brand identity and design cohesion. With all of the distinguishing marks removed, people who had seen a CNET site could immediately pick out a different CNET site from a lineup. Users considered this to be a benefit because they trusted the company and felt comfortable navigating its products. However, CNET's navigation was less consistent than its branding. When researched competitively (by Mike while working for Wired Digital), its users felt that they knew how to use a CNET site because it resembled other CNET products, but they actually had more trouble navigating some CNET sites than ones made by CNET's competitors. When researching a number of CNET sites, it was seen that both the strong branding and the bad navigation were consistently present in many of their products.

Traditional competitive analysis can, of course, also be revealing. It shouldn't be the only kind of analysis, but it can provide a useful shorthand. If, for example, users clearly value a certain set of features, then it may be appropriate to create a feature comparison matrix with those features. Such side-by-side comparisons, however, need to be between actually *comparable* items. Thus, a site map *somewhere* on a site should probably not be compared with one that has a map front and center on the home page.

Benchmarking

In the interest of creating a shorthand by which to evaluate competition, some competitive analysis techniques introduce numerical or letter grade competitive ratings. You can, for example, give each feature in a feature matrix a score—say 0–5, where 5 means the product does something well, and 0 means it doesn't do it at all. Adding up all the scores gives you a total for the competitiveness of the site. This allows you to quickly see which ones are, theoretically, most competitive because relative to the others they are the most successful at what they do.

Such techniques are useful when new competitors are constantly entering the field and you need to evaluate them quickly, but it obscures important information about which aspects of the competition influenced the final score, which may actually be more important than the overall value. However, the exercise can be useful when figuring out which strengths are serious threats and which weaknesses are important opportunities.

Example: A Quick Evaluation of Match.com

The following is an excerpt of a rapid competitive analysis that Elizabeth did during an online dating research project for Yahoo! Research. In the interest of saving space, the description of the research process and the way that these results feed into the larger list of core competencies have been omitted.

First, the team represented the various genres of online dating services on a two-by-two grid, Figure 5.2. They selected two dimensions to represent user experience: the extent to which each genre (such as "mobile social software") promotes in-person meetings (also known as "dates") and the extent to which each

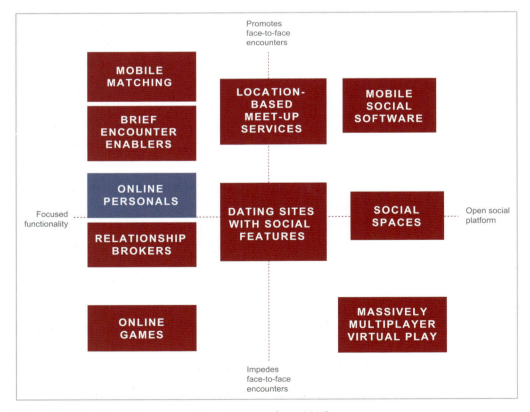

Figure 5.2 The online dating user experience landscape (circa 2007).

genre focuses on supporting just one kind of activity. They looked at a range of tools that help people meet each other—not just services aimed specifically at romantic matchmaking. For example, the team knew that people meet and even fall in love while playing massively multiple online games, so they included those in our competitive analysis. For this project, however, they did not include nondigital services such as traditional matchmakers and, of course, dance clubs.

Match.com (Figure 5.3) fitted squarely within the "online personals" genre. It provided a profile page with some structured information (such as age and gender) along with a limited area for free text self-description. Users were also encouraged to upload photos. It provided fewer types of structured interaction and opportunities for self-expression than dating sites with social features such as OkCupid.com. It promoted face-to-face encounters (e.g., getting to the first date) more than casual online gaming, but did so less intensively than mobile matching services that promise to connect users on the go.

- The general perception was that Match.com has one of the largest pool of users of any dating website. Unlike niche sites (such as those for specific religions, hobbies, or ethnic backgrounds), Match.com's population was seen as very diverse.

Figure 5.3 The Match.com front page (circa 2010).

- Users can search by gender, age, and location. Because of the very large user pool, the result was typically a very long list of potential matches—sometimes as many as 2000. Users had to filter the list themselves to find the most likely candidates. But they often found that a few photographs and brief profiles did not really give them enough information to feel comfortable with their decisions. Users of the free service, who did not pay for extra functionality, were more frustrated by this work.
- Longtime users' relationships to the site differed by gender. Men reported sending messages to many different women, hoping for a response from a few. Women sent many fewer messages. A result of this imbalance was that many women felt harassed by the number of messages they got—and many men became frustrated by a lack of response.
- Users often put a lot of confidence in the "matching" algorithms. Despite little information about it in the interface they cited it frequently as a reason for contacting one person over another.

Acting on Competitive Research

Finally, once you've collected all the data, analyzed the responses, and performed all the comparisons, you need to do something with it. To make the research usable—to create *actionable intelligence*—you need to refocus on your project. Take your list of advantages and hindrances and reflect them back on your goals. For every item on the list, explain its relationship to your product or service. Every advantage that a competitor's product provides can be seen as a threat to yours, and every problem as an opportunity. Everywhere the competition's product is more effective than yours reveals a weakness in your product, and vice versa.

Then create a theory explaining the motivation behind the design choices that were made by your competition, both good and bad. Why was the product made the way it was? What were the constraints? What was the likely rationale? Which choices do you agree with? Which do you not? Which are inexplicable?

Concentrate on the *whys* of your competitor's decision-making process, not necessarily on *what* was done.

In the case of Yahoo! Research's online dating project, the competitive analysis resulted in the realization that "online dating services" had a very narrow definition of the dating experience. At the time, all the Tier 1 competitors focused on pairing up compatible people. None of them helped daters navigate what interviews showed to be a critical point in matchmaking: the exciting and stressful "first date." The result was a call for strategic redefinition of what it meant to be an "online dating site," including new features to support daters as they prepared for that first face-to-face meeting. In the end, this single insight—that existing online dating websites didn't support much of what their users saw as "dating"—produced not just a working prototype but a patent application for the new technology.

The final outcome of competitive research is a deeper understanding of what makes a good user experience, admiration for your competitors' ability to solve problems, pride in your own product, and a plan that allows you to use this knowledge to your advantage. These are all worthwhile lessons, and there are few other ways to learn them.

Don't use your own results in your advertising.

Although it's tempting to use the results of your internal competitive research in your ads, it's generally not recommended. People won't give it a lot of credence, and your competitors may decide to sue if they think your results are incorrect.

If your internal research shows, for example, that four out of five people prefer your product over its competitors, and you're *convinced* that this is an accurate proportion of the population at large, hire an independent research agency to replicate your research. An independent agency is likely to use much more rigorous standards in their research, and their results will carry much more weight in consumers' (and judges'!) minds.

CHAPTER 6

Universal Tools:
Recruiting and Interviewing

No matter what the research, there are two things you're always going to be doing: looking for people who will give you the best feedback and asking them questions. These two elements, *recruiting* and *interviewing,* make up the backbone of every successful research project, and although some of this information is covered in other chapters, they deserve a chapter of their own.

Recruiting

Even if everything else is perfect, if you get the wrong people to talk about your product, your research can be worse than useless since it gives you confidence in results that don't represent the views and behaviors of your real users. Every product has a target audience, from toasters to missile guidance systems. You need to understand the experience of the people who are actually going to want to use, understand, and buy your product. Anyone else's experience will be of marginal use, or even deceptive. So if you're making a missile guidance system and you invite the North American Toaster Enthusiasts to speculate on how it should be improved, you're not going to get useful Army-related feedback. (And if you decide to take their speculating seriously, you may end up with a missile that has a 30-second pop-up timer.)

The process of finding, inviting, and scheduling the right people for your research is called *recruiting,* and it consists of three basic steps: determining the target audience, finding representative members of that audience, and convincing them to participate in your research.

The time required for recruiting can vary widely, depending on how accessible your target audience is and the location and duration of the research you have planned. For example, imagine a study in which you want to observe style-conscious young adults shopping for their favorite hair products in the stores they usually visit. You will be spending a fair amount of time with each participant (not to mention traveling to the stores) and you may need to pay them a lot for their time. To make this research valuable, you need to be choosy and screen each candidate individually before selecting them for the study. Table 6.1 shows the recruiting schedule you might follow.

Overall, this process could take two hours for each participant—more if you've never recruited that kind of participant before.

Now, imagine a very different study: you want to learn whether adding photos to your online hair care shopping guide helps users decide which products to buy. If you conduct the study online and have users participate remotely from their homes or workplaces, you may be able to recruit people *and* run the sessions inside of a day (see Table 6.2).

If you frequently need to conduct in-person studies, it is useful to have someone recruiting full time, rather than trying to do it in

Table 6.1 Typical Recruiting Schedule for a "Shop-Along" Field Study

Timing	Activity
$t - 3$ weeks to $t - 2$ weeks	Determine target audience(s).
$t - 2$ weeks	Recruit a pool of potential candidates, or find them in a database.
$t - 2$ weeks to $t - 1$ week	Screen for final candidates.
$t - 2$ weeks to $t - 1$ week	Send invitations to primary qualified candidates.
$t - 1$ week	Send invitations to secondary qualified candidates.
$t - 3$ days	Create schedule for all candidates and contact list for alternates.
$t + 1$ day	Follow up with participants and researchers.
$t =$ testing day (or days)	

Table 6.2 Typical Recruiting Schedule for a Remote Web Usability Study

Timing	Activity
$t-2$ weeks to $t-1$ week	Determine target audience(s).
$t-1$ week	Configure and test your recruiting and remote testing software.
t	Monitor participant screening process; conduct sessions as qualified participants show up.
$t+1$ day	Follow up with researchers.
$t =$ testing day (or days)	

between other work. Recruiting can be almost a full-time job in itself, and it always turns out to be more work than anticipated. To reduce costs, a temp or an intern can recruit full time if given some training.

Pick Your Audience

As a general rule, the longer your company has been providing a product or service, the better you will know its audience. If they have been selling laser printers for years, they should have detailed information about the people who buy them, which you can use in recruiting. On the other hand, if your company has just invented a new way to print photographic images on cupcakes, you may not have much to go on. If you are doing early-stage research to discover business opportunities, part of your job may be learning who the users could be. In that case, you should begin by finding out how your team currently defines its audience and recruit those people for an initial round of research to confirm your assumptions. If those participants turn out not to be interested in your product, you may need to recruit different people for another round, so plan accordingly.

So how do you define that group of "right people"? For most user research, the most important recruiting criteria are *behavioral*. That is, you are looking for people who actually do (or want to do) the things that your product or service supports. If your product is a new bicycle helmet with a fold-out rearview mirror, your research audience might be people who ride bikes regularly and use bike

As a researcher, it's important to question assumptions about audiences. For example, companies accustomed to traditional market research often want to have purchasers or final decision makers, such as chief executives, as usability participants. But the reality is that executives likely don't spend much time using your product—their employees do. If you recruit executives based on a client request and despite evidence that executives are not your product's main users, you risk designing for an audience that's not actually there.

This happens all the time and is a great source of pain for the people who actually have to use business software. In that sort of situation, you may need to argue for two studies—a usability test with frequent users and surveys or interviews with decision makers about purchasing behaviors.

safety accessories. They might also be people who don't ride regularly but would if they felt safer on the road. For some products, it may be especially important to know how intensively they use (or don't use) various computing and communications technologies, such as online games, mobile devices, or digital video. In that case, break that information out into a *technological profile*.

What about *demographics?* Shouldn't things like age, gender, geographic location, and household income be used to pick your participants? For a relatively new product or service with not many users yet, this can unnecessarily make your recruiting job harder. For an established product with many users, it can be important for your participants to resemble your existing users demographically. For example, say your company produces online bridge tournaments and the vast majority of your players are over 60. For your user research, you need to get people who play bridge and have played online, or you are unlikely to learn anything useful. Even if you do that, though, you are likely to miss some important findings if your participants are all under 40. (Plus, it will be hard to convince your stakeholders that your research is valid.) If your recruiting efforts consistently yield participants who don't resemble your users demographically, it's a sign that you need to find new channels for recruiting. In general, recruit based on behavioral criteria first, and if there are demographic attributes that are true of most of your target users, make sure at least some of your participants have them, too.

Put your profiles of the product's target audience into writing, if they aren't already written down. If you're making a website that helps people plan a night out, your primary audience may be single professionals who go on lots of dates and use the web on mobile phones as well as PCs.

Initial Date Planning Profile

Demographics
Ages: 25–55
Gender: male or female
Single
College educated
Income: $60K+

Behaviors
Go out on a date at least once a month

Technology Use and Experience
Use the web at least one hour per day
Access the web from a mobile device at least four times per week
Have gone online to get information about local restaurants, entertainment, or events in the past year

Now, ask yourself what makes the ideal research participants different from the target audience as a whole. What kind of people will give the best feedback for the specific research you are doing? Ask yourself:

- Which *segments* of your audience do you need to focus on? For example, the people planning dates, or the ones who get invited out?
- How much experience should they have with *your product*? If you're testing a new interface, do you want people who are used to the old version, or others who can see it "fresh"?
- How much experience should they have with *competing products*?
- Are you targeting a single group of users or multiple groups? For example, city-dwellers and suburbanites might be different enough that you should treat them as two groups.
- What are undesirable *characteristics* that should be avoided? In this example, people who consider themselves experts on their cities might not give useful feedback.

Explore the answers to these questions and modify your profile accordingly. Remove factors that are not going to affect how people use or view the product and add information. Focus on isolating the factors that will make them an ideal research audience.

Revised Date Planning Research Profile
Demographics
Ages: 25–55
Gender: male or female
Single
College educated
Income: $60K+

Behaviors

Invite someone out on a date at least once a month

Choose places and activities for dates

Consult friends and local media sources for ideas when planning dates

Technology Use and Experience

Use the web at least one hour per day

Access the web from a mobile device at least four times per week

Have gone online to get information about local restaurants, entertainment, or events in the past year

Not all research should be done with "average" users. If you are looking for new ideas to improve or differentiate your product, consider talking to some people who use it intensively, have an unusual way of using it, or have special needs. You may even want to interview people who have chosen not to use it.

Be careful not to overdetermine your target audiences. If you find yourself trying to define multiple conditions to the point where you're not sure you can find people who meet them, or if some of the restrictions are mutually exclusive, consider breaking the research into several groups. Thus, if you're making a mobile application for truck drivers and you need the perspectives of both long-haul and short-haul drivers, rather than mixing the two groups into one piece of research or finding drivers with experience in both fields, consider running the same research with two groups.

Find Your Audience

Once you have the research profile, you need to go out and look for those people. You have two groups to draw upon: people already in contact with your company and everyone else. Recruiting from the first group will always be the fastest and cheapest option. But what if this group is small, or doesn't include enough of the *right* people for your research? If you have plenty of time, you can do some outreach to find the participants yourself. If not, you can use a commercial recruiting service. This may be an agency that recruits the people you need, a software tool that puts you in touch with them online, or a combination of both.

Recruiting on Your Own from Existing Contacts

Existing contacts can include current customers; people who have created accounts on your website; people who have signed up for your newsletter or given you their business cards at trade shows or events; your company's friends/fans/followers on Facebook, Twitter, or other social networking services; your employees' own families and friends; and even brand-new employees.

Many of the channels you already use to interact with customers can also be used to recruit research participants. For example, you could post a call for participants on your company website (Figure 6.1), email newsletter, or Facebook fan page, or tweet it out on your Twitter account. Obviously, make sure to choose the channels where the people who fit your research profile can be found. If you're looking for expert users, don't announce it in the new user help forum.

For some research needs, you may have a very specific set of current users you want to contact; for example, customers who recently upgraded from the free version of your service to the pay version. In these cases you may want to email users and invite them to participate in your research. The advantage of this method is that you may already have information that you can use to prefilter the people you ask. For example, if you want to learn about new users' experiences, you can invite only people who have signed up for your service in

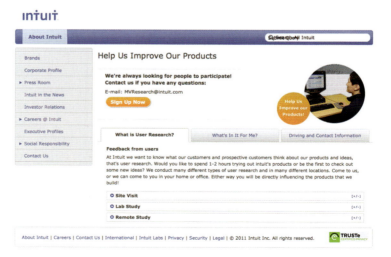

Figure 6.1 A call for research participants on Intuit's website (http://about.intuit.com/research/). The site explains why Intuit does research, how users can participate, and the incentives offered.

the past month. On the downside, some users may find it intrusive or annoying to be contacted in this way. To avoid alienating invitees, state the purpose of your contact in the subject line of your message, offer them an incentive for participating, and give them a way to opt out of being contacted for research in the future.

Recruiting on Your Own from a Wider Population

Maybe you don't yet have a product, or even a web presence. Perhaps you are a new company or are trying to enter a new market where you don't have many contacts yet. If you've done the work to define your audience precisely, it should not be too hard to find other ways to reach out to them. But it does take some effort! This is why people hire commercial recruiting companies—locating people on your own often costs less, but it can require some creativity and extra effort.

Say you want to do research with urban dog owners. You could post messages in online discussion forums for dog owners, buy ads on pet care websites, or post flyers in pet supply stores, vets' offices, and city dog parks. In other cases, it may be better to do your outreach more personally. If you are looking for parents of children with learning disabilities, you probably need to get to know a few of those people and earn their trust. Once they understand your objective, they may be able to introduce you to others.

Many of the techniques we introduce here can push the boundaries of the recruiting schedule in Table 6.1. If you try one on a short schedule and aren't having immediate luck finding people, be prepared to try another—fast.

- *Community email mailing lists and online forums.* Some communities have their own email mailing lists. Whether it's people who live in a certain area or people who use a certain product or people who are in the same industry, there are a lot of mailing lists in the world. After you've identified a list or forum, check how busy it is. Low-traffic sites might not have the membership numbers or interest to reward your effort in making contact. Once you've chosen a list, make sure that you know the community's rules and you have the organizers' permission before sending mail. It may help to start a conversation with the organizer first, then have the organizer send the message on your behalf. That way, community members can have more confidence that your request is legitimate. Never spam (send unsolicited email). Personalize the invitation

It's important to give people a reason to participate in your research, but that reason doesn't have to involve money. If you believe that your project has the potential to improve the lives of dogs and dog owners, or help dyslexic kids in school, say so. Overemphasizing financial benefits—especially if you have a very low project budget—can actually turn people away.

to the group, making it clear why you're sending the message and what the benefits of participation are.

- *Neighbors.* Your corporate neighbors are a great research resource. They may be familiar with your company, and it's easy for them to come into your offices during a lunch break. Send a note to your neighbors' office managers and ask them to post an invitation in a public place.
- *"Friends and family."* We put this in quotation marks because it's such an old standby. You don't want to pack a study with *your* friends and family—their relationship to you will slant how they behave. But recruiting people you don't know as well—say, friends of friends, or family members of friends—is perfectly legitimate. Friends can be especially helpful with niche recruiting requirements. If you're looking for martial arts experts, why not ask an acquaintance who teaches taekwondo? Send an email about the project to people you believe will have friends and family who fit the recruiting criteria. Ask them to forward it on. Keep the email short and to the point, or people won't forward it. The one big drawback to this method is that your friends probably resemble you in important ways. They're your friends, after all! So if you rely on *their* friends, you may well bias your results toward people who *also* resemble you. So be careful—but do call on your friends in a pinch.
- *Ads.* Online ads are easy, are often inexpensive, and hold the promise of reaching a vast number of people very quickly. You can take out ads on your site and on other sites (in 2012, Facebook is a common choice). However, we have had mixed results using online advertising to recruit participants. Our experience has been that ad recruitment is more successful when you are recruiting based on a hobby or deep personal interest. That is, an ad for martial arts experts will likely be more successful than one for people who go to the gym occasionally. However, that doesn't mean you shouldn't give ads a try. Make sure that the ads specify the location of your study and any incentives. And do make them attractive (as ads, they need to compete with all the other ads). An animated banner can, for example, read "Bay Area Black Belt? Want $60? Click here!" Clicking on the ad

then leads people to your project website, screening survey or contact form.

- *Traditional methods.* When you need people who can come into your office, consider traditional advertising methods. Classified ads online or in local newspapers can work, though an ad in the help wanted section might get confused for a job offer. If you're in an urban area, there may be leaflet distribution services that can put your invitation on every corkboard in town (college campuses are an especially good source of such bulletin boards and are a great way to recruit college students if they're part of your audience).

If you're at a loss for how to target a certain group of people, first find one person who matches your research participant profile. Then sit down with him or her and brainstorm about other ways that similar people can be reached. Talk about places he or she goes—online and offline—and habits and interests. Suggest some of the methods in the preceding list and ask how to tailor them specifically to his or her lifestyle.

Using a Commercial Recruiting Service

Commercial recruiters have databases with thousands of people from all walks of life. For them, the task of finding people is fairly straightforward: they search through their databases for basic demographic matches, and then they screen those people for the criteria that you've determined. We describe how to work with commercial recruiters later in the chapter.

The decision about whether to work with a commercial recruiting firm or do it yourself largely depends on available resources. Recruiting is a time-consuming process, especially for relatively rare groups or for people with complex schedules. However, basic recruiting can be a fairly straightforward process if organized well and given sufficient time.

Keeping Track of People Available for Recruiting

However you connect with potential research participants, you should keep a database of people who are willing to have you contact them directly for user research. Be sure to record how you got in touch with each person. You should also keep a list of people who have asked *not* to be contacted, so you can make sure not to bother them. Ideally, this should be integrated with whatever customer contact management system you use.

You should try to have at least ten times as many people in your contact list as you expect to invite to your next round of research.

Additional Recruiting Tips

Rather than including lengthy explanations in email, you can make a web page that explains the research program and then send email that points people to it. This can be the same page that collects their demo or web info, but it can be a purely informative page, too. The page should explain the purpose of the recruiting, the incentive, the occasional nature of the research (so people don't think it's a job), and how they can get more information. Add frequently asked questions to it as the recruiting process matures.

Clearly state the location of the research and the geographic area from which you'd like to recruit in all invitations. You can't predict who will read a request, and it's little use to have people offer to participate from halfway around the world (or even 100 miles away) unless you're willing to pay them for their transportation costs or you're doing research remotely.

Keep track of when and how people found out about your program. This will tell you which techniques work best and, moreover, how your recruiting methods may affect the perceptions of the participants. People who have purchased something from your company will know more about your product and have stronger opinions than people recruited through your neighbors, who will in turn have stronger opinions than people who saw an ad.

Don't get to the point where everyone you're recruiting has identical qualities or has been recruited in the same way. Every attribute in a profile has a range of values that could satisfy it, and recruiting should strive to get a diverse group of people within the range. For example, when participant ages are defined to be between 25 and 35, it would be better if the recruits ages encompassed the whole range rather than all being 35.

Try to keep the number of repeat recruits down. In most cases, it's generally acceptable to recruit someone who hasn't participated in any kind of usability or marketing research in six months. In some cases, however, this requirement will have to be waived—for example, when time is short or the person has a rare profile or he or she is in a popular market that gets recruited a lot (IT managers are few, and are the targets of much market research, for example).

When someone gives you especially good feedback, make sure to note it in the database (you can have a check box for "great response"). If you ever need a couple of people on short notice, you can just pull people who you know are articulate and insightful.

If time allows, run a small recruiting test. Recruit one or two people and run them through the research. If they provide good feedback and they're in the right audience, proceed with recruiting everyone else the same way.

The Screener

Your next task is to create an appropriate script for the recruiter to filter the general population for the criteria specific to your research. This is called a *screener*.

The screener is probably the most important part of the recruiting process. It's a script that filters out the people who will give you good responses from the ones who merely match your basic criteria. The screener can be a form posted on the web, a script read by the recruiter over the phone, or a questionnaire sent in an email. If you are doing an unmoderated study, such as an online survey, you can have people complete the screener at the beginning, with only screened participants proceeding to the actual research.

Getting the screener right can get you people who are likely to be interested in the product and can speak about their experiences intelligently and eloquently. Getting the screener wrong means getting people who are, at best, only marginally interested in what you have to offer and, at worst, uninterested and inarticulate.

Screeners vary from project to project and from recruiter to recruiter, but there are some general rules that apply to most.

- *Stick to 20 questions.* There's a reason that game exists. It's possible to find out almost anything about someone in 20 questions. Most target audiences can be defined in 10 to 15 questions, and if the people are prescreened through your database, you can get away with fewer than five.
- *Make it short.* It should be possible to get through a whole phone screener in five to 10 minutes.
- *Be clear and specific.* The person responding to the question should know exactly what kinds of answers are expected.
- *Never use jargon.* Use simple, straightforward, unambiguous language.
- *Ask for exact dates, quantities, and times.* This eliminates the problem of one person's "occasionally" being another's "all the time."
- *Every question should have a purpose.* Each question should help determine whether this person is in the audience or not. Don't ask questions that are incidental or "nice to know," since answers to them will not be useful in recruiting and take everyone's time. Save "nice to know" questions for when you actually meet a participant.
- *Start with the questions that will screen people out.* The earlier a question is in the screener, the more people it should eliminate from the pool of potential participants. This saves both the recruiter and the participant time since earlier questions weed out later questions that would be irrelevant otherwise. For example, if you know you only want people over 60, but you want a variety of experienced and inexperienced Internet users, put the age question before the Internet experience question.
- *Questions should not lead.* There should be no value judgments or answers implicit in the questions. "Are you bothered by the excessive lag times on the web?" implies that the person perceives lag times and that he or she should be bothered by them. Instead, phrase questions in a more general (but not more ambiguous) way, and then look for specific responses. "Are there things on the web that regularly bother you? If so, what?" could get at the same kinds of issues as the first question, without its bias.

- *Clearly state the format of the research.* State what the research is for, when it's going to happen, how long it's going to take, how much the incentive is, and whether the participants should do anything ahead of time (and whether they should do nothing ahead of time).
- *Build in flexibility.* Let the recruiter know the acceptable parameters for answering each question, so that you don't needlessly dismiss people who can provide valuable feedback.
- *Prioritize helpful participants.* There is nothing more frustrating than an interview with someone who hates talking or a usability test with someone who won't follow directions. Including open-ended questions can help the recruiter guess whether a person will be responsive and articulate.

Sample Phone Screener

This is a telephone screener for a site that offers an online calendar. The target audience is mostly existing users, but the screener has been expanded to include a couple of potential users and a power user (to get a taste for several different kinds of user experiences).

This screener consists of three sections: an introduction for the recruiter that specifies the ideal target audience, an introduction for the participants, and the main set of questions and selection criteria. It is a relatively complex screener that would probably be too involved for a first usability test.

Target Audience
6–9 people total: 4–6 current users, 1 power user, 1–2 nonusers (but likely potential users)

Current eCalendar Users

- People who use eCalendar on a regular basis and have used it recently
- Men or women
- Any age, but prefer 35–50
- Have Internet access on at least one personal computer or device
- Accesses the Internet daily or almost daily

- Have created at least five eCalendar events in last month
- Have used eCalendar for at least two months

eCalendar Power User

- Someone who uses eCalendar frequently and regularly uses the advanced features
- Any age, but prefer 40+
- Creates at least 20 eCalendar events per month
- Has used reminders and calendar overlays
- [rest of profile the same as current users]

Potential Users

- Have never used eCalendar, but may be aware of it
- Has at least five scheduled appointments per week
- [rest of profile the same as current users]

Note that some of the criteria are specific, such as the frequency of Internet access and the number of events entered into the calendar, whereas others (such as the gender and age) have ranges.

Logistics
- Available on January 20 or 21 between 8 AM and 6 PM
- Can come to the downtown San Francisco office
- Are not immediately affiliated with eCalendar or its competitors (but can be aware of it)
- Have not participated in any usability or marketing research in the last six months

Current User Screener

Hello, my name is [*screener facilitator name here*] from [*your company name here*]. We are seeking a few people who are interested in participating in a paid evaluation of a product that you may find useful. This is not a sales call, and no sales or solicitation efforts will be made at any time.

The evaluation will consist of a one-on-one interview on January 20 or 21 in downtown San Francisco. It will be during working hours and will last about one hour. If you participate, you will receive a cash stipend of $100. The interview will be strictly for research, and all of your comments will be confidential. If you are interested in participating, I need to ask you a few questions to see if you've had the kind of experiences we're looking for.

The introduction simultaneously sets people's expectations and serves as the first round of questioning since people will immediately say if they're unavailable on the given date or if they're unwilling to participate. It's also careful to describe the general nature of the research without going into specifics that may skew people's responses.

Alternatively, you can use a more generic introduction ("We are conducting a study, and I would like to ask you a few questions"), but you run the risk of going through the whole process just to find that the person is not available on a given day or is uninterested in participating in this type of research.

Question	Answers	Instructions
1. Do you or any member of your household work in any of the following businesses or industries?	Market research Advertising or media sales Public relations Usability or quality assurance User interface design or development	IF YES TO ANY, TERMINATE

Eliminate people who work in industries that can present a conflict of interest. People who are in advertising, usability, user interface design, and market research should almost always be eliminated since they're too aware of the kinds of issues that research is aiming to uncover and are unlikely to give an unbiased perspective (even if they want to).

"Terminate" is an instruction to the recruiter that tells him or her to stop the recruiting process and wrap up the interview. There is some termination text provided at the end of the screener.

2. We're looking for people of various ages. Which of the following categories includes your age?	Less than 30 30 to 34 35 to 39 40 to 45 46 to 50 More than 50	TERMINATE ASK Question 3 TERMINATE
3. Do you have access to the Internet?	Yes. No.	ASK Question 4 TERMINATE
4. What computers or devices do you use to access the Internet?		TERMINATE IF RESPONDENT *DOES NOT* MENTION AT LEAST ONE OF THE FOLLOWING: DESKTOP COMPUTER, LAPTOP COMPUTER, SMART PHONE SUCH AS IPHONE OR ANDROID PHONE; OTHERWISE, ASK Question 5
5. On average, how often do you access the Internet?		IF LESS THAN 5 DAYS A WEEK, TERMINATE; OTHERWISE, ASK Question 6

Although many of these questions will have already been filtered for if these names were pulled out of a database, it's still useful to make sure that the information is accurate, so it's a good idea to verify the information again. Additionally, the age and income questions may be considered to be invasive by some people. In many cases, that information doesn't affect people's behavior and the questions can be eliminated; in cases where the information is of secondary importance, it's possible to move the questions to the end.

6. How many scheduled meetings or events do you have to keep track of per week?		IF LESS THAN 5, TERMINATE; OTHERWISE, ASK Question 7
7. Have you kept track of any scheduled meetings with an online service in the last month?	Yes. No.	ASK Question 8 TERMINATE

8. How many?		IF LESS THAN 5, TERMINATE; OTHERWISE, ASK Question 9
9. Which online calendar service or services did you use?		IF eCalendar IS MENTIONED, ASK Question 10; OTHERWISE, TERMINATE
10. How long have you used eCalendar?		IF 2 MONTHS OR MORE, ASK Question 11; OTHERWISE, TERMINATE
11. Which of the following eCalendar features have you used in the past?	Reminders The address book Calendar overlays The buddy list	IF overlays AND reminders, CONSIDER FOR POWER USER SCHEDULING; ASK Question 12
12. Are you currently working on any projects with eCalendar.com or another company that makes online calendars?	Yes. No.	TERMINATE ASK Question 13
13. Have you ever participated in a market research interview or discussion group?	Yes. No.	ASK Question 14 SCHEDULE
14. When was the last time?		IF LESS THAN 6 MONTHS, TERMINATE; OTHERWISE, ASK Question 15

When people have participated in user research recently, they're more likely to give unconsciously biased responses since they'll be familiar with the format of the research and may try to anticipate the "appropriate" answers. Since you're almost always looking for unguarded, unbiased responses, it's generally a good idea to eliminate these people from the research unless you have no other choice. Moreover, some people see the incentive payments as a good way to supplement their income and may try to get into any kind of marketing or usability research project. Inviting such people should be avoided entirely since they're unlikely to provide natural or truthful responses.

When you are short on time or when you can interview only a couple of people, it's sometimes useful to filter for people you've interviewed before rather than filtering them out. People who are known to give good, honest, articulate feedback provide a shortcut to useful information. In such situations, it's important to inform the analyst about the participant's background since it'll probably affect the way he or she interprets the results.

15. In a couple of sentences, list your favorite websites lately and describe why you like them.	[NOTE DOWN] TERMINATE IF INARTICULATE; OTHERWISE, SCHEDULE

Open-ended questions like this serve two purposes. They give the recruiter an idea of how articulate a potential participant is, and they can collect information that's not easily formatted as a multiple-choice question. Save them for the end, and don't put more than one in any given screener since they're time-consuming and don't filter many people out. (That said, some recruiters prefer to ask the open-ended question at the beginning since it's less intimidating and can catch terminally inarticulate participants early in the process.)

TERMINATE	That's all the questions I have. Thank you very much for participating. Although we're not scheduling people who fit your profile right now, we may call you again for a different research project.

If you're using the more generic introduction, you can also replace the termination statement with something less specific, such as "That's all the questions I have. Thank you very much for participating in our study."

> That's it for the questions. Would you be willing to come into our downtown San Francisco offices for a one-hour paid interview on January 20 or 21? You will be reimbursed $100 for your time, and your help will be greatly appreciated by a development team that's currently making a product you may be interested in.

Online Screeners

Online screeners are similar to telephone screeners in terms of the kinds of questions that are asked, except that online screeners are designed to be answered directly by the participant. This makes them similar to a survey questionnaire in format. In fact, you can use the same writing style and online tools to create them that you would use to run a survey. See Chapter 12 for how to write survey questions and select an online survey tool.

Ideally, you should use a tool that lets you create screeners with branching logic, so that you can terminate people right away if their answers disqualify them, just as you would with a phone screener. Include a question at the beginning to determine whether they are available at the times and locations of the study and a form at the end for qualified respondents to provide their contact information.

Once your screener is online, you need to invite potential participants to fill it out; email is generally the easiest way of doing this. Your first task is to convince recipients not to ignore the invitation, so if you are paying an incentive, make that clear in the subject line. However, don't put the subject in all caps or use exclamation points, or your invitation will look like spam. Make it clear to readers why you are contacting them, describe the incentive they can earn if they qualify, and state how long the screener will take to complete. Since they haven't qualified yet, there is no need to describe the research in detail.

SUBJECT: Earn $100 helping us make a better online calendar

BODY:

eCalendar is looking for a few people to help us evaluate a new online scheduling product. Participants will receive a $100 gift card for completing a one-hour interview on January 20 or 21 in downtown San Francisco.

If you are interested, please go this web address to complete a five-minute questionnaire:

http://www.ourcompany.com/research/screener

If you qualify for the study, we will contact you to schedule your session.

You have received this e-mail because you are a current or former eCalendar user. If you would prefer not to be contacted about research studies, please let us know and we will remove your address from the list.

Scheduling

Scheduling procedures largely depend on how you will be conducting the research. Sessions conducted face to face should be scheduled at least a week in advance, longer for business users, if significant travel is required, or if multiple users will participate together. Remote sessions conducted by phone or videoconference can be planned on less notice than in-person research. In fact, some remote research platforms allow website users to be recruited "live"—while they are using the website—then get screened quickly and do the research session right away. Unmoderated research happens at the convenience of the users; you just have to give participants a deadline and remind them as needed.

Whatever the parameters, you should begin by defining a *scheduling window* in which the study will take place. What are the appropriate times for the researchers? Are there times that are inappropriate for your target audience? (Physicians and network administrators, for example, are almost impossible to schedule during weekday working hours.) Are there key observers who need to be there at certain times? Company meetings? Holidays?

Now, if your research is appointment-based, start scheduling. There are lots of ways to schedule people, and you should feel free to use whatever procedure is right for you. The following sequence was used successfully at Wired Digital and is similar to the procedures used by other recruiters:

1. Write the invitation.
2. Invite primary candidates.
3. Receive responses and schedule primary candidates.
4. Invite secondary candidates.
5. Receive responses and schedule secondary candidates.
6. Confirm primary candidates.
7. Confirm secondary candidates.
8. Send thank-you notes to unscheduled candidates.
9. Make email or telephone confirmation calls to all participants the day before their scheduled time.
10. Create and distribute a schedule of all participants.
11. Direct participants and/or researchers to the location where the study will be held.

For events with fixed schedules, such as focus groups or when critical observers have limited schedules, invitations are straightforward.

For more flexible situations, schedules should be constructed around the participant's preferences. It's often as effective to ask candidates for a list of times when they're available as it is to dictate times when they should show up. Allowing participants to drive the scheduling also shows them, upfront, that their input is valuable.

The Invitation

The invitation should reiterate what the research is about, why participation is important, how much the participant will be paid, where the research will take place, and when they should show up (or, in case of site visits, when they can expect the visitors to arrive). Here's an example of an invitation email:

> Thanks for your interest in eCalendar research. You are invited to participate in our next user study. One-hour sessions will be held on WEDNESDAY, DECEMBER 8 and THURSDAY, DECEMBER 9 at our offices on 123 Main Street in downtown San Francisco. An honorarium of $100.00 will be paid to you following the test session, and you will be required to sign a nondisclosure agreement prior to beginning the study.
>
> If you would like to participate, you MUST RESPOND TO THIS MESSAGE BY THIS THURSDAY, DECEMBER 2. Please answer the following:
>
> When are you available to attend a test session? Please indicate ALL the times you could attend:
>
> [ ] Wed, Dec. 8, 11:00 AM–12:00 PM
> [ ] Wed, Dec. 8, 12:30 PM–1:30 PM
> [ ] Wed, Dec. 8, 2:00 PM–3:00 PM
> [ ] Wed, Dec. 8, 3:30 PM–4:30 PM
> [ ] Wed, Dec. 8, 5:00 PM–6:00 PM
> [ ] Thur, Dec. 9, 11:00 AM–12:00 PM
> [ ] Thur, Dec. 9, 12:30 PM–1:30 PM
> [ ] Thur, Dec. 9, 2:00 PM–3:00 PM
> [ ] Thur, Dec. 9, 3:30 PM–4:30 PM
> [ ] Thur, Dec. 9, 5:00 PM–6:00 PM
>
> We'll get back to you on Friday, December 3 with the date and time of your session.

Confirmation and Reconfirmation

Since a lot of dates and times fly around during the scheduling process, it's a good idea to confirm the final date and time. Send a short, clear email or other message, like this:

Dear [*name here*],

Thank you for responding to our invitation to next week's usability study. We're confirming that your appointment is for:

Day: Monday, December 8, 2012

Time: 5:00 PM

VERY IMPORTANT—YOU MUST CONFIRM YOUR APPOINTMENT

In order to confirm this appointment time, please either REPLY TO THIS EMAIL or CALL 415-235-3468! If you don't respond, we will assume you are not coming, and we'll have to schedule another participant in your time slot.

All confirmations should also contain a line to the effect of "Because we have tight schedules, it's critical that you show up exactly at the time you're scheduled or a few minutes early," as well as specific transportation and parking instructions.

OUR ADDRESS

We're located at 582 Market Street at Montgomery, Suite 602, in the Hobart Building. There is a BART and Muni station right in front of the building, and all the trains stop there. The numbers 2, 7, 9, and 14 buses travel at street level. If you're driving, the closest parking is an underground pay lot at Mission and Second that is best approached from Mission Street going east.

OTHER GOOD STUFF TO KNOW. This session should last about one hour, and you'll receive an honorarium in the amount of $100.00 by check within two weeks following your participation. The schedule we have set up for this test is very tight, so if you think you're going to be running late, PLEASE CALL (415) 235-3468 TO INFORM US. If at all possible, plan to arrive 10 minutes before your scheduled appointment time, and you'll really be a star!

Thanks again and we'll see you next week!

In addition, we found it helpful to standardize the format of all correspondence with a one- to two-sentence summary of the message at the beginning; a standard layout for all messages; and a contact person's name, email address, and phone number at the end. Encourage the participants to contact that person as soon as they know they won't be able to make an appointment or if they have any questions. Keeping the text tight, but with humor and personality, helps make the process feel less clinical, and people are more likely to read it.

Finally, the single most effective way of preventing no-shows is a combination email and telephone reminder the day before the scheduled appointment. It reminds people, subtly reinforces the importance of their input, and gives you time to schedule an alternate in case they can't make it.

Choosing an Incentive

An incentive is something that encourages and rewards people for their help. As such, it needs to convince people that they should share their time and experience, and it needs to communicate their value to your company. Never shortchange people.

Although the chance to influence a favorite product can motivate people (and thus should always be emphasized), for most people the best incentive is cash. For increased security, widely accepted gift cards work, too. A starting point for incentives in major metro areas in 2012 is $1.50 for every minute of in-person consumer research and $2 per minute for business-to-business research. You can reduce incentives for phone interviews, videoconferences, or other research that doesn't require people to leave their homes or offices or you to visit theirs; unmoderated research can also pay small amounts.

Give extra incentives to people with unique perspectives or who are willing to come in at awkward hours. Calculate the "extra" based on the conditions. If you need someone to come in tomorrow, adding an additional $20 to $40 to the basic incentive may be appropriate. A busy manager may not be willing to break up his or her day for less than $200. It's often useful to budget for a range, and then let the recruiter up the incentive to get good candidates.

For certain people, no amount of money will be enough to encourage them to participate. For these people, you need to come up with alternative incentives. Executives may value meeting other executives in the same industry, so presenting the research as an opportunity to hobnob with peers may entice them. Charity donations are sometimes attractive, as are gift certificates to luxury restaurants or theater tickets. A luxury cruise line site had retired millionaires who liked to travel as its customers. It recruited them by giving them all-expenses-paid flights to New York. It cost the site several thousand dollars per participant, but they were able to get their exact target audience from all over the country. Merely offering the same amount in cash would not have showed the understanding and respect for the participants' priorities that convinced them to participate.

Sometimes people are willing to participate for less than you're offering, or even for free. But it's not a good idea to take advantage of them. For one thing, people who do research for cheap are a self-selecting bunch: they have a lot of time on their hands, or they're really eager to talk to you, or they need the money. The people who fit any of those criteria are unlikely to be representative of your target audience.

Recruiting Pitfalls

The Wrong People

Sometimes you recruit the wrong group. Maybe you misworded a key screener question, and everyone answered it opposite to what you had intended. Maybe you forgot a key element when determining the target audience. Maybe the recruiter always picked the minimal criteria when you only wanted a couple of people with that description. Regardless, sometimes you will mistakenly invite the wrong people. Every researcher has stories about coming into a room and realizing that it's full of people who shouldn't be there at all.

Preparation, a good screener, a carefully chosen target audience, and asking some key questions at the beginning of the research will minimize the chances of this situation, but it still happens. If you find yourself in such a situation, there are two things you can do: either cancel the session and re-recruit, or try to get as much information out of the group, hoping that some of their feedback will be usable. Sometimes the wrong group can be enlightening, since the comparison of answers with a group of the right people can lead to a better understanding of the whole population. Maybe your target audience isn't so unique after all. However, when time is short and accurate results are critical, cancellation is a perfectly acceptable option. Then you can channel your efforts into getting a group of the right people.

Before you decide to re-recruit (or you start blaming the recruiter), you have to determine why the recruiting failed. In some cases, it will be really obvious—you wanted job seekers, but not people who have never had a job—but sometimes it may not be clear why a certain group didn't fit your vision. Identify the elements that resulted in the wrong group: is it because of demographic factors? Is it because of their experience (or lack thereof) with the product? Perhaps you did not specify a key criterion ("factory workers" versus "factory workers who work on the shop floor," for example). Or maybe your expectation of how people behave may not match how your target audience thinks. In rare cases, there may be *no* way to recruit the perfect group because the factors you want simply don't exist together.

Always pay people who show up what you promised them, even if you made a mistake in recruiting them. They showed up in good faith. Likewise, pay the recruiter in full if the recruiter scheduled the wrong people and the problem lies with your screener.

No-shows

It seems to be human nature that about a quarter of any invited group won't show up, for one reason or another. You can compensate for this by scheduling extra people and adding unexcused no-shows to your list of people not to ask again.

If you would like to guarantee a full roster, you can double-schedule every time slot. This makes for twice the recruiting and scheduling work and twice the incentive expense (since you have to pay everyone who shows up, whether or not you need them to participate in research), so it's rarely worth the trouble. But it's useful in certain situations, such as when a senior stakeholder plans to observe the research. You can also use the extra people for other studies if you have the resources and a secondary research project. You could have a usability test as a primary research project and a questionnaire or card-sorting task as a secondary project, since these don't need as much interaction with a researcher as the usability test. You could even have members of the development team who aren't observing the usability test interview the participants (provided those team members have some user research experience).

Likewise, you can schedule a "floater" for a block of time, say, three hours, to hang out in case someone doesn't show up. However, qualified people who have two to three hours in the middle of their day are difficult to find, so this isn't as attractive an option as it may seem at first. Floaters should be paid the proportional amount of incentive for the amount of time they spend waiting (two to three times what someone scheduled for a single slot would get), and they, too, can participate in secondary research if they're not needed as substitutes.

If the schedule and facility rental budget permit, you can also create "makeup" slots a day or two after the initial batch of research. People who can't make their initially scheduled time may be amenable to rescheduling.

Note down the names of no-shows. Unless the people warned you or the recruiter ahead of time, do not pay them and remove them from your contact list, or tell the recruiter to do likewise.

Bias

Your recruiting methods will alter the kinds of people you find. If you rely on paper flyers in your local businesses, for example, you are limiting potential participation to people who visit those businesses. That's great if you're doing a study on people who probably spend a lot of time in your neighborhood. But those people might not have anything relevant to say about your research question.

A truly random sample is impossible, so there's no getting away from some amount of bias. The question is whether the bias matters for your project. Often it does not. Nevertheless, you should mind how bias in recruiting might affect the research results. Keep track of how each person was recruited and evaluate frequent sources for his or her potential to skew the results. If half of your participants come from the same place, you should consider whether that recruitment method is affecting your results.

Anonymity

Preconceptions about your company can also bias the attitudes of people coming to test with you. A famous name can be intimidating, and an unknown company or product can seem more trivial than it really is.

If you're expecting weather bad enough to close the roads, arrange an alternative day in advance. Pick a school near the study site and tell people to check whether it's closed. If that school is closed, odds are that roads are impassable, so people automatically know they're rescheduled for the alternative day.

If you don't want people to know your company's name as they are recruited and scheduled, it may be useful to maintain an alternative identity. Don't deceive people, but working through an alternative email address (say, one from a free service) and describing the company and research without giving any specifics can be useful. In general, people don't mind if you tell them that you'd rather not reveal the name of the company or its products.

Building and Space Preparation

Although not technically a recruiting pitfall, a common problem with scheduling participants for in-person research is that the venue isn't prepared to greet them. If they're arriving at an office, everyone they meet should be expecting them. Security staff should know where to send them; the receptionist should know they're coming. You can even make signs to direct them. If you are meeting in a public place (like a shopping mall or a park), make sure they have some way to coordinate on the go.

Working with a Professional Recruiter

A professional recruiter can take a lot of the headache out of doing the recruiting. Pros have access to a large number of people in a broad range of markets and can schedule them fast. They can be a great asset if you are short on time, don't have many current users to draw on, or aren't sure how to recruit a certain audience.

However, working with professionals is more involved than just picking up a phone and saying that you need people that match this-and-such a profile. Recruiters do not know your business or your research requirements. Careful preparation and collaboration on the part of the research team is necessary for the recruiter to get the people you need when you need them.

Where to Find a Recruiter

Recruiters are often associated with companies offering a broad range of market research services, from providing special

The American Marketing Association (www.ama.org), the Marketing Research Association (www.mra-net. org), and the European Society for Opinion and Market Research (www. esomar.org) can point you toward other resources. Also check www.mkp.com/ observing-the-user- experience for more suggestions on how to find recruiters.

conference rooms to focus group moderation to designing and running whole research projects. If you're in a major metropolitan area, finding one should not be hard. You can generally look up "marketing research" in your city and find half a dozen.

When choosing a recruiting firm, do some research. As with any service, ask for quotes from several different firms and request references from their last couple of user experience research clients. If you're recruiting for usability testing, ask them whether they do recruiting for "one-on-one interviews" (or, ideally, for usability testing) and if they recruit for offsite facilities. Follow up with the references they provide and ask about the accuracy of the recruiting, how receptive the recruiter was to changes, how many people were recruited, and how specific the recruiting criteria were. If you have a specific audience, such as martial arts experts or cardiologists, ask about the recruiter's expertise with that exact group. Different recruiters may have different areas of experience. Some have more contacts in medicine, for example, while some may have great sources in the hospitality industry.

Since recruiting may only be part of their business, full-featured marketing research companies may be reluctant to just recruit and may insist on renting out their research spaces (which can be expensive) or providing other services. If you're only interested in recruiting, you can definitely find a place willing to specialize in it.

For small, fast user research projects, the best bet is to find an independent recruiter who specializes in recruiting and scheduling. These types of companies are rarer than the general market research services, but they exist in most metropolitan areas. If you can't find one, ask some colleagues or check with one of the usability or human factors associations such as the Usability Professionals Association or Computer–Human Interaction Special Interest Group of the Association of Computing Machinery (ACM SIGCHI).

What Recruiters Can Provide

Every professional recruiter should handle all the aspects of finding the right people, scheduling them, answering their questions, and reminding them of their appointments. In addition, an experienced recruiter can also help you focus your research by narrowing your target audience to just to the people you're interested in. If you are not sure about how to specify the right market for your research, ask your recruiter to help you put together a profile.

Some recruiters will write a screener for you, and in practice, they'll often modify your screener to better fit their style and policies. You should participate in the process by requesting a copy before the recruiting begins to ensure that appropriate emphasis is placed on the elements that are of prime importance to you.

In addition to providing you with the profiles of the scheduled participants, many recruiters are willing to take notes about the responses of people who do not get scheduled. Although this tally does not qualify as a survey, it can be interesting information since it can reveal unexpected patterns in your target audience.

Many recruiters will administrate incentive payments, too, cutting checks or providing cash or gift cards as appropriate. In addition, larger recruiting companies can recruit in various geographic markets for you.

What Recruiters Need from You

The most important thing to provide a recruiter is a complete audience description. They will be happy to recruit based on just about any description you give them, but since they don't know your business, they can't filter based on unstated assumptions you have about your audience. If your description isn't sufficiently specific, you're likely to get people you don't want. If you say that you're looking for casual gamers without saying that you want them to have at least some familiarity with online games, the recruiter may get you a bunch of people who play cards. Be as specific as possible. If you're looking for white-collar workers, define what you mean by "white-collar workers."

Include a list of whom to exclude. What are industries that present a potential conflict of interest? How much past participation in research is too much? What companies make products competing with yours?

Budget enough time (many commercial vendors need two weeks minimum) and avoid changing the parameters of the recruiting in the middle. Changes are a hassle for the recruiter, and they're likely to pass the cost of that hassle on to you. If you cancel, be prepared to pay at least part of the incentive fee (all of it if you cancel on the same day) and all the recruiting costs.

Suggest where to get qualified candidates. If you already have a list of customers, such as people who have signed up for a newsletter, and you can filter it for your geographic area, offer the recruiter the list (though be aware that list members will likely know your product and have positive preconceptions about it; otherwise, they wouldn't have signed up for the newsletter). If you don't know where to find candidates, you should give the recruiter as much information as you can about where to look for the target audience and how prevalent you expect them to be in the population as a whole.

Provide direction for how to handle marginal candidates. Clearly note which qualities are flexible and how flexible they are. ("We prefer 25- to 35-year-olds, but will accept people between 20 and 40 if they match all the other criteria well.")

Describe the research to the recruiter. This will help the recruiter understand how to answer questions and may give him or her additional ideas for how to structure the target market description. Is it a series of groups? Is it a series of one-on-one interviews? Will it be done at a special facility? Will it be at the participant's house? Will it be focused on their attitudes, their experiences, or how well they can use a prototype? Tell the recruiter how much of this information is appropriate to tell the participants.

Finally, explain any terminology that's necessary so that the recruiter can interpret people's responses appropriately. If you're looking for IT managers who regularly buy "hot-swappable, fault-tolerant, low RF, Mil-Spec, U-racks," you should probably tell the recruiter something about what all those words mean. The recruiter probably won't need to use these words in conversation, but knowing what they mean will help the recruiter understand the questions he or she is asking.

What They Cost

In 2012, recruiting in major U.S. metro areas typically costs between $100 and $150 per participant scheduled, excluding any incentives you pay participants. Consumers fall on the lower end of the scale and professionals on the upper end. For common groups with few restrictions, such as grocery shoppers with kids, it may be even cheaper. For other groups, such as human resources vice presidents who run organizations with enterprise-wide knowledge management systems, the cost may rise significantly.

Other services, such as screener writing or response tabulation, can be rolled into the whole cost or charged on an hourly basis, with hourly rates of between $75 and $150.

When There Are Recruiting Problems

Don't accept bad recruiting. If it's clear that the priorities and questions in the screener were not strictly followed, ask for your money back or for some better recruiting. First, however, make sure that your audience description did not allow the recruiter to interpret it in a way you hadn't intended. Most recruiters, although not elated by the prospect, will re-recruit participants who didn't fall into the target description.

Further, as a final courtesy to the recruiter, tell him or her when a participant was particularly good or bad. This will help the recruiter in future recruiting efforts.

Gaining Informed Consent

Gaining informed consent is the cornerstone of ethical research practice. Research participants must understand what you are asking them to do and freely agree to participate. Getting participants' informed permission before starting research protects *you* as well as the research participant. Starting a research relationship off with full disclosure minimizes the chance that participants will wonder later if you took advantage of them in any way. This is particularly important in situations where people may feel as if a large company is going to profit from their participation.

It is your responsibility to give participants all the information they need in a way that makes sense to them. This is usually done by having participants read and sign a printed consent form. Consent forms typically include:

A brief description of the research activity and its motivation

This is a usability study of Forkopolis, a website devoted to selling forks. It is intended to improve shoppers' experience with the site. In this study, we will ask you to perform specific tasks using the website and tell us what you think.

An explanation of what data you want to capture and how you plan to use it

We would like to video record this usability test and share the results with our team for the purposes of improving the site. We will not share your name or any other identifying information with anyone else.

If you are planning to take photos, or video/audio record, the form should also ask participants to indicate which media they will allow you to record and to release their rights to it.

Please check the box if
[ ] you give us permission to record video and share it with the team.
[ ] you give us permission to quote any verbal statements you make during the test in our reports.

An assurance that the participant can leave the study at any time without penalty

You are free to leave at any time. If you end participation, we will delete any video we have captured and notes that we have taken.

An encouragement to the participant to raise any questions or concerns about the study as soon as possible

Please let us know as soon as possible if you have any questions or concerns.

Area for participant's printed name, signature, and date of signing

I understand and agree.

Name _____

Signature _____

*Date*_____

Over time, researchers tend to develop consent form wording and formats that work well for them, adapting a standard template to the needs of each project. The best consent forms are short and straightforward. Keep the form under a page if possible and avoid legalese or any unnecessarily formal language.

It can be helpful to think of a "consent" as a process, rather than a document. If a participant initially okays video recording but at the end of the interview asks you to delete the video, take that request seriously. Of course, you can—and should— ask why. Perhaps the participant has specific concerns that you can mitigate. But if the participant remains certain, honor the request and delete the video immediately. For the same reason, it can be a good idea to ask participants at the end of an interview if there is anything they said or showed you that they would not want shared.

If you are using a specialized research facility for focus groups or usability tests, the personnel there can handle consent forms as participants show up. Otherwise, you should get them signed *after* you introduce yourself and everyone gets comfortable, but *before* before you ask the first question or snap the first photograph.

There are some special consent cases that require extra work.

Minors. In much of the world, people under the age of 18 cannot legally consent to research. Their parents or other legal guardians must agree on their behalf. If your study involves minors, consent is a two-step process. First, create a consent form for the guardians specifying that they are consenting on behalf of a minor. Second, make sure to also get informed consent from the child or teenager. If the participant can read, make sure your consent form is at a suitable reading level. If the participant is too young to read, read the consent form aloud and ask questions to make sure the child really understands what's going on. Even though a child can't legally consent, making sure that he or she understands and agrees to participate is the right thing to do.

Illiteracy. You can't depend on written forms when you know or suspect that your participants can't read. In those cases, ask someone who can read—who's also *not* associated with the study—to serve as a witness ahead of time. Then just read the consent form aloud instead of handing it to the participant. Pause periodically so that the participant has time for questions. Ask the participant to make an "X" or other mark to indicate acceptance, and the witness will sign off to confirm that the participant agreed to the terms on the form.

For template consent forms and more resources on informed consent, visit www.mkp.com/ observing-the-user-experience.

Interviewing

Most of the research described in this book boils down to one technique: the interview. Observation is critical, but to really know the user's experience, you have to ask him or her about it, and that's an interview. User research interviewing differs from the kind of interview an investigative journalist or a prospective employer would hold. It's more formal and more standardized, and as a kind of *nondirected interview,* tries to minimize the perspective of the person asking the questions.

The Interview Structure

Nearly every user experience interview, whether it's a one-person lunchtime chat or a ten-person focus group, has a similar underlying structure. It's an hourglass shape that begins with the most general information and then moves to more and more specific questions before stepping back for a bigger perspective and concluding with a summary and wrap-up. Here is one way of dividing a standard interview process into six phases.

1. *Introduction.* All participants introduce themselves. In groups, it's important to know that the other people in the group are somewhat like you in order to feel comfortable, so a group introduction emphasizes the similarities between all the

participants, including the interviewer. In contrast, an individual interview introduction establishes the role of the interviewer as a neutral, but sympathetic, entity.

2. *Warm-up.* The warm-up in any interview is designed to get people to step away from their regular lives and focus on thinking about the product and the work of answering questions.

3. *General issues.* The initial product-specific round of questions concentrates on experiences with the product, as well as attitudes, expectations, and assumptions about it. Asking these kinds of questions early prevents the assumptions of the product development team from skewing people's perceptions. Often, the product isn't even named during this phase.

4. *Deep focus.* The product, service, or idea is introduced, and people concentrate on the details of what it does, how it works, whether they can use it, and what their immediate experience of it is. For usability testing, this phase makes up the bulk of the interview, but for site visits or exploratory interviews, it may never enter the discussion.

5. *Retrospective.* This phase allows people to evaluate the product or idea in a broader light. The discussion is comparable to the "general issues" phase, but the discussion is focused on how the ideas introduced in the "deep focus" phase affect the issues discussed earlier.

6. *Wrap-up.* This is generally the shortest phase of the interview. It formally completes the interview so that the participants aren't left hanging after the last question and returns to administrative topics.

Nondirected Interviewing

A famous scientist once asked the following question on a survey:

> *Does your employer or his representative resort to trickery in order to defraud you of a part of your earnings?**

Do a dry run with every new interview script. Run through it with a colleague or a sample participant, complete with all recording devices and prototypes, and then revise it appropriately.

---

*T.B. Bottomore and Maximilien Rubel, eds., *Karl Marx: Selected Writings in Sociology and Social Philosophy* (New York: McGraw-Hill, 1956), p. 208; as cited in Earl Babbie, *Survey Research Methods* (Belmont, California: Wadsworth, 1990), p. 37.

This is a leading question. Before you read on, think about what makes this a leading question. What in it implies a "right" answer? What is the actual information the author is trying to elicit? What would have to be different for the question to not be a leading question?

The scientist who wrote it was Karl Marx, and he clearly had an answer that he was expecting, and it wasn't "no."

Leading questions are the bane of all social research. They inject the prejudices of the person asking a question into a situation that should be completely about the person answering it. But avoiding directed questioning is easier said than done. It requires a constant vigilance on the part of the person asking the questions and expertise with nondirected interviewing.

Nondirected interviewing is the process of conducting interviews that do not lead or bias the answers. It minimizes the effects of the interviewer's preconceptions in order to explore the user's thoughts, feelings, and experiences.

The Neutral Interviewer

As the person writing and asking the questions in a nondirected interview, your job is to step outside everything you know and feel about your product. Forget all the hard work and creativity. Put away all hopes for success and all fears of failure. See it in a neutral light, as if it's not yours at all.

This seems harsh, but it's necessary in order to be able to understand the feedback people give you, both positive and negative, and be able to relate that to the process of making the product into what *they* want and need, not what you think they want and need. Otherwise, you'll always be seeing either the silver lining or the cloud at a time when you need to be seeing both.

Zen aside, asking questions so as to not bias the respondent's answer involves a lot of self-imposed distance and a rigorously critical examination of your assumptions. This can be especially difficult when you are intimately familiar with or emotionally invested in the product under examination. At first, it's going to feel like your questions take too much energy to formulate and sound stilted. Experience will clarify which questions lead people and how to phrase questions neutrally. Eventually—when you've achieved nondirected question enlightenment—your questions will sound natural, analysis will be easier, and the unbiased answers you get will give you greater confidence in your results.

Presenting a Neutral Face

Asking nondirected questions has been called an art of "talking without really saying anything." Interviewers need to encourage people to talk without telling them what to say.

Often, that means keeping quiet and letting the participant think. When you're tempted to interrupt, try squeezing your hands together instead. Or, when appropriate, take a sip from a glass of water instead of talking.

Experienced interviewers also have a repertoire of generic conversational cues. Some of them are nonverbal, such as "uh-huh" and "mm-hm." Others are sympathetic but bland, such as "that's interesting" and "oh, really." Others, such as "Can you tell me more about _____?" ask for more detail, but don't specify any correct answer.

Developing verbal cues is especially important for phone interviews, since there is no body language to communicate your engagement. In person, leaning forward and nodding occasionally can help. Whether verbally or nonverbally, it's important to make sure people know you are paying attention to them.

Composing Nondirected Questions

Most important, *every question should be focused on the person answering it*. It should focus on *experience,* not extrapolation. Our understanding of our own behavior rarely corresponds to how we really behave. When we try to put ourselves into others' shoes, we idealize and simplify. That's useful in trying to understand people's ideals, but it's rarely useful in understanding their behavior. A question such as, "Is this a useful feature?" can be easily misinterpreted as, "In the universe of all things, do you think that someone somewhere could find some use for this feature?" Even taken at face value, the potential for misunderstanding makes all replies questionable. "Is this feature valuable to the work you do right now?" clarifies the perspective.

Similarly, *questions should concentrate on immediate experience.* People's current behavior better predicts their future behavior than do their predictions. If you ask people, "Is this interesting to you?" they may imagine that at some point they could find it interesting and say yes. But some things that seem interesting in theory are quite different from things that people will remember and return to. If they find something compelling right now, they're likely to continue to find it compelling. Thus, the responses to "If it were available today, would you use it? Why?" will be more useful.

Questions should avoid judgmental language. The person answering the question should not think that you're expecting a specific answer or that any answer is wrong. You can (and should) state this explicitly, but it works better if the question reinforces that view. "Don't you think that this would be better if it was also available on smart phones?" implies that the person asking the question thinks will disapprove if they hear otherwise. "If this feature were available tomorrow on smart phones, would you use it?" doesn't imply an expected answer (though it's a binary question, which we'll describe later). An even better question would be, "Is there any other way you might use a feature like this?" and then ask about smart phones after they've stated their initial thoughts.

Focus questions on a single topic. An "and" or an "or" linking two ideas is ambiguous. It's hard to tell which concept the response addresses. Divide a question like "How would this product be useful to you in school or at work?" in two.

Keep questions open-ended. If forced to choose, people will pick something, even if none of the options match what they believe. "Which feature from the following list is most important to you?" assumes that there *are* features that are important, and it assumes that there is one that's more important than any other. A better way would be to say "Rate from 1 to 5 how important each of the following features is to you, where 1 is least important and 5 is most important. Put 0 if a feature is completely unimportant. Write down any features we may have missed." Or don't rate the features. Instead ask, "Does the product do anything that's particularly useful to you? If so, what is it? What makes it useful?"

Avoid binary questions. Binary questions are of the form "yes/ no" or "true/false" or "this/that," and they force people to make a black-and-white choice when their attitude may not lie near either extreme. "Is this a good product?" misses a lot of subtlety. Although it may be nice to quickly check people's off-the-cuff opinions, it's more valuable to know what they find good and bad about the idea, rather than just if the whole thing seems good or bad. "What, if anything, do you like about this product?"

Running a Nondirected Interview

There are a number of ways to increase the quality of the responses in a nondirected interview.

Define terms. "That thing" can refer to a button, a feature, or the whole site. Personal definitions of words differ from the dictionary definition and the development team's definition. Someone may speak of a simple function as a "module," whereas the development team may call complex clusters of functions "modules." When using a technical term, make sure that you clearly define it first. Whenever possible, use the respondent's definition of a word (even if it's not how you use it), but make sure that you understand what that definition is first (which may mean asking the respondent to define it). This is especially important in group interactions, where everyone can come in with different definitions.

Don't force opinions. There are topics about which we just don't have an opinion. We may have never thought about them, or we may not have enough information. When asked for an opinion, most people will express one. But it's not going to be carefully considered or deeply held. Before framing a question in terms like "Would this be better or worse if…," try to gauge whether the participant has any knowledge of "this."

Restate answers. Bouncing the respondent's answer back at him or her using different words can cut through problems with questions. It clarifies terminology and verifies that you and the participant understand each other. Immediately after someone has finished a thought, you can say something like "So I hear you saying that…" and state what you just heard using different words. Restating answers requires a little extra care because restatements themselves can lead the discussion. If you have a bias, it's easy to subtly restate in a way that better fits your assumptions.

Follow up with examples, but always wait for an undirected answer first. Sometimes people understand a question, but may not know how to start answering it. If you are precise with your wording, it shouldn't be an issue. Occasionally, though, you may want to ask a question that's intentionally broad, to see how people understand a concept or what their most general thoughts are. Prepare an example (or two) for the questions you feel may need examples. After the participants have given their initial answers, you can refocus their thoughts with an example. Say you're running a focus group that's brainstorming new features. If they're defining features too narrowly and seem to have reached an impasse, you can say, "Now what if it were to email you whenever items you liked were on sale?" and see if the participants can come up with other ideas along the same lines. Don't give more than a couple of examples since that tends to frame people's perceptions too strongly.

Use artifacts to keep people focused on the present and to trigger ideas. Artifacts are the material products of people's work: the notes, the papers, the tools, and so on. Bring participants back to their immediate environment by asking questions about the everyday objects that they deal with on a regular basis. When someone mentions "shopping carts" in the abstract, ask about "this shopping cart." When you're in the field and they're talking about how a certain procedure is done, ask them to show it to you with the actual objects. The idealized situation people imagine and discuss in the abstract is often different from the lived experience. Focusing on specific objects helps recall the grungy details missing from the ideal.

Be aware of your own expectations. Watch for situations that surprise you. Despite the exhortations at the beginning of this section, it's impossible to be a blank slate. There are going to be things you assume or expect from the interaction, and these are going to affect how you run the interview. If you're aware of these assumptions, it makes avoiding them easier.

Never say the participant is wrong. Even if someone's understanding of how a product works or what it's for is completely different from what was intended, never tell anyone that his or her perspective is wrong. Try to understand where it comes from and why he or she has it. Even the most minor, superficial contradictions can make participants feel clueless or unprepared and thus reluctant to volunteer their opinions. Steve Portigal, founder of the design research firm Portigal Consulting, tells the story of an interview he conducted about home entertainment technology with a participant who clearly considered himself very knowledgeable. At one point the interviewee called one brand-name digital video recorder a "Tie-vo," instead of pronouncing it "Tee-vo," as its makers do. Steve switched to saying "Tie-vo" himself rather than imply that the participant was incorrect.

Listen carefully to the questions people ask you. Questions reveal a lot about how people understand a product or a situation, and they're important for understanding experience and expectations. Probe why people are asking the question. For example, if someone asks, "Is that how it's supposed to work?" answer with a question: "Is that how you think it works?" or "Is that how you expected it to work?"

Keep questions simple, both in language and in intent. Use questions to uncover assumptions and perceptions, not prove points or justify actions. A good question does the minimum necessary to elicit an undirected response. Analyzing the answers will provide any proof or justification. Questions should focus on getting the clearest raw information.

Review your recordings when possible. It's easy to miss a key statement or a subtle distinction when relying on your memory and notes. Try to Spend some time with your tapes—whether audio or video—verifying that your views of the discussion accurately represent what happened. It's also the way to improve your interviewing skills, even though it can be painful to watch yourself.

Often, two people conduct interviews—one asking questions, and one taking notes. Cross-cultural research may also involve an interpreter (see Chapter 13 for more). In general, try to avoid having more than two interviewers (and, if necessary, an interpreter). Determine when and how the notetaker should ask questions in advance and introduce everyone involved to the interview participant at the beginning of the interview.

Common Interviewing Problems

- *Loaded words or words with multiple meanings.* Be precise in the words that you use. "When you're trying to find something in a site and you get hopelessly lost, what do you do?" "Hopelessly" is imprecise. It can be interpreted by one person as meaning "pretty lost" and by another as "lost without any possibility of ever finding anything." Rewriting the question as, "What do you do if, in the course of looking for something on a site, you realize that you don't know how to get back to an earlier point?"

- *Asking people to predict the future.* As mentioned earlier, when people try to project their actions into the future, they tend to oversimplify and idealize. People are much better at explaining what they're doing as they're doing it than at imagining their actions ahead of time. If you're interested in how someone will behave in a given situation, put him or her into that situation (or a suitable simulation).
- *Invoking authority or peer pressure.* For example, "Most people say that it's pretty easy to find information with this tool. Was that your experience, too?" You can almost always get a fuller and more honest answer with: "Describe your experience using this tool."
- *Assuming that they can answer the question.* Not everyone knows what they know and what they don't know. If you ask someone whether something is the best in its class, you're assuming that he or she is familiar enough with all the products in the class and that he or she can make a balanced, knowledgeable evaluation of all the products.

Problems don't just arise in the formulation of questions. The interpretation of answers also depends on the way questions are asked. There are a couple of behaviors to watch out for when asking questions, so that you can catch them and follow up quickly, making later analysis less ambiguous.

- *People won't always say what they believe.* Sometimes they'll say "yes" to avoid conflict when they mean "no." Watch for the clues in the form of hesitant answers or answers that are inconsistent with previous statements. More subtle cues include someone shaking his or her head while saying "yes," or suddenly stumbling over words. If you think this is happening, ask the person to clarify his or her answer. Often, just showing some interest gives him or her the confidence to say what he or she really means.
- *People will sometimes answer a different question than the one you asked.* In a situation where someone is thinking hard about a

If you are finding your interviews boring, you have a problem. Skilled interviewers can find almost anything interesting as long as participants themselves are interested. One boring interview can be a fluke, but two or three are a bad sign. Either you have a systematic recruiting failure, or your questions are not addressing what people want to talk about.

Don't persist with a script that doesn't work! If you are on your second or third boring interview, try going off-script for a few questions. Look for aspects of your research topic that get the participant talking. Then circle back with the team later to verify the recruiting strategy and maybe brainstorm some new questions for the script.

topic—maybe because he or she is in the middle of a task, or trying to remember a situation—he or she may easily mishear the specifics. Sometimes participants have their own agenda and really want to discuss it. If what they're saying is clearly off track, wait for a pause, say, "That's interesting. Now let me ask you…," and ask the question again with slightly different wording and emphasis. Don't be afraid to be persistent.

When to Break the Rules

You might feel that following all these rules can make for a pretty stiff conversation. And that's not good. People should feel comfortable talking to you and answering questions honestly. You should feel comfortable talking to them.

So take all these rules as suggestions. Feel free to improvise and humanize your interviews. Provide examples. One rule of thumb is that you can and should express enthusiasm and pleasure about anything that's *not* related to the research topic. Feel free to tell people that their children are cute, their vacation plans sound fun, or their home is beautiful. Let the participant off the hook if a question seems too difficult to answer. An interview can be both nondirected *and* comfortable.

Ultimately, the best interview is the one that provides the information you need when you need it. What it takes to do that will be different in every interview. These rules and guidelines will help you get the best information you can, but only you will know how best to implement them.

Documenting interviews
Video record your interviews if possible. Video can reveal crucial moments that audio can't capture, like a shrug while someone is saying "yes" when they really mean "no." Video also frees the interviewer from having to simultaneously take notes and think about asking questions. (Though it's still useful to note down any great quotes you hear and the times you hear them.) Later, you can mine the video for short clips to add richness and authenticity to your presentations.

If introduced quickly and placed carefully, cameras disappear into the background. As the interview begins, explain that you are using the video camera to get an accurate record and that the recording is for research purposes only. Stick the video camera on a tripod in an inconspicuous location, and while you're talking generally pretend it's not there. Do occasionally check the power and data storage, though. Better still, assign someone else to set up and monitor the camera.

If after you explain the purpose of camera, the interviewee does not wish to be video recorded, don't force the issue. You will just start off on difficult footing. Offer to record audio only. If that isn't acceptable, be prepared to take lots of notes and document your recollections immediately afterward.

Photography is often technically easier to manage and allows you to collect a close-up record of specific items and arrangements in an interview. A picture of the interviewee can be an essential memory cue later when you have interviewed many people over a short time span. In some situations—such as on-location interviews in security-conscious organizations—photographs and audio may be your only chance to document.

CHAPTER 7
Focus Groups

Focus groups are structured, attentively moderated group discussions that reveal a target audience's conscious preferences, recalled experiences, and stated priorities. They can tell you what features people value the most and why they value them. As a competitive research tool, they can uncover what people like best about competitors' products or services and where those products and services fail. Sometimes they even reveal entirely new competitors or applications for the product or service.

Originally called "focused interviews," focus groups emerged as a social research method in the 1930s, gained strength as a way to improve soldiers' lives during World War II, then finally took center stage as a marketing tool in the 1950s. As such, they're probably one of the oldest and most widely used techniques for researching the user experience.

Sometimes vilified as shallow and misleading, focus groups do not deserve their bad reputation. Focus groups are not a cure-all for bad products, but neither are they necessarily pseudoscientific voodoo. When guided by a good moderator, carefully analyzed, and appropriately contextualized, they are an excellent way to uncover what and how people think. In particular, they can reveal what people believe about themselves and their needs, which is crucial in determining how to present a product to the public.

Digital product development generally employs focus groups early in the development cycle, when generating ideas, prioritizing features, and understanding the needs of the target audience are paramount. As a quick way to hear a lot of personal stories in a short time, focus groups can give development teams an early foundation from which to analyze the product and its users' needs. Watchable and jargon-free, they engage company members who might not otherwise have the opportunity, expertise, or time to participate in user experience research.

Focus groups are popular in part because they are efficient. Two people working part time can set up a series of groups, run them, analyze the results, and have a report in three weeks. Conducting interviews with a similar number of participants, however, can take a full-time researcher almost twice as long. A survey would need to sample a much larger number of people—significantly increasing the complexity of the logistics and analysis, while providing less understanding about the motivations and attitudes of the respondents. And reading forums, blogs, and other sites of customer feedback doesn't provide the same opportunity for immediate, face-to-face questioning and conversation between company representatives and customers.

That is not to say that focus groups can neatly substitute for other techniques described in this book. By taking people out of their usual environments and putting them in a conference room, you are inevitably going to miss something. Focus groups cannot take the place of usability, in-context interviews, and diary studies. It's not wise to invest expensive resources based solely on self-reported beliefs and preferences. But with careful preparation focus groups provide an opportunity to see the world from the perspective of your users quickly and relatively cheaply.

When Focus Groups Are Appropriate

Knowing when to use focus groups is one of the keys to using them successfully. Although the technique is straightforward and flexible, it's not applicable to all cases or at all stages in the development of a product.

What Focus Groups Are Good For

Focus groups are good at finding desires, motivations, values, and memories. A focus group is an environment where people (ideally) feel comfortable revealing their thoughts and feelings. This allows them to share their view of the issues and assumptions that lie at the core of an experience and to relate them to real-world situations. The hallmark of a good user experience focus group, in fact, is concreteness. Knowing people's preferences and options is only helpful when you know where those beliefs come from.

Focus groups for user experience design (as opposed to focus groups for marketing existing products) are generally scheduled early in product development, though they can also be done during redesign or update cycles. That's when the development team is trying to nail down what problems their product is supposed to solve, how it's supposed to solve them, and why it's valuable for consumers to use their solutions versus all others. Likewise, by bringing users of competitive products in early in the process, it's possible to find out why people value the competition, what they feel are the most critical features, what regularly bothers them, and where they feel the competitors fail.

In combination with imaginative techniques such as probes, collages, and mappings (discussed in Chapter 10), focus group moderators can prompt a concrete, detailed discussion about products and services people want in their lives. Focus groups can also contribute to competitive analysis, allowing you to examine preferences and attitudes quickly across a range of products. Apart from the obvious marketing angle, this information can immediately influence feature and interaction development, defining a user experience that's closer to what the target audience wants before resources have been committed. Focus group data can (and usually should) be verified, either through a generalizable survey or through more in-depth and rich interviews or observation. However, identifying trends often gives teams enough data for initial decisions.

Later in the development cycle, the technique can help identify and prioritize features. Bringing a working prototype, visual mockups, or a concept video to a group discussion is a quick way to get feedback on a design direction before too much time and money are invested. Knowing why people value certain features and how they respond to what you present can help determine what gets developed and in what order. Moreover, since focus groups can act as brainstorming sessions, it's possible to achieve a synergy in which participants generate more ideas together than they could have come up with on their own.

One example from Elizabeth's practice was a tablet computer designed specifically for hospital nurses. She had a number of different designs for the tablet and needed to provide some data to help the product team choose between them. She knew that there were many different kinds of nursing tasks, and that an emergency department nurse might have different needs than an intensive care nurse. But she didn't have time to individually interview nurses from each major professional specialty. She just needed to know which design direction might be broadly acceptable to the widest number of nursing specialties, and, crucially, why. So she conducted three focus groups with six nurses each, representing as many different professional specialties as possible. In each focus group, she had the nurses discuss differences and similarities between their jobs, and then had them review five different form factor prototypes.

Through the discussion of nursing jobs, she discovered that the tools for nursing roles from telemetry to pediatrics needed to survive rough treatment. The participants shied away from equipment that seemed fragile. They wanted tools that could be quickly dropped if they needed both hands for patient care. Busy with paperwork, patients, and medication management, nurses in the study were impatient with tools that didn't work right the first time. Based on the focus groups, the team focused on designs that could be carried in one hand and made sure that programmable buttons provided quick access to frequently used functions.

Focus groups uncover perceptions. This does not mean that they uncover what people actually need or what their actions show they really value. Focus groups will only tell you what people will say they need and what they claim they care about. However, relativism aside, learning what people believe about themselves is as important as knowing what, in practice, they do and feel. Designers, product managers, and marketers need to take people's self-perceptions seriously in order to effectively communicate the product's function and define a style for the product that is recognizable and memorable. The closer a product's presentation of its services matches people's perceptions of their needs, the more they're likely to use it.

What Focus Groups Are Not Good For

First and foremost, focus groups are not a way to understand what people *actually* do. There's no way that people can predict whether they will actually want to use a product, service, or feature in practice, or whether they will even be able to use it effectively. That's why we have usability, observation of products in use, and diary studies.

Second, focus group results do not generalize to a larger population. They can't replace surveys. Data from multiple focus groups can help you make models of human perceptions and attitudes that may well apply to people similar to the participants. However, in almost every case, focus groups are not statistically significant samples. This concern cannot be overstated. When survey samples are both representative and statistically significant, their results can apply to larger populations. There's no guarantee that the proportion of responses in a focus group matches that of the larger population of users.

When taken literally, statements made in focus groups can mislead analysts. Just think of the many products (such as many feature films) that get worse, rather than better, by literal application of focus group results. Here's a funny, if potentially mythical, example from the history of comic books. In an attempt to give Superman fans what they wanted, a focus group of 10- to 12-year-old comics readers was asked what kinds of stories they liked. For a while in the 1960s, Superman's plot lines followed the kids' requests slavishly. What followed was surreal: the Man of Steel dressing up as a Native American and meeting George Washington, not to mention the transformation of Jimmy Olsen, a meek sidekick, into a giant space turtle. In the end, it led to creative bankruptcy. The impossibly convoluted storylines had to be scrapped entirely, and the comic started over as if none of the stories had happened. The lesson: People do not always understand the implications of what they request. They may not understand the trade-offs necessary to accomplish what they ask for. And they can't always accurately predict what they'll enjoy or find useful in practice, as the Superman writers discovered.

Four Types of Focus Groups

There are four common types of focus groups in user experience research. The type of group you choose depends on the types of questions you want to answer, which in turn will likely depend on the stage of development the product is in. Don't feel limited by these categories; they're provided only as rough guides.

Exploratory

These groups get at general attitudes on a given topic, helping developers see how the eventual users of the product will understand it, what words they use to talk about it, and what criteria they will use to judge it. For example, a furniture company is interested in what criteria people use to buy furniture in stores and how they buy similar items online. At the beginning of their development process, they run focus groups and find out that, at first, people insist on seeing furniture "in real life" before buying it (thus negating their entire business plan for selling it online). Further discussion reveals that it is only certain classes of products such as couches and beds that are mistrusted without direct experience. With other things (chairs, tables), most people have no problem buying based solely on pictures and descriptions and, in fact, would prefer to do so.

Feature Prioritization

These groups determine the features that are most attractive to the group and why. They are held, in general, right after the beginning of the development cycle, when it's already clear what the general outlines of the product are going to be. In these types of groups, the assumption is that the participants are interested in a certain kind of product, and the discussion centers on what kinds of things they would like that product to do for them. For example, the participants in a focus group for a homepage creation service were not nearly as interested in community services as they were in tools to help them build and market their own homepage. The "community feeling" that the site was trying to communicate and the tone with which it promoted itself meant little. For them the value in the site lay in the tools and free disk space.

Competitive Analysis

Just as it's important to know what people value in the feature set that a product provides, it's important to know what attracts and repels them with respect to competitors' sites. Often held anonymously (with the commissioning client left unmentioned), these focus groups attempt to understand people's associations with a competitor, what aspects of the competitor's user experience they find valuable, and where it doesn't satisfy their needs and desires. For example, a competitive focus group of online technology news sites revealed that people saw non-news content as largely superfluous. Most read only one news site for a few minutes a day. They valued daily updates and links to other sites, not opinions or in-depth background stories.

Trend Explanation

After spotting a behavioral trend, whether from survey responses, customer service feedback, or website analytics, it's often difficult to determine its primary cause. Focus groups can help explain the behavior by investigating the users' motivations and expectations. These types of focus groups are generally held either as part of a redesign cycle or in response to specific concerns. For example, a survey showed that parents of babies bought more children's products online than parents with older children. Focus groups with people who had taken the survey discovered that parents with babies liked to do their shopping when their babies were asleep, which was often after local shops closed. Older children were more mobile and had preferences of their own, so parents might look for sales online, then take the children in person to help make choices.

How to Conduct Focus Groups

Before you launch a focus group series, it's important to determine several things.

- *The topics that you want to research.* Not all groups feel equally comfortable talking about all subjects, and not all subjects lend themselves to group discussion.
- *The target audience.* These are the people you're going to invite. Specifically, you need to determine the subset of the target audience likely to give you the best and most relevant feedback.

- *The scope of your research.* Focus group series can have a few groups of a handful of people or as many as a dozen groups with ten or more participants apiece. The number of groups and people will depend on the complexity of your questions, the depth to which you want to explore the answers, and the certainty with which you want to know these answers.
- *A schedule.* The best results come from planning for likely contingencies. A good schedule (see Table 7.1) provides sufficient time for everything, especially recruiting, guide writing, and enough flexibility to be able to make a mistake or two.

A typical focus group series takes about three weeks from beginning to end.

Choosing Topics

For an average focus group, you should have three to five main topics to investigate. These should be phrased in terms of the project as a whole. "Understanding the mental model people use when researching insurance" could be a goal for an insurance brokerage site, while a service that recommended home building contractors could be interested in "Knowing at which point people turn to an external service when doing home repair." A high-end online auction site doing a competitive analysis could have "Understanding what repels high-end car sellers from listing their cars on eBay" or "Uncovering what factors will help our product idea to be seen in the same class as Sotheby's" as two of their goals.

A group should be able to adequately discuss each topic in about ten minutes. Topics should be broader than the actual questions you will ask participants, and they should not be goals that are better accomplished by other means (such as a survey). "Making a list of our competitors" would generally be too broad and probably better answered by a survey, whereas "Discovering what factors make the user experiences of our competitors more compelling than ours" is probably more appropriate.

Not all people are comfortable talking about all topics. Choose questions that your target audience will be comfortable discussing. Different audiences for the same product may react differently to the same topics.

Picking a Target Audience

It is not the actual differences between participants, but whether they perceive each other to be different, that determines their willingness to discuss a topic together.
David L. Morgan, *Focus Groups as Qualitative Research*

In focus groups, maybe more than in any of the other methods in this book, careful selection of participants is crucial. For people to feel comfortable talking about their experiences and their values, they need to know that other people in the group will not judge them and that they are with other people like them. Thus, unlike most other kinds of research, focus groups usually rely on homogeneous audiences.

However, the definition of "homogeneous" depends on the context of the research and the group. The participants don't need to be the same in every way, just in the ways that allow people to talk freely about their experiences. For example, generational differences can keep a group from completely opening up about their musical tastes, but might be comfortable and even desirable in a conversation about kitchen appliances.

From your ideal target audience, you should choose a subset or several subsets that are likely to give you the most useful feedback on your topics. The right group will vary from situation to situation. First, you need a solid profile of your target audience, backed up with information about their demographics and technology use. For example, if you're just looking to find out what existing users value about your service, you want to pick the people who represent the largest subset of your actual audience. However, if you're looking to find out why your service has problems retaining customers, you must be much more specific: you must focus only on the people who are just like your standard population but have used your service once and never again.

Often, it's useful to choose several groups to get an understanding of the breadth of experience and as a way to concentrate on specific groups' experiences. For example, if doctors are supposed to use your system but only medical students seem to be using it, then you probably want to talk to both groups. The doctors will tell you why they don't use it, and the medical students will tell you why they do. Maybe you need two separate focus group series.

Define "similarity" from the perspective of subgroup members. If you believe that certain groups of people would not feel comfortable chatting, then don't put them together. Start with demographics and technology use. Income, race, sex, class, age, job, and level of technical know-how are just a few of the factors that can play a role in group interactions and their reactions to a product or service. In order to create a group that can comfortably discuss the topic, we have to take these differences into account. Once the basic outlines are defined, further divide the groups based on behavior: Who does what? What else do they do? Sometimes differences that matter in one topic don't in another. Just remember: you are not looking for people who think identically—you are looking for people who will likely feel comfortable sharing different opinions and experiences.

Here are some examples.

- When studying automobile buying, researchers learned that men sometimes dominate conversations about cars in mixed-gender groups. Since the researchers wanted to ensure a diverse conversational mix, they created three groups: men, women, and a combined group.
- A medical service decided that doctors and doctor-administrators would likely have trouble feeling comfortable with each other because of their roles in the hierarchy of a hospital—even though they would likely both use the service. Thus, the focus groups were divided based the amount of time each participant spent on administrative work.
- A mobile interface to sports media decided that people living in the San Francisco Bay Area would be likely to see a disproportionate amount of information about new technologies when compared to seemingly similar people elsewhere in the United States. Research was conducted in Washington, DC, and St. Louis, Missouri.

You should feel free to define the subgroups in whatever way you feel comfortable. However, do not define subgroups based on the opinions or preferences of their participants. Prescreening participants for their previously stated values defeats the core purpose of the focus groups, which is to explore those values. For example, don't screen for people "who like shopping online"; instead, focus on people who shop online and then determine the full range of reasons why these people shop—especially if they don't enjoy it very much.

Recruiting

Once you've picked a target audience (or audiences), it's time to find participants and invite them. Recruiting for focus groups, much like recruiting for other kinds of research, should be done early and should begin as soon as you've picked your audience.

A couple of things distinguish recruiting a group of people from the standard recruiting process described in Chapter 6, which concentrates on finding individuals.

- The exact profile of the participants is more important. With much research, it's possible to have participants who are almost, but not exactly, ideal target audiences. With focus groups, it's critical that all the people in a given group fall into the desired profile since one person outside it can derail a whole discussion. Owners of small shops, for example, could potentially feel uncomfortable discussing their problems and feelings with an owner of a large store or a franchise.
- Never recruit people who already know each other. Friends— or even acquaintances—unbalance the group discussion dynamic. A raised eyebrow or a sigh says a lot between two people who know each other and can disrupt the discussion and inadvertently conceal important information. When recruiting using the friends and family method, avoid recruiting people who were all referred by the same person.
- Avoid people who frequently participate in focus groups. The group discussion depends on unguarded responses. Veterans of the process may attempt (often subconsciously) to give the kinds of answers that they feel are expected, or they may try to predict the next topic of discussion. Although not fatal, this can skew the discussion, necessitating extra moderation and analysis. If you have to recruit people with focus group experiences, the

experience should be neither frequent nor recent. For these same reasons, never include people who work for organizations that often employ focus groups. So no marketing company employees, no advertising agency people, and so on.

- Make sure none of the participants have significantly more knowledge about any of the topics than the others. If there's an "expert" in a group, that person's knowledge can intimidate the other participants, and his or her views can bias the whole group's perspective. Of course, an entire focus group of experts can be very worthwhile.
- And obviously, make sure you don't recruit anyone employed by any of the specific companies you'll be talking about!

Once you've decided your target audiences, write a profile of the kind of people you want to recruit. The following could be a profile for potential users of a home improvement recommendation website. It defines a group of people who are actively thinking about home improvement and would be likely to look for information about it online.

A Sample Focus Group Recruiting Profile

Demographics

Ages 20–55

Income not important if behavior criteria are met; otherwise, $70K+ household

Gender unimportant, as long as primary decision maker

Web Use

Use Internet at home or work

Use Internet on computer or mobile phone

Have 3+ years of Internet experience

Use the Internet 5–10 hours per week for personal tasks

Shop for products

Compare products or services

Visit websites that indicate an interest or need for home remodeling (e.g., DIY Network, House Beautiful, Martha Stewart.com)

Behavior

Have completed home improvements in the last 9–12 months or intend to perform improvements in the next 3 months

Total improvement cost at least $20K (estimated if in the future)

Defining Scope

You need to decide two things when determining the scope of the focus groups you're going to run: how many groups you're going to have and how many people you're going to have per group.

Never hold only one focus group for the same reasons you shouldn't base conclusions about a class of people on the words of a single person: there may be factors that seem important to the group but that turn out to be the product of the dynamics of one specific group of people. That said, more than four groups is rarely necessary. The first group is, essentially, a dress rehearsal. By the third group you should see confirmation of the views and statements (sometimes verbatim) from the first two groups. The fourth group should confirm trends in the first three. If there is still a lot of new information (especially dissension) coming in during the fourth group, it may be a sign that further groups are necessary or that the makeup of the groups is too broad.

Likewise, User experience research focus groups are generally smaller than their traditional marketing counterparts. Walking through a scenario, demonstrating a prototype, or having people perform a collage or mapping exercise takes time. Asking people for detailed responses—and then explanation of their responses—to these kinds of stimuli takes *more* time. Encouraging conversation takes even *more* time. Reducing the size of the group can help the moderator avoid a rushed and superficial discussion. Six to eight is a good size, balancing the collection of fine detail with a breadth of perspectives. In cases where you'd like to get a lot of depth from each participant, or if the individual focus groups are short, it may be useful to reduce the number to four. Use fewer than that, and the discussion feels more like an interview and doesn't produce as dynamic a situation.

See Chapter 8 for more information on collaging, mapping, and other creative techniques for user experience focus groups.

Writing a Guide

The discussion guide is a script for the moderator to follow. It creates a consistent framework and a schedule for the focus group series. Groups hear the same questions in roughly the same order with much the same context, and all the topics are given enough time. This allows a discussion to bring out the subtleties of the participants' views without shortchanging any of the topics.

Focus group questions should be:

- *Carefully ordered*. Questions put the participants in a certain frame of mind, thinking about certain issues and remembering certain events. A careful sequence of questions takes advantage of that frame of mind to make the flow of the group discussion feel more natural, which in turn helps the participants to maintain a creative stream of ideas and produce better insights. In general, questions should run from the most general to the most specific, with each question narrowing the discussion a bit and concentrating on a subset of what was discussed before. Plan transitions between topics unless a brand new topic is introduced and discussion begins from a general question again. In order to help the group achieve some comfort with each other before creating any friction, you will generally want to move from questions likely to produce consensus to more controversial topics.

- *Nondirected*. As described in Chapter 6, questions should not imply an answer or a value judgment. They should focus on allowing the participants to fill in their own thoughts and values. For example, asking, "Do you think Microsoft has a better search engine than Google?" assumes the participant thinks there are advantages of one over the other. Instead, the question should be framed neutrally: "Are there any things you like about using the Google search service? Are there things you like about using Microsoft? What are they? Are there any ways in which you can compare them? How do they compare?"

- *Open-ended*. Questions should not constrain the answers to fixed responses. They should encourage people to open up and share experiences. Longer responses tell a greater part of the story and tend to be less ambiguous than shorter responses. Thus, rather than phrasing a question in the form, "What's your favorite recipe site?" you could ask, "How do you search for recipes online?"

- *Focused on specifics.* The questions should encourage the participants to be specific in their answers. Richard A. Krueger, in his book *Focus Groups*, recommends breaking down "why" questions into multiple "what" questions, explicitly asking for the influences that informed participants' decision and the attributes of their decision. For example, "How did you decide to go shopping online for forks?" and "What factors went into picking this site?" will provide better insight than asking, "Why did you pick this site?"
- *Personal.* People often attempt to generalize their experiences to the general public or some larger hypothetical group. Since you want to know *individual* views, values, and experiences, emphasize *individual* experiences. Questions should be formulated to concentrate on people's current behavior and opinions, without presenting the option to project their experiences. Thus, "If you had to redo your kitchen right now, which of these features would you use to find a home contractor?" is preferable to "Which of these features do you think are useful?"
- *Unambiguous.* There should be as few shades of meaning as possible, especially when the participants are introduced to new terminology.

Granted, fulfilling all these criteria with all questions is often difficult (writing questions that are simultaneously specific and open-ended is a particularly tricky challenge), but they should be kept in mind as guidelines that should be followed whenever possible. Next to carefully selecting participants, writing a clear, thorough discussion guide is the most crucial ingredient in a successful focus group.

Sample Discussion Guide

The guide is broken up into three major sections: the introduction, the main discussion, and the wrap-up.

The guide that follows is from a focus group for an online news site that is (primarily) interested in understanding the criteria its existing users use to pick the news sites that they read.

Warm-up and intro (10 minutes)

The introduction sets the tone for the discussion, breaks the ice for the participants, and explains the process. It's important to explain who you are—and especially that you are not personally invested in the project. Many people will not want to say negative things if they worry about hurting your feelings.

> Hi. Welcome.
>
> My name is [*first name*]. I am a researcher working with [*company*], who have asked me to help them get some of your thoughts and opinions about some products and some ideas they have. I am not associated with the development of any of the products we'll be talking about, and I have no emotional attachment to any of these things, so you can say whatever you want.
>
> We invited you here because you all read a fair amount of news online. What we're going to do today is talk about some of your experiences so that they can create a service that is best tailored to people like you.

Telling people how they were chosen helps them feel comfortable with one another. Informing them of the end goal of the research helps them start focusing their thoughts.

> The discussion is going to be a pretty casual conversation, but there will be a couple of times when I will ask you to concentrate on certain things.
>
> While we're talking, it's important that you be as candid as possible. You won't hurt anyone's feelings with anything you say, so please say exactly what you feel.
>
> Furthermore, we want *your* opinion. No opinion is right or wrong here—especially about the things we're going to talk about—it's just an opinion, so even if you disagree with someone in the room we'd like to hear that.
>
> But, we'd like you to speak one at a time.

Set out the ground rules for conversation ahead of time and explicitly allow disagreement. This encourages people to feel comfortable voicing their thoughts later.

Also, since we have a lot of ground to cover today and none of us want to be here for hours, I may have to ask you to wrap up a thought or put it aside so that we can move on.

People don't take being interrupted as personally if the expectation has been set early on.

Behind that glass wall, as you can imagine, are a couple people from the company whose idea we'll be talking about and [*assistant moderator's first name*], who is working with me. Occasionally, [*assistant moderator's first name*] may come in here with a note or something we need. Regardless, feel free to ignore them.

Explicitly noting the mirrored wall (assuming there is one in the room) helps to diffuse any anxiety participants may have about it. Sometimes it's even appropriate to have the participants wave or make faces at the people behind the mirror during the introduction. Once mentioned, it shouldn't be brought up again.

As I said, we brought you here to hear what you think, so you won't hurt anyone's feeling by whatever you say. We are video recording this conversation, in case you're wondering, so that [*first name*] and I don't have to sit here scribbling notes and can concentrate on listening to you. It's purely for research purposes. It may be seen by members of the product development team, but it's not for any kind of publicity or promotion or broadcast.

If the session is video recorded, that should be mentioned, even if participants have signed a consent form before the focus group began.

Now I'd like to read you what's called a statement of informed consent. It's a standard thing I read to everyone I interview. It sets out your rights as a person who is participating in this kind of research.
   As a participant in this research:
   You may stop at any time.

> You may ask questions at any time.
> You may leave at any time.
> There is no deception involved.
> Your answers are kept confidential.
> Here is a form that gives us permission to video record this discussion and to use the recording in our research.

It's critical to inform participants of their rights and to get releases that allow you to video record them. Don't skip it. Doing otherwise is both unethical and, in some situations, illegal. Don't be dour when introducing the camera, however, since it can create an overly formal atmosphere. Mike usually makes a joke at this point by saying (while pointing at the snack dish that is in virtually every focus group room) that we're not doing a secret candy taste test.

> Any questions about any of that? [Pause for about 3 seconds to let people speak] Let's start!
> Now I'd like all of us to introduce ourselves. By way of introduction, I'd like you to tell us four things.
> Your first name
> Which city you live in
> What TV shows or publications you absolutely can't live without every week
> Anything that regularly irks you about the Internet
> (Assistant moderator and moderator do introduction first, everyone goes around.)

The introductory questions introduce everyone and break the ice by sharing something personal but not private, such as a favorite TV show or a pet peeve. As such, it's appropriate for these questions to be specific, (somewhat) directed, and unrelated to the topics of inquiry.

> **General News Reading (20 minutes)**
> How do you get the news most frequently?
> Probe: Are there some other ways you regularly get news?
> Which news sites do you regularly read? (Make a list on the whiteboard.)
> Probe: Are there some that you read more than others?

Probe: What attracts you to the sites you read more often? (Ask individuals about specific sites.)

Have you ever switched from one favorite to another? How often? Did it just happen once or have you had several favorites?

Probe: What made you decide to switch?

Probe: How did you pick the site you switched to?

Probes are follow-up questions that dig deeper into a given topic.

Switching gears, what kinds of news are there? (Make a list.)

Are there any good sites for sports? How about for politics? Technology?

Even though the primary topic is technology news, asking about several different kinds of news keeps the discussion from focusing on technology prematurely.

Are there sites that specialize in any of these (business, entertainment, technology)? Can you name some, even if you don't read them regularly?

Changing gears again, have you ever come across a situation where you think that advertising has affected the news you're reading?

Probe: Can you give an example?

Prioritization Exercise (20 minutes)

Pass out paper with the following exercise:

Rate each of the following things based on how important they are to you. Rate them from 1 to 5, with 1 being least important. Also, if you can think of a site that does that one thing better than any other site, write its name or URL next to the statement. You don't have to put a different site down for every one, and you may not want to put any sites down for some.

The number of different stories on a given topic

The number of different topics covered

How quickly the page downloads

Who is presenting the news

How comprehensively each story is covered

Regular columnists

The quality of the site's search engine

The visual appearance of the site

How quickly stories are covered after they happened

How easy it is to get around in the site

(Going around) Say which ones you picked as the most important.

Probe: What about it makes it so important?

Probe: Is there a site that does it well? Does anyone else have that site written down?

Are there any attributes of news sites that you think are important but that are not on the list?

This exercise is designed to start a discussion about what makes a good news site by focusing on specific features.

Competitor Site Review (20 minutes)

We've been talking about general news reading, but let's talk about a couple specific news sites for a few minutes.

Turn on projector.

Are any of you familiar with (*competitor site*)?

Probe (for people who are): Have you ever read it? How often? Under what circumstances do you read it versus other news sources?

Describe [*competitor site's*] personality.

Does [*competitor site*] fall into any kind of specialization?

What kinds of stories would you expect to find here?

Probe: Are there situations where you think you would read it versus other sites?

Probe: Are there kinds of technology news that you wouldn't go here for?

Probe: What about columns? Are there any that would entice you to read them on a regular basis?

(Go through questions again for another competitor; present competitors in a different order to every group.)

Blue Sky and Wrap-Up (10 minutes)

We're almost done. I'd like to do a quick brainstorming exercise. I only have one question, but I'd like everyone to think about it for a few seconds and say what comes to mind.

If you could have anything you wanted in a news service, what would you really like a news service to do that none of them currently offer?

(Wait 30 seconds, then go around and discuss, write ideas on board.)

All right, that's the last of our questions about news.

I know you're all excited about talking about online news, but we really have to wrap up. If there's something you think of on your way home that you'd really like to tell us, please feel free to send a note to the following email address [write email on board].

I have one final question: is there anything that we could do better, either in terms of scheduling or in terms of running these groups? Should we have different food, whatever?

Once the content for the site had been established, subsequent focus groups concentrated on the desirability of specific features and how people use news sites in their daily lives.

After you've written the guide, it's important to review it and time it. Members of the product development team, especially the product and project managers, are good guide reviewers. They can point out ambiguities, serve as a second perspective, and prepare the rest of the team for observing the groups.

Guides should always be tested. An easy way to test the guide is to get a couple of people (it doesn't have to be as many people as the actual group) who haven't seen it and walk them through it, paying attention to how they answer the questions and how accurate the timing is. In addition, treat the first group as a dress rehearsal, reviewing the effectiveness of the guide and adjusting it appropriately.

Setting a Schedule

A typical schedule (see Table 7.1) for a focus group should provide sufficient time for recruiting and writing the discussion guide.

Table 7.1 A Typical Focus Group Schedule

Timing	Activity
$t-2$ weeks	Determine audience and scope; start recruiting immediately.
$t-2$ weeks	Determine broad topics to be investigated; start writing guide.
$t-1$ week	Write first version of discussion guide; discuss exact topic wording with development team; check on recruiting.
$t-3$ days	Write second version of discussion guide with timing; discuss with development team; recruiting should be completed.
$t-2$ days	Complete guide; schedule run-through; set up and check all equipment.
$t-1$ days	Run through in the morning; check times and adjust guide questions as appropriate; do final recruiting check.
t	Conduct groups (usually one to three days depending on scheduling); discuss with observers; collect copies of all notes.
$t+1$ day	Relax; do something else.
$t+3$ days	Watch all tapes; take notes.
$t+1$ week	Combine notes; write analysis.

Conducting the Group

The Physical Layout

If a focus group runs for more than 90 minutes, give people at least a five-minute break halfway through—enough time to get to a restroom, call their families if it's late at night, or check on their cars or bikes.

Hold groups in a comfortable room with good ventilation, good temperature control, and few distractions. Make sure it's large enough for the group, without being so big that people feel lost in it. Make sure that all the participants can see each other around the table and that there's no obviously "best" seat. As well, make sure that the observation room (if there is one) is also comfortable. Hot, cramped, poorly ventilated rooms aren't conducive to positive, engaged attention.

Typical setups look like conference rooms or living rooms, depending on whether the participants are supposed to feel they're in a comfortable work area or at home. Actual conference rooms or lounge areas are easily converted to focus group facilities. If the groups are to be held in a conference room with windows to the inside of the office, the windows should be covered or the group should be held as far away from the windows as possible. Outside windows are fine, unless they're on the first floor, in which case they can be too distracting.

After the group starts, no one except the assistant moderator should enter the room. (Post a sign on the outside door to this effect.) Mike once had a focus group interrupted by a pizza delivery. After some confusion, it became clear that the pizza was for the observers behind the mirror. Although the participants joked about it ("We don't get pizza!"), the disruption set up an unfortunate dynamic. Even entrances and exits by the assistant moderator should be kept to a minimum, in order to avoid any such disruption to the flow of conversation.

Focus Group Supplies Checklist

Here's a starter list for the basics you'll need to bring to a focus group. If you are using a commercial research facility, they may be able to take care of many of these elements for you—check ahead to see what your facility will provide and what it will cost.

- Consent forms and incentive receipts
- Paper for table tents
- Food and drinks for the participants and observers
- Supplies for any object-based activities (see Chapter 8), including big sheets of paper, markers, Post-its™, etc.
- Note-taking supplies
- Recording tools (video and/or audio), along with any accessories you need (e.g., batteries, power cables, tripods, microphones). Bring extra batteries just in case.

Less frequent, but still important, issues:

- Need a projector? Check to see whether your focus group room has one built in or if you'll need to bring one.
- Planning to do some brainstorming or list making? Check whether your focus group room has a whiteboard. If not, you may have to invest in some poster-size paper pads and big markers. An easel is handy as well, so the whole group can see what you're writing. You can also take notes by projecting from a computer screen, but paper is still more reliable, easier to set up, and more flexible.

Eating together can break the tension when people first meet, so provide food and drink when possible. For late evening groups, people are likely to have eaten dinner, so providing high-energy snacks (such as cookies) can often keep a sleepy group talking. Make sure to provide vegetarian choices and plenty of water. Crunchy food can be quite loud when recorded, so things like celery and potato chips are best avoided. Have plenty of noncarbonated drinks; people drinking carbonated beverages have a tendency to stay silent because they're afraid they'll burp in the middle of a sentence.

How to Create a Seating Order

Krueger recommends the following procedure to place people around the table:

- Print *table tents* with the participants' names on them. Table tents are folded sheets of paper that sit upright on the table. Each participant's first name is printed on both sides of the tent, large enough that it can be read from the observation room and on camera (1.5-inch letters printed in black seem to work pretty well).
- Identify the quiet and outspoken people by visiting participants in the waiting area and making small talk with the group.
- Figure out a placement for each person. Long-winded people go next to the moderator, so he or she can break eye contact without disturbing the group dynamic; quiet people go across from the moderator, so the moderator can make eye contact easily and elicit their comments.
- Organize the table tents according to this order.
- Then, when bringing people into the room, drop the table tents seemingly randomly on the table, but actually according to the predesignated order.

If observers are present, they will need some way to unobtrusively watch the proceedings. This can be the traditional two-way mirrored wall, with a soundproof room behind the mirrors that observers can sit in. The observer's room should have its own entrance, so that observers can come and go without entering the

Visit the book's website at www.mkp.com/observing-the-user-experience for tips on remote observation tools, focus group consent forms, and other resources.

discussion room. If such a room is unavailable, closed–circuit video is an inexpensive and easy solution. A long video cable and a television in a nearby room generally suffice, as long as the observation room is acoustically isolated from the discussion room. If the observers will not physically be on site, streaming video over the Internet will allow them to watch from multiple locations (see sidebar).

Remote Observation of Focus Groups

In the past, observers had to be onsite to actively participate in focus groups. Now, using live streaming video and online messaging, observers need only an Internet connection to participate. While watching the video, they can send occasional questions to the assistant moderator as online chat or text messages.

At the time of writing, there are a number of paid and free services that simplify setting up a live video stream. However, since the easiest methods for streaming live video change quickly, we won't specify any tools here. Suffice it to say that you will need to decide ahead of time:

- The number of connections to the video stream you are likely to have
- How high-quality your video needs to be
- Whether you will be recording the video stream or whether you will have a separate camera for the actual recording
- Also remember to test your video streaming setup onsite *before* your first focus group, giving yourself enough time to do any necessary troubleshooting. Setups that work perfectly in your office may fail in the field due to unexpectedly unreliable Internet access, hasty cable connections, and poor lighting.

Video record focus groups when possible. Unlike an audio recording, it's easy to see who's saying what on video and to see the body language that sometimes betrays a negation of a concept or discomfort with a topic. If the video process is made unobtrusive, it quickly disappears into the background of the conversation.

Only one camera is usually necessary to adequately capture a focus group, though you will need to take some care to get good audio. Place the camera roughly behind the moderator. If it has a good wide-angle lens, it's not necessary to have a camera operator, which reduces the cost of the process, as well as the hassle and intimidation of having a person swinging a camera constantly between one side of the table and the other.

Two cardiod microphones are generally sufficient to capture all the participants' comments without a lot of extraneous noise. Cardiod microphones are directional microphones that have a broad area of sound capture in front and a much smaller area facing back. Thus, unlike the omnidirectional microphones that are attached to most video cameras, they can be pointed away from sources of noise such as outside windows and air vents (see Figure 7.1).

The Moderator

Focus group moderation is a skill. The moderator must encourage participation, without allowing any one person to dominate others. To do this without biasing the results takes practice, aptitude, and the right frame of mind.

The basic skills that a moderator must have are a respect for the participants, the ability to listen closely, and the ability to think fast. Often, a moderator must be able to predict where a conversation is headed and either drive it that way or move it in a more desired direction, without the participants realizing that they are being

For temporary setups (as in Figure 7.2), two opposing microphones set on the table work well. However, they're vulnerable to vibration (a pencil tapping, a coffee cup being set down, or a computer humming will sound much louder to the microphone than they do in the room). Putting some cloth or a mouse pad between the stand and the table can ameliorate this problem.

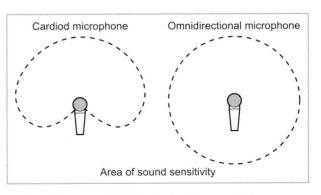

Figure 7.1 Cardiod versus omnidirectional microphone sensitivity.

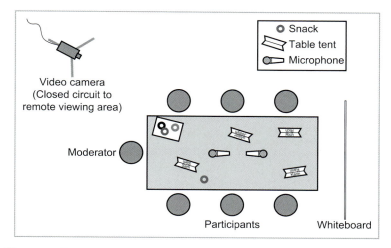

Figure 7.2 Temporary conference room-style focus group layout.

moderated. This can involve many subtle cues in what the moderator says, the tone he or she uses, and even his or her body language.

More specifically, the moderator must be:

- *Always in control.* Most of the time the moderator can use body language and verbal emphasis to maintain control, subtly directing the discussion to certain participants and topics. However, if a digression is moving in an unproductive direction for too long, the moderator should not hesitate to exert more overt control and refocus the discussion on the necessary topics. For example, if in the course of discussing home renovation services, the discussion digresses into stories about home renovation disasters, the moderator should refocus it on the product rather than on extraneous gripes.
- *Always moving forward.* The moderator should monitor the flow of the conversation and introduce topics at appropriate times, making the transition feel natural rather than controlling the flow by stopping discussion or abruptly changing the topic. That way the discussion doesn't turn into an interview, with the participants answering the questions the moderator poses, one after another.

It's impossible and almost certainly unhelpful to remain completely immobile, of course. However, it can be a good exercise to limit extraneous nods, shrugs, and smiles at first.

- *Nonjudgmental.* The moderator acts as mediator, helping the participants express their views without stifling their eagerness to do so. Therefore, the moderator should not express his or her views but facilitate the views of the group to come out. This sometimes involves suppressing the habits we have learned in maintaining civil conversation. For example, many people nod while someone is talking as encouragement, whether they agree or not. This communicates agreement and an endorsement of the viewpoint being expressed. Since the moderator is seen as the "official" at the table, the participants may feel that this is an authoritative endorsement of a certain position and may feel uncomfortable voicing a dissenting opinion.
- *Respectful.* The moderator must have the utmost respect for the participants at all times even if he or she does not agree with them. Every participant in a focus group has a perspective that's useful to the development team, even if it doesn't match with the team's views. For all participants to feel comfortable speaking their minds, they need to know that the moderator will treat their input as valid as everyone else's. This can be accomplished through the use of nonjudgmental statements and strict control of body language, but it's best communicated through the honest belief that everyone needs to be heard.
- *Prepared.* The moderator should know enough about the topics discussed to be able to follow up on participants' statement with specific questions. This does not mean acquiring expertise in the subject matter, but the moderator should have a good working knowledge of the general concepts, the terminology, and the implications of the issues being discussed. The moderator should also have some knowledge of the habits and environment of the people in the group.

In addition, the moderator should have a good sense of timing (knowing when to transition from one participant and one topic to another), a good short-term memory (referring to people's earlier statements and using their own words to describe concepts), and an aptitude for diffusing uncomfortable situations, preferably with humor.

Sometimes it's useful to have multiple moderators. If there are a lot of groups, or they're particularly long, or they're done in different languages, it's sometimes useful to use several people as moderators. If multiple people are going to be moderating, it's important that they go through every question and determine how they're going to ask it and what they will probe.

If there is no assistant moderator, the burden of moderating the participants, managing the observers, and analyzing the final results can fall on a single person. In such situations, it's useful to create situations where the moderator can leave the participants alone for five to ten minutes and walk back to the observation area to review the discussion with the observers, helping frame the discussion for them.

The Assistant Moderator

Although it's certainly possible to conduct a focus group without an assistant moderator, having one helps the process.

The assistant moderator is a key analyst and the connection between the focus group and the outside world. The assistant takes care of the needs of the focus group participants and collects information, leaving the moderator to focus on maintaining a productive discussion.

Before the discussion begins, the assistant should greet the participants when they first come in, bring them into the discussion room, present any initial paperwork (such as nondisclosure agreements), and bring them refreshments. As the discussion progresses, the assistant can bring in notes from the observers and take care of requests.

During the discussion, the assistant moderator should take extensive notes on the interesting parts of the discussion (such as key quotations, issues voiced by the participants, and his or her own observations) and manage the observers' discussion (taking notes on that, too). After the group ends, the assistant moderator can use these notes to spur a debriefing with the observers and the moderator.

Moderating the Discussion

Moderating a discussion is the process of balancing the participants' comfort level and keeping the discussion producing useful information for the research. There are few strict rules for how to moderate a discussion since every group and every topic will demand a different approach Different moderators have different styles that work equally well.

There are, however, several general guidelines that apply to most user experience focus groups.

Actively Manage Group Dynamics

Spending five minutes chatting with participants ahead of time will give you a sense of social relationships—especially the participants who might be too quiet, too bossy, and so on. You can also have the assistant moderator do the talking and discreetly brief the moderator ahead of time.

During the discussion, check for people who talk too little or too much. Are silent people feeling shy? Intimidated? Bored? Try calling on them by name in order to demonstrate your interest. When you ask a general question to the group, look directly at any silent people to let them know you're listening. At the same time, make sure certain people don't talk too much. When someone is having trouble articulating an interesting idea, try judiciously interrupting with follow-up questions. When people are just talking without a purpose, ask them to conclude so that you can ask a different question: "This has been interesting, but we do need to move on to the next topic." Calling on new people by name can also help you derail an overly talkative participant.

One dominant or bullying participant (also known as an "Alpha Jerk") can ruin a whole focus group. Ideally, the best way to avoid the problem is to remove him or her before the group starts. Hostility or aggression can be obvious when meeting and observing participants in the waiting room. During the group, if the bully obviously tries to take "control" of the group from the moderator, it's critical to draw attention away from the challenger. The techniques are basically the same as for a talkative person, but they need to be applied more firmly (and, often, more frequently) than for someone who's merely wordy. In addition, physically dominating the discussion space by walking to a whiteboard and taking notes helps to regain the floor and control of the discussion.

Sometimes the conversation falls dead. To avoid this, try keep the energy level high. Mix in different types of activities, such as watching videos, filling out questionnaires, or using some of the object-based techniques from Chapter 8. If it seems like the group is bored, frustrated, or just tired, consider breaking a little early. If all else fails, temporarily abandon the discussion guide. Return to any questions that did seem to interest the group, or turn the session into an open-ended brainstorm.

Probe for Different Perspectives

When someone says something that's either unclear or contradicts an earlier statement, restate the idea or ask for clarification. Ask for examples of what the person means or definitions of terms he or she is using. Ask the group for agreement or dissent if someone introduces a new interpretation of the topic. Ask about different experiences or opinions.

Go with the Flow...Up to a Point

Group discussions have a tendency to spiral off on tangents, leaving your planned questions far behind. When they bring up important dimensions of a topic that you may have not yet considered, tangents can be very fruitful. But when the tangent moves on to points of marginal interest, end it quickly. Mention that people seem to be interested in a topic—no topic should ever be discouraged flat-out—then ask the group to end the discussion or to postpone it. As well, feel free to skip around your discussion guide if participants bring up a topic or question you had planned for later. Of course, if there are questions that absolutely have to be asked in a certain order, then (politely) insist upon it.

Help People Express Themselves

Give people time to think before you talk. Wait about five seconds after a participant finishes talking before asking a follow-up. Maybe someone else has something to add. When you ask a question, do the same thing before people answer. Doing it explicitly gives people permission to pause a bit before they talk: "Remember the last time you ordered spare parts? Think for a couple of seconds about what led up to that." Five to 10 seconds is all that's generally necessary. In the same way, remember to keep your body language nonjudgmental when people do talk. However, that doesn't mean you need to act like a robot. Laughing along with a joke is also part of helping people feel comfortable. Be relaxed. Smile. Enjoy the opportunity to share in people's lives. Have fun with it.

Watch videotapes of yourself moderating. Is your body language unconsciously expressing your personal preferences? Are you leaving room for people to think and talk?

Asking Questions

Asking questions is a subset of moderating, but there are enough elements that strictly relate to questions that we feel it deserves its own section. Several techniques help in asking questions and in clarifying the responses to questions.

Speak the Language of Your Participants

Avoid introducing new terminology and concepts to the group. New words and ideas tend to frame and bias discussion. If the group uses nonstandard words for a concept or creates its own definitions, let it. When you ask follow-up questions, use the participants' own terminology and concepts, when possible. *Don't use industry jargon.* Even if you think your questions are completely comprehensible, pretest to be sure. As a backup, have some examples ready to explain any potentially unfamiliar words or ideas. Try to elicit responses without the example first, so you don't unnecessarily slant the discussion. But bring out the example if people seem confused. For instance, if the group doesn't know where to start a feature brainstorm, give them an example of what is considered a new feature (e.g., "The car texts you a reminder when it needs an oil change.").

But Ask Key Questions Verbatim

We know; we just told you to use the same terminology as the group. However, there's an important exception. If you have a crucial idea to test, such as a value proposition or a design concept, present it identically to all groups. In order to reduce the ambiguity of the results, you need to make sure that all the groups are responding to the same stimuli.

Writing Before Talking

When people have written something down, they're much less likely to change their minds and follow groupthink or a dominating personality during discussion. For example, participants who first rate a list of topics on paper have more individual and earnest responses in a subsequent group discussion of the ratings. For that reason, individual writing exercises can be especially useful in feature prioritization focus groups, where getting reliable rankings is the whole point of the session.

Prioritize Lists

If you have participants make a list—whether of concerns, needs, features, or what have you—always follow up by having them prioritize it. You don't want to have to guess the most important item later. You can have them vote on the most important thing on the list (randomize when walking through the list!) or do a spontaneous finger tally for each item (everyone holds up a number of fingers to rate the item, the moderator quickly comes up with a rough average of the group's ratings).

Chauncey Wilson, a senior user researcher at Autodesk, suggests the following technique for feature prioritization: give people a "menu" of features on a page with a description of each feature and "price" that's based on an estimate of how much each feature costs to implement, in fictitious dollar amounts. For example, $100 for something that's relatively straightforward and $500 for something that's very involved. Then ask each person to "buy" up to $1000 dollars' worth of features, writing their choices down on a piece of paper. After all participants have made their choices, discuss why people made certain choices.

Handling Focus Group Problems

Misleading Results

The most common problem in focus groups is misleading or inaccurate results. People are conditioned (or predisposed, depending on whose theories you follow) to avoid conflict in small groups. People have a tendency to go along with what they think other people in the group want, even if they don't really agree. This is called *groupthink*, and it presents the illusion of consensus where none actually exists. Failing to question this apparent consensus leads to dangerously unreliable results. To minimize groupthink, first make it clear to the participants that you encourage sincere, polite disagreement. Then include individual writing or sketching exercises as a first introduction to a new topic on which no consensus has yet developed. Careful recruitment will minimize other groupthink problems. Cultural patterns of respect for people of certain ages, genders, income levels, and professions can all lead to some individuals determining a group consensus, often without conscious intent.

Sometimes, however, the problem lies with the team. Focus groups also produce misleading results when the discussion guide incorporates fundamental misunderstandings about people's experience. Hopefully, you will pay attention to any obvious warning signals—perhaps an overly quiet group, or a few people who insist on talking about what matters to them, rather than your questions.

Then you can adjust your approach. The worst outcome is a group that meekly follows your lead, and hence never mentions a critical aspect of their experience. The best way to avoid this is by interviewing a representative of the target audience beforehand. If you discover a misunderstanding after the focus group series has begun, rewrite the guide as soon as possible. If necessary, schedule more groups to be sure you've asked enough people the right questions.

Rough Emotions

The unpredictable mix of personalities in focus groups can create uncomfortable situations. After pretesting your discussion guide, you can probably anticipate which topics might be emotionally difficult. The best way of dealing with powerful feelings is by focusing on the ideas behind them, as long as emotional release doesn't dominate the entire session. If you expect strong feelings, block out some time for participants to discuss their emotional reactions. If a topic unexpectedly stirs up emotional reactions, it's respectful to let participants discuss them, even if it means skipping a couple of questions in the guide. However, the moderator should tactfully move the discussion as soon as possible to a more distanced analysis of any experiential factors contributing to the emotions.

Defuse hostility toward other participants, however, as soon as possible. When a participant says something that other participants find offensive, sometimes a fruitful discussion ensues. But sometimes the group shatters into hostile partisan groups or unites in attacking the offender. Both are extraordinarily damaging to your plans for the group, not to mention upsetting for everyone. To head off attacks, first ask if anyone else shares that view. Then ask if anyone has a different view. Use follow-up questions to get at the rationales underlying the controversial opinions. Ask angry participants why they disagree with the statement. Stay as neutral as you can, even if you yourself are personally offended.

Dismissing Participants

On rare occasions, you will need to eject someone from the group. Whether innocently or not, occasionally a participant will mislead the recruiters and fit the audience profile so poorly that it's disrupting conversation. For example, you might have scheduled a focus group with first-time brides-to-be on wedding planning services…

only to find that one participant actually has a lot of experience helping friends and family plan their ceremonies. You had screened out professional wedding planners as well as people who had been married before, but you hadn't anticipated this special case. So instead of answering questions from their own perspectives, participants keep asking her for advice and deferring to her expert knowledge. It's not her fault, but it's destroying the utility of the group. More unpleasantly, every once in a blue moon you can get a participant whose hostility or bullying is making it impossible for other people to speak their minds. Whether the person is pleasant or obnoxious, always be polite when you request that he or she leave.

Dismissing participants is a last-ditch solution. Do it only when both the moderator and the assistant agree that it's necessary for the focus group's effectiveness.

The assistant moderator should do the dirty work of asking the person to leave. To manage it discreetly, the assistant moderator asks the participant to leave during a scheduled break in the group. As the group is completing a demographic form or a nondisclosure agreement you can duck out and discuss any potential problem with the assistant moderator. In the middle, unfortunately, you may just need to pass notes. Later on, the moderator will announce a "five-minute stretch" or a similar pretext for breaking the action. As it starts, the assistant moderator should come into the room and politely ask the person to go with him or her. The assistant thanks the person for participating, hands over the promised honorarium, and says good-bye. Everyone will know what happened, but the excitement of seeing someone "get kicked out" will quickly fade. If people ask you questions, simply tell them that you felt that the person wasn't a good fit for the group. Don't commiserate or apologize.

Don't let in latecomers who arrive after the introductions. Give them their full honorarium and say good-bye. Bringing new people up to speed is disruptive, and the presence of a "stranger" puts people back on guard after all the icebreaking you did earlier.

Managing Observers

As many people from the development team should attend as many focus groups in a series as possible. This gives the team instant information about their ideas, and it provides the analyst access to valuable technical expertise. For the same reasons that there should be more than one group per topic, people should be encouraged to observe at least two groups if they're planning to observe any. It's much easier to know which phenomena are unique to a given group of people and which may be more general phenomena when you've seen several groups discussing a given topic.

Observers can communicate with the focus group moderator through notes, chat, or text messages. If you are using paper notes, collect questions during stretch breaks to minimize any disruption to the group. Using text or chat to ask questions is potentially less disruptive, but requires constant monitoring by the moderator and assistant. If you are using text or chat, use an account or number that does not get a lot of traffic. You don't want to be fielding messages from your friends and family when your attention should be on the focus group.

Focus Group Observer Instructions

Since observers are an active part of the analysis process, it's important that they know how to approach the observation process. There's a right way to observe a focus group and many wrong ways. Make a point of meeting with new observers beforehand and prepare them for observing the focus group. The following instructions help prepare observers and can be presented as part of the initial orientation or as a written list.

- *Listen.* As tempting as it is to immediately discuss what you're observing, make sure to listen to what people are really saying. Feel free to comment, but don't forget to listen.
- *Don't write people off.* Sometimes, a participant may say things that indicate that he or she isn't getting it. Never assume that someone has nothing important to say just because they aren't interesting or insightful from the start. Understanding why one participant "doesn't get it" can hold the key to understanding the perspectives of everyone who "does."
- *People are contradictory.* Listen to how people are thinking about the topics and what criteria they use to come to conclusions, not necessarily the specific desires they voice. A person may not realize that two desires are impossible to have simultaneously, or he or she may not care. Two people may think they're agreeing, when they're actually saying the exact opposite.
- For that reason, *don't take requests too literally.* Use people's statements as guides to how they think about the topic and what they value, but don't treat the specifics of their

statements as gospel. If everyone in a group says they like or hate something, that doesn't mean that the whole world thinks that way. It is, however, a good indicator that you should be paying attention.

- *Focus groups are not statistically representative.* If four out of five people say something, that doesn't mean that 80% of the population feels that way. It means that a number of people may feel that way, but it doesn't mean anything in terms of the proportions found in the population as a whole. Nothing. Zilch.

- *Focus group participants are experts.* The participants in a focus group know what they want to do and how they currently do it. Listen to their needs and their experiences. Treat them as consultants who are telling you what your customers need, not as novices who need to be educated or the targets of a sales pitch.

- *Focus groups are not a magic bullet.* A couple of good ideas from every group is enough to make that group worthwhile, but not every statement that the group participants make should be followed to the letter.

- Feel free to *pass questions to the moderator, but don't overdo it.* Occasional questions to the group are okay, but there should not be more than a couple in a session. Write your question clearly and concisely, and phrase it as if you were talking to the moderator. When appropriate for the flow of conversation, the moderator will introduce the question. However, the moderator may decide to never introduce your question if the timing or topic is inappropriate.

- *Save some pizza for the moderator.*

Hiring Experts

At this point, you've likely concluded that focus groups are not as simple as they seem. Effective focus group moderation is particularly difficult. It's significantly more complicated than a one-on-one interview. You can hire a company that specializes in focus groups rather than expending the time and energy to do the process in-house. There are several things to consider when hiring a company to run your focus group.

Does the moderator know the subject? A moderator needs to be able to think on his or her feet about the subject and probe appropriately. The company should have some experience with the subject. If the moderator does not, then you should prepare to brief him or her in depth on the subject, the terminology, and the associated issues.

Can the company recruit the right people? Getting the right people for the focus group is critical to that group's success, thus the recruitment method is important. Ask the company how they get their database and how they will screen people for your focus group. Make sure to review the screener, or write your own screener for them. Information on writing screeners is in Chapter 6.

How long is the turnaround time? The analysis method varies from company to company. Depending on the final deliverable, it can take from days to weeks. Make sure to find out what they are planning to do and how long it will take. You may want to forgo a fancy report and slide presentation for a list of findings and a discussion with the moderator and analyst.

As with any contract work, ask for references to the last couple of projects that the company has completed and follow up on them. Do not be shy about asking for satisfaction. If anything is amiss—the recruiting, the moderating, the analysis—call them on it. If necessary, request that additional groups be run at their cost.

Debrief the moderator, assistant moderator, and the observers in between every group. Groups quickly get mixed up in people's memory as time passes, so getting people's thoughts on each group immediately after it's over makes for less work later. Copy everyone's notes and take notes on the debriefing. The guide is an effective tool for organizing and triggering people's memories. Walking through the guide section by section, ask the moderator and observers about what happened. What was unexpected? What was expected but didn't happen? What attitudes did people display? What values did they espouse? What interesting statements did they make (and why were they interesting)? What trends did they observe? Which participants provided interesting feedback? What were the problems with the group? These observations often serve as the backbone of later analysis.

CHAPTER 8

More Than Words: Object-Based Techniques

The stuff that dreams are made of is often difficult to express in words but may be imaginable as pictures in your head.
Elizabeth Sanders, *Generative Tools for CoDesigning*

Talking and listening underpin most user research techniques. However, there's a lot that people know and feel about the world that they have difficulty expressing in words. Maybe they have difficulty remembering the concrete details that will bring a vague memory of a vacation to life. Maybe they can't quite articulate what would improve their experiences with a frustrating wait for medical attention in a hospital emergency center. Maybe they aren't quite sure how to explain something as psychologically complicated as their relationship to saving money. Or maybe you just want to know how other people might draw connections between different parts of a website that currently are not linked.

That's what these techniques are for. They supplement what you can learn by interviewing and observing people by adding objects that participants can use as props to think with and through. This chapter will cover three main types of object-based techniques:

1. *Photo elicitation* is a *dialogic technique* that prompts conversation between researchers and participants.
2. *Collage* and *mapping* are *generative techniques* that invite participants to externally represent internal thoughts and feelings.

3. *Card sorting* is an *associative technique* that asks participants to group objects together in order to surface how they order and make sense of the world.

When to Use Them

Because they do not typically give targeted answers to precise questions, generative and dialogic techniques are most useful in formative, exploratory research. They help you understand how people come to think, feel, and know about their lives. They are not good for testing hypotheses or answering specific tactical questions about product direction. What they are good for is early-stage, "fuzzy front-end" development, when the goal is to open up a space for exploration rather than to justify selecting one direction over another. Design scholars refer to this widening of perspective as *divergent thinking,* as opposed to the *convergent activity* of narrowing one's options. As Pieter Jan Stappers and his colleagues at the Delft University of Technology write "The researcher uses these methods not to answer precisely framed questions, but in order to generate the questions themselves, in directions he or she does not control: in order to find the blind spots."

Why would you want to find your blind spots? Well, if you're trying to expand your current market, develop a totally new product or service, or even substantially update what already exists, it's important to question your assumptions. That's how you avoid mistakes and come up with unexpected breakthroughs. These exploratory techniques also produce lots of rich, inspirational data about people's aspirations, values, and aesthetics—the kind of information that designers can use to generate new concepts and shape decisions about form and function. They can also help researchers map more intangible characteristics or qualities of an organization such as relationships between stakeholder, information flow between elements or stakeholders in a system, and competencies within a value chain.

The associative technique of card sorting, as we'll discuss later in this chapter, is a little different. It is most often used for tactical, convergent decision making about products that are already in the process of active development. Because researchers need to put together a collection of words, phrases, or images to be sorted, it's more effective at organizing information you already have, rather than opening up new areas for investigation.

All of these techniques typically take an hour or less and usually happen in conjunction with interviews or focus groups. For this chapter, we are assuming that you have already chosen a primary research activity.

Dialogic Techniques

One of the simplest ways to stimulate discussion is to show people things, from images to performances, and have them respond. With a concrete example in front of them, people can immediately comment rather than struggle to imagine an example and communicate it to you. Examples give both the researcher and the participant a shared reference point. One of the most commonly used dialogic techniques for user research is *photo elicitation*.

Photo Elicitation

People often say that a picture is worth a thousand words. In photo elicitation, that's not quite true. The goal of photo elicitation is not to substitute images for words, but to use pictures to stimulate vivid, concrete, meaningful words. In photo elicitation, participants respond to a set of images that researchers show them. The idea, based on decades of qualitative social science, is that photographs don't speak for themselves; they require active interpretation by the viewer. As viewers discuss images, you can begin to understand what they see in them, and apply those interpretations to your own project.

Let's return to the example of the hospital emergency center project. You are trying to get people to recall an experience that was probably physically and emotionally difficult—one that they may have tried to forget but that may still provoke intense reactions. Some critical details may have been forgotten, while others might remain so vivid as to obscure other important points.

This would be a good opportunity for a diary study (see Chapter 10), to capture the experience as it's happening—except that people obviously can't plan when they will have a medical emergency. So it would be very hard to recruit them ahead of time. Moreover, asking participants take photographs of other sick people, or of clinicians who have not given their permission, creates a host of legal and ethical problems. In that sort of situation, photo elicitation comes to the rescue.

How to Do It

Assembling the Images

First, you will need to collect a set of images that you think will help you answer your research questions (see Chapter 4 for a discussion of how to formulate research questions). The images used in elicitation are either *user-generated* or *researcher-assembled*. Initial research, such as stakeholder and pilot user interviews (Chapter 6) or competitive analysis (Chapter 5), can produce a list of standard images to stimulate discussion that you assemble yourself. To get user-generated photographs, you will need to contact participants ahead of the interview. They will produce the photographs either through the course of usual activities or in pre-interview exercises initiated by the research team. For example, if you are designing a new camera for documentary photography, you might want to ask photographers for examples of their own existing work. However, if you are interested in learning more about how busy working parents feel about their cars, you'll probably want to ask the car owners to take some specific photographs of car seats, trunk storage, and garaging ahead of time.

Participant-generated photograph elicitation activities resemble simple diary studies or probes. Chapter 10 discusses how to set up a self-documentation exercise with participants.

In the case of the emergency center, you could assemble your own collection of hospital images by downloading photographs from stock photography websites. You might also search for photographs of emergency centers on websites where people share personal photography. The latter can be especially useful to prompt discussion, as stock images are often too polished to include the messy details that can really prompt recollection. Second, with the permission of hospital staff, you might also take your own photographs of the emergency center, documenting those people, places, and objects you know you will want to discuss with participants. Third, depending on your research aims, you might collect some hospital informational and marketing materials to see how they match the experience of your participants.

Make sure you have the legal right to use any photographs you download for research purposes.

Once you've got about 20 or 30 images, it's time to decide which ones you will present, and in which order. Generally, you will want about six to nine images, allotting about five minutes of discussion per image. At this point, you will probably have many more images than you could possibly address in an hour. It's time to cut.

One good way to start creating a manageable collection is to write down all the research questions on separate pieces of paper. Then print out all the possible images. Place each photo next to the research question it supports. If a photo supports more than one research question, just print out another copy. Then sort the photos under each question in order of relevance. Make sure that each research question has at least one image that seems to directly address it. For example, research on hospital emergency centers might be concerned with both what people do to pass the time while they wait and how they feel about waiting. A photo of an angry-looking person pacing next to a person sleeping on a chair might allow you to probe both questions at once.

Just like interview questions, image order is sensitizing: it will direct your participants' attention to certain subjects and away from others. If you are interested in an activity or event (e.g., fixing a car, visiting the hospital) you may want to follow the chronological order of that activity in order to help people recall it. Alternatively, if you are interested in a state or activity with no specific chronological order (e.g., attitudes toward water conservation or photograph editing tools), you could move from more general, atmospheric photos to more specific, concrete ones in order to query participants on more general attitudes before digging into the details of behavior.

Writing the Script

With the images assembled, it's time to write the script. Sometimes called a "protocol," sometimes a "discussion guide," the script is really just that—a list of instructions for the moderator to follow so that the interviews are consistent and everything gets done. For the purposes of keeping this script simple, we're assuming that you've already introduced yourself to the participant, gained informed consent, and proceeded with some introductory questions.

Introduction (3–5 minutes)

The introduction is a way to break the ice and give the participant some context.

[Don't start showing images until after you've finished the introduction.]

What I'd like to do now is show you some photographs. These are photographs that you took for us, remember? When I show you the photograph, I'd like you to speak your reactions out loud. I'm going to ask you some follow-up questions as well. If there's anything in the photograph that you do not want to discuss, please feel free to ask me to move on to the next question.

In the introduction, you want to make sure that you remind participants of how you got the photographs (they gave them to you!) and that they don't have to answer any questions they don't want to. People don't always realize what's in the background of their photographs, and you don't want to shut down your interview by accidentally asking a series of questions about objects or people your participant finds embarrassing or disturbing. This establishes a comfort level about the process and their role in it.

For researcher-generated photographs, you will use much the same language, but make sure that you explain whether the photographs have been customized to them in any way. For example:

Now, I'd like to show you some photographs of hospital emergency centers. Some of them will be from a hospital near where you live. But others may be from hospitals that are far away, and so they may not look familiar to you. They are just here to help us have a conversation about your experience with emergency centers.

Give a basic explanation of the origin of any researcher-assembled images early on so that participants don't interrupt the interview with questions about where the photographs came from or why you chose them.

Then you'll move on to prompting discussion with the photographs. This is the bulk of the activity and, depending on your schedule and the talkativeness of your participants, can take up to five minutes per photograph. You don't want to make people look at too many photographs or they'll get bored. You will also need to take into consideration what other activities you have planned for the interview or focus group.

Elicitation (30–45 minutes)

Showing people objects during the initial introduction can be distracting, as is showing all of your collected objects at once. Instead, proceed one by one, asking (at least initially) identical questions about each photograph. A standard set of questions might be:

> Can you tell me more about what was happening when you took this photograph?
>
> Why did you choose this place (or object, or person)?

People interpret photographs as objects differently. For many people, photographs exist as a straightforward documentation of reality. They may not think about whether the photograph is specially cropped or digitally altered. Experts, however, may pay as much attention to the construction of photographs as to their subject matter.

That means you may want to ask specific questions about how the photographs were made, if that seems appropriate:

> Have you altered the photo in any way with software? Can you tell me about what you did?

For researcher-generated photographs:

> What is the first thing that comes to mind when you see these images?
>
> What are some words you would use to describe how you would feel if you were part of this scene?

When you're done with the photographs, you'll conclude and move on to the next section of your interview protocol, if there is one.

> **Conclusion (2–7 minutes)**
> Thanks for looking through these with me. Before we move on, do you want to return to any of the photos and say anything more?

Offer participants a chance to go back and discuss any of the photographs, just in case there's something they didn't get the chance to say.

Conducting an Elicitation

The format of the images you choose to show will depend on how much control you have over the interview environment. It may seem more convenient to simply bring a computer along to show your images. However, printing them on smooth paper and attaching them to sturdy cardboard allows participants to really get close to them: to handle them, sort them, and stack them in ways that aid their storytelling and help you understand how they are making associations between them. Participant-led image elicitation may require a large number of images that cannot be so easily printed out; in that case, make sure that you have software that can show the images sequentially (as in a slide show), give an overview of the whole collection, or search for a specific image.

If you are using printed photos, you may want to make sure you have a flat area on which you can spread them out. If you are using a computer, make sure you have power.

Unless you have completely reliable Internet access, do not depend on image-sharing websites or other online tools for image elicitation. When in doubt, test your connection first to make sure that you have the correct passwords, firewall access, and download speeds.

Other Types of Dialogic Research

You don't have to show your participants only photographs. Dialogic exercises can use any materials related to the project that could elicit an emotional response (Figure 8.1).

Elizabeth studied relationships to shopping and advertising in families by bringing a collection of advertisements to interviews—from newspaper coupons to print advertisements in glossy magazines. She also asked participants to show her their favorite websites and asked them to discuss the ads featured there.

Figure 8.1 Lextant, a design research and user experience design firm, uses "multi-sensory stimuli" to elicit reactions from research participants. These stimuli can include working portable consumer products, such as mobile phones, as well as material samples to show texture, finish, and even smell. Here, a research participant groups and labels a collection of multi-sensory stimuli. Image courtesy of Lextant.

She spent half of the interview on researcher–generated prompts (the print advertisements) and the other half on the online advertisements. A common set of prompts between interviews allowed some comparison of responses, while visits to personally chosen websites stimulated more in–depth discussion of habits and attitudes.

Table 8.1 Image Elicitation Options

Step 1: Preparing stimuli (images, text, video, etc.)					Step 2: Eliciting responses	
User-generated, produced during		Researcher-assembled, from			Media interpreted as	
Usual activities	Research activity	Stock media	Media sharing websites	Research visits	Existing client materials	Crafted objects	Direct documentation of reality

You can also show participants videos, or even have them react to scenes performed live in front of them by trained actors. Whatever you show participants, you will likely face some similar questions in writing a research plan. Table 8.1 summarizes the many options for elicitation exercises.

Generative Techniques: Making Things

Generative techniques allow participants to externalize emotions and thoughts by creating objects that express them. In discussing the objects with participants as they make them and then analyzing them later on their own, researchers learn more about desires, sensations, and aspirations that are often hard to explain.

Uday Dandavate, of the design research firm SonicRim, often explains generative techniques as ways to access people's *schemas*. Schemas are mental frameworks that organize our experience. While individual schemas can change over time, in the moment they shape people's assumptions about how the world can and should work. Developed by psychologist Frederic Bartlett in the early 20th century, the concept of schemas is now used widely in psychology, cognitive science—and user experience research. Through generative activities, Dandavate says, participants help researchers "gain access to their preconceived abstract mental structures that form the basis of their understanding" of a service or product.

Generative techniques either deploy a toolkit of basic elements provided by the researcher or guide the participant in an open-ended process of making something completely new. This section

The most practically helpful guide to using generative techniques we have found is Contextmapping: Experiences from Practice, *available online from the Delft Technical University.*

covers the activities of collage, which is typically toolkit-based, and mapping, which is usually more open-ended.

Collage

In collage, individuals or groups of people make a new composition out of a pre-existing set of elements. Often called "mood boards" by product designers, collages are useful for just that—expressing attitudes, desires, or emotions. They are easy and fun to make but can deeply inform future design through collaborative interpretation by researchers and participants.

The goal of collaging is not so much to make a coherent and consistent statement whose meaning is obviously clear. Instead, the goal is to help participants express themselves, first through the making of the collage, and next through conversation about the collage. Dr. Gerald Zaltman, of the Harvard Business school, calls this "metaphor elicitation": the structured use of significant images to invoke personal associations and analogues.

How to Do It

Assembling Components

Project-Based Toolkits

You can put almost anything that's printed on paper into a collage— not just photographs, but also shapes (e.g., squares, circles), icons (e.g., arrows, smiley face symbols), and words (e.g., "boring," "escape"). Many sites charge very little to license stock photographs for limited use. Some best practices (adapted from advice given by the Delft Technical University) for picking images to produce rich and stimulating collages include:

- Use preliminary research (e.g. competitive analysis, pilot interviews, books and articles about the subject domain) to help you pick components. Look for words that show up frequently or that seem to have contradictory meanings.
- Vary the image subjects (e.g., plants, animals, people, and things). Also vary the human environments portrayed (e.g., different areas of the home, different kinds of workplaces, and

exotic or unfamiliar landscapes). Include images of people of both sexes, as well as different ages and ethnicities.

- Balance positive and negative emotionally tinged images (e.g., a laughing baby and a frowning adult), as well as realistic and abstract images.
- Avoid any consistent style or mood. That is, don't work to collect images that will look aesthetically pleasing together. The point is to give participants varied ingredients with which to articulate something that's hard for them to state outright, not to create professional-looking outputs.
- Include only a few images that literally show the research topic (e.g., if you're studying hospital emergency rooms don't have too many pictures of doctors, stethoscopes, pills, etc.). You may want those images as a base, but too many of them will constrain the discussion.

Then add some generic components, such as icons and geometric shapes. Most of these generic components can be reused from project to project. Many icons and shapes are available as free files online.

Typical toolkits include about 100 photographs and 100 words. You want to give participants a wide choice of shapes, icons, photographs, and words, but you don't want to overwhelm them. The images in Figure 8.2 demonstrate the range of possible choices.

Participant-Chosen Images

You can also ask participants ahead of time to bring their own photos. In that case, contact your participants a week or more ahead of the planned collage date and ask them to spend two to five hours finding images that represent their feelings about the topic of the interview. If the photographs are in a digital format, have them email the photographs to you in advance so that you can print them out and/or work with them digitally.

Participant-chosen images make for a highly variable result. The advantage is that participants may tell more personally meaningful and detailed stories. The disadvantage is that all the collages will have different components, with no real basis for comparison. If you are interested in, for example, identifying the colors and

Figure 8.2 Sample pages from image collection for collage exercise. Pages were printed out on sticky-back paper. Image courtesy of Adaptive Path.

textures that your target audience associates with "safety" in hospital emergency centers, you may be more interested in what images are chosen from a common set of stimuli rather than the specific details in individual collages.

Preparing the Components

You'll need enough sets of components for all your participants, and then a few extras just in case. The most efficient way to present those components is to lay out many images on the same page, as in Figure 8.2. You can either print the pages on sticky-back paper or use plain paper and provide glue.

What else do you need? Think elementary school arts and crafts.

- Scissors and glue
- Geometric paper cutouts such as stars, squares, and circles
- Colored markers and pens for annotation and drawing
- Sheets of plain paper (11×17 or larger) as the backing for the collage

Writing the Script

Here's a brief guide to a collaging session with one person. At this point, we assume that you've already introduced yourself and the study and signed the consent forms. If you are leading a group collage exercise, plan time in the beginning for everyone to introduce themselves by first name and tell something about themselves (such as a favorite color) to break the ice. This will help them feel more comfortable about sharing other experiences with strangers.

Introduction (3–5 minutes)

What we're going to do next is called a collage exercise. We're really interested in your personal experience with [*subject topic here*]. We'd like to learn about [*subject topic here*] through your eyes. Please choose some of the images and words in your kits and arrange them on the big piece of paper in front of you in a way that represents your own experience with [*subject topic here*]. You can do whatever you want—there's no right way to do this exercise. If you have any questions, feel free to ask. We'll take about 20 minutes.

The most important role of the introduction is to emphasize that people are free to interpret the instructions as they like. Second, it should ask for only personal memories and perceptions, not what participants believe is the general opinion.

Collage (20–30 minutes)

During this period, participants work silently. They may occasionally ask you questions. Try not to imply that there is a right or wrong way to choose and place pictures.

Interview and Discussion (20–30 minutes)

I'd like you to tell me/us about your collage and why you chose the images and words you did.

Have participants present their collages as in a show-and-tell exercise. As they talk, ask them to explain why they chose those particular images and words and what they mean to him or her. Why is one image next to another one? Are they related? You may also want to probe whether there is an overall order or logic to the visual layout of the collage.

If you are running a group exercise, the group can then discuss the entire exercise as a group once every person has spoken.

One workshop can include multiple generative exercises. Just make sure that you include time for open group discussion after each one if you are running a group session.

Wrap-up (3–10 minutes)

Thank your participants for helping out, and ask if there's anything more they want to tell you about the collage or about the experience.

Conducting a Collage Exercise

Just as with the earlier section on photo elicitation, we assume that you've already done the research planning and recruiting for this activity. You know what your major research questions are and have people who you think can help you answer them.

Because you need to give people time to make a collage and then discuss it, allot one to two hours for the entire exercise. As with focus groups, it can be helpful to have a moderator and a note taker present to manage group collage exercises. The note taker can also serve as a timekeeper, since keeping a group collage exercise moving on schedule can involve gently moving people from one part of the activity to the next.

Make sure you have a big enough table for all your participants to work comfortably on. Depending on the participants' comfort

with the idea, people can also work on the floor. Before the participants show up, put a stack of components, scissors, glue (if necessary), and pens in front of each chair.

Have a video camera on a tripod behind the moderator to
record the discussion. Once again, an external microphone on the
table will help you in getting slightly better audio.

Analyzing a Collage Exercise: Avoiding Temptation

You may be tempted to speed up your analysis by interpreting the
collages as solely visual objects, without reference to your notes or
recorded media from the discussion. You may also be tempted to
count the number of times the same image appears in multiple collages and use that as a measure of the "meaning" of the activity.
And, indeed, many consumer researchers use both of those tactics.

Our advice: be careful! Yes, it is possible to look for quantitative
(e.g., numerical) trends in the data. If most of your participants choose
the same image from your toolkit when asked to make a collage about
"safety" in hospital rooms, don't ignore that pattern. But you cannot
simply assume that you know what the placement of the photograph
means to each participant—or that the same photograph means the
same thing to different people. For example, one photo elicitation
study conducted by Froukje Sleeswijk Visser and design research firm
P5 Consultants found the following explanations (emphasis ours) of
the same photo of a swimmer preparing to dive into a pool:

> P1: "I always shave myself in the evening. So I dive into my
> bed, completely **fresh and clean.**"
> P4: "I feel very **sharp** after shaving."
> P3: "I always shave myself before going to work. I work in the
> swimming pool as a **swimming teacher.**"

So while only looking at photographs may be inspirational for
design, it will not necessarily assist in understanding potential users.
In the same way, counting the incidence of any given component
can also be misleading if you assume that each component always
represents a single meaning. Instead, go through your notes or
audio and make sure you link verbal explanations and discussions
with each individual photo. For example, P1 and P4 seem to have
a similar psychological response to shaving: it feels "sharp" and

"clean." P3 approaches the swimmer more literally, as a reminder of when and why he shaves. In the end, you are looking for patterns not just in the photos but in the relationship of multiple people's words to the photos they choose.

Mapping

A map is just a visual representation of relationships between people, objects, and spaces. Maps have three main uses in user research. First, they help participants add concrete details to what might otherwise be abstract answers about habits and preferences. They can help prompt richer, more interesting stories. Second, it can be easier to visually analyze and compare different maps of the same place—or the same sort of place, like a home or a workplace—than it would be to compare verbal descriptions. Third, and most importantly, maps reflect people's beliefs about the spaces and objects around them: how they define those spaces, how they categorize them, and what they feel about them. If you are designing context-aware mobile applications, domestic appliances, or interactive environments, understanding how people relate to places is crucial to the success of your product.

Spatial Mapping

What's your route from home to work? Where's the nearest place to get some coffee? How would you tell a guest cooking in your kitchen where to find a frying pan, eggs, salt, some butter, and a plate?

Most of us have some practice at reading and drawing simple spatial maps, so it's one of the easiest mapping techniques to explain and carry out. It also (unlike photo elicitation and collage) requires little advance work to assemble materials.

How to Do It

To begin, all you'll need is a piece of paper (preferably 11×17 or larger), some pens, and some colored markers. Abstract shapes and graphic icons (as assembled for the photo collage exercise) can be helpful, but they're not necessary. You'll also need a flat space large enough for participants to comfortably spread out. Place an audio recorder nearby or use a video camera to document the drawing process.

The exercise takes about as long as the photo collage, and the same basic principles apply. You can do this exercise with individuals or groups, as long as you allot some time for the groups to present their maps to the group and discuss the maps as a group.

It is helpful, if possible, to get a sense of the space before asking the participant to map it, whether you're interested in a room, home, workplace, or even an entire city. It's hard to ask good questions when you have no idea whether participants are exaggerating the relative sizes or distances of regions or objects, or whether they are leaving out certain regions or objects altogether. For a neighborhood or city, you might look at maps beforehand. If you are interested in the layout of someone's home, you might first schedule a set of getting-to-know-you questions to break the ice, and then ask for a tour of the house. After the tour, you can sit down and start mapping.

A typical one-on-one mapping exercise during an interview looks like this:

Introduction to the exercise (3-5 minutes)

Explain the purpose of the mapping exercise. Make sure to explain that you are interested in the participant's personal experience, not that of the "average" visitor or inhabitant.

Mapping (30-45 minutes)

First, ask participants to sketch a map of the place in question. Don't ask for precision or accuracy. What's important is understanding why people represent size and distance in certain ways. So if you notice that a participant's bedroom looks twice as large as the kitchen (when you know the opposite is true), follow up with a question:

Can you tell me why you drew the bedroom that size?

In following up on absences or strange proportions, avoid implying that the map is badly drawn or somehow "wrong." You didn't ask for an architectural blueprint, after all.

Once you have a basic plan view of the space, ask participants to draw in other significant objects. Think of them as landmarks. The identity of those objects depends on what you're studying. If you're interested in children's play, you might have participants indicate where all the toys and other play objects in the house are located. If you're interested in physical security in the workplace, you might ask the participant to mark locked doors and guard stations. Ask questions as they go to make sure you understand what everything is.

With a base map and landmarks, participants have a solid basis from which to recall activities and attribute meaning to regions on the map. You can ask people to trace the paths of their habitual movements, activities, or routines on the map, step by step. This can involve differently colored arrows, lines, and written annotations (see Figure 8.3 for an example). This kind of question is particularly useful for understanding a physical "journey" through a space or experience, as with someone's weekly grocery shopping or a visit to the doctor's office.

You can also ask people to mark regions and zones that are important to them, such as favorite and least favorite places to do certain tasks, places of play and work, or places where physical access is limited or forbidden. Keep on asking follow-up questions. Make sure to suggest that participants use differently colored markers for each activity or region—that will help you keep track of the different questions later.

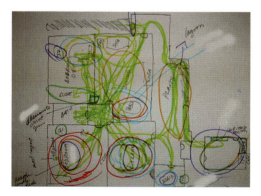

Figure 8.3 A "cognitive map" of a Brazilian household, created during an Intel research project on domestic life around the world. Image courtesy of Intel Corporation.

Conclusion (5-7 minutes)

In the conclusion, as usual, ask if there's anything more participants want to add. Is there anything they forgot to draw in? Is there an expected question that you didn't ask?

Social Mapping

Social network maps have become very popular in the past few years; they're the node-and-link style visual diagrams that represent people as points and relationships as lines between them. Social network maps are usually generated by software that traces explicit, named relationships on social websites, or which extracts implicit relationships from people's communications over email, chat, or telephone. They represent human relationships from the viewpoint of communication systems and they can have hundreds or even thousands of nodes and links.

Here, we are talking about the reverse: getting a picture of communication from the viewpoint of humans. These diagrams are handmade by participants and focus on the most consciously meaningful relationships in their lives. They are a way to get people thinking and talking about the tools they use to make and sustain important relationships in their lives. If you are designing any kind of product or service that facilitates social interaction between people, these kinds of maps can help you understand the dynamics you are developing for.

How to Do It

Like spatial mapping, you'll need a sheet of paper (preferably 11×17 or larger), pens, and colored markers. Get a few packs of Post-it™ notes and small stickers in four or five colors. Make sure the stickers are small enough to fit three or four on a Post-it note and leave some space for writing.

Once again, you'll also need a flat space. Place an audio recorder nearby or use a video camera to document the drawing process.

A typical one-on-one social mapping exercise might go like this:

Introduction to the exercise (3-5 minutes)

Explain the purpose of the exercise, emphasizing that you're interested in the participant's personal experience.

Mapping (30-45 minutes)

First, give the participant a stack of Post-it notes. Ask her to write her name on it and put it anywhere she wants on the paper.

Now, ask her to write down the names of other people in her life, one per Post-it. The wording of this question will affect the results, of course. You should give participants some specific, concrete instructions so they know whom to add. You don't want to suggest that you're interested in hearing about a best friend if you're interested in getting a picture of workplace communication. For example:

- If you're studying communication, ask about "people you are in contact with once a week or more." At this point, it may be helpful to suggest that people take out mobile phones or computers (or paper mail!) and check to see whom they've contacted lately.
- If you're studying emotional attachment, ask about "people who you would talk to about a personal success or trouble." Again, it may be helpful for the participant to refer back to their usual communication tools.

When your participant has gotten going with the names, ask her to stick the Post-its to the paper. Have the participant place the Post-its in proximity to the her name based on, for example, frequency of communication or degree of emotional intimacy. Then ask the participant to group together people who have something in common. As she places Post-its, ask questions like, "How do you know that person?"

As the participant places Post-its on the page, she will probably remember more people to write down and place. That's fine. Have her rearrange the Post-its until all the groupings make sense. Ask her to name the groups. The goal is not perfect accuracy—it's just to get a sense of which people are important and how the participant puts them into groups.

Next, have the participant list the main communication tools she uses on one corner of the page. You will then put a different colored sticker next to each tool. To maintain consistency between interviews, it helps if you have already matched each color to a tool you expect to hear about.

Give her the sheets of colored stickers and have her use the list to place stickers on each person to represent the tools they use for communication. As she places the stickers, probe for further information with questions like:

> How did you start using [*name of tool*] to communicate with [*name of person*]?
>
> Can you give me an example of the last time you were in contact with him/her?
>
> What was the subject of the conversation?
>
> Oh, so you sent him a picture? Where was the picture from?
>
> Does your mother often send you links in email?

In addition to asking for specific examples, a good way to get more concrete detail in answers is to ask the participant to review her major means of communication (for example, text messages, phone call list, email, or social website) and discuss the past few days' activity.

You could probably keep going with these sorts of questions forever, but 45 minutes is about as much as most people can take (Figure 8.4).

Conclusion (5-7 minutes)

In the conclusion, as usual, ask if there's anything more participants want to add. Is there anything they forgot to draw?

In Conclusion

You don't just have to map space—you can also map time. That's what we call a "time line." Asking people to chronologically list the major activities of their day (also known as a "day in the life" exercise) can give you tremendous insights into habits, routines, and everyday struggles.

Sketching relationships of closeness and distance on paper can help your participants discover and explain phenomena that they take for granted. In turn, it can help you make better recommendations— whether you need to know where to install information kiosks in a transit station, or which people your likely users email most.

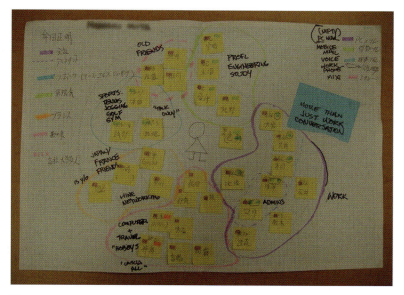

Figure 8.4 Results of social mapping exercise. Image courtesy of Paul Adams, from his 2010 presentation, The Real Life Social Network v2.

Remember, however, that maps don't speak for themselves. They need interpretation. Part of the map's value is in how you use it to prompt follow-up questions about behavior and values. Analyzing a map on its own, without notes from the conversation, is difficult and misleading.

Maps also suffer from all the limitations of our own memory and perceptions. Maps reveal perspective. For example, a child's map of her school will likely not include the maintenance office. That doesn't mean the maintenance office isn't important, but it does give you a child's-eye view of what matters.

Associative Techniques: Card Sorting

Card sorting is a technique that helps uncover how people organize information. It works exactly like it sounds. Participants sort cards with words or phrases in them into groups. How cards get organized—and what labels participants give to each group—can tell you

For a thorough guide to card sorting, we suggest Card Sorting: Designing Usable Categories, *by Donna Spencer.*

a lot about how participants relate and categorize concepts. That, in turn, can help you create visual and structural relationships that make sense to users. You can then use those relationships to understand the sequence of tasks in an activity, structure databases, organize navigational elements, or name features and interface elements.

When to Do Card Sorting

Unlike the other object-based techniques in this chapter, card sorting is best at answering tightly scoped information organization questions. For existing products, it typically serves as a means to solve a clear problem. Maybe there is evidence that users aren't finding what they want on a website, or perhaps two websites need to be combined into one. Card sorting is most effective when you know what kind of information needs to be organized, but before you have figured out how to do it. At that point, a product's purpose, audience, and features are established, but there is not yet a fixed information architecture or interface design. However, since it's fast and easy, you can also use card sorting whenever you need to change an information structure.

There are two kinds of card sorting: *open* and *closed*. In open card sorting, participants sort the cards in any way they want. In closed card sorting, participants assign the cards to predefined groups. Open card sorts are more generally useful as a user research technique, because they produce richer information about user-made categories. However, closed card sorts can be tactically useful in adding to an existing information structure or in answering minor questions about an information structure that you know is working well.

How to Do It

Recruiting

Like the other techniques in this chapter, card sorting is suitable for both individuals and groups. Group card-sorting activities can prompt valuable discussion and debate about what cards "go together," but will also require additional attention to coordination and moderation to make sure that the views of one or two participants don't dominate the sort.

Card sorting is often a quiet individual activity. You can schedule several people simultaneously if you can give the participants enough room to work alone without feeling crowded and if you make sure that moderators circulate to make sure that participants have their questions quickly answered. If you have only one person as a monitor, stagger the schedules about every 15 minutes so that the monitor has time to give each participant an introduction to the technique. An hour is more than sufficient for most card-sorting studies.

Preparing Cards

The core of the card-sorting technique is, not surprisingly, the cards themselves. First, assemble a collection of words and phrases that represent the information you are interested in organizing. If you're trying to uncover how people organize concepts, explain the concepts on the cards with a sentence or two. However, if you're trying to see how people understand a set of terms without necessarily knowing your definitions for them, you can just write them on the cards.

These words and phrases can come from many places: from content you already possess, from terms that the development team uses to describe sections and functions, from interviews with stakeholders or potential users, or from competitive analysis. However, just as with any research technique, your outcomes will only be as good as the prompts you give participants. Donna Spencer recommends ensuring that:

- *Your terms make sense to participants.* This sounds obvious, but sometimes it's hard to know in advance if a common technical term will mean nothing to a nonprofessional. If your product has multiple groups of users who have very different vocabularies (for example, students and teachers, or doctors and patients), you might have to create multiple sets of cards.
- *Your collection contains some reasonable groups.* A test run of your card sort exercise should verify that the items can form some clear groups. If you ask participants to cluster items that don't share any qualities, you are wasting your time and theirs.

- *Your terms are at the same granularity* (level of detail). People facing cards titled "forks," "spoons," and "silverware," will be tempted to make a group of "forks" and "spoons," then label it with "silverware." While seemingly a successful card sort, you aren't learning anything new about the kinds of groups people make *without* your prompting. One tip, from Michael Hawley of the research firm Mad*Pow, is to select terms one layer down in an information hierarchy from the level you're interested in. The groups in the card sort should then suggest how to organize and label the more higher-level type of content.
- *Your terms represent the most important content or functionality.* Talk to stakeholders to make sure that your sort includes the most relevant concepts.
- *Your prompts aren't biasing.* For example, repeating the similar words across multiple cards is likely to lead people to group those cards together, even if there's some evidence that the cards could or should be separated. Additionally, avoid specific brand or product names as labels. Those can bias people toward existing corporate marketing messages or organizational structures. Instead, substitute a more generic description of the product or service.

You can have as few or as many terms as you want. However, the size of a standard card deck (52) strikes a good balance between not providing enough cards to make adequate categories and providing so many that it's overwhelming. If you have hundreds of terms, consider breaking them up across multiple tests.

Next, write your collection of terms on a deck of sturdy note cards. Depending on the size of your collection, it may save time to enter the names into a word processing program or spreadsheet and print the items onto mailing labels that you then stick to the cards. To minimize distraction, use cards that are identical, except for their titles. Also, it will simplify later analysis if you number each card in one corner at this point.

As always, do a test run with a friendly outsider to diagnose any problems: card titles that are biased or unclear, or perhaps misleading instructions. You will also want to test your chosen analysis tool. Will it handle the amount and kind of data that all the combinations of cards will generate? Will it produce the kind of analytic results that you will need to bring to project stakeholders?

The Sort

After bringing in participants and going through all the initial formalities, introduce them to the concept. Say something along the lines of this:

> Each card in this stack has the name of something that you might see on the website. I'd like you to organize the cards into groups that make sense to you. Take as much time as you need. There are no right or wrong groupings. Try to organize all the cards, but not everything needs to belong in a group. You won't have to provide a reason why cards belong in the same group, so if a group feels right, go with it. You also don't need to think about how this group might relate to the design of a website. Focus on what makes sense to you, not what may make sense to anyone else.

Provide a stack of Post-it notes, several pens, and a pile of small binder clips or rubber bands. After they're done grouping, ask them to label the groups if they can, but remind them that not every group necessarily needs a label. Don't tell participants that they'll be labeling ahead of time since that tends to bias people to organize based on labels rather than on what they feel are natural groupings. When they're done, ask them to clip or rubber-band the cards and place the label on the groupings. If you have numbered the cards, you can then just quickly note the numbers for each card on the Post-it label instead of writing or typing each title.

Then ask a brief set of follow-up questions, perhaps something like:

> Can you tell me why you made each of these groups?
>
> Which card is the best example of each group?
>
> Which groups were easiest to assemble? Which were hardest? Why?

The answers to these questions will tell you more about the logic of the groupings, which will matter later as you conduct the analysis. Make sure you audio record or take good notes.

Card Sorting to Prioritize

Card sorting is primarily an organizational or naming technique, but you can also use it to understand how people prioritize features.

Label the cards with current and potential features. First, have the participants place the cards into one of four piles describing how valuable they felt the feature would be to them—from "most valuable" to "not valuable." Then, take the "most valuable" pile and have the participants sort those cards by frequency of predicted use. That allows you to differentiate between immediate interest in a feature and its potential usefulness. Now put the cards into six numerical categories:

0 – Not valuable
1 – Least valuable
2 – Somewhat valuable
3 – Most valuable, rarely used
4 – Most valuable, sometimes used
5 – Most valuable, used often

Then calculate the median value of each card over all the participants. If a number of choices have the same median, calculate the standard deviation of the choices. Lower standard deviations will represent greater agreement among participants about the value of the feature. (See Chapter 12 for definitions of these terms.) Ranking first by user preference, then by agreement, can help teams prioritize features for development.

Card Sort Analysis

You can analyze card sorts either qualitatively and quantitatively.

Qualitative Analysis

When you have the clusters from all the participants, look at them. Copy the clusters to a whiteboard or a spreadsheet. If using a whiteboard, it can be handy to simply refer to each card by number.

By eyeballing the trends in the clusters, you can infer how people understand relationships between the various elements. For example, if people put "News," "About us," and "What we like" together, it tells you they're interested in putting all the information coming from the company's perspective into a single place. However, if they group "News" with "Latest Deals" and "Holiday Gift Guide," then maybe they associate time-related information together.

Try three different types of analysis. First, look at the clusters as a whole. Can you discern any logic behind their organization? Don't treat the clusters literally. People's existing organizations may not make a scalable or functional architecture. Instead, look for underlying themes tying them together. Pay attention to the cards that people didn't categorize or that were categorized differently by everyone. What about the card is giving people trouble? Is it the name? Is it the underlying concept? Is it the relationship to other elements?

Second, follow one card at a time through its various groupings. Are there any cards that consistently appear together? These activities are easier if you have entered the cards into a spreadsheet, which you can then sort in various ways.

Third, look at the labels. Do any words or phrases appear consistently to describe the same cards? Are there common groups that nonetheless got very different labels? Looking at the labeling and the labels' relationships to the clusters underneath can underpin a structure that matches your users' expectations. Even if not used in an interface or information architecture, the terminology can be useful when explaining the product to potential clients and users.

Throughout this process, pay attention to participant comments. What do they say about their reasons for organizing the cards as they did?

Quantitative Analysis

Percentage

Instead of creating their own spreadsheets, many professionals rely on spreadsheet templates. Check www.mkp.com/ observing-the-user-experience for templates, recommendations for specialized card-sorting software, and other card-sorting resources.

With a few simple formulas, spreadsheets can make it easy to calculate more numerical measures of similarity and difference. For example, it's helpful to automatically calculate the percentage of times a card appears in one of the standardized categories, or which categories have the most agreed-upon sets of cards. With the help of a spreadsheet, this isn't difficult, but it does require a detailed setup.

If you performed an open sort, your participants generated their own descriptions for each group of cards. This can present some problems during percentage-based quantitative analysis, since there will likely be multiple groups with similar names that suggest similar concepts. If you preserve those different names, it may be harder to see patterns during qualitative or percentage-based quantitative analysis. In many cases, you will need to start by creating a standard set of labeled categories to which multiple cards can belong.

Are there any cluster of groups with noticeably overlapping labels? For example, take a set of categories with names like "Schedule," "Program schedule," "Event program," and "Event times and places." At least for the moment, you can probably give all those groups the same label, derived from the most generally used words in the cluster. In this case, it would be likely be "Event schedule." Don't worry, you can change the final name of the category later. Just record which category labels you condensed together.

Under no circumstances should you create a group called "Miscellaneous" or "Random stuff." If your users have created such groups, you should either decide that those types of information are irrelevant to the project (it happens!) or assign them to categories. In information organization, naming a group "Miscellaneous" is a sign of laziness or despair. It's preferable to spend extra time trying to figure out why some cards are hard to categorize rather than include a quick fix that just adds confusion to your organizing system.

Statistical

Cluster analysis is a branch of statistics that measures the "distance" between items in a multivariate environment and attempts to find groupings that are close together in the variable space. This allows you to uncover groups of objects that are similar across many dimensions, but that may not be obviously alike in any one of those dimensions. Since people have trouble visualizing more than three dimensions, and there are often more than three variables that can determine similarity, the technique is used to "see" clusters that would otherwise go undiscovered.

In card sorting, cluster analysis locates underlying logics by looking at the clusters people make. Are certain things grouped together more often than other things? Are there hidden relationships between certain cards? These are all things that are hard to see

Cluster analysis does not remove the human analyst from the process. As Donna Spencer points out, while statistical methods "can help you spot patterns, they don't allow you to identify why a pattern exists."

by just looking at the cards. Unfortunately, the mathematics of cluster analysis is difficult without special software. Statistical software packages contain modules that can do cluster analysis, but these are expensive and require an understanding of the statistical procedures used in the analysis. Specialized card-sorting software (see sidebar) is a better choice if you're not a statistics whiz.

The card-sorting process sheds light on people's existing understandings and preferences, and it can show subtle relationships that may not be obvious by just examining a list of clusters. It also provides an idea of how concepts relate to each other, since what may seem like a strong relationship when casually examined may turn out to be weaker when actually analyzed.

Card-Sorting Software

While many professionals prefer the hands-on approach of paper index cards, there are a number of software tools for card sorting. You can use them while the participant and moderator are in the same room, but remote card sorting is increasingly popular. Remote card sorting, by contrast, is typically *unmoderated*. That is, participants perform the card sort on their own time, with no interaction with a researcher. You can reach a much larger number of participants in a shorter amount of time with remote card sorting, but you will not have an opportunity for real-time conversation about sorting decisions.

Note that software packages will produce statistical measures of similarity for you, which can make them especially good choices if you need quantitative analysis and you are in a hurry. You'll find links to card sorting software on the website for this book.

CHAPTER 9

Field Visits: Learning from Observation

Let's say you wanted to design a new, better showerhead—one that would really improve people's experience of bathing, without changing what they already like about it. Keeping clean is one of those seemingly universal behaviors that nonetheless means very different things to people. Where would you start?

You have probably taken at least a few showers in your life. So have all your friends and your family, too. You could design a showerhead based on how you and your friends take showers—but as we've seen elsewhere in this book, this kind of egocentric design can be a mistake. After all, the way you (or your friends) feel about showers might not be typical of the people you want to buy your hypothetical showerhead.

You could also interview a wide range of people about their preferences in shower accessories. While interviews might reduce your egocentrism, just asking people what they want can produce extremely convincing—but misleading—suggestions. Psychology research tells us that people often idealize their needs and desires. Statements about personal preferences often don't correspond to actual needs, values, and behavior.

"But surely," you think, "Showering is a very private activity. You can't just watch people!"

As it turns out, you can.

That's how Moen, a venerable bathroom fixture manufacturer, designed their Revolution showerhead. Realizing that they didn't know much about how people shower and what they look for in a showerhead, they partnered with QualiData, a research company. With QualiData, they recruited a group of ordinary people who wouldn't mind being watched in the shower: *nudists*.

With participants' permission, the researchers installed small waterproof cameras in their bathrooms. They watched participants shower, exactly as they normally would—without clothes, and without observers crowding the room. Then they interviewed the participants to learn about the experience. "You can see what they're protecting and what they're exposing," QualiData researcher Hy Mariampolski told *The Washington Post*. "It turns out that the shower is this emotional and almost spiritual experience."

The participants in their study, of course, wanted to get clean. But they also had other goals: to relax after a hard day; to get energized for a new one; to ease aches and pains. What QualiData and Moen realized through their observation, however, is that people's showerheads were frustrating these goals. The warm water from showerheads didn't seem to cover participants' bodies consistently; people trying to adjust the flow found themselves blinded by steam and soap. Ironically, they would wriggle and contort their bodies in order to get the sensations they associated with relaxation and calm.

Based on this research, Moen engineered a showerhead with wider water coverage and with an adjustment knob that was easy to use even with the eyes closed. That showerhead, the Revolution, became one of Moen's top sellers and won a Businessweek/IDSA silver medal in 2002.

We usually engage in user research to design a new product or improve an existing one—and often we enter a research project already aware of potential solutions. However, we can't limit our consideration of users' experiences to what seems directly relevant to the product. Products and services work well when they blend into our lives. The task of much user research is not just to discover product requirements but to understand how people live—and how they might like to live differently. Thus, from the user's perspective, the Netflix media streaming service is not simply about accessing lots of movies. It's about having a quiet evening with a spouse, killing time in an airport, or maybe indulging in a beloved TV show. The Netflix website recommendations and the streaming service are tools that make media consumption easier, but the real value lies with the experiences they facilitate.

One of the best ways to understand people's experiences is to see them for ourselves. The techniques in this chapter will help you experience how potential users of your product or service live, how they think, and what problems they run into. As QualiData found out, with a little bit of ingenuity, you can observe almost anything.

What Are Field Visits?

Field visits are just what you think: going out of the office to meet people where they're most comfortable—that is, at their habitual places and activities. Field visits move research into offices, homes, shops, cars, public transportation, hospitals, factories, and gyms—any place important to your target audience (Figures 9.1–9.3). However, that doesn't mean your research can't also involve other techniques, such as diary studies or card sorting. The goal of field visits, like that of other methods, is to understand both *how* and *why* people do what they do.

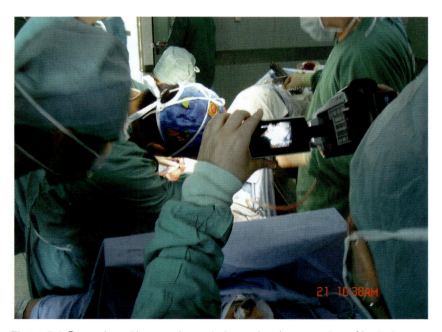

Figure 9.1 Researchers video record a surgical procedure. Image courtesy of Lextant.

Figure 9.2 Field visit with a farmer. Image courtesy of Lextant.

Figure 9.3 Tour of a home office.

In other words, field visits give you information about the environment people live in and work in that you couldn't otherwise get. It helps you interpret their lives within the context of that environment—and not as they recall their lives while sitting in a lab or conference room. It uncovers what people really do, how they define what is actually valuable to them, and what will compete with your product for their time and attention.

In experiencing the world alongside them, you can better understand the problems people face and how your product can fit into their lives. This basic research method involves visiting people once or multiple times, asking them questions, and often following them as they go about their normal activities.

How Are Field Visits Used?

Most projects begin with an idea about an initial problem or situation and some rough ideas about how to respond to it. Field visits clarify and focus these ideas by giving concrete insights into the situation, what the situation entails, and how people cope with it. Thus, as with the showerhead example, they are usually done before the process of creating solutions has begun—most often the very beginning of the development cycle.

However, field visits are also useful in between development cycles or as part of a redesign. In those situations, they can tell you how people are using the product, when they're using it, and what they're using it for. This serves as a check of your initial assumptions, a way to evaluate the suitability of the product to its actual use, and a method of discovering areas into which the product can naturally expand.

For example, a major mobile device company was trying to understand why there were so many data entry errors on a mobile device for long-haul truck drivers. Many people in the company tended to blame the truckers, whom they assumed were uneducated. None of them had ever actually met a trucker, but they figured it couldn't be too hard to type in a word or two. One winter, a senior user interface (UI) designer decided to see for himself.

The designer spent a week at a truck stop watching truck drivers use the device and talking to them about it. He quickly discovered that the truckers could spell perfectly. Instead, the problem was the device. The truckers tended to be big men, with big fingers. To make matters worse, they often wore bulky gloves in the winter. The device had tiny buttons, making typing with big fingers in warm gloves frustrating. The team redesigned the UI so that it required less typing and added a big OK button that was easy to hit while wearing gloves. The error rates dropped dramatically. More importantly, the team realized it had been basing important design decisions on faulty assumptions.

Field visits typically have one or more of these outcomes:

- *Specifying concrete details about actual use.* Researchers often observe how people work and play in order to help write concrete requirements that engineers can implement. In the mobile UI example, the designer discovered that the buttons were too small for the truck drivers to easily use. This kind of project is often called *requirements gathering*, though "gathering" is a misleading term. It's important to note that requirements are *produced* through skilled analysis and interpretation of research data. They don't just wait around like flowers to be picked.

- *Surfacing hidden understandings.* In everyday life, people have experiences that they can't recall or explain abstractly when asked. Take the question of showering: In the abstract, people may not be able to remember or explain how they take a shower, nor what they enjoy about it. Engaging with people in context helps us not just identify those moments of hard-to-explain emotions and activities, but also elicit discussion and description of how tools and technologies play a role in social relationships and internal states.

- *Challenging assumptions.* One of the roles of the user researcher is to (politely!) challenge incorrect, and sometimes insulting, assumptions about the intelligence, competence, and dignity of "users"—who are, after all, just ordinary people trying to use your product to accomplish their goals. We challenge these assumptions not just because it's the right thing to do, but also because our job is to help make more useful, more desirable, and more usable products. Informed empathy lies at the heart of better design. If the mobile UI designer had not visited the truck stop, his team would have had no better insight into the errors.

Table 9.1 A Typical Observation Schedule

Timing	Activity
$t - 3$ weeks	Recruit and schedule participants.
t	Observation and interviewing.
$t + 1$ week	Complete all follow-up interviews. Sort and organize research data for analysis. Begin analysis.
$t + 2$ weeks	Continue analysis.
$t + 3$ weeks	Write initial report.

Different types of field visits have different purposes and assumptions. The point of this chapter is not necessarily to advocate for one approach over another. Instead, the point is to help you choose the best approach for your project and then help you get started. Revealing hidden understandings is not necessarily in conflict with requirements gathering. However, it may be a waste of your time to try to get deep into the values and aspirations of your users when what you really need to identify—fast—is why truckers are making so many data entry errors.

What Ethnography Is…and *Isn't*

Over the past decade, many people have come to use "ethnography" as a catchall description for any kind of qualitative research taking place outside of a lab or other specialized research facility.

How you *do* research is much more important than what you *call* it. Nevertheless, there's been a lot of debate within the research community over using "ethnography" to describe on-site qualitative research. Understanding what the word "ethnography" has historically meant within social science and how commercial design researchers now use it will save you a lot of trouble and confusion. It will also help you do more interesting, more thoughtful, and more credible work if you plan to do ethnographically influenced observational research.

The term "ethnography" has a specific meaning and history to the social sciences, anthropology in particular. What we now call "ethnography" began with attempts in 19th-century Europe to study places and peoples that seemed strange and exotic. Today, ethnography is widely practiced as a means to understand the worldview of many groups—from teenagers with mobile phones to waitstaff in bars.

Many scholarly ethnographers would not call ethnography a technique or method. Rather, they treat it as a goal of research. This makes sense if you think about the origin of the word "ethnography"—from the Greek "ethno" (people) and "graphy" (writing). So, ethnography is more about how ethnographers represent their subjects than any specific research activity. A quick rule of thumb: If you are using words that you, your boss, or your client invented to describe experiences and activities that you have never had and that are specific to your users or customers, you're probably not doing ethnography.

Ethnographers often characterize this distinction in terms of *emic* concepts (those native to a group) and *etic* concepts (those from outside). Ethnographers try to interpret and represent the differences between the two from their own perspective and from that of research participants. For that reason ethnography is often associated with the method of *participant observation*, in which the researcher actively takes part in a group's activities to learn from members experientially. However, for ethnographers trained in the social sciences, doing ethnography also requires knowledge of the history and theories of their discipline. This connection gives ethnographers a framework for asking questions, interpreting what they see, and situating it within a larger cultural context.

So, just performing participant observation—the main inspiration for the methods described in this chapter—will not automatically make what you are doing an ethnography in terms of social science. And that's okay! A lot of necessary, useful, inspirational, and valuable consumer research is not traditionally ethnographic in nature. But if your goals for a project include representing how people understand what they do and why they do it, then you'll find that at least a basic grasp on the history and theory of ethnography in social science is very helpful. There's a reading list on the book's website, but we recommend Michael Agar's *The Professional Stranger* as an expert and nuanced introduction.

The Field Visit Process

Since you'll be going out of your office and into the workplaces and homes of your customers, it's especially important to be thoroughly prepared. You won't have the option to go back and get something you've forgotten, and you—not your company's cool new leather waiting room furniture—will be the one making the first impression about your company.

Selecting Participants

Chapter 6 describes how to choose an appropriate set of participants in detail. But here's the short version: Pick people like the ones you think will want to use your product. Maybe they use the product already. Maybe they use a competitor's product. Maybe the people who use the product are different from the people who buy the product, so there are actually multiple important groups to consider. Regardless, your participants should resemble the people who will eventually use and/or purchase your product.

You should specify this target audience in as much detail as you can, concentrating on their behavior.

- What is their demographic makeup?
- What activities are most significant to their relationship with the product?
- What tools (digital and otherwise) do they regularly use in those activities?
- Are there tools they must occasionally use to solve specific problems?
- How do they use them?

Take this list and narrow it down to a few key factors. They may be demographic, such as location and income, or behavioral, such as tools used and attitudes toward the product/activity. In the showerhead example, Moen knew that it was aiming for North America and had a good idea of the stores (and hence likely customer budget) where it would sell its new showerhead.

There are two main strategies for selecting sites and people for observation. Your choice of strategy will reflect the priority of your project. If your goal is to develop a wide range of new opportunities for design, you may want to follow the *extreme* or *lead user* strategy. If your goal is to solve a specific problem, you may want to follow the *typical user* strategy.

Typical User Strategy

After specifying your target audience, identify the most important activities and groups of customers. Your product may appeal to a varied group of people, but there are only going to be a couple of key target markets defined by the factors you earlier identified. In fact, there may be only one. Focus your research on participants who share the most common key factors until you feel that you know what there is to know about their behavior, and then move on to secondary markets.

Extreme/Lead User Strategy

After identifying a domain of interest and specifying the possible audiences, ensure as much diversity in key factors as possible. Instead of looking for "typical" users, look for people who are extreme in some way—extremely enthusiastic users, extremely negative or resistant nonusers, or "lead users"—people who are ahead of most in adopting a new technology. For example, an extreme user strategy for designing a new showerhead might be to look for people who really love showering and who have invested a lot in their perfect shower, then contrast them with people who hate showering and who only take baths.

You may find that extreme users make visible behaviors or desires that are present in users that are more "typical" but are harder to see. You may also find that widely divergent participants may suggest a broader set of opportunities than a narrow (though deep) study of one particular group.

Recruiting

Once you have your profile, you need to find people who match it. A complete description of recruiting is in Chapter 6, but here are some things to consider.

First, decide how many people you want to visit. The number will depend on how much time you have allocated to the research and the resources available. We think designer Kim Goodwin's suggestion of four people per important factor in your analysis of the target audience is a good starting point for a quick project. So if you're interested in showering, you might interview four people who shower a lot and four people who don't like to shower at all.

If you have more time, five to eight people per factor should give you a pretty good idea of how a big chunk of the target audience does their work (or entertains themselves, or shops, or whatever the focus of your product happens to be) and should be enough for a first round of inquiry. If you find that you have not met the goals of the research or you don't feel comfortable with the results of the first round, schedule a second round.

Scheduling

After finding some candidates, you need to schedule time to visit them. Observational research sessions can last from a couple of hours to multiple full workdays, depending on the length of the tasks and how much ancillary information you'll be collecting. The most important criterion in scheduling is that the people need to be doing the kinds of activity you're going to study *while you're observing them.* You may need to negotiate timing in order to show up when they're doing the relevant tasks. You may need to ask them to wait until you arrive. If you are doing an on-site interview (rather than a full observation activity), it may only take you an hour or two.

If you are interested in complex activities achieved by multiple people working together, it is a good idea to schedule multiple days of visits, with a team of more than two people. That way, you get a more complete perspective on how people's jobs fit together. During the day, You should also make time at least once to meet with other people on your team to share what you're seeing and discuss any emerging insights into patterns of behavior.

Since the research is going to be on-site, give the participants some idea of what to expect when you arrive. Before you show up, tell them the general goals of the research, how long it will take, the equipment you will use, and what kinds of activities you want

If you do not have the time, budget, or team members to make all the visits you think are necessary, it's time to revisit your research plan (see Chapter 4) and rethink how you will answer your research questions—or if you need to rescope your goals for the project.

to observe. You don't have to be specific (and, in fact, leaving some specifics out can produce a more spontaneous response), but they should have a good idea of what you are asking of them. That way, you minimize the chance of unwelcome surprises for both you and the participants. You will need to get consent from all participants before taking photographs or video of them, so it's an especially good idea to clarify your documentation plans ahead of time. Finally, ask them not to prepare for your arrival at all. People tend to tidy up their living and working space when a stranger arrives, so make it clear that it's important for you to see their daily environment, warts and all.

When studying people in office environments, it's often necessary to get releases and to sign nondisclosure agreements. Sometimes it's possible to do stealth research under the promise of anonymity, but this approach brings real ethical and pragmatic problems. When you do not tell people you are a researcher, you are essentially spying on them. You are violating their privacy. Pragmatically, field visits are hard to overlook. People are unlikely to ignore a stranger taking photos, waving around a video camera, or obsessively taking notes. If there's any doubt that your visit might come as a surprise, ask the people you've scheduled to tell everyone who needs to know about your arrival and to get you all the forms you need to have as early as possible.

The incentive payment to each participant should reflect the length of the observation. Generally, this means something between $100 and $200 for most visits. Some companies may have policies restricting such payments to their employees, which should be determined ahead of time (this is especially true when the company being studied is the same company commissioning the research—as is often the case for intranet or in-house software projects).

If you are working within a company that already does a lot of marketing or user research, you should check if there are rules about payments to research participants. Some companies prefer giving cash; others use cash equivalents, such as gift cards. Accounting for payments also differs across companies. Some use a signed consent form as a receipt; others will want a separate signed receipt. Learning the rules ahead of time will make project accounting a lot easier on everyone.

Remember, research participants are doing *you* a favor by welcoming you into their homes and workplaces. If cash payment is forbidden, then a small gift may be appropriate (though not for government agencies or regulated industries). Follow-up interviews should be treated likewise unless you agree with the participants ahead of time on a single lump sum (in which case, it should reflect the total amount of time spent).

Learn the Domain

In order to be able to understand what people are doing and to properly analyze your data, you need to be familiar with what they do. This means getting to know the terminology, the tools, and the techniques that they are likely to be using in their work. You don't have to know all the details of their job, but you should be somewhat familiar with the domain.

If you know nothing about an activity or domain, before you visit you'll probably want to start with some preliminary research. Online forums or discussion sites, in which experts give each other advice, will help familiarize you with everyday terms and concerns. Personal photography sites, in which people share snapshots of their everyday lives, can also provide a window into any unfamiliar environments you will be visiting. Once you've done some initial reading, you have some sense of what you've gotten yourself into. You can go further by asking a friendly expert who is not connected with the project to walk through the basics of their job. He or she doesn't have to go into complicated technical explanations, just enough to familiarize you.

If possible, try a typical task yourself. This is the most basic form of participant observation. If it requires some physical skill, you may need to get special access to tools and equipment (this works well for things like making pizza, but not so well for things like brain surgery). You can often get access to software and a training manual for a couple of hours. Sometimes you can experiment with a similar—but easier—activity in order to start engaging with the experience. For example, researchers studying a biology lab made themselves measure and chart all the activities involved in making a cup of tea, just as if they were titrating a solution. Of course, making tea is not laboratory biology. But it helped them put themselves in the position of someone who had to document every single part of a task. If the environment you're studying is a technical one, ask a member of technical support or quality assurance to walk you through some typical tasks to see how they, as expert in-house users, do them.

In general, it's a good idea to start with "beginner's mind"—to act as if you are just coming to a topic or audience, even if you think it's very familiar to you. That way, you can make yourself more sensitive to details you might otherwise take for granted. If you are preparing to study a clearly unfamiliar cultural group—perhaps people who speak a different language, live in a different country, or follow different religious traditions—take a look at the recommendations for cross-cultural and global research in Chapter 13.

Make Your Expectations Explicit

As part of your preparation, get clear about your expectations. Write down how and when you expect people to do things that are important to your product, and what attitudes you expect they will have toward certain elements. You can do this with other members of the development team, asking them to profile the specific actions you expect people to take. When you're in the field, keep these scenarios in mind. Use the situations where what you see doesn't match your expectations to trigger more investigation. This is especially important when, as with the typing truck drivers, it's clear that you aren't the only one in your company who expected to see something different.

Preparing for the Visit

In addition to all the research-related preparation, do these things just because you're leaving the comfort of your office:

- Make a list of everything you're going to bring—every pencil, consent form, and notebook. Start the list a week before you're going to visit your first site. Then, whenever you remember something else you should bring, add it to the list. A day before you visit the site, make sure you have everything on the list and get everything you don't. On the day of the visit, cross off everything as it's loaded into your backpack or car.

Some people will tell you to take a "neutral" or "unbiased" position to field visits. However, we think total objectivity is an unrealistic expectation. Everyone has experiences in the past and expectations for the future that influence their view of the world. That's what being human is all about! Instead of futilely trying to rid yourself of personal beliefs and preferences, we recommend reflexivity *instead. Be clear to yourself and others about your expectations for the project, then work actively to counteract them. That way, you can enter each new situation with a more open mind to its possibilities.*

Sometimes real-life situations unfold very differently from your expectations. You may be counting on one kind of situation—say, a typical day using the typical tools—and you find something completely different, such as a crisis where the main system is down or workers are scrambling to meet an unexpected deadline.

In such situations, pay attention to how the unexpected situation is resolved and compare that to the situation you had expected and that others experience. If the situation is very atypical—it happens only every five years, or the people you're interviewing have been pulled into a job that doesn't relate to a task you're studying—try to get them to describe their normal routine, maybe in contrast to what they're doing at the moment. If the situation seems like it's too far off from what you're trying to accomplish, reschedule the visit for a time where their experience may be more relevant to your research goals.

- Make sure you have twice as many media releases and/or consent forms as you expect to need. During the field visit, more people could show up than you planned for—and if you don't get their consent, you won't be able to share all those amazing things they tell you.
- Put everything you need to make and track incentive payments in one container that you can carry with you inconspicuously, like a large envelope or small bag.
- Know how to operate your equipment. Set up a test site that will simulate the user's work environment ahead of time. A day or two before, set up everything as you're going to use it on-site, complete with all cords plugged in, all tripods extended, all cameras running, and all laptops booted. Then, break it down and set it back up again. Get a set of good headphones to check the quality of the audio. Good audio quality can make the difference between usable and useless media files.
- Have more than enough supplies. Bring an extension cord with multiple outlets, extra recording media, two extra pads of paper, and a couple of extra pens. You never know when a card will fail or an interview ends up being so exciting that you go through two notepads. Take extra batteries for every piece of electronics you own that requires separate batteries.
- Plan for meal breaks and debrief time. Closely watching someone for several hours can be draining, and you don't want to run around an office frantically looking for a drinking fountain while worried that you're missing a key moment. Bring bottled water and plan to eat between sessions. It's sometimes helpful to have lunch with your participants, which can be a good opportunity to get background on their jobs in a less formal setting.

Caution: Videographer on the Loose

Video is useful for capturing the details of both environments and behavior. It doesn't have to be Hollywood-quality; it just needs to be good enough to share with stakeholders as part of your reporting.

There are some reasons to be careful about using video, however.

perhaps the workaround is a fantastic solution that should be implemented everywhere. Nevertheless, workarounds mean that *there once was a problem*. But with the immediate need met, your participants may have forgotten that the problem ever existed. Workarounds are one of the main reasons why field visits are so useful. It's hard to get people in a focus group to identify a problem they've forgotten they ever had.

Some signs of a workaround:

- Objects used for unintended purposes (e.g., the stacked books)
- Widespread, casual, accepted rule breaking (e.g., the shared passwords)
- Improvised physical interventions (e.g., the taped light switch)

When you see something that looks like a workaround, ask how it got there. That may give you some insight into the original problem.

When asking about workarounds, try not to sound judgmental or accusing, especially if your participants are actually breaking a rule (as with the sharing of passwords). People will not help you if they think you're going to get them in trouble.

Collect Artifacts

When we say "artifacts," we mean the nondigital tools people use to help them accomplish their tasks. Documenting and collecting people's artifacts can be extremely enlightening. For example, if you're interested in how people plan activities, it may be appropriate to photograph their calendars to see what kinds of annotations they make, or to videotape them using shared calendars like the ones written on many office whiteboards. If you're interested in how they shop for food, you may want to collect their shopping lists and videotape them at the supermarket picking out items. Pay attention to all the artifacts at work in an activity, even if they don't seem entirely related to your project. It's doubtful that you'd want to collect a surgeon's instruments after an operation, but you may want to record how they're arranged.

Sometimes, as in health care environments, there may be privacy concerns that prevent you from viewing or collecting an artifact. However, a faked paper form or doctor's note is undesirable. It will likely be idealized and miss some of the mess and variety of the real one. Ask permission to watch a participant work with the

Always make sure to ask for permission before you copy or collect artifacts.

real thing, and then take a blank form as a reminder of how the information was organized.

Note Taking

How to take notes during observation is a key question to consider ahead of time, even if you are video and audio recording. We find that taking occasional notes while concentrating on participants' words and actions works well, but it requires watching the videotape to get juicy quotations and capture the subtlety of the interaction. Others recommend taking lots of notes on-site and using the videotape as backup.

Note taking isn't just about you. It also affects your relationship with participants. There are very real negative consequences to paying too much attention to what you're writing. While the etiquette of listening differs from place to place, interviews depend on how we appropriately signal attentiveness and respect. Looking people in the eye, smiling, turning your body toward them—all of those can be meaningful signals. If you are constantly looking down at a notebook, participants may feel like you don't care about what they're saying. You will also miss lots of meaningful body language and hence lots of opportunities to probe more deeply when what participants are saying doesn't quite match how they're saying it.

You will want a clear method to highlight your follow-up questions. One way is to write them in a separate place from the rest of his notes. Another way is to keep follow-ups scattered throughout the notes, but mark them so you can find them again.

You will also need to clearly differentiate what you see and hear from your interpretations about what it all means. Confusing observation with your personal interpretation leads to inaccurate analysis later, because you can so easily end up replicating your own biases and assumptions. The easiest way to avoid this problem is to visibly separate different kinds of notes as you go. You can do that by:

Taking notes doesn't require fancy gadgets. In fact, what you want is something simple, cheap, and unbreakable. Most researchers still rely on pen and paper.

- Writing observational notes on one side of the paper, interpretation on the other
- Highlighting interpretation with brackets, asterisks, or other typographic marks like [this] or **this**
- Using a different colors of pens or pencil

For an example of what field notes look like, here is a snippet from an observation of a health insurance broker using an existing online system to create a request for proposal (RFP):

> Looks at paper [needs summary] form for coverage desired. Circles coverage section with pen.
>
> Goes to Plan Search screen.
>
> Opens "New Search" window.
>
> "I know I want a 90/70 with a 5/10 drug, but I'm going to get all of the 90/70 plans no matter what."
>
> Types in plan details without looking back at form. **Because he's so familiar with it?**
>
> Looks at search results page.
>
> Points at top plan: "Aetna has a 90/70 that covers chiro, so I'm looking at their plan as a benchmark, which is enough to give me an idea of what to expect from the RFP."
>
> Clicks on Aetna plan for full details.
>
> Prints out plan details on printer in hall (about three cubes away) using browser Print button. Retrieves printout and places it on top of needs summary form.
>
> Would like to get details on similar recent quotes.
>
> Goes back to search results. Scrolls through results and clicks on Blue Shield plan.

Why Can't You Just Ask People?

Field visits take more time and effort than other techniques. Observational research generates enormous amounts of data that you then have to analyze. Moreover, despite a long and quite successful history of use in ergonomics, product design, and information systems design, it can seem exotic to people more accustomed to surveys and usability labs. So it's understandable that people often ask, "Well, why *can't* you just ask people what they want?"

We touched on this question briefly early in this chapter. But it's important to return to it, because there are some common concerns that those planning observational research often need to address. These concerns (and their responses) draw in large part from an article by corporate ethnographers Brigitte Jordan and Brinda Dalal.

"This Takes Too Long"

There's a lot to learn from field visits, even if you just have an afternoon. You can use what you learn from a brief period of observation to argue for dedicating more resources to visiting your audience on their home turf.

"This Costs Too Much"

The question is, "Compared to what?" How is the budget being spent now? Doing some field visits early can help avoid sinking huge amounts of time and money into products that turn out to be undesirable or unusable. It can be helpful, suggest Jordan and Dalal, to ask clients or managers to express their fears so that you can address them specifically. It can help to talk about other projects that required costly fixes late in the development cycle because the product did not match the realities on the ground.

"Don't Bother. We Can Do This Faster and Cheaper with Market Research and Focus Groups"

Traditional market research and user research are complementary. Market research attempts to map the size of the potential consumer base in order to drive business decisions. In order to make those decisions, market research requires a well-defined product. Field visits are one of the tools we use to design that product.

Focus groups and surveys are useful, but they are prone to multiple biases. First, people aren't always good at remembering and reporting all the details of what they do. Second, it turns out that people aren't very good at predicting what they will do in the future. For example, take the case of complex personalization features. Many product teams have been perplexed as to why no one uses personalization features after the vast majority of survey respondents claimed to want them. The reason is simple. Ideally, people would love products tuned perfectly to their preferences and needs. But the actual tuning process is much harder than first imagined. So although survey respondents would indeed love a service personalized as they imagine it, when faced with the pragmatics of customization, they give up and use the plain vanilla service. Observational research helps you get a better sense of what kinds of efforts people are prepared to make.

"Couldn't I Just Go Myself and Watch for a While?"

It's true that it can be helpful for clients and other stakeholders to experience the contexts in which the products they design will be put to use—especially if those contexts are unfamiliar to them. But, as we're sure you're beginning to realize, user research requires effort and learned expertise. Field visits may look like "hanging out," but the observation, the analysis, and the communication of results require rigorous thought and skill. Sometimes, you may need to have someone your questioner finds credible to explain (in writing, if possible) why field visits are more than just "watching for a while."

"You Can't Generalize from This!"

It's also true that time and budget constraints will mean that observational research will only include a limited sample. Typically, field visits include multiple sites to look for shared patterns, and researchers ask about typical and atypical events in order to check that what they are seeing is typical. But the real question is, how far does the research need to generalize? Often, Jordan and Dalal point out, the research doesn't need to generalize very far. For example, does this work need to apply to all call centers? Or just call centers for this one industry? Or just for this one company?

"What Kind of Results Can You Give Me?"

This one, Jordan and Dalal suggest, actually stands in for multiple questions. One question is about return on investment and getting some measurable benefit for the time and money. Alternatively, this might be a question about the sorts of deliverables that field visits produce and how to share them. In that case, you need to discuss what kinds of information designers, marketers, engineers, and businesspeople actually need, and what kinds of collaboration might help productively influence the development process as it proceeds.

Conclusion

> *Sometimes the obvious is not always apparent. The obvious things don't bubble to the surface all the time.*
> Jack Suvak, marketing director for Moen, Inc., in *The Washington Post*

We observe people in the field because what's obvious, as Suvak says, isn't always apparent. Indeed, design directions often only *become* obvious through the hard work of close observation and analysis. This chapter has outlined the first part—what ethnographers call "fieldwork" and we call "field visits." Field visits are labor intensive, but they can help you generate insights that no other technique can reproduce.

The Fieldwork Way

1. *Stay close to the work.* Fieldworkers should strive to stay close to where work takes place and to directly observe people doing that work.
2. *Do not dismiss anything as trivial or boring.* It is important to open one's mind and see, hear, sense, and smell as much as possible and to record your impressions faithfully.
3. *Be an observer and stay out of the way.* Know when to ask questions and when to listen.
4. *Be an apprentice and take a learning stance.* See the natives as teachers. What would you have to learn and be able to do if you were to this job yourself?
5. *There is always something going on.* Pay attention to what's happening around you, even if it doesn't seem relevant.

6. *Reflect on what you have collected.* Resist the urge to just collect more data; instead take time to reflect. A little fieldwork goes a long way.

Adapted from *Teaching Organizational Ethnography*, by Nozomi Ikeya, Erik Vinkhuyzen, Jack Whalen, and Yutaka Yamauchi.

CHAPTER 10

Diary Studies

Dear Diary…

Imagine you want to learn more about how people commute by car. Following all those people in person from their homes to workplaces over days, weeks, or even months would take up all your time—not to mention how much it would irritate them. This isn't an unusual problem. Most, if not all, processes or activities don't happen only once. Nor do they unfold in convenient locations.

The solution is to use a diary study. Diary studies, as the name implies, ask a group of people to report their activities over time. Diarists track which mistakes they make, what they learn, how often they use a product, and anything else that is of interest to the project. Diarists can also give you a more general window into their lives, documenting the places and people they encounter.

Letting people track their own progress can give you an unobtrusive view into their experience without actually having to stare over their shoulders—literally or metaphorically—for months at a time. Even with minimal analysis, diary studies can provide a source of feedback that reveals patterns that would be difficult to identify otherwise. They can help you observe infrequent or brief events. Moreover, they reduce the time between an event and its documentation. Memory is reliably unreliable; diary studies help avoid asking people to remember events of interest.

Diaries are also one of the few geographically distributed qualitative research methods. You can have people complete diary entries around the country (or the world, for that matter) without leaving your office. This allows you to perform research into internationalization and into how cultural and geographic differences affect people's experiences of your product. And unlike such methods as log file analysis (Chapter 16) and remote usability testing (Chapter 11), a diary study will help you observe activity on- *and* offline.

For example, in 2011, Beverly Freeman of the PayPal user research team conducted a "Managing Expenses" online diary study to better understand how nannies, caregivers, and small business employees handle business expenses with their employers. Participants across the United States completed online activities that involved sharing photos and commenting on various actions such as communicating with others, paying for expenses, and getting paid back. Freeman told us, "Because these actions occurred across multiple roles, times, and locations (both online and offline), the diary study proved to be a practical data-collection tool for revealing the good, bad, and ugly of today's situation. In addition, projective exercises such as 'Please take a picture of something that represents how you feel about your role in managing expenses' helped crystallize the emotional aspects of a topic that extends far beyond the mere exchange of money" (Figures 10.1 and 10.2).

When to Do a Diary Study

Diary studies can track usage of a product, document particular activities, or follow a specific type of experience. As such, they typically occur at two main places in a product development cycle. Early in design, diary studies can help you follow behaviors and activities. They can help you scope a survey or serve as the basis for more in-depth later interviews. Later in the process, a diary study can serve as a kind of extended remote usability test for a working prototype.

Steve August, maker of the qualitative research tool Revelation (www.revelationglobal.com), proposes four main types of diary

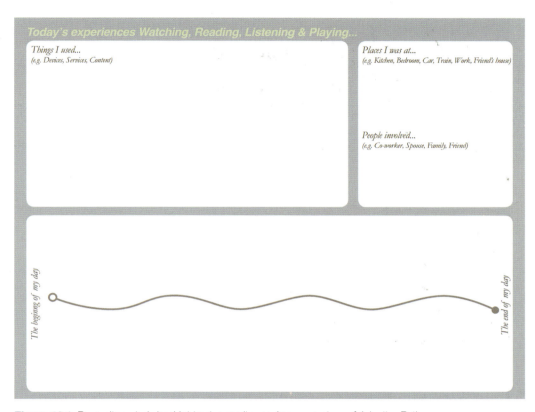

Figure 10.1 Paper diary study booklet tracing media use. Image courtesy of Adaptive Path.

studies. His taxonomy is a useful starting point for deciding where and how a diary study might help you.

- *Usage diaries* document specific moments of interaction with a product or service. The subject can be a website, a restaurant, an ATM, or a railway. The interactions can be organic—activities the participant would perform outside the diary study—or activities that you specify. If the latter, the usage diary can serve as a type of remote usability test.
- *Spotter diaries* identify where and how the presence of companies, products, or services matter in people's lives. Unlike usage diaries, spotter diaries map the place of these objects in the broader context of people's lives.

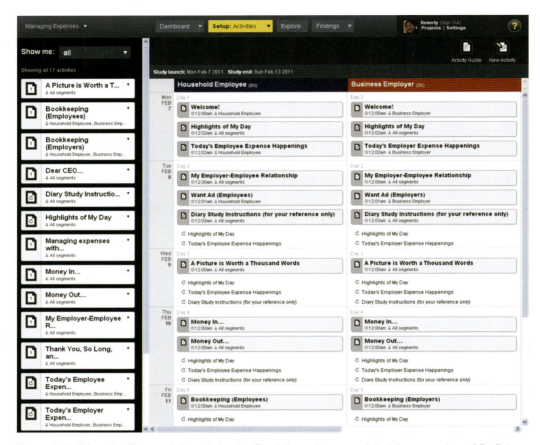

Figure 10.2 "Managing Expenses" diary study using Revelation online research tool. Image courtesy of PayPal.

- *Process/purchase diaries* follow activities that unfold over time and space. They involve longer narratives, such as those of buying a car or planning a wedding.
- *Behavior diaries* are more exploratory in scope. They examine a range of activities or objects that comprise a specific topic. For example, a behavior diary could examine how participants deal with money in their lives—the tools and activities of earning, spending, and saving.

Usage diaries and spotter diaries are useful when you already have a product, company, or service that is stable enough to support long-term engagement. Process and behavior diaries, however, are often helpful earlier in the design process to explore a potential design space.

How to Do a Diary Study

Preparation

Because you have to design and manufacture a customized digital or paper workbook for participants, diary studies require more advance preparation than a simple interview or even a field visit. Even experienced researchers don't try to put together exercises for a diary study in a hurry—they allot plenty of time for recruiting and pretesting (as in Table 10.1).

Pretesting for paper-based diary studies is particularly important because once you send the activities out to your participants, you won't have much opportunity to clarify vague instructions or modify an activity that isn't delivering interesting results. Once it's in the field, you just have to live with what you get back. Online diary platforms offer slightly more flexibility. They make it easier to run a study in which participants begin and end at different times, which lets you pilot your activities with early participants.

However, do not underestimate how much time it will take to monitor an online diary study while it is in progress. A typical study has 10 participants and seven days of activity. If there are three diary exercises per day, you will have 210 entries. You will need to review entries as they come in. Participants will often have questions, and you may need to coach them if their participation wanes in the middle of the study.

Recruitment

Diary study recruiting resembles any other user research activity. However, diary studies require self-directed action from participants, sometimes over weeks. Given the demands of diary studies, recruiters should filter potential participants not just by eligibility and availability over the study, but also for likely reliability and articulateness. Ask yourself: do potential participants respond promptly

Table 10.1 A Typical Diary Study Schedule

Timing	Activity
$t - 2$ weeks	Start recruiting. Brainstorm activities. Try them out quickly within the team or with friends. Make first draft of diary collateral and instructions.
$t - 1$ weeks	Pretest diary study activities, especially all digital tools. Revise instructions and diary workbook.
$t - 4$ days	Recruiting completed. Distribute diary study pack to participants.
t	Diary study in progress. Monitor participation. Replace any dropouts. Share incoming data with stakeholders.
$t + 1$ week	Hold follow-up interviews (optional). Combine notes; write analysis.
$t + 2$ weeks	Present to stakeholders; discuss and note directions for further research.

Recruiting people who are dedicated enough to fill out diaries over an extended period of time will likely bias your sample. Their diligence may come with other qualities that are not representative of your general user population. It's still worth doing diary studies, but be aware of the potential bias when analyzing your results.

See Chapter 6 for more information about recruiting.

to messages? Do they seem willing to perform the activities involved? Are they good at expressing their thoughts and emotions in words or pictures? Since even careful screening cannot prevent all mid-study dropouts, save yourself some stress by securing backup participants early on. A typical diary study has about 10 participants, so a careful researcher will recruit two extras if possible.

Designing the Study

Whatever the purpose of your study, there are two main types of activities: *feedback activities* and *elicitation activities*. Human-computer interaction researchers Scott Carter and Jennifer Mankoff explain the difference this way: In feedback activities, participants complete a questionnaire. For example, a participant might record date, time, location, purpose, and purchases at every visit to a grocery store. In elicitation activities, participants capture media, which later prompts interview questions. For example, a participant might be asked to take a photo or record some sound during that shopping trip.

Because they are so prolonged, diary studies tend to have their own rhythms. They often have multiple phases, such as an initial phone interview, the study itself, and then a follow-up interview. The study itself has its own internal tempo created by the frequency and duration of the activities. For that reason, designing diary studies requires some attention not just to the activities that will best answer your questions, but also to how you and your participants will experience them over time.

The type of study you are planning and the kinds of activities you think will best capture your interests will influence the final three decisions: *duration, schedule,* and *sampling rate.*

- *What is the duration of the study?* There should probably be at least a half dozen diary entries for trends to be observable (though the exact number, of course, depends on many factors). If your topic of interest happens once a week, the study will need to go on for about two months to be able to measure a change. However, if there will be a relevant event every day, then a week may be sufficient to see changes in people's use.
- *What kind of schedule will entries follow?* You can ask people to make entries at fixed times (such as every hour) or variably. Variable entries can take place at random intervals (usually prompted by a telephone call or text message from the researcher) or whenever the participant starts or finishes a specific activity. The Arbitron radio diary, for example, is a long-running American market research study with hourly data on participants' radio listening activities. However, radio listening is a fairly easy phenomenon to track. What about less clear phenomena, like "being happy"? People aren't always able to recognize and respond to their moods in the moment. If you wanted to track mood swings, it might make sense to employ a variable schedule and prompt participants to report their moods at random intervals during the course of the study. If you were just interested in how people cook dinner, obviously you would ask for neither hourly or random entries. Instead, people would complete the diaries as they begin to prepare food.
- *How many entries do you predict?* The study's sampling rate determines the level of detail that you can observe. The more

frequently people respond, the more subtle the changes you can notice in their experience. However, changes happen at all levels of detail, and there are important monthly and yearly trends even in products that get used many times a day.

Since people aren't diary-filling machines, picking a sampling rate, schedule, and duration that won't bore them or take too much effort is likely to get you better quality information. For example, a study of how search engine users learn a new search engine recruited people who searched roughly once per day (with a different search engine than the one being researched). Picking daily searchers defined the maximum sampling rate since asking them to fill out more than one diary entry per day would not have produced any additional information.

The balance of feedback and elicitation activities will also affect the rhythm and duration of the study. The need to fill out a questionnaire tends to mean that feedback activities take more time in the moment of action. If you are following a variable schedule, this could cause inconvenience, as you prompt participants at random intervals to make entries. However, feedback activities do not necessarily require any conversation after the diary is completed. Elicitation activities, on the other hand, tend to take less time for participants in the moment (it only takes a few seconds to snap a photo, after all). But follow-up interviews require scheduling and time.

Inventing Good Exercises

The first step in creating good diary exercises is to write down everything you might possibly want to know about participants' activities. Then come up with diary tasks that can help you track them.

Like survey questions (see Chapter 12 for more on question writing), diary exercises produce both structured and unstructured data. Structured data are the result of choosing responses from a limited set of possibilities. The Arbitron diary study (Figure 10.4) produces mostly structured data: hours of the day and radio stations. Unstructured data are, essentially, unconstrained. Unstructured data in diaries can result from notes or sketches on paper, text messages or voice calls, or photography and video. Cultural probes (Figure 10.3) produce mostly unstructured data. Structured data

Figure 10.3 A cultural probe investigating the lives of 10- to 13-year-olds in Lebanon (a). Designed to appeal to both boys and girls, it includes postcards (b), a disposable camera, an audio recorder (c), a food and eating diary (a) and a set of "like/dislike" stickers to place on a collection of images (a). The project's client is a nonprofit organization working to promote health awareness in kids. Images courtesy of MENA Design Research Center.

(c)

Figure 10.3 *Continued...*

are well suited to the quantitative data analysis methods described in Chapter 12, unstructured data to the qualitative methods in Chapter 15.

Diary studies are extremely flexible as a method. You can ask people to do anything that you think will help you understand their lives. Typical diary activities include:

- Taking photos of places (such as the kitchen) and activities (such as cooking)—and writing captions for them
- Using stickers or icons to indicate one's mood
- Drawing maps of the home or workplace
- Noting the time, location, and purpose of each occurrence of an activity of interest (such as checking email)

You count in the radio ratings!

No matter how much or how little you listen, you're important!

You're one of the few people picked in your area to have the chance to tell radio stations what you listen to.

This is *your* ratings diary. Please make sure you fill it out yourself.

Here's what we mean by "listening":

Listening is any time you can hear a radio – whether you choose the station or not. You may be listening to radio on AM, FM, the Internet or satellite. Be sure to include all your listening.

Any time you hear radio from **Thursday, Date 1a, through Wednesday, Date 1b,** write it down – whether you're at home, in a car, at work or someplace else.

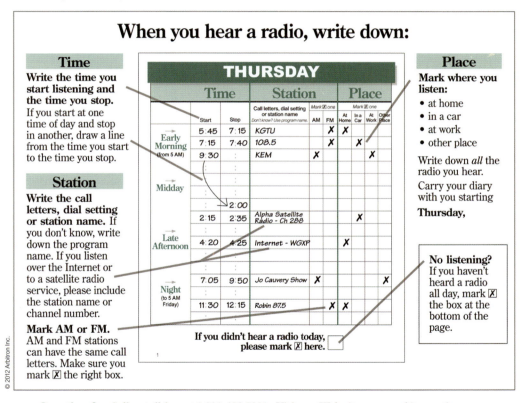

When you hear a radio, write down:

Time

Write the time you start listening and the time you stop.

If you start at one time of day and stop in another, draw a line from the time you start to the time you stop.

Station

Write the call letters, dial setting or station name. If you don't know, write down the program name. If you listen over the Internet or to a satellite radio service, please include the station name or channel number.

Mark AM or FM. AM and FM stations can have the same call letters. Make sure you mark ☒ the right box.

Place

Mark where you listen:
- at home
- in a car
- at work
- other place

Write down *all* the radio you hear.

Carry your diary with you starting **Thursday,**

No listening? If you haven't heard a radio all day, mark ☒ the box at the bottom of the page.

© 2012 Arbitron Inc.

Questions? Call us toll-free at 1-800-638-7091. Visit our Web site: www.arbitronratings.com

Figure 10.4 Instructions for the Arbitron radio diary form, which collects information about U.S. radio-listening habits. Image courtesy of Arbitron, Inc.

- Tracking emotions or energy level at key events (such as at the beginning or end of a daily commute)
- Writing or recording longer reflections about an activity or event at the end of each day

Diary studies also commonly include one-time activities, such as photographing one's workplace or home or answering a set of initial attitudinal or behavioral questions.

Cultural Probes

Traditional diary studies are descriptive—they ask participants to record activities accurately, as they happen. By and large, they do not encourage speculation, whimsy, personal idiosyncrasy, or flamboyance from participants. More recently, many researchers have begun to use a type of diary activity—the cultural probe— that encourages imaginative personal reflection through structured, but playful, exercises.

As explained by their original creators at Britain's Royal College of Art in 1999, cultural probes deliver "inspiration, not information." They are not intended to produce an "objective picture" of the conditions of people's lives. Instead, cultural probes are used to stimulate creative discussion between designers and potential users—to provoke the imagination and generate empathy.

That's why MENA Design Research Center chose to use a cultural probe to learn about Lebanese children's lives for a project on promoting health awareness. Doreen Toutikian, MENA's director, said, "All these various multi-sensual and interactive methods allow the child to be more responsive and intuitive. This form of design research has proven to be far more effective than concrete interviews with researchers in sterile observation rooms with stalking cameras. It allows the child to feel free in his/her environment and explore his/her world with creativity and insight."

Common probe materials and activities include:

- Pre-addressed, stamped *postcards* with an evocative image on the front and an open-ended question on the back. Postcards in MENA's cultural probe (see Figure 10.3b), called the KonfiKit, asked questions such as, "If you ever met an alien from outer space, what would you ask it?" As an informal way to communicate with friends, postcards can feel more casual and intimate than a survey form on a website. For people who mostly use digital mail, they can also simultaneously feel exciting and special.

- *Maps* of familiar places, such as neighborhoods and cities. A probe might ask participants to mark up maps with sketches and stickers to answer questions like, "Where would you go to be bored? Where are you afraid?" A probe might also ask the participant to sketch a map in lieu of a pre-printed one.
- *Cameras* (disposable or digital). MENA's KonfiKits, like the original cultural probes, use disposable cameras whose cardboard cases had been recovered with new paper to match the other materials. Instead of documenting specific activities, probe "shot lists," like those in the KonfiKits, might include requests like, "Take a photo of your favorite clothes" or "Take a photo of your favorite game."
- Space for *sketches* and *collage*. Paper probe packets often include space for participants to make their own compositions—to draw representations of their relationships to people and places, or maybe to select and collage images that represent parts of their lives.

Probes exist to stimulate multiple interpretations. As evocative objects, they often serve to elicit discussion in interviews. See Chapter 8 for more instructions on using probe materials in interviews.

Because diary studies are so flexible, there are no firm guidelines for their design. However, here are some characteristics of good diary activities that you can use to evaluate your own.

- *Relevant*. Just as good survey questions do not ask people to guess at information they do not possess, good diary activities don't waste participants' time—and your own—by demanding actions that are not natural to them. Partially, this is a matter of recruiting. When studying kitchen appliances, don't recruit people who mostly eat out. But the larger question is: How can people effectively document a phenomenon of interest? To

A note on terms: Some people use "cultural probe" as a synonym for "diary study." Others classify a diary study as a type of cultural probe. However, diary studies were frequently used in social science research long before the publication of the original cultural probe study in 1999. Given the history of the diary study, we think it makes most sense to call the cultural probe a diary study variant—one that focuses on reflection and interpretation rather than factual documentation. Given this varying terminology, make sure that all your stakeholders understand what you mean when you propose doing a cultural probe.

design kitchen appliances, you probably should ask people to document not only cooking, but cleaning and storing appliances as well. However, adding extra activities creates new problems, such as disruption.

- *Nondisruptive.* The other side of relevance is disruption. The struggle to follow directions can distort or obstruct diarists' normal activities. As the study's demands escalate, participants might give more attention to the study than to the activities it documents. At that point, your study can self-destruct. Sometimes, the resulting irritation can lead participants to skip exercises, falsify data, or even drop out altogether. Obviously, all diary studies disrupt people's everyday activities to some extent. The question is, how disruptive is too disruptive? The best way to tell if your study is too disruptive is to pretest it yourself or have a sympathetic friend give it a shot.

- *Nonbiasing.* During a project on physical fitness, Elizabeth realized that participants' embarrassment about "not exercising enough" might keep them from accurately reporting their own gym-going. Moreover, they did not classify some physically demanding work, such as moving furniture, as "exercise" and thus might not report it. So direct questions about physical exercise were likely to produce unhelpful responses (see sidebar on self-reporting). Instead, Elizabeth avoided the words "fitness" and "physical exercise" in diary instructions. She simply asked participants to wear a pedometer all day while listing their activities. The pedometer helped establish a ground truth about participants' level of physical activity movements, while the written accounts gave more detail. Between the two, she could estimate participants' level of physical exercise without asking directly.

Self-reporting

When you ask people to report their own experiences, you ask them to step outside their normal perception of themselves and comment on their behavior. Some people will provide accurate answers. Others will have more difficulty. Even if they want to help you and think that they're telling you everything, they may not feel comfortable admitting failure or revealing that they don't know something. This problem applies to any self-reported information, such as support comments, survey questions, or interview responses. But it's especially problematic in diaries. When the diary entry is your only contact with the person, there's no way to ascertain what's called the "ground truth" of their behavior.

One way to mitigate the effects of self-reporting bias is to gather multiple perspectives on the same event. Andrea once conducted a diary study to learn more about how close friends and family members share information. She recruited diary study participants in pairs (mother and daughter, boyfriend and girlfriend, and so on) who communicated daily. Every day of the study, each participant wrote about an interaction they had had that day with the other member of the pair. This not only helped Andrea to understand what had actually happened, but also highlighted the differences between what each person remembered and considered important.

Another way to mitigate self-reporting bias is to follow-up with additional interviews. Use the interviews to ask for clarification of important statements. And always keep a grain of salt handy.

Choosing Your Platform

Paper booklets, voice messaging, and online tools can all help people document their experiences. You can use them singly or in combination. For example, you could use a paper booklet to direct people to upload digital photos to a website (see Figure 10.5).

Paper Booklet

Traditionally, diary studies have relied upon giving participants a paper booklet with entry forms (see Figure 10.1 and Figure 10.3) to return at the end of the study. In fact, they are still widely used. Participants can fill out timesheets (as in Figure 10.4), sketch maps, or even collect and collage paper documents.

It pays to put some thought into the aesthetics of your booklet. The design of the booklet affects readability and ease of completion, especially if you are providing forms (as in Figure 10.4). Furthermore, the appearance of the booklet is a demonstration of your attitude and commitment. Participants are more likely to spend time on attractive booklets that look professionally prepared. Figure 10.1 is a good example of a well-designed paper booklet that is easy to produce. It uses a standard-sized piece of paper folded in half.

The advantages of paper booklets are many: they are cheap to produce, require no technical know-how to complete, and support a variety of writing, collage, and sketching activities. However, during the course of the study there is no practical way to monitor completion. Researchers must wait until the diaries are completed and mailed back, which means that there is no way to correct any misunderstandings or mistakes.

Voice Messaging

With the prevalence of mobile phones, voice messaging can be very useful—especially when engaging with people who are not comfortable writing. Voice message diaries are simple to set up; they only require a phone number and voice mailbox. You can even send instructions and reminders by text message (although you'll probably want to give people an initial email or paper letter with full directions).

Save yourself some time by using a voice-to-text service to have the voice entries transcribed as they come in.

Voice diaries are expressive. People often talk more freely than they write. They may choose to update their diaries more often, in more concrete detail, and with more emotional richness. Because people carry mobile telephones with them, voice diaries remove the need for them to remember a paper booklet. As well, participants can call in while they are on the go, which keeps the time between an event and its documentation to a minimum. Text message reminders can help bridge that gap even more quickly than email to a computer.

Voice messaging, however, will not always be the most appropriate solution. You may want to make sure you get precise data, such as the call signs for radio stations, from your participants. Maybe each entry requires complex steps. Or maybe you know that in some locations and activities, speaking aloud is not an option.

Online Applications

It's becoming more and more common to have participants fill out their entries using email, a website, or mobile application. Online

Visit the book's website at www.mkp.com/observing-the-user-experience for more information on tools for online diary studies.

If you do use an email-to-web solution, make absolutely sure you password protect access to the resulting website. The same thing goes for every other online tool you use. Don't allow participants to see each other's data, and don't make data publicly viewable. Your participants didn't sign up to have the details of their lives potentially exposed.

entries allow researchers to monitor participation and ask for any adjustments in the moment. Online entries also streamline the incorporation of digital media, especially video. If your participants have a computer with a camera, you can instruct them on how to record video messages—thus adding expressiveness and conversational spontaneity to any text entries.

An email form is perhaps the simplest digital tool. You simply email your participants a form and have them respond to the email with their answers. Not only is email free, but it's a familiar way of communicating for many people. It's a neat trick: the diary entry email reminds people to reply promptly. You can also have participants attach photographs and video to the email. If you then set up a blog (at time of writing, Tumblr. com and Posterous.com are popular choices) to accept email posts, you can automatically have those emails posted to the web for easy aggregate viewing by you and potentially your clients. Using the blog commenting functionality, you can even start up a conversation about specific entries during the run of the study.

If most of the data you'd like to capture is relatively structured, you can also use a spreadsheet (either an online document or an individual file on a desktop). You name the columns, and respondents fill in the rows with their own data. The Arbitron radio diary essentially follows a spreadsheet format.

You can also create your own diary entry forms using one of the many free online survey tools (Google Forms is popular). Diarists complete entries by "responding" to the survey. All you have to do is make sure that the survey includes a free text entry area for participants to identify themselves. Then you can use any built-in survey analytics to analyze the resulting data.

There are also custom online tools for diary studies. At the time of writing this book, a popular one is Revelation (www.revelationglobal.com). They simplify the task of designing and deploying online diaries by offering a standard library of exercises to choose from. Participants can report the details of an event, upload photographs, or capture video. They also simplify analysis by providing built-in tools for aggregating the data and extracting trends. Mobile versions of such applications can sometimes use the phone's capabilities to add location data to each entry as well. However, such tools are generally not free. Also, you may want the greater flexibility that assembling your own diary may give you.

A final online tool is not a tool so much as an overall strategy. You can study people's lives through the social tools they already use, such as Facebook, text messaging, and Twitter. Just ask your respondents to give you temporary access to their daily communications. They can use whatever built-in access controls are already available to keep certain messages private—but you will see the vast majority of the everyday activity they would share with friends.

This type of diary study, called "lifestreaming," by Chris Khalil, Director of User Experience at **News Digital Media**, does not demand artificial action from participants. When participants are asked to step back and comment on their own activities, they can unwittingly bias their responses in order to fit them into the diary study "frame." That frame also means that diary studies can fail to capture some of the most important minutiae, simply because participants don't think it's important. With lifestreaming, that frame is absent. Participants are simply permitting the researchers to watch them going about their daily business. There is no need for them to judge whether an event is "important enough." If a feeling or event is important enough to post to Facebook, then the lifestreaming diary study will catch it.

As with an email diary, you can set up a blog to automatically bring together these sources into one "stream." At the time of writing, most blogging services include plug-ins that automatically integrate feeds of new content from a variety of websites. Then you can ask participants to add their own commentary later.

Incorporating Images and Video

In the days before cheap digital cameras, diary studies relied on disposable film cameras. Researchers would distribute the cameras along with detailed written instructions on what to photograph. Then they had to wait until the end of the study to discover what participants had done. As you can imagine, the developed rolls of film often brought unwelcome surprises: out-of-focus or poorly exposed shots, unhelpful or irrelevant images, or even an entire blank roll.

Luckily, there are many relatively low-cost digital cameras these days. We recommend digital so you don't have to wait until the end of the study to see how your participants are doing. And with a digital camera, there is no such thing as "running out of film." If you have the funds, you can even allow participants to keep their cameras after the study as an incentive for participation.

Nevertheless, don't fret if your budget does not run to buying 10 or 15 digital cameras. You can ask participants to use their own cameras, if you believe they own their own and are likely to find this acceptable. For some participants, using their own cameras may actually be more comfortable than learning an unfamiliar interface. Alternately, disposable cameras are still better than nothing. You can customize them by making your own cardboard cover, as in Figure 10.3a.

Assembling the Diary Components

Since your participants will be completing diary entries outside of your presence, you will need to provide whatever materials you think will help them consistently give you the information you want.

A typical diary (or probe) has four components:

1. Introductory message
2. Instructions
3. Diary/key incident forms or questionnaires
4. Recording device(s) (camera, camera phone, stickers)

Throughout this section, we will use as an example text from an email diary designed to track use of HotBot, a search engine.

Introductory Letter

After being recruited, screened, and invited to participate, participants will still need a full introduction to the study. It's likely that they've gotten this information in bits and pieces already, but it's always good to condense all the key facts into one place. An introductory letter addresses:

- Basic study information: its goals, motivation, and sponsorship
- Why participants were recruited (optional)
- Compensation and warning of any potential harms
- Permission/consent letter (if not already completed during recruitment)
- Contact information for researchers
- Thanks and appreciation for their effort

If you are using an online tool, the introductory message should also include a link to the website you are using.

The introductory letter is also a good place to remind diarists of why—besides any money—they agreed to do all this work for you. However, no one wants to read a lengthy exposition; this letter should be short and sweet.

> Thank you for participating in our evaluation of the HotBot search engine. We are in the process of evaluating it for redesign, and we would like your input so that we can base the design changes on people's daily experiences with it. We are asking for your help as someone who uses our search engine frequently and who might be interested in helping us improve your experience with it.
>
> If you have any questions or comments, please feel free to contact Mike Kuniavsky at mike@adaptivepath.com.
>
> Once again, thanks for your time and effort!

Explicit instructions to diarists make it more likely that they will comment on what's important to you. However, detailed instructions can bias the responses. The participants may look at parts of the product they have not looked at before, describe it in ways that they normally wouldn't, or use it in novel ways. Stay conscious of how your wording might bias your results.

Instructions

After the introductory letter, diarists will need some instructions. The instructions should be specific, brief, and complete. They should give the diarists a set of guiding principles about what kind of behavior to record while encouraging active participation (Figures 10.5 and 10.6).

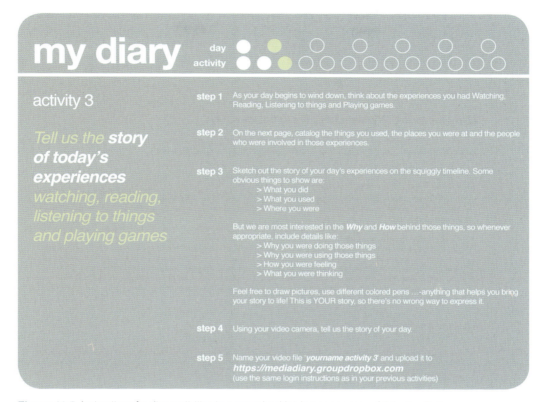

Figure 10.5 Instructions for diary activities in a paper booklet. Image courtesy of Adaptive Path.

The most important thing is to keep the directions simple and short. Remember that your participants are completing your questions in breaks between other activities.

As with surveys, question wording really matters, because you will not be present with participants to clarify any instructions they find confusing. Depending on your participants' projected education, you may want to aim your instructional text at a sixth-grade (11-year-old) to high school (16-year old) reading level.

The forms for diary study entries resemble survey questionnaires. The following sample set of instructions comes from an email study, but you can have people answer your questions on paper, on a website, or using a custom application.

Fry's Readability Graph is a standard method for measuring the reading level of American English. Directions for using Fry's Readability Graph are available at www.idph.state.ia.us/ health_literacy/common/ pdf/tools/fry.pdf.

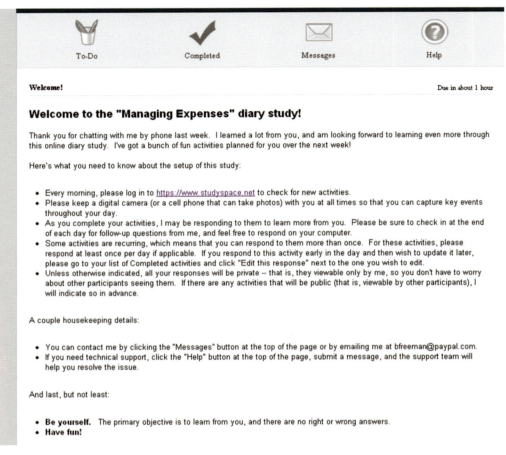

Figure 10.6 Participants' view of instructions for intro activity using Revelation. Image courtesy of PayPal.

Here's a sample set of instructions:

> Please use HotBot for as many Internet information research needs as you can. Your thoughts and experiences are very valuable to us.
>
> For the next month, you will receive this instruction sheet along with a diary form twice a week (on Mondays and Thursdays) in email.

It's a good idea to remind people of their obligations and to set some expectations. Attaching the instructions to every email reminds the participants of how they should think about filling out the diaries.

We would like you to fill out the diary form and email it to diary@adaptivepath.com before the next one arrives (mailing it on the same day is fine). We estimate that it will take 20–30 minutes to fill out completely.

If you can't email the diary to us by the time the next form arrives contact us as soon as possible. Contact information is at the bottom of this sheet.

Of course, you already gave diarists your contact information in your introduction. Just keep on reminding them. Including contact information prominently with every communication will help remind people that you are there to answer questions and lower any barriers to contacting you.

The form is designed to help you describe your experiences while using HotBot to look for information. You don't have to fill it out at any specific time and you can write as much as you want, but we would like you to fill out as much as you can.

Here are some things to keep in mind while you're filling out the form.

- Relate as much as you can about your experiences, positive and negative, big and small. We are interested in all of it, no matter how minor it may seem at the time. We are especially interested in experiences that were surprising or unexpected.
- Our goal is to make HotBot work better for you. If you can't get some feature to work, it is not your fault. Please describe any such situations in detail.

As with all situations where people report their experiences, they should be assured that they're not the ones being tested, it's the product, but that it's their responsibility to accurately report such failings.

- Whenever you try a feature of HotBot that you have not used before, please tell us about it, whether or not you were able to get it to work. Describe the situation in which you used it in detail.

People may not know when they're using something new, but it doesn't hurt to encourage them to look for and record novel situations.

> • If you have a problem with HotBot, but are then able to solve it, please describe the problem and your solution in detail.
> • Please include the specific search terms you used whenever possible.

Encourage specifics when possible. Search terms and products are relatively easy to note down, so it's feasible for people to record them, but avoid more abstract or labor-intensive tasks. If people are asked to write down everything they clicked on and every checkbox they selected, they're likely to spend all of their time writing about the minute elements of their experience instead of the more important issues. And they'll get sick of doing it.

> If you're not sure about whether to put something in the diary or not, please put it in.
>
> If you have not performed any searches by the due date of the form, please mark it as such and return it.
>
> If you have any questions, please don't hesitate to contact Mike Kuniavsky at mikek@adaptivepath.com or (415) 235-3468.

Questionnaire Forms

The previous example collected relatively unstructured data on the use of a search engine. However, it's possible to treat the diary entry more as a structured questionnaire. Here's a sample questionnaire-structured diary email form.

> **HotBot diary**
>
> Please return this diary entry on or before **Thursday, June 22, 2013**
> Today's date:
> The current time:
>
> 1. Approximate number of searches since your last diary entry:
>
> 2. Of those, the approximate number of searches using HotBot:
>
> Please describe what you searched for most recently, providing the search topic and the exact search terms you used, along with any + or - modifiers.

As described earlier, asking people for the specifics of their actions is worthwhile as long as it's not burdensome. Note that this questionnaire directs users' attention to a specific part of the interface, which turns this diary study into a kind of remote usability study.

3. How successful was this search?
(Please rate the search from 1 to 5, where 1 means that it was unsuccessful, 3 means that the information you found was adequate, and 5 means that you found exactly what you were looking for.)

4. How well is HotBot working for you?
(Please rate your experience from 1 to 5, where 1 means that it's not working at all, and 5 means that it's working very well.)

5. In your recent searches, did you use any of the search options in the left-hand margin of the main search page (the first page you see if you go to *www.hotbot.com*)? If so, which ones?

6. If you used any of the tools in the left margin, how well did they work?
(Please rate their effectiveness from 1 to 5, where 1 means that they did not help your search at all, and 5 means that they were critical to its success.)

7. Please describe your personal strategy for narrowing your search, if at first it is unsuccessful. Has this changed in the recent past?

Open-ended questions give participants the opportunity to explain their experiences in depth. Asking people to present a narrative of the changes in their experience, although prone to the bias of selective memory, can compress the analysis process, providing direct insight into how people's views and thoughts are changing.

8. Have any of your views about HotBot changed since the last diary entry? If so, how have they changed, and was there a specific experience that caused the change?

9. Other comments. Are there any other issues you'd like to tell us about or questions you'd like us to answer?

10. When you've completed this form, please email it to diary@adaptivepath.com. Thank you very much for helping us make HotBot a better product.

If you have any questions or comments about this form, please contact Mike Kuniavsky at mikek@adaptivepath.com or (415) 235-3468.

This form adds several questions about a feature cluster on the front door interface. This allows the researchers to get feedback on a specific part of the product.

Of course, the specific content and layout of your diary forms will depend on the product and your goals for the research. Feel free to experiment.

Pretesting

Before you finalize your diary design, test whether the instructions are clear and the activities are doable. The question that you think is clear may confuse your audience; the activity that you think will take five minutes may actually take fifteen. You should at least try them yourself. If you have the time, get someone else to run through a day of the study.

Conducting a Diary Study

Diary studies may allow the researcher to do other things while they run, but they do require some continuing attention. After the diaries are distributed, a successful diary study rarely runs on auto-pilot. You will need to stay in touch with participants—not just to remind them of their commitment to the study, but also to trouble-shoot any technical problems they might have with forms or devices. Moreover, diary studies, especially lifestreaming studies, can produce a surprisingly large amount of data very quickly. If you are not using an online tool for diary management, you will give yourself extra work at the end of the study if you don't organize diary entries as they come in.

Managing Participation over the Study

One of the keys to a successful diary study is the management of responses and respondents. During the course of a diary study, day-to-day contacts with participants will require less sustained attention than an interview or site visit. But because they are so drawn out, diary studies challenge researchers' skills in creating and sustaining participant engagement.

After sending out the instructions, you might review them with the diarists either in person or through some other real-time method (the phone, instant messaging, etc.) to clarify any subtleties.

Review the early responses carefully. If they do not meet the goals of the research, adjust the question phrasing or activity design. This is easy to do with online tools. If the changes are drastic, you may have to mail out a new paper booklet.

Don't be surprised by dropouts. Often, a small percentage of people who sign up for your diary study will quit midway through. Some participants didn't understand how much work the study entails. Some participants feel that the incentives don't sufficiently compensate them for the disruption to their everyday life. And some participants are just flaky. Don't be offended or upset if some participants just quit without any warning. You probably didn't do anything wrong—it happens to everyone.

However, a very high dropout rate should worry you. First, it indicates a problem with the study design. Second, those who finish the study are probably unusual in some way. They are likely not representative of your target audience.

Incentives

Align incentives to the amount of time required to complete the work. Six entries may well take a total of three hours to complete, with an extra hour of overhead spent managing them. Diarists should be paid at a rate somewhere between 60% and 100% of what you would pay participants who came to your lab. Assuming a standard rate of $60 per hour, this means that each participant in a two-month study that requires two diaries per week should receive roughly $200 as an honorarium at the end of the study. It is possible to do this less expensively, but you risk high dropout rates. Mike remembers a very long diary study that paid $50 and a t-shirt—but only one person out of eight finished it. You can encourage completion, with smaller "surprise" incentives (t-shirts, restaurant gift certificates, etc.) placed throughout the process. Staged incentives—paying out a little at a time—can also help. It's better to pay too much than too little in order to ensure good results after you invest all that time and effort.

When working with an organization where incentives may be inappropriate, consider asking the participants' managers to allocate time to fill out the diaries.

Reminders

Reminders can be important tools in bridging the gap that happens when you're not doing research face to face. Since much of the study work is self-initiated, it's easy for people to treat the diaries as optional. Reminding participants of their promise to complete the diary and of the importance of their effort to the product can inspire them to provide better feedback—and to put the diary on their to-do list. Text messages or email follow-up to missed entries tells the participants that you're still there and that their feedback is important to you. Thanking them for their responses and promptly answering their questions lets participants know that you are committed to the study as well. To maximize response, you have to give people incentives and remind them of their obligations. But please, don't spam them with a dozen "keep up the good work!" messages a day.

Schedule some time every day for checking for uploads, monitoring compliance with instructions, and organizing the collected data. Keeping up with these project management tasks will help you move more smoothly into data analysis.

Distributing and Collecting Diaries

If you are using paper booklets, you will need to include a pre-addressed, stamped envelope for any diary materials you need returned. You will also—since people have busy lives and will probably forget—need to send a reminder to mail the diary back at the end. If you have loaned any media devices, such as video cameras, to participants, make sure they know you're expecting to get them back as well.

Follow-up Activities

Coupling your diary study with follow-up focus groups or interviews allows you to clarify their responses, ask follow-up questions, and check any frameworks you are beginning to develop. This is where elicitation activities come in handy as the generators for "show and tell" discussions. Here are some sample elicitation questions:

See Chapter 8 for pointers on using media prompts in interviews.

> You took this photo while you were making dinner? Can you tell me more about what's happening in this picture?
>
> What prompted you to take this photo?

Make sure to schedule these follow-up activities relatively soon after the events described in the diary.

Conclusion

Diary studies assist in studying everyday activities, long-term processes, and rare events. They minimize recollection bias and maximize geographic coverage. Paper diaries need no batteries; mobile phone diaries are always in one's pocket. They can even go places—like a crowded train commute and the locker room—where a researcher might be unwelcome. They encourage participants to share deep thoughts and casual observations. All in all, diary studies solve some thorny problems in research. But they do not run on autopilot.

We've given you a number of tips for designing and managing a successful diary study. In closing, remember these basic suggestions:

1. Recruit for responsible and articulate participants.
2. Select a few extra participants.
3. Make your diary materials look attractive and professional.
4. Pretest, pretest, pretest!
5. Regularly contact participants to catch problems that they don't think to report.
6. Encourage the kind of participation you want. Praise and thank participants, remind them of deadlines, and let them know if you want more or different responses.
7. Remind participants that they are getting paid and helping improve the world.
8. Schedule your follow-up interviews promptly, while the events in the diary are still fresh.

CHAPTER 11
Usability Tests

This chapter covers tests focused on task completion, rather than activities that address broad questions about how people use certain products. Techniques such as interviews, diary studies, surveys, log analysis, and field visits best accomplish those kinds of broad goals.

Usability tests are structured interviews focused on specific features in an interface prototype. A one-on-one usability test can quickly reveal an immense amount of information about how people use a prototype, whether functional, mockup, or just paper. The heart of the interview is a series of tasks performed by the interface's evaluator (typically, a person who resembles the product's imagined audience). Researchers analyze recordings and notes from the interview for the evaluator's successes, misunderstandings, mistakes, and opinions. After a number of these tests, researchers compare the observations, collecting the most common issues into a list of functionality and presentation problems.

Using usability tests, the development team can immediately see whether their assumptions about how people will understand and use their designs as they are hold true. Unfortunately, the technique has acquired the aura of a final check before the project is complete. Usability tests often happen at the end of the development cycle—with the feature set already locked, the target markets already determined, and the product ready for shipping. Although prerelease testing can certainly inform the product's next revision, the full power of the technique remains untapped. Usability tests are more useful when they provide feedback earlier in the development cycle. Then they can check the usability of specific features, investigate new ideas, and evaluate hunches.

When to Test

Usability testing examines how people perform specific tasks, guiding the definition and implementation of functionality. For that reason, usability tests are not a good way to study an entire experience with a product or service. Usability testing is most effective in the early to middle stages of development, before a feature is locked in and its interaction with other features is set. Testing a finalized feature is more of an investment in the next version than in the current one.

Unlike some of the other techniques in this book, usability testing is almost never a one-time event in a development cycle for a product. Every round of testing should focus on a small set of features (usually no more than five). A series of tests can encompass a whole interface or fine-tune a specific set of features.

It makes sense to start usability testing when the development cycle is underway, but not so late that it is impossible to implement extensive changes if testing indicates their necessity. Occasionally, usability testing reveals problems that require a lot of work to correct, so the team should be prepared to rethink and re-implement (and, ideally, retest) what they have tested. For websites and other software, this generally takes at least a couple of weeks, which is why iterative usability testing often occurs about once a month. Changes to hardware, plastic casing, and other nondigital product elements can take longer to re-implement, making tests less frequent.

There are four main types of usability testing.

- *Exploratory*, to test preliminary concepts and evaluate their promise
- *Assessment*, to test features during implementation
- *Comparison*, to assess one design against another
- *Validation*, to certify that features meet certain standards and benchmarks late in the development process

Figuring out which type of test your planned activity most resembles will help you figure out which features you want to examine, and how.

A solid usability testing program will include iterative usability testing of every major feature. Tests scheduled throughout the development process reinforce and deepen knowledge about people's behavior, ensuring that designs get more effective with each cycle of testing.

For example, take an iterative usability testing process at Wikipedia, the user-created online encyclopedia. Wikipedia wanted to make it easier for new users to participate in the project by editing or contributing new content. Over a year, the organization partnered with two user research companies to conduct three tests of their user contribution interface. Wikipedia was most interested in the problems novice users might encounter in creating and editing articles. The organization also wanted to know if the help documentation was useful during that process. Third, the developers had questions about the usability of specific features. Finally, the organization also wanted to surface any unknown user experience problems unrelated to those in creating and editing articles.

The first, *exploratory,* test diagnosed both specific problems for new users ("Clutter"), and some broader reactions to the interface that put them off ("Feeling stupid"). After extensive redesigns, a second test combined *validation* of the changes, further *assessment* of specific features, and more *exploration* of patterns in user experience. The third and final test, which we'll return to later in the chapter, validated changes made in the third redesign.

Completely open-ended testing, or "fishing," is rarely valuable. When you go fishing during a round of user research—often prompted by someone saying, "Let's test the whole thing"—the results are neither particularly clear nor insightful. Know why you're testing before you begin (see Chapter 4 for a guide to research planning).

How to Do It

Preparation

Although it's similar to the "friends and family" test described in Chapter 2, a full usability test takes significantly longer to plan, execute, and analyze (see Table 11.1). You should start preparing for a usability testing cycle at least three weeks before you expect to need the results.

Before the process can begin, you need to know whom to recruit and which features to have them evaluate. Both of these things should be decided several weeks before the testing begins.

Recruiting

Recruiting is the most crucial piece to start early. It needs to be carefully timed and precise, especially when outsourced

Table 11.1 A Typical Usability Testing Schedule

Timing	Activity
$t - 2$ weeks	Determine test audience; start recruiting immediately.
$t - 2$ weeks	Determine feature set to be tested.
$t - 1$ week	Write first version of script; construct test tasks; discuss with development team; check on recruiting.
$t - 3$ days	Write second version of guide; review tasks; discuss with development team; recruiting should be completed.
$t - 2$ days	Complete guide; schedule practice test; set up and check all equipment.
$t - 1$ day	Do practice test in the morning; adjust guide and tasks as appropriate.
t	Test (usually 1–2 days, depending on scheduling).
$t + 1$ day	Discuss with observers; collect copies of all notes.
$t + 2$ days	Relax; take a day off and do something else if possible.
$t + 3$ days	Watch all recordings; take notes. (Watching all recordings might not be realistic if you are following a rapid, iterative testing cycle.)
$t + 1$ week	Combine notes; write analysis.
$t + 1$ week	Present to development team; discuss and note directions for further research.

to a specialist recruiting company. Finding the right people and matching their schedules to yours takes time and effort. The more time you can devote to the recruiting process, the better (although more than two weeks in advance is generally too early, since people often don't know their schedules that far in advance). You also need to choose your screening criteria carefully. The initial impulse is simply to recruit people who fall into the product's imagined target audience, but that's usually too broad. You need to hone in on the representatives of the target audience who are going to give you the most useful feedback. (We're presenting a condensed explanation of the recruiting process here. See Chapter 6 for a more in-depth discussion.)

Say you're designing a website that sells forks. Your imagined audience consists of people who want to buy forks.

In recruiting for a usability test, that's a pretty broad range of people. Narrowing your focus helps preserve clarity, since different groups can exhibit different reactions to the same features. Age, expertise, and motivation, just to name a few common differences, can result in very different user experiences. Choosing the "most representative" group can reduce the amount of research you have to do in the end and focus your results.

The best people to invite are those who are going to need the service you are providing in the near future or who have used a competing service in the recent past. These people will have the highest level of interest and knowledge in the subject matter, so they can concentrate on how well the interface works rather than on the minutia of the information. People who have no interest in the content can still point out interaction flaws, but they are not nearly as good at pointing out problems with the information architecture or any kind of content-specific features since they have little motivation to concentrate and make it work.

Say your research of the fork market shows that there are two strong subgroups within that broad range: people who are replacing their old silverware and people who are buying wedding presents. The first group, according to your research, is mostly women in their 40s, whereas the second group is split evenly between men and women, mostly in their mid-20s and 30s.

You decide that the people who are buying sets of forks to replace those they already own represent the heart of your user community. They are likely to know about the subject matter and may have done some research already. They're motivated to use the service, which makes them more likely to use it as they would in a regular situation. So you decide to recruit women in their 40s who want to buy replacement forks in the near future or who have recently bought some. In addition, you want to get people who enjoy shopping online, so that you do not confuse problems with this specific website with dislike of online shopping in general. Including all these conditions, your final set of recruiting criteria looks as follows:

Men or women, preferably women
25 years old or older, preferably 35–50
Have Internet access at home or work
Use the web five or more hours a week
Have made at least three online purchases
Have bought something online in the last three months
Are interested in buying silverware online

Notice that there is some flexibility in the age and gender criteria. This is to make the recruiter's life a little easier. You may insist that the participants be all female and that they must be between 40 and 50 years old, but if a candidate comes up who matches the rest of the criteria and happens to be 33 and a man, you probably don't want to disqualify him immediately. Purchasing experience, on the other hand, requires precise requirements, since getting people who aren't going to be puzzled or surprised by the details of purchasing online is key to making the test successful. Testing an e-commerce system with someone who's never bought anything online tests the concept of online shopping as much as the specific product. You rarely want that level of detail, so it's best to avoid situations that inspire it in the first place.

Recruiters will try to follow your criteria to the letter, but if you can tell them which criteria are flexible (and how flexible they are) and which are immutable, it's easier for them. Ultimately, that makes it easier for you, too.

How many participants do you need? Unfortunately, there's no simple answer. More evaluators means catching more potential problems—but at a certain point the cost of recruiting and the extra effort needed to run the tests and analyze the results lead to rapidly diminishing returns. For many years, the conventional choice, following a study by Jakob Nielsen, has been at least five evaluators per simple test. Larger groups still produce useful results, especially for complex tests with many different elements, but after eight or nine users, you may find that the majority of problems appear several times.

However, careful recruiting and task coverage matters. Research from scientists Gitte Lindgaard and Jarinee Chattratichart suggests that the number of tasks and type of evaluators are as important as the number of evaluators. A large number of evaluators who are unrepresentative of your target users will likely be less effective than a smaller number of representative evaluators. Similarly, a large number of representative evaluators performing a very limited number of tasks—or tasks that are irrelevant to actual use—will likely catch fewer severe problems than the same number performing more tasks.

So, to check your understanding of your primary audience, you can recruit one or two people from secondary target audiences—in the fork case, for example, a younger buyer or someone who's not a recent online shopper—to see whether there's a hint of a radically different perspective in those groups. This won't give you conclusive results, but if you get someone who seems to be reasonable and consistently says something contrary to the main group, it's an indicator that you should probably rethink your recruiting criteria. If the secondary audience is particularly important, it should have its own set of tests, regardless.

To offset no-shows, it's a good idea to schedule a couple of extra people beyond the basic five. And to make absolutely sure you have enough people, you could double-book every time slot. This doubles your recruiting and incentive costs, but it ensures that there's minimal downtime in testing. So, for focused task-based usability testing, you should recruit from six to ten people to make sure you have at least five evaluators for each round of testing.

Having decided whom—and how many—to recruit, it's time to write a screener and send it to the recruiter. (Chapter 6 of this book describes screeners and recruiting.) Make sure to discuss the screener with your recruiter and to walk through it with at least two people in-house to get a reality check.

Then pick a couple of test dates and send out invitations to the people who match your criteria. Schedule interviews at times that are convenient to both you and the participant and leave at least half an hour between them. That gives the moderator enough buffer time to have people come in late, for the test to run long, and for the moderator to get a glass of water and to discuss the test with the observers. With 60-minute interviews, this means that you can do four or five in a single day, and sometimes as many as six. With 90-minute interviews, you can do three or four evaluators, and maybe five if you push it and skip lunch.

If you're testing for the first time, schedule fewer people and put extra time in between. Usability testing can be exhausting, especially if you're new to it.

At this point, you will have your evaluators picked and scheduled. To help keep everything straight, we suggest making a master spreadsheet (see Table 11.2) that contains all the pertinent information—time of test, name, responses to the screener questions, and which test conditions each person saw (if you are testing multiple versions of the products). This will help you later, when you need to analyze the data and want some context for your analysis. It will also help speed up writing evaluator profiles for the report.

Choosing Features

If you have very distinct, different markets for your product, consider creating a different set of tasks for each major market, as people in each market are likely to use your product quite differently.

The second step is to determine which features to test. These, in turn, determine the tasks you create and the order in which you present them. Give yourself enough lead time to fine-tune the procedure. A 60- to 90-minute interview can cover five features (or feature clusters). Typical tests range from one to two hours. Initial or broad-based testing requires two-hour tests, while in-depth research into specific features or ideas can take less time (though it's perfectly acceptable to do a 90-minute broad-based test).

Table 11.2 A Sample Spreadsheet Layout

Time	Name	Gender	Age	Online Shopping Frequency	Reason to Buy Silverware	Main Internet Access
Thu May 27 9:30 AM	Tina	F	42	> 4/month	Replacement	Phone, Mac at home
Thu May 27 11:00 AM	Kristie	M	40	7–8/year	Replacement	PC at home and work
Thu May 27 1:00 PM	Ben	F	45	2/month	Replacement	PC at home and work
Thu May 27 2:30 PM	Sonia	F	48	1/month	Replacement	PC at home
Thu May 27 4:00 PM	Kim	M	30	2/month	Wedding	Phone, PC at home and work

Test individual functions in the context of feature clusters. It's rarely useful to test elements of a set without looking at least a little at the whole set. Here's a good rule of thumb: something is testable if you would draw it while making a 30-second sketch of the interface. If you would sketch a blob labeled "nav bar," then think of testing the entire navigation bar, not just the new link to the home page.

The best way to start the process is by meeting with the development staff (at least the product manager, the interaction designers, and the information architects) and making a list of the five most important features to test. To start discussing which features to include, look at features that are:

Used often

New

Highly publicized

Considered troublesome, based on feedback from earlier
    versions

Potentially dangerous or have bad side effects if used
    incorrectly

Considered important by users

A Feature Prioritization Exercise

This exercise is a structured way of coming up with a feature prioritization list. It's useful when the group doesn't have a lot of experience prioritizing features or is having trouble.

Step 1: Have the group make a list of the most important things on the interface that are new or have been drastically changed since the last round of testing. Importance doesn't just mean visible prominence; it can change relative to the corporate bottom line or managerial priority. Thus, if next quarter's profitability has been staked on the success of a new Fork of the Week section, it's important, even if it's a small part of the interface.

Step 2: Make a column and label it "Importance." Look at each feature and rate it on a scale of 1 to 5, where 5 means it's critical to the success of the product, and 1 means it's not very important.

Next, make a second column and label it "Doubt." Look at each feature and rate how comfortable the team is with the

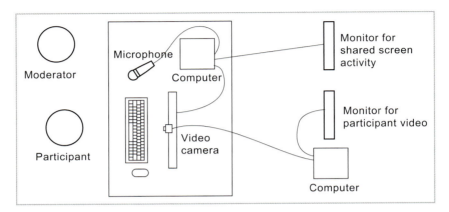

Figure 11.4 Running live video and screen activity to on-site observers in a separate room.

If your observers are on site, it may be more practical to use a combination of external video camera and shared monitors. That is, you would record screen activity as usual on the participant's computer. Then you would run another cable to the separate room and share the participant's screen with another monitor. Finally, you would set up an external video camera to capture audio and facial expressions, then show the live video on a separate computer and monitor in the observation room (e.g., Figure 11.4).

Testing Mobile Devices

Most of this chapter assumes that you are testing software on a conventional desktop computer. But what if you're working with a mobile device?

The same principles apply to usability testing for mobile devices as for desktop applications. However, in practice the many contexts in which we use mobile devices and the different modes of interactions they require trigger new questions. You may be interested, for example, in how people use tiny keyboards, buttons placed on the backs and sides of cases, and screen buttons. You may be studying device interactions that take place through shaking, bumping, or waving. Or you may need to understand how people complete tasks on the go, outside of home, lab, or office.

Obviously, you're going to have to make some changes to the traditional usability setup. Depending on the goals of the project, your mobile usability test will need to record:

- Screen activity
- Participants' finger movements
- Participants' faces (optional)

As of the time of this edition's publication, there is no standard commercial equipment for mobile usability testing. There are some commercial sleds made by companies such as Noldus and Tracksys, but they are typically quite expensive and limited in functionality. Cheaper or more extensive solutions are a decidedly DIY activity, rewarding creativity and gumption.

If you can keep the device tethered to a computer, one solution is a sled (Figure 11.5). The "sled" is a piece of plastic or metal that securely holds one or more cameras in position to record the evaluator's fingers moving and, if desired, the evaluator's face. You can use video editing software to combine the input from the webcam(s) later.

You can also use what's called a "document camera"—a desk-mounted camera that points downward onto a flat surface. The usability participant must hold the device below the camera. Document cameras are usually far more expensive than the tiny webcams used in sleds, and they limit participants' range of movement. However, they do provide much better image quality.

But mobile usability tests also leave the lab, moving through streets, into cars, and onto public transportation. In that case, mobile usability testing is necessarily a two or more person activity, with one person documenting the activity through video, and another handling the interviewing. It's still possible to use a sled, however—you just hook up the cameras to a laptop in a backpack. Alternatively, you can make your own creative alternative—there are many ways to record what you need.

Whatever you choose, the most important thing to remember about mobile usability testing is the old real estate agent catchphrase: location, location, location. You can learn a lot about your application or product from testing in the lab. Going out into the world takes more preparation and more creativity. But if you really want to get the most out of your testing, you're going to have to go where the action is.

- *Investigate mistakes.* When evaluators make mistakes, wait to see if they've realized that they've made an error. Next, immediately probe their thoughts and expectations. Why did they do something one way? What were they hoping it would do? How did they expect it to work? What happened that made them realize that it didn't work?

- *Probe nonverbal cues.* Sometimes people will react physically to an experience in a way that they wouldn't normally voice. When something is surprising, unexpected, or unpleasant, someone may flinch, but not say anything. Likewise, a smile or a lean forward may signify satisfaction or interest. Watch for such actions and follow up, if appropriate. For example, "You frowned when that dialog box came up. Is there anything about it that caused you to do that?"

- *Keep the interview task centered.* People naturally tend to digress. Performing a task may remind participants of an idea or an experience that they want to explore. Allowing people to explore their experiences is important, but you also need to keep the test focused on the product and the task. When someone leans back, takes his or her hands off the keyboard, stops looking at the monitor, and starts speaking in the abstract, it's generally time to introduce a new task or return to the task at hand.

- *Respect the evaluator's ideas.* When people are off topic, let them go for a bit (maybe a minute or so) and see if they can wrap up their thoughts on their own. If they're not wrapping up, steer the conversation back to the task or topic at hand. If that doesn't seem to work, then you can be more explicit: "That's interesting and maybe we'll cover it more later, but let's take a look at the Fork of the Week page."

- *Focus on their personal experience.* People have a tendency to idealize their experience and to extrapolate it to others' needs or to their far future needs. Immediate experience, however, is much more telling about people's actual attitudes, needs, and behaviors and is usually much more useful than their extrapolations. When Peter says, "I think it may be useful to someone," ask him if it's useful to him. If Maria says that she understands it, but others may not, tell her that it's most important to understand how she views it, not what others think. If Ken says that something "may be useful someday," ask him if it's useful to him *now*.

Managing Observers

Getting as many members of the development team to observe the tests is one of the fastest ways to relate the findings of the test and win them over.

Make the appropriate staff watch the usability tests in real time, if possible. There's nothing more enlightening to a developer (or even a vice president of product development) than watching their interfaces misused and their assumptions misunderstood and not being able to do anything about it.

Bring in plenty of food (sandwiches usually work). The team can then lounge in comfort and discuss the tests as they proceed (while not forgetting to watch how the participants are actually behaving). Since they know the product inside and out, they will see behaviors and attitudes that neither the moderator nor the analyst will, which is invaluable as source material for the analyst and for the team's understanding of their customers.

If neither a two-way mirror nor live video is available, it's possible to have members of the team observe the tests directly. However, there should never be more than one observer per test. It's intimidating enough for evaluators to be in a lab situation. To have several people behind them, sometimes scribbling, sometimes whispering, can be too creepy for even the most even-keeled. If an observer is in the room, introduce him or her by name. An introduction allows the participant to treat the observer as a legitimate, nonthreatening presence, not as "that guy watching me silently from the corner."

Give observers some instructions on acceptable behavior. This will also set their expectations for what's going to happen.

The standard technologies for managing, recording, and sharing usability tests change every few years. Please check www.mkp.com/observing-the-user-experience for up-to-date information.

We have found that multiple observers in the same room usually makes participants uncomfortable and hence compromises evaluation quality. It may be possible to for participants to act naturally and comfortably with a bunch of people staring at them—stage actors do this all the time, after all. However, we try to avoid complications by avoiding having any observers in the room at all.

Usability test observer instructions

Listen. As tempting as it is to immediately discuss what you're observing, make sure to listen to what people are really saying. Feel free to discuss what you're seeing, but don't forget to listen.

Usability tests are not statistically representative. If three out of four people say something, that doesn't mean that 75% of the population feels that way. It does mean that a number of people may feel that way, but it doesn't mean anything in the context of your larger user population.

Don't take every word as gospel. These are just the views of a couple of people. It's great if they have strong opinions, but trust your intuition in judging their importance unless there's significant evidence otherwise. So if someone says, "I hate the green," that doesn't mean that you change the color (though if everyone says, "I hate the green," then it's something to research further).

People are contradictory. Listen to how people are thinking about the topics and how they come to conclusions, not necessarily their specific desires. A person may not realize that two desires are mutually incompatible, or he or she may not care. Be prepared to be occasionally bored or confused. People's actions aren't always interesting or insightful.

Don't expect revolutions. If you can get one or two good ideas out of each usability test, then it has served its purpose.

Watch for what people *don't* do or *don't* notice as much as you watch what they do and notice.

For in-room observers, add the following instructions:

Feel free to ask questions when the moderator gives you an explicit opportunity. Ask questions that do not imply a value judgment about the product one way or another. So instead of asking, "Is this the best-of-breed product in its class?" ask "Are there other products that do what this one does? Do you have any opinions about any of them?"

Do not mention your direct involvement with the product. It's easier for people to comment about the effectiveness of a product when they don't feel that someone with a lot invested in it is in the same room.

If the observers are members of the development team, encourage them to wait until they've watched all the participants before generalizing and designing solutions. People naturally want to start fixing problems as soon as possible, but teams need to determine the context, magnitude, and prevalence of a problem before expending energy to fix it.

Tips and Tricks

- Do a dry run of the interview a day or two beforehand. Get everything set up as for a real test, complete with all the appropriate hardware and prototypes installed. Then get someone who is roughly the kind of person you're recruiting, but who isn't intimately involved in the development of the product, and conduct a full interview with him or her. Use this time to make sure that the script, the hardware, and the tasks are all working as designed. Go through the whole interview and buy the evaluator lunch afterward.
- Reset the computer and the test environment in between every test. Make sure every user gets the same initial experience by clearing the browser cache, resetting the history (so all links come up as new and cookies are erased), and restarting the browser so that it's on a blank page (you can set most browsers so that they open to a blank page by default). Clear off any notes or paperwork from the previous person and turn off the monitor.
- If you are testing a product that runs on different platforms (say, both Macintosh and PC), allow the evaluator to use whichever makes him or her the most comfortable. You can even include a question about it in the screener and know ahead of time which one the participants typically use.
- Don't take extensive notes during the test. This allows you to focus on what the user is doing and probe particular behaviors. Also, the participants won't jump to conclusions about periods of frantic scribbling, which they often interpret as an indicator that they just did something wrong.
- Take notes immediately after, writing down all interesting behaviors, errors, likes, and dislikes. Discuss the test with any observers for 10–20 minutes immediately after and take notes on their observations, too.

Remote Usability Testing

What we've just described is a tried-and-true method for basic in-person usability testing. However, it's possible—and often desirable—to test products remotely by interacting through the Internet and telephone.

Proponents of remote usability research point out that it is both more efficient—you don't have to get researchers and evaluators in the same place—and more natural. If you intercept people when they are visiting your website, your evaluation can come from someone at the precise moment of interest in the product—what remote research specialists Nate Bolt and Tony Tulathimutte call "time-aware research." Even if you pre-recruit and thus are not "time-aware," you can also increase the number and geographic diversity of your participants, making for a richer sample. So it would seem that remote research is preferable to in-person tests.

But wait! Remember, we wrote earlier that the two goals of a usability test are to get the most natural responses from evaluators and to get the most complete responses. Remote testing can advance the first, but don't forget the second: complete responses. Remote usability can miss parts of face-to-face research, such as the richness and spontaneity of body language and gesture. Many experienced remote research practitioners believe that they gather as much emotional information from vocal tone as in-person researchers do from body language. But even die-hard remote research evangelists will tell you that their sensitivity to vocal intonations took practice to develop.

If you really need to see a participant's full body in action, or you have specialized equipment that you need to run in person, then voice-based remote research isn't for you. As of the time of writing, remote usability is less useful for interfaces to consumer electronics, such as appliances or mobile devices. For those who don't advocate remote usability, the lack of face-to-face presence can also inhibit the development of empathetic rapport between evaluator and researcher.

According to Bolt and Tulathimutte, there are two main kinds of remote research—*moderated* and *automated*. In moderated research, a researcher actively leads evaluators through a series of tasks, asking questions and monitoring their reactions to the product. It requires the same kind of engagement as in-person testing, but the human interaction takes place over the telephone or through online chat. For that reason, moderated testing most resembles the in-person usability tests we describe in this chapter. Moderated testing produces similar kinds of rich qualitative data, as well. Automated usability research, on the other hand, relies on specialized software to prompt completion of simple tasks and record results. It results in sparser results but can feasibly engage many more evaluators in the same amount of time.

Remote Usability Basics

The initial tasks of remote usability, such as choosing tasks and writing a protocol, generally resemble those of in-person testing. There are some small differences, though. A remote usability protocol will have more up front explanations of the study, any incentive payments, how to use the screen sharing tool, and the necessity for clear verbal communication at all times.

From there, recruiting and interviewing require different tools. Both moderated and automated tests usually involve a custom pop-up window that "intercepts" potential participants as they visit a website. This means that you will need access to the website you are testing in order to install the pop-up code. The pop-up usually has a screening questionnaire (see Chapter 6 for more on how to write one) that asks a few simple demographic questions, ascertains willingness to participate in a usability test, and gets voice contact information. The researcher then telephones any eligible, willing candidates immediately or at an agreed-upon later time and date. If there are observers, they can listen through conference call functionality. Of course, you will need to prepare some initial explanations of what you're doing, since most people don't anticipate being called by strangers who want to look at their computer screen!

In order to see what the evaluator is doing, the researcher asks the evaluator to share a view of his or her computer screen— typically with an online tool, such as Adobe Connect. Software on the evaluator's computer then records this screen activity. Some screen-sharing tools have built-in recording functionality. Otherwise, you will need to install a program to capture the screen activity on your own computer. As well, some programs may allow you to access the evaluators' webcams in order to record their faces as they speak. However, taking over someone's webcam to record his or her face may be seen as too invasive—you've only just introduced yourself. Of course, the evaluator needs to give explicit permission before you make and store any kind of recording.

Then the evaluator follows the protocol, much as in an in-person test (see Chapter 6 for a discussion of telephone interviewing techniques). At the end of the test, the evaluator terminates the phone call and the screen sharing, assuring the evaluator that his or her screen is no longer visible and confirming the necessary contact information for sending the evaluator an incentive payment.

We can only provide a brief introduction to remote usability techniques here. For a thorough guide, we recommend Remote Research, *by Nate Bolt and Tony Tulathimutte, which is the source of many of our recommendations. You can see some examples of their work at www.remoteusability. com.*

Remote Usability Tips and Tricks

Here's some advice from Jodi Bollaert, of the advertising agency Team Detroit:

- You may find it difficult to recruit enough eligible and interested participants if you have a low-traffic website.
- For higher-quality recordings, screen participants for high-bandwidth connections and make sure to call them on landline telephones.
- Remind observers to turn their phones to "mute"—you don't want the participant to hear any backchat!
- You don't have to use working websites! Remote observation also can help in evaluating wireframes and concept sketches.

Eye Tracking

Interview-based usability testing evaluates user experiences at a conscious level. That is, participants perform a task and reflect verbally on their experiences, while the moderator watches and conscientiously notes his or her observations of the interaction. But there are some aspects of computer-human interaction that escape this technique. They happen too quickly, and the user is typically not aware that they are occurring.

A user may be looking directly at the product page of a shirt for sale on your website, but he still reports that he cannot find any sizing information, even though sizes are specified in a table on the right. In the seconds during which he was looking at the web page, did he literally *not see* the sizing table, or did he fail to notice it, read it, or understand it? What specific changes to the page might make him notice, read, and understand that information? These are the types of questions that eye-tracking usability studies can address.

Eye tracking uses an invisible infrared light source and a special video camera mounted on a specially constructed computer monitor. The video camera senses the infrared light reflected from the eyes, tracking even tiny movements of the user's eyes. As the participant uses the computer to perform a task, software measures those movements and logs where on the screen the user looks, the path of the gaze from one point to another, and the length of time the user's gaze is fixated on one point. Originally developed to study how people read, eye tracking can now be used to analyze a person's visual processing of any media that can be presented on a digital screen. (At this time, eye tracking is not widely used to evaluate small-screen or mobile device interfaces, but this may be changing.)

The best-known results of eye-tracking studies are *heat map* graphics (Figure 11.6), in which a screenshot is overlaid with a multicolored map showing the regions on which study participants tended to focus most and least. Another well-known result is a *gaze plot* (Figure 11.7). Unlike the heat map, which represents overall trends, the gaze plot shows the trajectory of one person's eye around a screen. Circles represent points of fixation, and lines represent the paths, called *saccades*, that the eye took between them.

Eye-tracking activities usually occur in conjunction with, or following, conventional interview-based usability. Eye tracking produces a lot of compelling data, but heat maps and gaze plots can be deceptively simple. Just because you know *where* someone is looking doesn't mean you know *what* they're thinking about—or if they're thinking at all. A very long fixation on one spot of the screen could indicate deep thought…or daydreaming. Since asking questions during an eye-tracking session can potentially distract the participant, ask retrospective questions after the session ends.

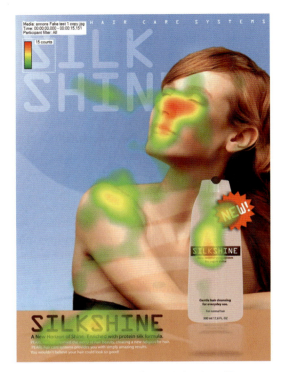

Figure 11.6 Heat map. Image courtesy of Tobii Technology AB.

Conducting usability studies with eye tracking is a highly specialized skill and can be very costly. It requires pricey equipment, significant computing power, and extensive training of the moderator. Because eye-tracking data are "noisy" (i.e., people's eye movement patterns are unpredictable and vary for many reasons), eye-tracking studies usually require more participants than conventional usability studies. The large quantities of numerical data they generate require a knowledgeable analyst to produce useful insights.

You should consider conducting eye-tracking studies if *all* the following are true:

1. You have a specific objective or task you want to enable, and the task has a clear measure of success.

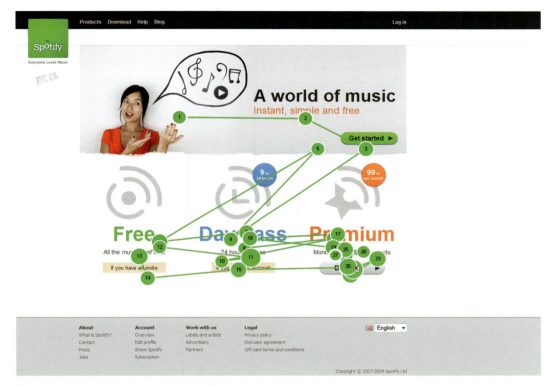

Figure 11.7 Gaze plot. Image courtesy of Tobii Technology AB.

2. Your objective has to do with the way users visually process a website or software interface. For example, you want them to notice and read the lead article, or browse more of the products on a catalog page.
3. You have already determined that the content is of interest to users, conducted interview-based usability testing and A/B testing (See Chapter 16 for more on A/B testing.), and optimized your page design based on the results, and you have not seen the improvements you seek.

Offered by a number of usability consultancies, eye tracking is a well-accepted part of the usability toolkit. Choose an eye-tracking research vendor the way you would select any other

We *don't go into much detail on the technical details of eye tracking because the technology changes so frequently. If you're thinking about doing an eye-tracking study, check out the resources at www.mkp.com/ observing-the-user-experience.*

We refer to the moderator and analyst as separate people here, but in practice the same person often performs both roles.

consultant: by meeting them and evaluating examples of their work. While the technology may be shiny, don't underestimate the analysis component. Your vendor should be able to do more than provide pretty heat maps. They should be able to tell you how they will address your specific questions and demonstrate that they can run the tests and analysis you need to make a difference to your product's usability and effectiveness.

How to Analyze Usability Tests

Although some conclusions are going to be obvious, a formal analysis is necessary to get to underlying causes and to extract the most value from the interviews. Analyzing the output is a three-stage process: collecting observations, organizing observations, and extracting trends from the observations. The analysis process described in this chapter is specific to usability testing; there is a longer and much more thorough description of general qualitative data analysis in Chapter 15.

Collecting Observations

There are three sets of observations to be collected: the moderator's, the observers', and the analyst's.

Collecting the moderator's and observers' notes is pretty straightforward. Get their notes (or copies) and have them walk you through them, explaining what each one means. In addition, interview them for additional observations that were not in their notes. These are frequently large-scale perspectives on the situation that the person made in the days or hours following the last test.

The analyst's notes are the most important and time-consuming part of the data collection process. The analyst should go through at least four of the videotapes and note down all situations where there were mistakes or confusion or where the evaluators expressed an opinion about the product or its features. He or she should note which features the evaluators had problems with, under what circumstances they encountered those problems, and provide a detailed description of the problem. You will likely find the majority of the usability problems in the product during this phase, as the patterns in people's behavior and expectations emerge.

Quantitative information, although not generalizable to the whole target market at large, is often useful when summarizing and comparing behavior (however, it's fraught with potential problems, as people reading reports can latch on to largely meaningless numbers as some kind of absolute truth). To collect quantitative information, first create a measurement range for each question that everyone in the analysis team agrees upon. Don't use a stopwatch and take exact numbers. The statistical error present in the small sample of people in a usability test negates the accuracy of a stopwatch. The most useful metrics are the ones that are the most general. Flow Interactive, Limited, a UK user experience design and evaluation consulting company, uses the following range to measure how long people take to perform a task:

0. Fail
1. Succeed very slowly in a roundabout way
2. Succeed a little slowly
3. Succeed quickly

Most of the time, you don't need any more precision, since making critical comparisons only requires an order-of-magnitude measure. Each scale should have three or five steps (don't use two, four, or six since it's hard to find a middle value; don't use more than five because it tends to get confusing) and a separate value for failure.

Make a grid for each participant consisting of the task metrics you're going to collect. As you watch the videos, note the severity in each cell (when appropriate, define severity using the same language and scale that is used by the development team to define how serious code bugs are). For the fork tasks, the following table would reflect one person's performance.

Then, when compiling the final analysis, create a table for each metric that summarizes the whole user group's experience. For the completion time metric, two summary tables could look as in Table 11.5 and Table 11.6.

Table 11.5 Tina's Task Performance

Task	Time to Read	Errors	Time to Complete
Find Louis XIV	1	3	1
Buy replacement	3	1	2
Find similar forks	1	2	0
Key	0. Don't read 1. Read very slowly 2. Read moderately slowly 3. Read quickly	0. Fail because of errors 1. Many errors 2. Some errors 3. Few or no errors	0. Fail 1. Succeed very slowly in a roundabout way 2. Succeed a little slowly 3. Succeed quickly

Table 11.6 Task Performance Time Measures Summary

	Tina	Kristie	Ben	Sonia	Kim	Avg.
Find Louis XIV	1	2	1	0	2	1.2
Buy replacement	2	3	2	1	1	1.8
Find similar forks	0	0	1	1	0	0.4

The average numbers, although not meaningful in an absolute context, provide a way to compare tasks to each other and between designs.

Note feature requests and verbatim quotations from the evaluators, especially ones that encapsulate a particular behavior (e.g., "I don't understand what "Forkopolis" means, so I wouldn't click there"). Feature requests are often attempts to articulate a problem that the evaluator can't express in any other way. However, they can also be innovative solutions to those same problems, so capture them, regardless.

If time and budget allow, a transcription of the session is helpful, but use it only as an aid in watching the video. Transcriptions miss the vocal inflection and behavior that can clarify some situations. For example, the statement "A-ha! There it is!" doesn't sufficiently convey the effect of a confused pause of five seconds while an evaluator passes his pointer over every single visual element on the screen looking for somewhere to click.

Much as with other forms of qualitative data analysis (see Chapter 15 for a deeper discussion) organizing usability testing information and extracting trends can be done in a group with the development team (and other stakeholders, as appropriate). This allows the group to use its collected knowledge to flesh out the understanding of the problem and to begin working on solutions.

Organizing Observations

First, read through all the notes once to get a feeling for the material. Look for repeated concerns as well as multiple issues that may have their origin in common underlying problems.

Then put all the observations into a pile (literally, or in a single large document). Opening a separate document in a word processor, go through each observation and group it with other similar observations in the new document. Similarity can be in terms of superficial similarity ("Term not understood"), feature cluster ("Shopping cart problems"), or in terms of underlying cause ("Confusing information architecture"). Group the observations with the most broadly sweeping, underlying causes. Pull quotations out and group them with the causes that they best illustrate.

Extracting Trends

Having grouped all the observations, go through the groups and consolidate them, separating the groups of unrelated topics. Throw away those that only have one or two individual observations. For each group, try to categorize the problem in a single short sentence, with a couple of sentences to fully describe the phenomenon. Explain the underlying cause as much as possible, separating the explanation of the phenomenon from your hypothesis of its cause. Concentrate on describing the problem, its immediate impact on the user experience, and the place where the problem occurred. Be very careful when suggesting solutions. Ultimately, the development team knows more about the technology and the assumptions that went into the product, and the responsibility for isolating underlying causes and finding solutions is theirs. Your recommendations should serve as a guide to where solutions could exist, not edicts about what must be done.

Describe the severity of the problem from the user's perspective, but don't give observations numerical severity grades. If a shorthand for the characterization of observations is desired or requested, categorize the observations in terms of the effects they have on the user experience, rather than assigning them an arbitrary number. Such an effect scale could be "Prevents an activity," "Causes confusion," "Does not match expectations," "Seen as unnecessary."

It's easy to turn user severity measures into project development priorities. This is usually inappropriate. What's most important to a user's success with the product is not necessarily what's most important to the product's success. Inform the product team of problem severity from the user's perspective. Problem severity can tell you how to determine project priorities, but the two aren't the same.

Once all this is done, you should have a list of observations, hypotheses for what caused the phenomena, and quotations that reinforce and summarize the observations. Some of those observations will likely please your stakeholders. But usability reports can be controversial, as well. Nobody likes hearing bad news, but it's almost unavoidable with usability tests. No product is perfect all the time, and usability tests are designed to find trouble spots. By this time, you will likely have a good sense of which, if any, of your observations will be controversial or difficult for your stakeholders to accept.

As you assemble your report, consider these common-sense tips for breaking bad news:

- *Don't present an entirely negative report.* There's bound to be some positive comments you can find to soften a harsh set of findings. Don't invent positivity where there is none—but by the same token, don't assume that your job is only to present only problems. Celebrate successes where you can.
- *Put the focus on real people.* Demonstrate that the source of critical findings is *not* the usability research team. Quotations from users, especially in a video-highlights clip, establish the credibility of your findings and give them more weight. It's harder to doubt the existence of a problem when a video clip shows a succession of real people struggling with your product.
- *Be constructive.* We know we told you to be wary of making design edicts. But that doesn't mean you should never make any recommendations. If a problem has an obvious fix, especially if suggested by evaluators, say so! Even if your recommendation isn't taken up, you have at least acknowledged that there are potential solutions.

The problem with consistently bringing only bad news is two-fold. If your stakeholders are already fearful about the product, it can make the problems seem hopeless. Second, you can damage the credibility of usability research in general. Usability can become synonymous with criticism, and people understandably end up resenting it. The goal is for stakeholders to welcome your reports, not dread them.

Luckily, it's usually not that hard to balance calls for improvement with praise for success. Let's take a look at a usability report prepared for the Wikipedia Foundation by the design and research firm gotomedia. (Note: We've edited this report down because our space is limited, but what you see here remains basically identical to what was delivered.)

Anatomy of a Usability Test Report

There is no one right way to report usability test results. You can put them in email, make a word processing document, or a presentation. What's important is that you use a medium that gets the message across to your stakeholders in a convincing and timely way. Here, we're focusing on the content of the report, and not the design. See Chapter 18 for more tips on formatting and presenting reports.

This is the last usability test of three that Wikipedia conducted to redesign their article editing and creating interfaces.

Project Overview

As a part of the Wikipedia Usability Initiative, the Wikimedia Foundation asked gotomedia to conduct a series of usability tests to evaluate progress toward the Initiative's overall goal of "measurably increase(ing) the usability of Wikipedia for new contributors."

The primary research goals were to:

- evaluate the progress/improvements made by the team in reducing the obstacles that novice users encounter in editing a Wikipedia article, including—but not limited to—adding personal content, fixing a typo, adding a reference, formatting content, and creating an article.
- evaluate the new prototype interaction with templates
- evaluate the effects of template collapsing.

In previous rounds of testing, Wikipedia and Bolt | Peters uncovered and documented many usability issues that exist in Wikipedia generally, and in the editing process specifically.

Our research reaffirmed these previously documented issues such as:

- **People love Wikipedia.** Wikipedia is extremely popular with users. All of the participants we spoke to use the site at least several times a week, and many use it several times a day.

- **People don't think they have anything to add.** Nearly everyone we interviewed reported that they are reticent to add to Wikipedia because they are not confident in the quality or validity of their own potential contribution.
- **Wikitext is easy…and hard.** Users are able to make simple text changes to a Wikipedia article with relative ease, but more advanced editing tasks such as creating links, footnotes, and tables proved to be more challenging.
- **Users learn by example.** When confronted with a task that they did not immediately understand, most users looked for examples in the Wikitext and attempted to mimic what other editors had done.
- **Users are not able to create a new article.** Only one of our participants was able to figure out how to start a new article on Wikipedia.

These issues are well documented. We did not find anything in our research that significantly contradicts any of the findings of the previous studies. We will focus our comments on more specific editing issues, new functionality that was introduced since the previous tests were conducted, and additional observations not previously documented.

Overviews are very useful when communicating results. The vice president of product development may never read the report but might skim a couple of paragraphs giving a high-level overview. Highlight the main points, maybe by **bolding** them, maybe by making them a different color. When attaching the report in an email, the executive summary should be included in the email, while the rest of the report—including the executive summary—is included as an attachment.

Procedure

Sessions began with a brief interview about participants' computer use in general and their past experience with Wikipedia. Sessions then progressed to Usability Testing of the prototype editing interface. In Usability Testing, participants from a representative sample of website users are observed as they perform a set of predetermined tasks from a script. The 75-minute sessions were led and moderated by an experienced Usability Specialist. Throughout the session, the UX Specialist asked additional questions to clarify and expand on participant responses. This process helps create an understanding of how users interact with the website and illuminates potential usability problems.

The interview scripts were developed by a gotomedia User Experience Specialist and are outlined in Appendix A. Participants were chosen based on the segmentation agreed upon by gotomedia and Wikipedia, focusing on Wikipedia users who had limited or no editing experience.

Though the script was generally task based, the questions were open ended and left room for interpretation, encouraging subjects to not try to complete the tasks in any "correct" way, but rather to go about them naturally, if they had felt the motivation to do so on their own. Open-ended interview questions including "How did you find that process?" regularly follow every "task." The script was piloted on one staff member of gotomedia, a reader (but not editor) of Wikipedia prior to any official testing.

A quick description of the procedure demystifies the process and provides important context for report recipients to be able to understand the results.

Testing Environment and Recruiting Criteria

Ten participants were interviewed at Fleischman Field Research in San Francisco on March 25–26, 2010. Nine additional participants were interviewed remotely via web conference. Remote participants were all from the continental United States, and all but one were from the center of the country or the east coast. Participants were selected according to the target demographics defined in cooperation with Wikipedia.

The participants were divided into two primary groups: Wikipedia users with no editing experience and Wikipedia users with limited editing experience. The recruiting criteria are outlined below. Participant grids are available in Appendix B.
Recruit:

* 12 participants from Group 1 (half remote, half in-person)
* 6 participants from Group 2 (half remote, half in-person)

All Participants

* Are suitably articulate to share their opinions in the testing setting
* Are easy to understand (no thick accents)
* Are comfortable using the Firefox web browser

Group 1—No Successful Editing Experience

* Have not attempted to edit a Wikipedia article, but are interested in doing so **OR:**
* Have attempted to edit an article but were not successful

Group 2—Limited Editing Experience

* Have edited less than 25 articles

As in past studies, we recruited over 2,000 San Francisco residents for the in-person testing and over 1,000 U.S. residents for the remote testing. A banner/alert was placed and displayed at the top of every 1 in 100 Wikipedia pages for the duration of 3 days. When users viewed our message by clicking, they were forwarded to an Ethnio recruiting system where we asked them a series of questions. Specifically, users were asked about what they were doing on Wikipedia, how often they used Wikipedia, if they had ever contributed to Wikipedia (and in what manner), their age, gender, location, and availability. Based on these criteria, the 3,000+ users who responded to our survey were filtered down to 500 viable subjects based on their answers to these questions. The team and gotomedia worked with Fleischman Field Research to contact, filter, and schedule these participants based on a further phone conversation covering their Wikipedia usage patterns, reasons for not contributing, talkativeness, and occupation.

It's important to explain exactly who was recruited, and how. This section follows proper inverted pyramid style: It begins with the most important and general information, then introduces more detail with each paragraph. Finally, actual information about each participant appears in an appendix at the end. (Depending on your stakeholders' expectations and your own preferences, information about the actual participants can go in this section as well.) Remember: Usability tests aren't experimental science; it's more important to respond to the needs of your immediate situation than to exactly replicate this format.

Key Findings
General Editing Issues
Wikitext presents significant barriers to editing. The best way to really open up the editing process to all users would be to hide Wikitext from users altogether. Wikipedia participation will only be truly open to everyone when a true WYSIWYG interface can be developed. There are many technical, cultural, and financial reasons why a true WYSIWYG interface probably won't be implemented at Wikipedia any time soon, and there are legitimate arguments about whether or not making editing that easy would ultimately be good for Wikipedia. However, if the goal is to truly open up editing to all users, a true WYSIWYG interface would be the best way to accomplish that goal.

> *"I am not a technical person so I have no idea (how to do this)."* —Carrie, 32, Account Manager

> *"...seems like that would be so much easier than dealing with code. The way it's doing it now, it seems to be keeping some people out. It seems exclusionary."* —Phil, 22, Freelance Writer

"I know my mother couldn't use this!" —Oliver, 48, Business Analyst

New editors need more help. Several users expressed a desire for a short video or tutorial that would give them a basic understanding of the editing process. Many users were observed looking for help in the left-hand column of the page, and those that did so expected to find edit-specific information under the Toolbox menu in that left column.

"Some of the things aren't actually intuitive. So either they could make it more obvious for a novice or lay people, or make a tutorial. (And) make that tutorial really, really obvious for when features are just rolled out." —Bianca, 22, Intern

"I think they should highlight the Help and how to contribute. It should be super obvious on the front page. I had no idea and had never tried, but I think if it were more obvious (how easy editing is) then more people like myself would." —Adam, 21, Student

"I would likely look at a video. I know Google does that for their suite of apps…" —Clayton, 22, Tutor

Recommendations: A tutorial would be very valuable for new users, particularly those who are not used to dealing with markup languages. If tutorials are produced, they should be modular in nature and short in duration. Users are less likely to sit through and understand a long tutorial that addresses many editing tasks. A short tutorial should explain the very basics of making a text edit, using Preview, and Publish. Additional self-contained tutorials should address specific issues such as linking, references, tables, images, etc. A tutorial should offer a quick way to learn a needed skill in real time, not a 20 minute distraction from the task at hand. Users should be able to view a short tutorial about the specific task they are trying to accomplish at the time they are trying to accomplish it. Tutorials should display in a new window so editors can view it side by side with the editing interface.

Also, Wikimedia should consider adding clearly labeled links to edit-specific help in the left-hand column of the page while in Edit mode.

[some findings omitted]

Editing Toolbar
The editing toolbar (Figure 11.8) definitely represents an improvement for editors over the tools previously available to them, and the changes made to the toolbar since the previous rounds of testing do appear to facilitate easier editing. Toolbar visibility was improved over the previous design. Some participants still overlooked the toolbar, but most users did eventually find the toolbar on their own.

Figure 11.8 Editing toolbar.

The findings section summarizes the main themes. In general, organize the findings section into subsections according to the technical features in question. In this case, boldface headings subdivide the technical features even further. This helps readers easily navigate the mass of text.

You should also include quotations. Some well-chosen words from evaluators are more compelling than a paragraph of explanation. The readers can see how evidence from actual people supports all of your points. When placed next to each point, they reinforce each one's meaning. When presented all at once, they communicate the overall "feel" of a usability test.

Where relevant, include screenshots or other documentation of what you tested. That way, readers don't have to fumble through their own files trying to figure out exactly what evaluators tested. If necessary, you can annotate these with drawn-on boxes, text, and arrows to make sure everyone understands exactly what evaluators are discussing.

Finally, remember that usability tests don't always have to surface problems. If there is good news, the findings section should also highlight it.

We've shortened the report to fit in this chapter. However, here's one example of a typical participant grid (all names are pseudonyms):

Appendix B

Time	Name	Occupation	Age	Gender	Edited before?	Wikipedia Usage	Mac or Windows
3/25: 9:00	Kelsey W.	Office Manager	35	Female	No/ Interested: Yes	Daily	Windows
3/25: 10:30	Carlos W.	K-12 Tutor	22	Male	No/ Interested: Yes	Daily	Windows
3/25: 12:00	Melissa S.	Student	20	Female	No/ Interested: Yes	3 times/week	Windows
3/25: 3:00	Carolyn O.	Account Manager	32	Female	No/ Interested: Yes	3–4 times/week	Windows
3/25: 4:30	Tran M.	MBA Student	30	Female	Yes/ 1–2 articles	3–4 times/week	Windows

Evaluator profiles are often in table form like this one, but they can also be in paragraph form. Evaluator profiles are useful both to help the report reader understand the context in which people's statements were made and as a way to personify the participants to those who were unable to observe the tests. Like personas (described in Chapter 17), these profiles help personalize the abstract concept of a product's users and make the results that much more immediate. This is where it comes in handy to have a spreadsheet to keep all the relevant evaluator information in one place.

Conclusion

Usability tests are one of the workhorses of user experience research. They can be done quickly and inexpensively and provide a lot of immediately actionable information. Too often, they serve as the only form of user feedback, but when used correctly, they're invaluable.

CHAPTER 12

Surveys

You may know whom you want as your ideal target audience, but do you know who is actually using your product? Are your actual users the people you imagined while building the product, or are they completely different? You may know some things about which parts of your product are used and what people complain about. But how widespread are those complaints? Are people using your product as anticipated, or are they using it for something else? Unless you can get the opinions of a large section of your audience, you won't know what makes your product popular (or disliked).

Qualitative techniques such as interviews, think–aloud usability tests, and observational research give you insight into why people do the things they do when using your product and how some people use your product, but they can't accurately tell you the prevalence of characteristics and tendencies in user population. Only *quantitative* techniques can predict how many of your users are teenagers and whether those teenagers in your audience generally desire the new features you're considering. Knowing your audience's makeup can tell you on whom to concentrate your qualitative research and, more important, can give you information about what qualities define your audience.

The best tool to find out who your users are and what opinions they hold is the survey. A survey is a set of questions that allows a large group of people to describe themselves, their interests, and their preferences in a structured way. Using statistical tools on the results, you can reveal broad characteristics about your users and extract interesting patterns. When done correctly, surveys can give you a higher degree of certainty about your overall user population than using only qualitative research methods.

Surveys can answer such questions as:

- How old are your users?
- What kind of Internet connection do they have?
- Is your user population homogeneous, or does it consist of a number of distinct groups?
- What do they want? Does the product provide it?
- What do they like about the product? What do they dislike?

However, surveys can easily go wrong. If not designed carefully, they can ask the wrong people the wrong questions, producing results that are inaccurate, inconclusive, or, at worst, deceptive. Web-based surveys are especially vulnerable because, lacking any direct contact with respondents themselves, their accuracy depends on the perceptions people have of themselves and their ability and willingness to honestly report those perceptions. Without direct contact (whether through in-person visits or analysis of behavioral data), you cannot tell what services respondents really use or whether their descriptions of themselves are accurate. Respondents can only tell you what they think.

When to Conduct Surveys

If you already have a group of people using your product, then the kind of questions you want to ask them will determine when you do a survey. A *profile*, for example, can be done any-time you want a snapshot of the composition of your current user population. A *satisfaction survey* could be run before a major redesign in order to make sure the redesign resolves the main problems people are experiencing. A *value survey*, investigating what people find important, could be run before a major marketing campaign to shape how it describes and promotes the product.

Surveys come in all sizes and structures. Ultimately, it depends on what kind of survey you want to field and what you want to get out of it.

Although it's possible to use simple surveys to gain a basic understanding of your audience, statistically accurate survey creation is very complex. This chapter covers only fielding a basic survey through a website. For anything more complicated than a simple profile survey, for telephone or email surveys, or for important product decisions that require accurate numerical results, we recommend reading the following books or hiring a professional survey company.

Survey Research Methods by Earl Babbie

The Handbook of Online Marketing Research by Joshua Grossnickle and Oliver Raskin

It can be particularly useful to field a survey after preliminary qualitative research. Methods such as focus groups, interviews, and observational research can give you detailed, specific information about values and behaviors to guide writing survey questions that examine their prevalence. For example, a series of interviews with owners of toy robots can suggest some behaviors to track that you might not imagine yourself: treating the toys like family pets, restricting children from playing with them, giving them as gifts to family and friends, throwing them away after a few days, etc. They can also help guide the kind of terminology you use, so that you're not writing questions using words participants find confusing.

How to Field a Survey

Before designing a survey, you need to know what you're trying to accomplish. Start by writing a sentence or two about why you're doing this survey—your goal. For example, say that you have a mature product, a website that's been around for several years. Although revenue is decent, the growth of new users has slowed. You have an idea of the size of your audience—but you're assuming that the kinds of people using your site now are the same as when the site launched. Further, although your site has some unique features, several competitors have similar feature sets. You've been counting on your unique features to drive user growth. Though the log files show that the features get used, it's difficult to tell whether the unique features are the reason people use your product or whether they're icing on the cake. Completing the sentence "We are going to run a survey," the reasoning could read as follows:

> To understand if our user base has changed since last year, and if so, how, and to understand which features they find most attractive.

Setting the Schedule

Once you've decided on the overall goal for the survey, you need to construct a schedule. Since the preparation of a survey is critical to its success, a typical survey research schedule includes enough time for questions to be written and reviewed and for the survey to be tested and revised as necessary. Once a survey has been sent out, no changes can be made to maintain statistical validity, so leaving time for survey testing and redesign is crucial.

Writing the Survey

You should start by enumerating the goals of your survey as specifically as possible, based on desired outcomes. These might include:

- Create a demographic, technological, and web use profile of our audience.
- Get a prioritized rating of the utility of our main features to the survey audience.
- Get a list of other sites they commonly use.

With this list, you should have enough information to choose the kind of survey you're going to be fielding.

Table 15.1 A Sample Survey Schedule

Timing	Activity
$t - 3$ weeks	Determine test audience, goals.
$t - 3$ weeks	Start writing questions.
$t - 2$ weeks	Finish writing questions and review with a few people. Rewrite as necessary. Write report draft. Choose an online survey provider.
$t - 1$ weeks	Set up your survey using the service you chose. Pilot test, using both collection and tabulation software. Write report based on pilot test results.
$t - 3$ days	Rewrite questions based on pilot test feedback; review with a few people.
$t - 2$ days	Finish preparing online questions. Test survey for functionality under multiple conditions.
t	Field the survey (usually 114 days, depending on whether there's important daily variation). When done, remove the survey site immediately and shut down data collection.
$t + 1$ day	Begin analysis.
$t + 3$ days	Complete analysis. Begin report.
$t + 1$ week	Complete report. Present to team, discuss, and note directions for further research.

Brainstorm Your Questions

With the survey goals in mind, brainstorm your questions (you can do this by yourself or with a group). Without stopping, write down every question you can think of that you want to answer with the survey. Don't try to phrase them in "survey-ese," just write down what you want to know.

As you're brainstorming, keep in mind that there are two different kinds of survey goals, *descriptive* and *explanatory*.

Descriptive goals aim to profile the audience. They summarize your audience's composition in terms of their personal characteristics, what they own, what they want, and how they claim to behave. Although such profiles can be quite extensive and sophisticated, they do not attempt to understand how any of the characteristics affect each other.

Explanatory goals explain people's beliefs and behaviors by uncovering relationships between their answers. For example, a mostly descriptive survey would seek to know which features people use and what their average incomes are, whereas an explanatory survey would try to explain how the size of their income affects the features they prefer. Such goals aim to find inherent relationships between characteristics. The more these relationships can be isolated, the more precise the explanation.

Survey questions themselves come in a variety of flavors. General question categories can be divided into *characteristic* questions that describe who someone is and what his or her physical and software environment is like, *behavior* questions that outline how someone behaves, and *attitudinal* questions that inquire into what people want and believe.

Each of these major categories can have lots of subcategories. We provide some common subcategories to give you an idea of what you might ask.

Characteristic Categories

Demographic. These are questions about who the respondents are. How old are they? What do they do for a living? How educated are they?

Technological. These questions ask about their digital technology setup and experience. What kind of mobile phone do they own? How expert are they at managing online privacy settings?

Behavioral Categories

Technology use. These questions ask people how they use the technologies you care about. How often are they online every week? What kinds of things do they use their washing machine for? What kind of computer experience do they have?

Usage. What product features do they (claim to) use? How often do they use them? What are the reasons they come to your site? How long have they been using it?

Competitive. What other sites do they visit? How often? How long have they been using them? What features do they use?

Attitudinal Categories

Satisfaction. Do they like your product? Does it do what they had expected? Are they able to do what they want with it?

Preference. What do they find most compelling about your product? Which features do they tell their friends about? What do they consider unnecessary or distracting?

Desire. What do they want? What features do they feel are lacking?

Now, with your list of questions in mind, ask other members of your development team to come up with a list of their own. You may want to show them your list, but first ask them to do it from scratch so that they're not biased by your ideas. Then, when you've collected everyone's questions, share them and see if any additional questions appear from the mix.

This initial list could look like this.

How old are you?
How much do you make?
What's your education level?
What operating system do you use?
Have you ever heard of Linux?
Have you ever used Linux?
Do you ever use eBay?
What speed is your connection?
How much time do you spend on the web?
How long are you willing to wait to get an answer?

> Have you ever used Quicken?
> How long have you had your current computer?
> Do you own a mobile phone?
> How much do you spend on your mobile phone per month?
> Do you have a phone plan or do you top up?
> What time zone do you live in?

Write the Questions

> *Ask people only questions that they are likely to know the answers to, ask about things relevant to them, and be clear in what you're asking. The danger is that people will give you answers—whether reliable or not.*
> —Earl Babbie, *Survey Research Methods,*

Now it's time to write the questions. In Chapter 6, there are a number of rules for asking nondirected questions, questions that don't lead the person answering them to think that there's a "right" answer. Most of the suggestions in that section concentrate on the moderator's immediate behavior and helping staying nonjudgmental, but they apply equally well to survey questions. However, whereas qualitative research questions need to be *flexible* in order to avoid cramping respondents' answers, survey questions need to be more precise and restricted in order to be *unambiguous*. Unlike most interviews, where the questions should be *open ended* (in other words, they should not limit the set of responses to a list compiled by the interviewer), most survey questions are *closed ended*. In general, open-ended questions require much more effort from the person answering them and from the analyst. This is desirable in long interview situations with a few people, but much more difficult in a survey situation when there may be potentially thousands of participants. Open-ended questions may be used in surveys—they can provide answers in situations where you have no idea how to write the question in a closed-ended way—but they need to be used carefully and sparingly.

The most common type of closed-ended survey question is the single-answer *multiple-choice question*. We've all seen this type of question: it has a range of choices for the respondent, only one of which may be picked.

How long have you been using Internet email?
- ○ Less than a year
- ○ 1–2 years
- ○ 2–5 years
- ○ 5 years or more

Another common type of question is the *checklist*. This question consists of a list of answers, any number of which can be chosen.

What kinds of news stories have you read in the last week? (Check all that apply.)
- ☐ International news
- ☐ Domestic news
- ☐ Entertainment
- ☐ Predictions
- ☐ Sports
- ☐ Industry analysis
- ☐ Political commentary
- ☐ Fine arts
- ☐ Financial
- ☐ Other
- ☐ I haven't read any news stories in the last week.

In order for closed-ended questions to be comfortably answerable by the respondents, the answers to them need to be *specific*, *exhaustive*, and *mutually exclusive*. Specificity reduces the amount of uncertainty when the time comes to analyze the answer. If your audience consists of dance music DJs and you're asking about what kind of music they spin, it is important to make sure that you don't just ask about "dance music," because DJs themselves may distinguish between two dozen different subgenres. Exhaustive answer lists include all possible answers. For example, the responses to the question above include both "other" and "I haven't read any news stories." They reduce respondent frustration and errors, because people won't be as likely to choose a random answer after searching fruitlessly for the one that matches what they really mean. If you can't make an exhaustive list of answers, the question should not be closed ended. Answers should also be mutually exclusive to reduce the amount of ambiguity among the choices. If you want to know where people shop, and you ask them to choose between "in my neighborhood" and "nearby," they could honestly pick either answer—leaving you with inaccurate data.

Obviously, requiring closed-ended questions limits what you can ask. You will have to rephrase your questions to make them closed-ended and eliminate the ones that can't be rewritten.

Now, make a grid with four columns. For each question, write the question, the instructions you're going to give to the respondent, the possible answers, and why you're asking the question. The "reasons" column is especially important, because you need to make sure that you have a specific justification for each and every question. Why is it important? What is the information going to be used for? Who wants to know? Long surveys can discourage people from completing them, so you want to make sure you have a very good reason for each question.

You may also want to make a second list of information that can be gathered automatically. Web server log files can collect the time a survey was taken, the operating system of the machine used to take the survey, the kind of browser they were using, what Internet domain the machine was on, and so on. Cookies can keep track

Sample Survey Question Grid

Question	Instructions	Answers	Reasons
What is your age?	*None*	Radio buttons: Under 18 18–20 21–24 25–34 35–44 45–55 55 and over Prefer not to state	Need to stop underage respondents from taking the survey. For comparison with last year's survey. Compare with experience.
What is your gender?	*None*	Pop-up: Male Female Prefer not to state	For comparison with last year's survey.

Question	Instructions	Answers	Reasons
What kinds of stories have you read on the website in the last week?	Check all that apply.	Checklist: Telecommunications New products Hackers Fashion Travel Hardware reviews Software reviews Predictions Sports Computer industry analysis Political commentary Fine arts Fiction Investment Personality profiles	A measure of reader information desires. Compare perceived reading habits to actual behavior based on log analysis. Summarize for ad sales.
What operating system do you use most frequently to access the web?	*None.*	Pop-up: Windows Macintosh Linux Android Other Don't know	Compare with last year's survey. Compare with log analysis. Summarize for design. Summarize for editorial.

of who has visited your site before, who has purchased from you before, what their preferences are, and the like.

When writing questions, *don't make people predict* their behavior. People's past behavior is usually better at predicting their future behavior than their statements are. If you're interested in whether someone would use an online calendaring system, don't ask

In some cases, people may have little or no appropriate past experience to base their answers on. For example, the process of buying a home (or getting open-heart surgery or enrolling in a university) is relatively infrequent for most people, and past experience may have little relation to their future behavior. This is the one time when asking a hypothetical question may be better than asking about past behavior, since past behavior would be unlikely to yield any useful information.

Will you use an online calendaring system?

Ask instead

Have you ever used or ever wanted to use an online calendar system such as Yahoo! Calendar or Google Calendar?

Avoid negative questions. Negative questions are more difficult to understand and easy to mistake for the positive versions of themselves.

> Which of the following features are you not interested in?

can be easily read as

> Which of the following features are you interested in?

It's much simpler to ask

> Which of the following features are you interested in?

and then to infer the ones that are not checked are uninteresting to the respondents.

Don't overload questions. Each question should contain at most one concept that you're investigating. Although multiple concepts may be linked, they should still be divided into separate, clear individual questions. Compound questions are frustrating for the respondent who only agrees with half of the question, and more complicated for the analyst who needs to infer the respondent's perspective on both parts of the question.

> Do you find yourself frustrated with the performance of the website because it is slow to load?

can be rewritten as

> Are you frustrated by the website's performance?
>   If so, which of the following aspects of the website's performance frustrate you?
>   ☐ Page length
>   ☐ Download time
>   ☐ Picture size
>   etc.

Be specific. Avoid words with multiple or fuzzy meanings ("sometimes," "around," "roughly," "any"). When speaking in units other than money, percentages, or other common abbreviations, make sure that the whole name of the unit is written out ("hours" instead of "hrs.," "thousands" instead of "K," etc.). Use exact time periods.

So rather than writing a question about how often someone reads news as

One of the virtues of staying specific is that you avoid the common mistake of asking people to judge their own expertise. The research of communications scholar Eszter Hargittai suggests that asking people to rate their own knowledge, skill, or effectiveness runs into the same problems of self-perception as asking people to predict their future actions. Asking questions about frequency of use or time spent doing certain activities at least allows a more objective comparison between participants. As well, try asking questions that require people to demonstrate, rather than claim, knowledge. Hargittai suggests asking people to choose the one fake term from a list of technical-sounding words.

> How much time have you spent reading news on the web recently?
> ○ Some
> ○ A lot
> ○ Every day

the question can be written as

> How much time did you spend reading news and information on the web in the last week?
> ○ None
> ○ 0 to 5 hours
> ○ 6 to 10 hours
> ○ 11 to 20 hours
> ○ More than 20 hours

Never shut people out. Questions should always give people an option that they feel applies to them. The following question, for example, assumes a lot of things about the respondents and their attitudes.

> What do you love most about CNN's website?

Should be rewritten as

> Which of the following features are important to you in CNN's website? (Check all that apply.)

The latter phrasing avoids most of the problems with the earlier question—especially if it provides an option for "None"—and provides most of the same answers.

Stay consistent. Ask questions the same way every time. This means more than just using similar wording for similar questions. You should also strive to maintain consistency in meaning in the order of answer options and in the way the questions are presented.

Avoid extremes. Extreme situations rarely happen, and most people infrequently find themselves exhibiting extreme behavior, so avoid situations that require or imply the need for extreme behavior.

> Do you visit a news website *every time* you go online?

This would probably produce almost exclusively negative responses since it's likely that only a few people check news every single time they surf. A better way would be to ask

> How often do you visit news websites?
> - ○ Several times a day
> - ○ Once a day
> - ○ More than once a week
> - ○ Once a week
> - ○ Once a month
> - ○ Less than once a month
> - ○ Never

and compare the responses to how often people say they surf the web to see the proportion.

Make questions relevant. If people are confronted with a list of questions that don't relate to their experience or their life, they're not likely to finish the survey. For example, a group of computer service technicians will respond differently to questions about the minutia of their computer configuration than will a group of taxi drivers. If the respondent can't answer many of the questions or if they're not interested in the answers, they're not likely to be interested in finishing the survey.

Use Likert scales. Likert scales are a familiar method of presenting multiple-choice answers. They consist of a statement or series of statements followed by a choice of three, five, or seven options (most surveys use three or five) that define a possible range of answers, including a neutral middle option.

> Rate the following aspects of news and information websites for how interesting they are to you.

	Very interesting	Somewhat interesting	Neutral	Somewhat Uninteresting	Very Uninteresting
The number of different stories on a given topic	○	○	○	○	○
The number of different topics covered	○	○	○	○	○
How quickly the page downloads	○	○	○	○	○
The reputation of the news outlet	○	○	○	○	○
How comprehensively each story is covered	○	○	○	○	○
A unique editorial perspective	○	○	○	○	○
The quality of the site's search engine	○	○	○	○	○
The visual appearance of the site	○	○	○	○	○
How quickly stories are covered after they happened	○	○	○	○	○
How easy it is to get around in the site	○	○	○	○	○

A list of common questions is provided on the book's website, at www.mkp.com/ observing-the-user-experience. However, don't hesitate to experiment with new questions and question types. Much online research still shows its roots in the paper survey world, with online questions essentially the same as their printed

Create follow-up questions. When technologically possible, ask questions that further expand on a given answer. Ideally, follow-up questions should appear only after a specific answer for a given question. This is technologically possible with many online survey services. When it's impossible, it should be clear that the follow-up questions are related to a given answer and that they should not be answered otherwise.

If one question asks

> Check all the sites that you read regularly.

a follow-up can then contain a list of sites that were marked as being read regularly.

> Rate how important each of the following sites are to you, from "Crucial" to "Unimportant."

ancestors. Using the possibilities of technology offers a lot of possibilities for innovative questions. A simple example: Rather than asking people for the size of their web browser window (something that many people may not know), it's possible to put a picture of a ruler onscreen and ask "In the image above, what's the largest number you can see without scrolling?"

Include an opt-out option. Always include an option for people to signify that a question does not apply to them or that none of the suggested options are appropriate. These are typically phrased as variations on "None of the above," "Don't know," or "No answer," depending on what's appropriate for the question.

Leave space for comments. Although most people won't use them, you should include a space at the end of the survey for people to provide comments about it.

Edit and Order the Questions

The first thing you need to do is to pare down the survey size. One way to maximize the number of responses to a survey is to keep it short. Most people should be able to complete your survey in 20 minutes or less. Surveys that take more than 20 minutes begin feeling like a burden, and respondents have to schedule time to do them. Since reading the instructions takes about 5 minutes and each question takes 30 seconds or so to read and answer, this limits you to about 30 questions total. Keeping a survey to 20 questions leaves you with a safe margin. Besides, as the old game implies, you can find out almost anything about anyone in 20 questions, provided you choose the questions carefully.

Once you've written and culled your questions, it's time to edit and organize them. The question order is as important as the wording. A survey is a dialogue, with every question revealing something to the person taking the survey and providing information to the person receiving the results. Question order should pace, focus, and selectively reveal information.

In some ways, a survey is like a short story. The beginning grabs the readers' attention, drawing them in. As they read the survey, they begin to get an idea of what kind of information the survey is trying to find out. In the middle, big ideas are explored and "twists" on the basic plot are introduced as certain avenues of inquiry are followed. Finally, loose ends are tied up, and the survey ends. Admittedly, even at their best, surveys do not make exciting stories, but writing them with even a small narrative arc can make them more interesting for the participants, which reduces the number of people who drop out due to boredom.

As in a story, you can gradually reveal what the survey is about, not explaining too much upfront in order to get people's responses about general topics. Earlier topics may influence people's expectations and thoughts. If your survey is trying to understand how people buy toys online, you may not want to reveal that your survey is about toys until after you've gotten a general picture of their buying behavior.

For example, a survey is trying to understand the relationship between people's food-buying and toy-buying habits. The following two questions are logical ones to pose.

If question A is asked before question B, then people may think

A. What was the total price of groceries you bought last year?
B. How carefully do you track your purchases?

B applies only to groceries, which they may track very carefully, but the survey is more interested in people's general purchasing behavior. By asking B before A, the survey collects people's general impressions without constraining their perception of the survey's scope.

A typical survey has four parts.

1. An *introduction* that presents the purpose of the survey, instructions for filling it out, the duration of it, and contact information in case questions arise.
2. A *beginning* with teaser questions. These questions should be interesting to the person taking the survey, drawing them in. They should not be demographic questions, which often bore people and, at this early stage, can be seen as intrusive.
3. A *middle,* where it's a good idea to keep things moving by alternating questions that are likely to be interesting to the respondents with questions that are not. Questions are grouped thematically, such as "General News Reading Behavior," "Online News Reading Behavior," "Quality of News Sources," and "Unmet Needs and Desires."
4. The *end,* which concludes with all the remaining demographic questions, provides an open-ended field for general response, and reiterates the contact information.

Within this structure, the survey should be flexible. When there isn't a logical progression in a list of answers to a multiple-choice question (best-to-worst, most-to-least, first-to-last, etc.), the list should be randomized whenever possible. This reduces the chances that the order of the answers will affect how people choose. Some online survey software products do this automatically, but it's also possible to create several versions of the survey with answers in a different order and randomly assign people to them when creating invitations.

Write the Instructions

There are two different kinds of instructions in a survey: general instructions and individual question instructions.

The general survey instructions should be brief and straightforward. They should run a paragraph at the longest and contain several pieces of information:

- *That the survey is important.* "We want to make vFork a better service for you. Your participation in this survey is very important to us."
- *What it's for.* "The survey is to help us understand the needs and desires of the people using vFork."
- *Why people's answers are safe.* "All of your answers are confidential and will be used strictly for research. There will be no sales or marketing follow-up because of your participation in this survey."
- *What the reward is.* "By completing this survey, you will have our gratitude and a 1 in 100 chance of winning an iPad."
- *Who is responsible* for the survey, if not the company in question. "This survey is being administered for vFork by YourCompany LLC."
- *How long the survey is running.* "This survey will run from July 17, 2010, until July 24, 2010."
- *Who to contact with questions.* "If you have any questions or comments about this survey, you may enter them into the form at the bottom of the survey or mail them to Mike Kuniavsky at mikek@yourcompany.com." This also personalizes it (the survey is no longer an anonymous form), which tends to increase the response rate.

Many places, such as most of the United States, have laws governing sweepstakes (which is what a survey offering a "one in X" chance to win something becomes). Sweepstakes laws require posting their rules clearly along with the survey description. You can get most of what you need by copying the rules from other sweepstakes, but you should absolutely have a lawyer look at what you've written before you publicly launch your survey.

Likewise, many places have rules about interviewing children. You should make it clear that only people 18 and older should take the survey. If necessary, ask respondents to verify, through a checkbox on an entry page, that they are over 18 before allowing them to progress into the survey proper. If your survey must involve kids, you should consult a lawyer about how to allow them to take the survey (often this requires written permission from their parents).

Question instructions should likewise be simple and straightforward. Most closed-ended questions won't need special instructions, but open-ended questions should say exactly what kind of answers you want. Rather than writing

List your favorite websites.

the instructions could say

Make a list of the URLs (web addresses) of sites that you go to often or that you really like. Write up to 10 addresses.

For questions where you want a single answer, but people may feel that any of several options may be adequate, make it clear that they have to select what they feel is the strongest option.

Likert scale grids generally need a couple of sentences of explanation.

The following is a list of features that can be found on vFork and other online fork sites. If you believe that you have used one of these features on vFork, please rate how important the service is to you when buying forks online. If you have never used a feature on vFork please select "Never Used." If you don't know whether you have used it, select "Don't Know."

You should also make additional instructions visible whenever it's appropriate, such as for error pages or for sections of questions that resemble other sections but function differently. For example, if a page reloads because of an error, highlight the reasons for the reloaded page and any new instructions on the first screen people see after the new page appears.

Lay Out the Report

The report? But we haven't started yet! That's right, lay out the report. One of the best ways to know what questions to ask is to make a list of the answers you want.

The data you collect should be dependent on what analysis you want to perform, what questions you want to answer. You should never ask questions "just in case" (although it's okay to ask exploratory questions for which you don't have a good idea about how people will answer).

Your report should begin with your goals and your methods. Writing as if the survey has already been completed, describe why you've run this survey, your goals, and the design of your research. Include information about your estimates of the size of the total population from which you sampled, your sampling method, the size of the sample, the completion rate, and how you analyzed the data. Then write your conclusions. Of course, before you start analyzing your data, you won't know what your real conclusions will be, so these will be your hypotheses, but you will have some idea of what kinds of conclusions you want to have. So write those down.

> *Sixty-five percent of the people who bought forks in the last month buy forks three times a year or more.*

This tells you that you need to collect information about when the last fork was bought, how many times people buy forks a year, and the people who bought forks in the last month need to be large enough for analysis based on it to produce statistically significant results.

Once you've written down your placeholder conclusions, you should make all the tables and graphs you're going to use to back up your conclusions. As the following example shows, the tables should say exactly what variables are being plotted against what other variables and what's being displayed.

Opinion of Features Based on Length of Time on the Web

Feature	Length of Time on the Web			
	<6 months	6 months–1 year	1–2 years	2+ years
Fork Finder				
Shopping Wiz				
Main Catalog				

Because the process of writing the report can affect the content of the survey, make sure you budget enough time to at least outline the report beforehand. That way you can make changes to the survey method or the kind of data you collect.

After you've run your pilot survey, use your report mockup and run all the pilot data through the same processes you're planning for the real data, making the same tables and drawing conclusions as you would with the real thing. This will help shake out issues with your analysis procedure.

Web Survey Tips

Now you're ready to build the survey on the Internet. We won't go into the technical aspects of creating online surveys since the process will depend on what service or software you chose. However, the basic structure of all web surveys is the same: an HTML page containing a form and a backend program or email-based script to collect the results. Tabulation is accomplished via a custom program, a statistical program, or for simpler surveys, a spreadsheet.

Web Survey Tools

There are a wide variety of online survey options as of 2012. Some are services hosted by an independent website. Others are software packages that you can install and run on your own website. Different services offer different features—from more varied input types to more complicated internal question branching and skipping options. They also offer differing tabulation and reporting options. Part of the work of setting up an online survey is figuring out what services support the type and complexity of questions you need. Note that hosting services often offer free survey packages. These provide more limited functionality (usually, fewer features and a limited number of responses). These free services are great for small, simple projects. Trying out free options can also help you decide whether you want to commit to a paid subscription for a more large-scale and complex survey.

There are some things to keep in mind when building any kind of web-based survey.

- *Error checking.* The backend system can check how people responded. If any are missing or incorrectly filled out (for example, if someone checked a checkbox for a specific choice and "None of the Above"), the page should be reproduced with the incorrectly filled-in responses clearly flagged.
- *Functionality.* If you are hosting your own survey system, survey pages should be checked like any other page for functioning HTML, even more than usual. The survey page should download quickly and look right on as many browsers, operating systems, screen sizes, and bandwidth speeds as possible. If you expect a segment of your user base to be behind a firewall, make sure you check the performance with those systems, too.
- *Usability.* Usability test the survey just as if it were a new feature. This helps to make sure that everything works and that people's experience of it matches their expectations.
- *Timing.* Since you can keep track of when responses are returned, do so. This will help keep track of what responses arrived within the research period, and it provides another piece of information about the behavior of your user population. If a large group of your respondents claim to be in the Eastern Standard time zone and their responses arrived between 9 AMand 5 PM EST, you can hypothesize that they were accessing your site from work.
- *Mortality.* Keep track of the people who drop out of the survey. Note at which points they dropped out, and try to draw some conclusions about how they differ based on the answers they completed.
- *Response rate.* Similar to mortality, this is a count of people who were offered to take the survey versus how many actually responded. This is critical information when projecting your analysis to a larger population.

Test the Survey

A survey can often only be run once. Rerunning a whole survey is almost as expensive as running the survey the first time; surveys shouldn't be changed on the fly. Pretesting (also known as *pilot testing*) the survey is a critical part of its development and can eliminate a lot of costly mistakes.

A pretest is run just like the real thing, using all the same software, the same recruiting methods, the same data collection methods, and the same analysis methods as the final survey. You should even make a pretest report using your report template, drawing conclusions just as you would with the final data. The difference is in terms of sample size. A pilot sample contains 5–10 responses from people who are, ideally, representative of the group who will be responding to the survey (if you can't get people who match that profile, it's okay to use people who may match only some of the key criteria). Don't tell the participants that it's a pretest. Use the same invitation materials you would use for the regular test, and see if the answers they provide are what you had expected.

If you have the resources or if this is going to be a particularly involved survey, consider running a prepilot, where you present 5–10 people with the survey questions phrased in an open-ended way. If all of their responses fit within the responses you have written for in your prepared survey, you can be pretty sure you've covered the appropriate ground.

Afterward, or simultaneously, do two or three in-person user tests of the survey, watching people as they take the survey. Keep track of how long it takes them to take it and what problems and questions they have about it. You can also follow up with an email to the pilot participants, asking them to discuss how the survey went, what kinds of problems they had, and so forth.

Since a large amount of survey analysis involves understanding the uncertainty of the collection method, one of your chief goals in survey design should be to reduce the number of variables that need to be considered and controlled. Everything can influence how people respond to the survey, from who sees the survey to how fast the description page downloads. Thus, as you're creating the survey and the mechanisms for gathering respondents and collecting responses, continually think of ways of reducing the number of unknown variables.

The Incentive

Unless your survey is extremely short, you should provide an incentive for people to take it. You will want to provide an incentive that's related to the complexity of your survey and the interests of your audience. Knowing your audience is important to picking the right incentive. The incentive for a site for teenagers and one for middle-aged millionaires will be different, but the goal is the same: it's a reward for giving up a portion of their time and personal information. An online gaming information site offered a chance to get one Microsoft Xbox in exchange for its visitors' participation in a survey. Ninety-five percent of the people visiting the site took the survey, a proportion that beats many censuses.

The way you present your incentive is important. If you're offering something that's worth $2 for a completed response and your survey takes half an hour to complete, many people may not think that it's worth their time to fill out. However, if you offer a 1 in 100 chance to win something that costs $200, you're likely to get more responses. Although the end costs to you are the same, it's been shown that people would rather gamble with their time for something that's worth more than take a sure thing that's worth less.

Fielding the Survey

Fielding a survey is the process of inviting people to take it. It sounds simple, but it's not. Surveys are neither censuses, which attempt to get responses from the entire population, nor questions answered by a haphazard group of people. They attempt to contact a randomly selected, evenly distributed subset of the population in a controlled way.

So before thinking about how to field your survey, it's important to discuss what it means to pick a sample from a population.

The Sample and the Sampling Frame

The group of people who fill out your survey is called a *sample*, but what is it a sample of? It's a randomly chosen subset of the group of people your sampling method can put you in contact with. This group is called the *sampling frame* (see Figure 12.1). In other words, out of the universe of all of your users, there's a subset your methods allow you to contact and a subset they don't. The subset you can hypothetically contact is your sampling frame; a random selection of people from your sampling frame is your sample.

Ideally, the sampling frame matches the whole population of people you're interested in. If it doesn't, then your results can be inaccurate and misleading since they will not represent the views of your entire audience. For example, if you field a survey only to the people who have complained about your product, you're not likely to get a good representation of your whole audience's opinion. Likewise, if you talk only to people who have signed up for a mailing list or who have purchased something from your site, you're talking only to a group of people who have expressed an active interest in your product, and those people likely form a minority of all the people who may be interested in what you have to offer.

Sampling frame mismatches come in many flavors. If a survey is run only on Monday and Tuesday for a shopping sales notification website that gets the majority of its use on Thursday and Friday, the results will not be representative since the weekend shopping audience is likely to be different from the midweek audience. Likewise, just running the survey on Thursday and Friday may miss a key market of hardcore shopping enthusiasts. Knowing the composition of your sampling frame is critical to knowing how valid your results are. Unfortunately, there are many, many ways to sample badly and get the wrong sampling frame.

First, define the groups of users you're most interested in. Usage frequency is a good place to start. Are they regular users? (How do you define "regular"? Every day? Every week?) First-time users? Infrequent users?

Now add other characteristics that are important and that can affect the way you recruit people for your survey. Are they people who have bought products from your site? Are they from a specific geographic region? Are they students? People who are thinking of switching from your competitors' products? Power users?

Your survey may end up being the combination of several subgroups (power users and frequent users, older shoppers, and others).

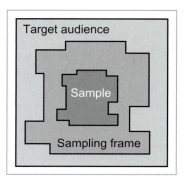

Figure 12.1 Sample and sampling frame.

Having decided who your users are, you will have to create a way that will comprehensively invite the people who make up your target audience, without missing or overrepresenting any groups. Each characteristic will create a different method of inviting people and a different set of potential problems in terms of data collection.

For example, say you're interested in the usability problems of frequent users, so you'd like to profile people who use your application all the time. Although it may be interesting to know if there's an observable difference between people who visit often and people who visit and buy your products, you need to stay focused on your target audience choices. So, for example, you decide that your target audience is "users who use the website at least once a week and who have bought something as a result."

So how do you contact these people? You could use a tracking cookie and ask questions of people whose cookies are less than a week old. But that's dependent on people not having switched machines, deleted their cookies, or changed browsers. What's more, it assumes that you have tracking cookies. It may be easier to randomly invite users using a pop-up window and filter out the responses of anyone who doesn't say they visit at least once a week. Moreover, you will need to run your survey for at least a week or in week-long increments, so as to not overrepresent the visitors who show up on any given day. But is that still guaranteed to target all the users who fit your target profile? No. Some of them may be on vacation; others may skip a week and miss your survey. However, since people do these things randomly, it's unlikely that this will affect your results. There may also be other groups of users—say, people who shop infrequently but buy a lot—who are also important to you, but you're not aware of their existence. Missing these people can really affect your results. So how are you going to know about and contact all these people? You won't and you can't, but you should strive to contact enough people that their responses can make a positive change in your product.

All this is to say that the more you know about your population and their habits, the better you can choose your sampling frame. However, if you know little about your audience, don't panic. You can field your first survey to reveal a lot about your audience's profile, and qualitative research (interviews, focus groups, site visits) can reveal things about their behavior so that subsequent surveys can be more accurately targeted.

Sample Size

So how many people do you invite?

Surveys always contain some amount of uncertainty. There always is a possibility of error in a sample since you're not asking every single member of the population the same questions in the same way. The size of the uncertainty can be estimated mathematically, but the amount that's acceptable will have to be decided by you.

Ultimately, surveys depend on the variation in your population. If all of your users are identical, then you need to ask only one of them to understand how all of them would respond. But all of your users aren't identical, so you have to estimate how many to ask based on how varied the population is. This is a classic chicken-and-egg problem: You can't find out how varied your audience is without surveying them, and you can't survey them unless you know how varied they are. Fortunately, it's possible to estimate how many people to invite by assuming that your population has a pretty "standard" variation and then adjusting future surveys if the estimate turns out to be too low (asking too many people is rarely a problem, other than the extra work it involves).

Let's start with the assumption that your entire user population has 10,000 people in it. That means that if you count everyone who has ever used your site or is ever likely to use it (within reason, say, within the next year), you'll get 10,000 people. Now you want to find out how many of them you need to survey in order to be able to get an idea of how all (or the majority) would answer your questions. You'll never get the "real" values unless you survey all 10,000 people, but (without going into the math—that's covered later in this chapter) by asking 300 of them, you can be 95% confident that the answers you get from them will fall in a 10% range ("plus or minus 5%," as they say on TV) of what you'd get if you asked everyone. What does "95% confident" mean? It, too, is explained later in the chapter, but for now you can read it as "pretty darned confident."

Three hundred people is fine, it's not such a big number, but what if your audience has a million people in it? Thirty thousand is a lot of people to have in a survey. Fortunately, the relationship between the number of people in your population and the number of people you need to talk to is not proportional in that way. The way the math works, you need to sample only 2000, which is significantly easier. So, without consulting a statistician, you can use the following table to estimate the number of people you need in your sample.

Approximate Sample Sizes*

Population	Sample Size
1000	150
10,000	300
100,000	800

*Assuming 5% standard error, 95% confidence, and normal variation.

These numbers are a very rough minimum number of responses necessary for you to be able to extrapolate a survey statistic to the population at large. Statisticians will chastise me for butchering the statistics involved (and, believe me, they are butchered), but the numbers are close enough to make some educated guesses.

To complicate things a bit more, these numbers don't apply to your whole sample size, but to any single group you're going to be studying. If you're going to be segmenting your audience into sub-groups (such as by gender or by experience or by region) and doing calculations on the subgroups, then *each subgroup* needs to be that big. For example, if your product has 10,000 unique users and you're planning to analyze frequent users separately from infrequent users, *both* sets of data have to have at least 300 entries. This means you'll have to have at least 600 responses in your total sample.

Bias

Sampling bias is the Great Satan of survey research. It's clever, insidious, omnipresent, and impossible to eradicate. Sampling bias occurs when the people who you thought would respond—the members of your sampling frame—are not members of the population that you're trying to sample (as illustrated in Figure 12.2). This is very dangerous.

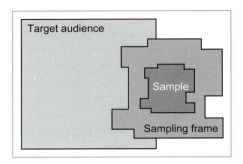

Figure 12.2 Sampling bias.

For a sample to provide useful information about the population as a whole, it needs to resemble that population and their views. If it does not, then certain subgroups or views will be over-represented while other groups and views get shortchanged. When the data from a biased survey are tabulated, the results don't describe the population. Since the purpose of a survey is to describe your users, misrepresenting elements of your audience undermines the whole endeavor.

To some extent, you are always going to exclude certain people. Just by fielding an online survey, you are cutting out people who are not online. By writing your survey in English, you are cutting out those who don't read English. The keys are to know whom you are excluding (or misrepresenting) and to make sure that they are not members of your target audience and that you do not include them in your analysis.

One of the most common and important kinds of bias is *non-responder bias*. Some number of people will always ignore your invitation, but if there's a pattern to those who do, it's bias. If your survey is repelling a certain group, then they'll never be represented in your research. For example, if you're surveying people about their time use, and your survey takes 45 minutes to complete, you may be missing the most important segment of your market simply because they don't have time to fill out your survey. There many other different kinds of nonresponder bias.

- *Timing bias.* Does the time you invited people affect the way they answered? If you ask people about how much they enjoy shopping for gifts on the day before Christmas, you may get a different response than if you ask at a time when people aren't frantically grabbing toys off the shelf.

- *Duration bias.* Some behavior is cyclical: it consistently peaks during a certain part of the day or week or month. If your target audience consists of commodities traders and you run your survey from 9 AM to 5 PM, when most traders are too busy to fill out surveys, you will likely miss a large portion of your audience.

- *Invitation bias.* How did you invite people to participate in the survey? The places, times, incentive, and wording all affect who is going to respond. If you're trying to invite skateboarders and you begin your invitation with "Dear Sir or Madam, you are cordially invited to…" you will likely lose much of your audience (unless the invitation is obviously ironic).
  If you offer t-shirts as an incentive to senior managers, you're not likely to get a representative group.

- *Self-selection.* A special kind of invitation bias and a common mistake in web surveys is the practice of letting people choose whether they want to participate in a survey without explicitly inviting them. "Click here to take our survey!" is often how this is presented. Who is going to take that survey? Why will they take it? In an opt-in situation like this, you have no idea who the people who aren't clicking on the link are. They could be the same kind of people who click on the link, but it's doubtful. Opt-in surveys tend to attract people who have extreme opinions and specialized interests, which is rarely the only group that you want to attract. It's better to have people have to opt out of a survey by closing a pop-up window than opt in. That way you know that a random distribution saw the invitation, how many people were invited, and how many chose not to take it.

- *Presentation bias.* The way you present the survey, the survey's look and feel, also determines who feels interested in answering it. Technologically, if you use Flash to perform a certain key function and a portion of your key population has Flash turned off, they won't be able to take your survey. Aesthetically, if you present the survey with a bunch of cute cartoon characters around it, businesspeople may be reluctant to take it (conversely, if you present a plain black-and-white screen full of text to a group of teenagers, they may think it's too boring to even read). The visual polish of surveys should match that of the sites they're linked from. If a slick site links to a survey that is too stylistically unsophisticated, it may cause confusion. If the shift is too harsh, it may even damage people's perception of the site brand.

- *Expectation bias.* People have expectations of what a survey is going to be about and why they should take it. If those expectations are not met, they may abandon it. In a pretest of a survey, one user said, "Oh, I thought that this was going to be about me and it's asking all these questions about how I change the oil. I don't care about that."

The art of survey design is in tracking response rates to minimize and understand all the preceding factors while maximizing participation. Tabulating results and drawing conclusions are pretty straightforward in comparison. Typical online survey response rates vary between 20% and 40% (which means that between 20% and 40% of the people who are offered to take the survey take it and finish it). Much less than 20% and the results of a survey are highly dubious. As Joshua Grossnickle, co-author of *The Handbook of Online Marketing Research*, says, "a survey with a 1% response rate is worthless data." Testing your survey and understanding the implications of your design in terms of the groups that it is excluding are key ways of minimizing the amount of bias.

Invitation

After bias reduction, the next task to consider is how to randomize your sample. Finding a truly random sample can be tough and depends on how you invite people. There are a number of common ways of inviting people to take your survey, and each method has its own benefits and carries its own problems.

Invitation Link

This is the easiest but least accurate online survey invitation method. It consists of a link from a key page (generally the home page) inviting people to participate in a survey. Its benefits are that it's cheap and unobtrusive, but it suffers heavily from self-selection bias. There's no guarantee that a random selection of users to the site sees it, and there's no attempt to distribute the invitation among visitors, so the people who take it are likely to be people who want to communicate something about the site. These groups are likely to be experienced users who have strong opinions. Their views are useful, but are rarely representative of the typical user's views.

If you do use a front-door invitation link, keep track of all the unique visitors to that page and compare it to the number of people who responded. This will give you some idea of how many have seen the invitation versus how many filled out the survey. If the response rate is small (say 5% of the number of people who have seen the site), then there's a high chance that the responses are not representative of your audience. The survey may still produce useful information, but it's unlikely that the conclusions can be extrapolated to the population at large.

Email

If you have a list of known users, you can select a random subset of them and invite them to take the survey. Such an invitation list won't reach users who aren't in your database (and therefore haven't used the services of your site that get them into your database), and it won't reach people who have opted-out of having email sent to them, but it will let you contact people who almost certainly use your site. More important, it lets you issue explicit invitations so that you know that all potential users were exposed to the same invitation (thus reducing the problems of self-selection), and it lets you track exactly how many invitations resulted in responses.

When using tracking identifiers, make it clear that the survey software possesses this capability so that respondents who expect the survey to be anonymous know that it's not. Also make it clear that even though it's not anonymous, responses will be still be confidential.

There are two basic kinds of email survey invitation: one that's just an invitation to visit a web-based survey and one that results in an email-based survey. Although email-based surveys can reach a wider group of people, they involve more work on the data collection side since the responses have to be parsed (either by hand or with software). Web-based surveys are generally preferred.

Ideally, each email survey invitation will have a unique identifier that will allow you to track which and how many people responded.

Interruption

An interruption invitation works by inviting random users to take a survey as they are visiting your site. Every user has an equal chance of being invited (either every time they visit the site or once per user), and the invitation interrupts their experience of your site such that they have to actively accept or decline the invitation to continue using the site. Interruption invitations tell you exactly how many people were invited, ensure that they were all equally aware of the survey, and guarantee a random sample of all users.

Random interruptions can sample either by *probability* or *systemically*. Sampling by probability involves choosing visitors according to a probability that will make the total amount of visitors that meet that probability roughly equal to the expected number of responses. In practice, this generally involves picking a random number for each visitor. If the random number matches a predetermined "magic number," then the person sees the invitation. Otherwise, they experience the site normally, never knowing that a survey is underway for others. So if you have determined that you need 1000 responses for a week-long survey and the site gets about 100,000 unique visitors per week, then each visitor during that week should have a 1 in 100 probability of being invited to take the survey.

Random Selection

A useful way of creating a consistent probability sample is to include a piece of code on every page. This code performs the necessary calculations about whether the current visitor should be offered the survey and leaves a cookie in his or her browser so that the visitor isn't considered for invitation more than once per survey (unless, of course, the survey is measuring behavior per visit, rather than per visitor, but those types of surveys are considerably rarer).

In order to accurately measure all visitors, not just those who visit the home page, the code needs to be inserted into every page that someone can get to by typing in a URL. This is easiest with dynamically generated sites, or sites that include a uniform navigation header (in which case the code can be inserted as part of the header), but even sites that are "flat," made with plain HTML, should still have it inserted at all the likely entry points into a site.

This means that you will need access to the site's code in order to insert your pop-up. There's no way around it. Commercial surveying packages will make it a lot easier to insert this code.

Systemic interruptions are sometimes simpler. A systemic sample works by inviting every *n*th visitor. In our example, this would equate to picking a random number between 1 and 100 and then taking every 100th visitor after that person until 1000 visitors have been invited. This is more of a traditional paper survey technique, where it has the advantage of being simpler to implement, but it's not as flexible.

Telephone, In-Person, and Standard Mail Surveys

Traditional survey techniques such as telephone, in-person, and paper mailed surveys are beyond the scope of this book, but they should not be forgotten. These are the typical survey techniques used by political and market research. They are *the* most effective ways to get a truly random sample of the population. One typical tool is the random phone call: a machine randomly dials phone numbers within a certain area code and telephone exchange until someone answers, then a person takes over and begins reading a telephone survey script. However, users of a specific software product or visitors to a certain website are likely harder to find by randomly dialing phone numbers than people who belong to a certain political party or who buy a certain product, so the technique isn't as efficient for finding users. Although collecting data in person seems to defy the global nature of the Internet, if your audience is easily accessible—such as for an application that serves the teachers in a local school district—then the flexibility and information-gathering potential of an in-person survey is hard to beat. These methods are generally more time consuming and expensive than web-based surveys, but they should not be forgotten just because they're not digital.

How to Analyze Survey Responses

The world abounds with bad survey research that's bandied about just because it contains numbers. Do not be deceived by numbers, and do not try to deceive with numbers. Seeing numbers used as evidence does not mean that a rigorous process produced them.

Survey analysis and interpretation is as much of an art as a science. Although it deals with numbers, proportions, and relationships, it also measures statements, and the relationship between statements and actions is notoriously difficult to understand. From the ambiguities of recruiting bias, to misunderstandings in question wording, to the tendency of people to exaggerate, the whole process involves approximations and estimates. Ultimately, every person is different, and the final analysis will miss the subtleties of any single person's perceptions, behavior, or experience. However, this is all right. In most cases, results can be valuable and useful without complete certainty, and often it's important to only know the odds in order to make an informed decision.

Thus the analysis of survey data should strive for accuracy and immediate utility. Although sophisticated techniques can sometimes extract important subtleties in data, simpler analysis is preferable in most cases. Simpler methods reduce the possibility of error and labor and are sufficient to answer the majority of questions that come up in typical product development situations.

The two common analysis techniques can be summarized simply as *counting* and *comparing*.

Counting

The easiest, and often the only, thing that you can do with results is to count them (to *tabulate* them, in survey-speak). When basic response data are counted, it can reveal simple trends and uncover data entry errors. It consists of counting all the response values to each question.

You should start by looking through the raw data. The raw information can give you ideas of trends that may be present in the data before you start numerically abstracting the results. How are the results distributed? Is there an obvious way that some responses cluster? Are there any really clearly bogus or atypical responses (such as teenagers with $150,000 personal incomes or skateboarding octogenarians)? Spending time with the raw data can give you a gut-level feeling for it, which will prove useful later.

Once you've looked through the raw data, a simple count of all the answers to a given question can be useful. For example, adding up the answers to the question "Which of the following categories includes your household income?" could yield the information shown in Table 12.2.

Table 12.2 Example 1

Less than $20,000	0
$20,001–$29,999	2
$30,000–$39,999	3
$40,000–$49,999	10
$50,000–$59,999	12
$60,000–$69,999	20
$70,000–$79,999	25
$80,000–$99,999	28
$100,000–$119,999	22
$120,000–$149,999	17
$150,000 or over	5
No answer	10

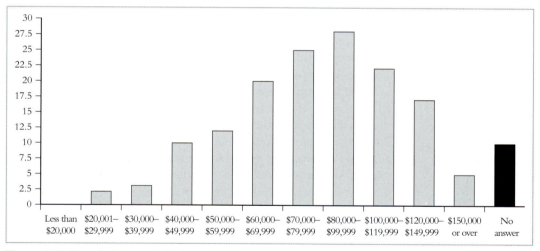

Figure 12.3 Example 1, a normal distribution.

Displayed as a simple histogram, this reveals some interesting information about the distribution of your audience's income (Figure 12.3). From Figure 12.3, it looks like the audience's income peaks somewhere between $80,000 and $100,000, and that people with incomes between $60,000 and $150,000 make up the majority of the users. If your site was aimed at lower-middle-income partici-pants, then it's clear that your site isn't attracting those people in the way you had hoped.

Taking the data from the table, it's possible to calculate the *mean* and *mode* of the data. The mean is the average of the values, in the traditional algebraic sense. It's calculated by adding all the values of the responses to a given question and then dividing by the number of responses. In the case of ranges of numbers, such as the one above, you can use the midpoint of every range as your starting point. For this example, the mean would be about $86,000, calculated as such

$$= \frac{(25,000 \cdot 2) + (35,000 \cdot 3) + \cdots + (150,000 \cdot 5)}{144}$$

$$= \frac{12,425,000}{144}$$

$$= 86,285$$

It is "about" $86,000 because the ranges are broad, and the highest range of "$150,000 or over" is unbounded at the upper end (the lower bound was used in calculations). For practical purposes, this is generally enough.

A small number of extreme results can easily skew a mean. It's the "billionaire" problem: If you're sampling the actual values of annual salaries and you happen to survey the CEO of Apple, your "average" value is likely to be significantly higher than what the majority of people in your sample make. This is where looking at the raw data is important since it will give you a gut-level expecta-tion for the results. Your gut could still be wrong, but if you looked at a bunch of responses where people had $40,000 and $50,000 incomes and your mean turns out to be $120,000, then something is likely pushing the value up. You should start looking for *outliers*, or responses that are well outside the general variation of data since a few extreme values may be affecting the mean.

The *mode*, the most common value, can be compared to the mean to see if the mean is being distorted by a small number of extreme values (in our example, it's "$80,000–$99,000," which has 28 responses). When your responses fall into a *normal distribution*, where the data rise up to a single maximum and then symmetrically fall off (forming the so-called bell curve), the mean and mode are the same (as they are in the example). The larger the sample, the more likely you are to have a normal distribution. However, sometimes you don't. If for some reason, your site manages to attract two different groups of people, the mean and mode may be different numbers. Take, for example, a site that's used extensively by practicing doctors and medical school students. The income distributions may look something like that shown in Table 12.3.

The mean of incomes based on this table is about $70,000, but the mode is about $90,000. This is a large enough difference that it says that the distribution of responses is not a balanced bell curve (in fact, it's what's called a bimodal distribution), so it's a tip-off that additional analysis is necessary. A histogram (Figure 12.4) shows this clearly.

Since it's important to know whether you have a single homogeneous population or if you have multiple subgroups within your group of users, looking at the difference between the mode and mean can be an easy, fast check.

Likewise, the *median*, the value at the halfway point if you sort all the results, can also tell you if your mean is being affected by extreme values. The median of Example 2 is about $75,000 and

Table 12.3 Example 2

Less than $20,000	20
$20,001–$29,999	17
$30,000–$39,999	14
$40,000–$49,999	6
$50,000–$59,999	10
$60,000–$69,999	12
$70,000–$79,999	18
$80,000–$99,999	22
$100,000–$119,999	20
$120,000–$149,999	15
$150,000 or over	9
No answer	3

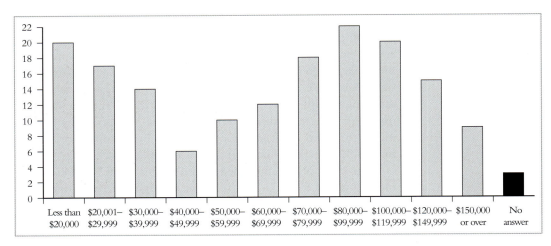

Figure 12.4 Example 2, a bimodal distribution.

the mode is $90,000, which tells you that the mean value of $72,000 is being affected by a large cluster of lower numbers, which the histogram clearly shows. Because outliers affected the median less than the mean, the median is the standard typically cited and compared when discussing standard demographic descriptors such as income and age.

How to Deal with Missing Data

Not everyone will answer every question. How should you deal with that? The simplest common method is to report the missing elements when tabulating variables and eliminate those responses from calculations that use those variables in comparisons. Elimination creates the problem that different calculations and conclusions will rely on different numbers of responses. If the sample is sufficiently large and the number of eliminated responses is relatively small, the calculations should still be usable and comparable, but it becomes an issue when the amount of missing data overwhelms the margin of error. Regardless, when the number of responses differ, always list the actual number of responses used. This is generally reported as $N = x$, where x is the number of responses used in the calculation.

Comparing

Tabulating single variables can be informative and useful, but the real power of survey research lies in comparing the contents of several variables to each other. For example, you may be interested in how the frequency with which people use your site affects what kinds of features they use. Do people who use the site all the time use a different set of features than people who use it occasionally? Knowing this could allow you to better emphasize features and create introductory help. This type of relationship is difficult to discern by just looking at the data, so you need to start using a comparison technique. The most common comparison technique is *cross-tabulation*. Cross-tabulation uncovers the relationship between two variables by comparing the value of one to the value of another.

Although there are a number of ways to create a cross-tab, a typical technique works as follows:

- Start by identifying the *independent* variable. This is the factor that you feel is doing the "affecting" and the one that is the subject of your question. In "How is the frequency of visitation affecting the kinds of features our users use?" the independent variable is the frequency of visitation since that is likely affecting the features that people are using (rather than the other way around, where using certain features causes people to visit the site more—this is possible, but not as likely, based on what you know of people's use of the site).
- Group the responses to the question according to the values of the independent variable. For example, if your question asked, "How often do you use [the site]?" and the multiple-choice answers were less than once a month, once a month, several times a month, and so on, then grouping the responses according to the answers is a good place to start.
- Tabulate the answers to the other variable, the dependent variable, individually within each independent variable group. Thus, if another survey question said, "Which of the following features did you use in your last visit to [the site]?" then people's answers to it would form the dependent variable. If the answers to this question were the Shopping Cart, the News Page, and the Comparison Assistant, you would tabulate how many people checked off one of those answers for each group.

- Create a table with the tabulated values. For example, the following table compares the features that various groups of people report using in their last visit to the site:

	<1/month	1/month	Several/month	Etc.
Shopping Cart	5%	8%	20%	
News Page	20%	25%	15%	
Comparison Assistant	2%	10%	54%	

At this point, it should be possible to see simple relationships between the two variables, if any are there to be seen. For example, people who use the site multiple times a month use the Comparison Assistant significantly more than people who use the site less frequently, which likely means that the more people use the site, the more that feature becomes valuable to them. (Why? That's a question that surveys can't easily answer. A full research project would likely follow up the survey with interviews to answer questions like that.) Likewise, the News Page seems to be somewhat less important to frequent users than to others, which isn't surprising considering they visit enough so that less is new to them with each visit. Additional relationships can be found by comparing other variables to each other (for example, length of use to frequency of use: Do people use the site more frequently the longer they've been using it?).

The following table compares the answers to the question "How often do you visit this website?" with "Why are you visiting this site today?" in order to understand whether frequency of visitation affects the reasons why people come to a site. It summarizes only the responses to "Why are you visiting this site today" that have 500 responses or more (because that was determined as the minimum number necessary to be statistically significant).

Displayed as percentages, it's a little more informative.

A proportion chart, shown in Figure 12.5, however, tells the most compelling story.

Just glancing at the chart reveals several observations.

- Regular visitors visit to listen more than more casual visitors. This implies that one of the driving "stickiness" factors may be the fact that the site offers audio streaming capability.
- Infrequent users tend to look for program information more than regular users. Maybe this is because they don't know that there's more there. If so, this could impact both the site's design and its marketing. Such users also have a tendency to look for "other" things, which may be a further indicator that the site insufficiently communicates what is available since that value drops only a small bit for people who have visited more than once.

	This Is My First Time	Less Than Once a Month	Once a Month	Once a Week	More Than Once a Week	Row Total
Looking for information about a specific radio program	260	229	167	129	115	900
Other	220	159	104	56	78	617
Want to listen to a radio program	344	245	251	298	630	1768
Want to read news or information	140	120	106	96	109	571
Column total	964	753	628	579	932	3856

	This Is My First Time	Less Than Once a Month	Once a Month	Once a Week	More Than Once a Week	Total
Looking for information about a specific radio program	29%	25%	19%	14%	13%	100%
Other	36%	26%	17%	9%	13%	100%
Want to listen to a radio program	19%	14%	14%	17%	36%	100%
Want to read news or information	25%	21%	19%	17%	19%	100%
Mean response	25%	20%	16%	15%	24%	100%

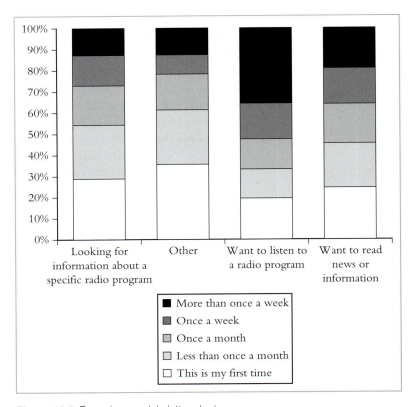

Figure 12.5 Example cross-tabulation chart.

If you are using Microsoft Excel for tabulation, much of the grunge work of doing cross-tabs is eliminated by pivot tables. Pivot tables allow you to take lists of raw survey data, one complete set of responses per row, and automatically cross-tab one variable against another. This can be a great timesaver, but be careful: It's easy to get lost in comparisons and easy to compare things that–logically–should not be compared.

Of course, there are other conclusions that can be drawn and many more sophisticated ways of manipulating and displaying relationships between variables, but these topics are beyond the scope of this book (for that, see the excellent information visualization books by Edward Tufte).

When constructing the table, you should always make it clear how many total responses there are to each independent variable group. The customary way to do this is to add a "total" column (though that's less useful when discussing percentages, in which case the total is usually 100%; in those cases, use the $N =$ notation, where N is the number of responses).

This is also the time when the calculation for a minimum number of responses comes into play. If the total number of responses in any independent variable group is less than the minimum sample size you calculated at the beginning of the survey, you should not draw *any* conclusions about that variable. The results are insignificant and should be marked as such, or left out of the report entirely. You can, however, merge groups to create larger groups that have the requisite sample size. When you do that, you should label the new "supergroup" clearly. Thus, if there weren't enough results in "18–24 years old" to draw any conclusions, you could leave it out of the report entirely, or you could merge it with "25–30 years old" and create an "18–30 years old" group. This, of course, works only with groups where it makes sense to combine the categories.

Estimating Error

Since every survey uses a sample of the whole population, every measurement is only an estimate. Without doing a census, it's impossible to know the actual values, and a lot of confusion can come from the apparent precision of numerical data. Unfortunately, precision does not mean accuracy. Just because you can make a calculation to the sixth decimal place *does not* mean that it's actually that accurate. Fortunately, there are ways of estimating how close your observed data is to the actual data and the precision that's significant. This doesn't make your calculations and measurements any better, but it can tell you the precision that matters.

Standard error is a measurement of uncertainty. It's a definition of the blurriness around your calculated value, and a measure of the precision of your calculations. The smaller the standard error, the more precise your measurement—the larger, the less you know about the exact value. Standard error is calculated from the size of your survey sample and the proportion of your measured value to the whole. It's calculated as

$$\sigma = \sqrt{\frac{PQ}{n}}$$

where P is the value of the percentage relative to the whole, as expressed as a decimal, Q is (1 − P), and *n* is the number of samples.

So if you sample 1000 people, 400 of whom say that they prefer to shop naked at night to any other kind of shopping, your standard error would be calculated as the square root of (0.4 * 0.6) / 1000, or 0.016. This means that the actual value is probably is within a 1.6% spread in either direction of the measured value ("plus or minus 1.6% of the measured value"). This is sufficiently accurate for most situations.

Standard error is also useful for figuring out how much precision matters. Thus, if your calculation is precise to six decimal places (e.g., 0.000001), but your standard error is 1% (e.g., 0.01), then all that precision is for naught since the inherent ambiguity in your data prevents anything after the second decimal place from mattering.

The easiest way to decrease the standard error of your calculations is simply to sample more people. Instead of sampling 1000 people, as in the example above, sampling 2000 gives you a standard error of 1.1% and asking 5000 people reduces it to 0.7%. However, note that it is never zero—unless you ask every single person in the target population, there will always be some uncertainty.

Standard deviation is a measure of confidence. It tells you the *probability* that the real answer (which you can never know for sure) is found within the spread defined by the standard error. With a normal "bell curve" distribution, the numbers are standard: The real value has a 68% chance of being within one standard deviation (one standard error spread) on either side of the measured value, a 95% chance of being within two standard deviations, and a 99% chance of being within three.

The range that a standard deviation specifies around the measured value is called the *confidence interval* (see Figure 12.6). It's how standard error and standard deviation are related. Standard error defines the width of the range where you can expect the value to fall, whereas standard deviation gives you the odds that it's in there at all.

Say, for example, a survey measures that 50% of the population is made with a 3% standard error. This means that you can have 68% confidence (one standard deviation, as shown in Figure 12.7) that the actual male percentage of the population is somewhere between 47% and 53%, 95% confidence that the actual percentage

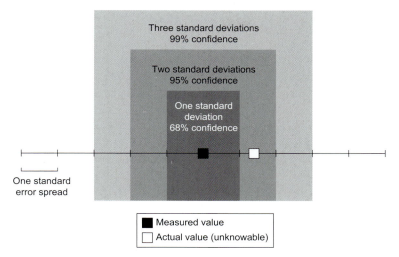

Figure 12.6 Confidence intervals.

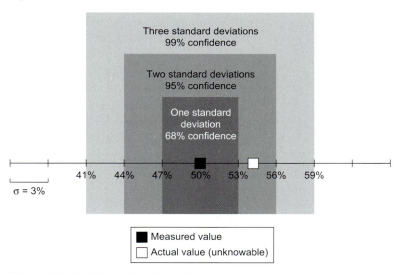

Figure 12.7 Confidence interval example.

is between 44% and 56% (two standard deviations), and 99% confidence that it's between 41% and 59% (three standard deviations). You can't know where in that range it is (maybe it's 54.967353%), but if you need to make decisions based on that amount, at least you'll know how close your guess is to reality.

Measurement Errors

By calculating the standard error and confidence level of a sample, you can get some idea of how close your measured data is to the (often unknowable) objective truth. That doesn't mean, however, that your data actually represent what it's supposed to represent. It's still possible to systematically collect data in a logical, careful, statistically accurate way and still be completely wrong.

As an example of problems that cannot be compensated or predicted with statistics, witness the crash of NASA's Mars Climate Orbiter. The Orbiter was a state-of-the art piece of equipment built by some of the smartest people in the world. It was launched from Earth in December 1998 and was scheduled to reach Martian orbit in the fall of 1999. The margin of error for such a trip is exceedingly small since the craft carries almost no fuel for corrections should something go wrong. For most of the journey, everything looked great. It flew the whole way flawlessly, its systems regularly reporting its position and velocity back to Earth. The last critical phase before it began its scientific mission was its entry into Martian orbit, which was to be carried out automatically by its systems. As it approached the planet, it began its automatic deceleration sequence. At first it got closer and closer to the planet, as it should have, but then it began to go lower and lower, dropping first below its designated orbit, then below any moderately stable orbit, then below any survivable altitude, and finally into the atmosphere, where it disappeared forever. In the investigation that followed, it was discovered that although one development team was using the English measure of force to measure thrust, pounds per second, another was using the metric measure newtons per second, which is four times weaker. So, although both sets of software were working as designed, the spacecraft thought that it was using one measurement system when, in fact, it was using another, causing a multi-hundred-million-dollar spacecraft to crash into Mars rather than going into orbit around it.

Something similar happens all the time in survey research. A financial website may want to know how often people make new equity investments. The question "How often do you buy new stocks?" may make sense in light of this, but if it's asked to a group of grocery store owners without first preparing them for a financial answer, it may be interpreted as referring to their inventory. The analysts believe they're measuring one thing, while the participants are referring to something entirely different.

This is called *systematic error* since it affects all the data equally. The Mars Climate Observer suffered from an extreme case of systematic error. No matter how accurate the measurements were made, the measurements weren't measuring what the engineers thought they were. However, there is also *random error*, the natural variation in responses. Measurements of standard error are, in a sense, a way to compensate for random error; they tell you roughly how much random error you can expect based on the number of samples you've collected. Since random errors can appear in any direction, they can cancel each other out, which is why standard error shrinks as the number of samples grows.

Drawing Conclusions

The conclusions you draw from your results should answer the questions you asked at the beginning of the research, the questions that are most important to the future of the product. Fishing through data for unexpected relationships is rarely fruitful.

Before you begin making conclusions, you need to refresh your understanding of the tables you put together at the beginning, and which you are filling out as part of the analysis. What variables do they display? What do those variables measure? Why are those measurements important? Redefine your tables as necessary if your priorities have changed over the course of your analysis.

When you are comparing data, you may want to use numerical tests to determine whether the differences in responses between two groups of responses are significant. In the radio example, the difference between people who came to read news once a week and those who came to read news more than once a week is 2%. Is that a significant difference? The *chi-square* test and the *Z-test* are two tests that can be used to determine this though explaining the math behind them is beyond the scope of this book.

When making conclusions from data, there are a number of common problems that you should avoid.

- *Confusing correlation and causation.* Just because two things happen close together in time does not mean that one causes the other. A rooster crowing at dawn doesn't make the sun come up though it does usually precede it. This is one of the most commonly made mistakes (look for it and you'll find it all over the media and in bad research) and is probably one of the strongest reasons for surveys and statistics getting a bad name. It's a simple problem, but it's insidious and confusing. Just because a group of people likes a product and uses it a lot doesn't mean that liking the product makes people use it more or that frequent use makes people like it better. Just think about the case of a company in which everyone is required to use the same email program, whether they like it or not. The two phenomena could be unrelated.
- *Not differentiating between subpopulations.* Sometimes what looks like a single trend is actually the result of multiple trends in different populations. To see if this may be the case, look at the way answers are distributed rather than just the composite figures. The distributions can often tell a different story than the summary data. For example, if you're doing a satisfaction survey and half the people say they're "extremely satisfied" and the other half say they're "extremely dissatisfied," looking only at the mean will not give you a good picture of your audience's perception.
- *Confusing belief with truth.* Survey questions measure belief, not truth. When you ask, "Have you ever seen this banner ad?" on a survey, you'll get an answer about what people believe, but their beliefs may not have any relationship to reality. Banner ads, for example, are notoriously liable to a phenomenon called "ad blindness," in which people who see many advertisements actually stop noticing them. This is also why questions about future behavior rarely predict actual actions: People may honestly believe they can predict how they behave, but their state of mind and apprehension of what's at stake may be very different when the time actually comes for them to act.

Even if you draw significant distinctions between responses and you present them with the appropriate qualifications, there are still a number of issues with the nature of people's responses that interpretations of survey data must take into account.

- *People want everything.* Given a large enough population, there's going to be a group of people who want every possible combination of features, and given a list of possible features abstracted from an actual product, everyone will pretty much want everything. And why not? What's wrong with wanting it cheap, good, *and* fast, even though you know it's impossible? Thus, surveys usually can't identify one universally approved combination of features—but a survey can tell you how people prioritize features and which ones they value most highly.
- *People exaggerate.* When presenting ourselves—even anonymously—we nearly always present ourselves as we would like ourselves to be rather than how we actually are. We exaggerate our positive features and deemphasize our failings. Taking people's perspectives on their opinions and their behavior at face value almost always paints a rosier picture than their actual thoughts and actions.
- *People will choose an answer even if they don't feel strongly about it.* There's a strong social pressure to have an opinion. When asked to choose from a list of options, even if people feel that their feelings, thoughts, or experiences lie outside the available options, they'll choose an answer. This is one of the failings of the multiple-choice survey, and it's why the choices to a question need to be carefully researched and written, and why providing "None," "Does Not Apply," or "Don't Care" options is so important.
- *People try to outguess the survey.* When answering any question, it's common to try to guess the reasons behind the question and what the questioner expects to hear. For that reason, it's important to avoid leading questions. However, you should also keep the phenomenon in mind when interpreting people's answers. Pretesting and interviewing survey respondents is a good way to avoid questions that provoke attempts to outmaneuver them.
- *People lie.* Certainly not all people lie all the time about everything, but people do exaggerate and falsify information

when they have no incentive to tell the truth or when they feel uncomfortable. For example, if you ask for an address that you can send a prize to, it's unlikely that people will lie about being able to receive mail there, but if you ask about their household income and they feel that it doesn't benefit them to answer honestly, they're less likely to be as truthful.

Ultimately, the best way to analyze a survey is to hire a professional statistician who has appropriate survey research experience and to work with him or her to answer your questions about your product. Ideally, you can begin working with the statistician before you even write the survey. The more you work with a statistician, the more you will realize what kinds of questions can be asked and what kinds of answers can be obtained.

But don't shy away from running surveys if you don't have access to a statistician. Without a pro, it's still possible to field surveys that produce valid, useful, significant results, but it's important to stay with straightforward questions and simple analyses. A limited survey with a small number of questions fielded to a well-understood group of customers can reveal a lot about your user base, enough to form a foundation from which you can then do other research.

Follow-up and Ongoing Research

Once you've run one survey, you should not consider your surveying complete and the survey process over. As your product grows and changes, so will your audience and your knowledge of them. Following up with qualitative research and tracking your audience's changes can help guide your other research and predict the needs of your audience rather than just reacting to them.

Follow-up Qualitative Research

Survey research tells you what people feel and think about themselves, their behavior, and your product, but it's too limited a technique to say much about why they feel that way and the nuances of their actions. For that, you need to follow up with qualitative research.

When trying to understand people's values and their causes, good tools include interviews (Chapter 6), focus groups (Chapter 7), and site visits (Chapter 9). For example, if you are running a satisfaction survey and your audience says that they're unsatisfied with a certain feature or features, it's almost impossible to understand why they're unsatisfied. Is it the idea of the feature? Is it the implementation? Is it the way that it interacts with other features? It's difficult to understand this without asking people directly, but without first running a survey, interviews—and, in particular, focus groups—may concentrate on less important features than those that really matter to the audience.

To understand people's actual behavior, rather than how they report their behavior in the survey, direct observation is important. Site visits (Chapter 9) can reveal how people make certain decisions in context. If, in your survey, people say that they read online news two to three times an hour, it's possible to get an idea of the accuracy of that by actually observing a group of people for a couple of hours during the day. If only a few follow the "two to three times an hour" pattern, then you may take that fact with a grain of salt when interpreting the results. Automatically gathered data (Chapter 16) reveal the pure patterns of their online activities. If a surveyed population overwhelmingly reports visits two or three times an hour, but log file analysis doesn't support it, you also have cause to doubt what they're telling you.

Usability testing (Chapter 11) and other think–aloud techniques can reveal people's decision making and what functionality leads to their perceptions of the product. If they don't like it, maybe it's because they can't use it. Or maybe they like it because it's fast. Or maybe the speed doesn't matter and they don't like it because the button text is red on black or they can't find what they're looking for. It's difficult to know what causes opinions from a survey, but once you know what those opinions are, it helps focus the questions of later research.

Tracking Surveys

By running the same survey in the same way at regular intervals, it's possible to track how your product's audience changes. So, for example, as a certain kind of service becomes more popular, it's likely to attract more and more mainstream users. But how many more? What defines "mainstream"? Repeatedly presenting the same survey to a similar number of people who are invited in the same way reveals whether the profiles change and, if they do, in what ways.

Refined Surveys

If you determine a set of "core" characteristics that define your audience, you can field additional surveys that ask additional questions that deepen your knowledge. So if you determine that the most important factors that define your audience are the level of their computer experience, the frequency of their computer use, and what software they use, you can field surveys that—in addition to asking these questions—ask further questions to probe their preferences, their satisfaction, the common ways they use your product, and so on. Asking all this on one survey may be impossible for purposes of length, but spreading the "noncore" questions among similarly sized groups with a similar composition can give you deeper knowledge than you could acquire otherwise.

Pre/Post Surveys

There are times when you want to know how your audience changes in reaction to a specific change. It could be a major interface change, or it could be an advertising campaign. Identical surveys conducted before and after a significant change in a site or its marketing can reveal how the users' opinions or how the makeup of the users' population changes because of the product changes.

A *pre/post survey* is, as its name implies, run before and after a certain event. The results are compared to see what, if any, effect these changes had on the population. Was a new demographic group attracted to the product after an ad campaign? Are the users more satisfied since the redesign?

Before running a pre/post survey, it's important to determine what variables you will be observing. What do you expect will change as a result of the changes you're about to implement? What do you not want to change? Write your survey with those issues in mind, making sure to include appropriate questions that will address these issues.

It's also important to try to understand the effects of timing on these surveys so that the "pre" survey is fielded before the effects of the change have affected the audience, and the "post" fielded when the effects are greatest. When do you expect that the most significant change will happen? Will it be immediate, or will it take a while to affect the population? Do you expect there to be buzz around the changes you're about to make? Taking these things into consideration well ahead of the change can minimize the "noise" in observations between the two groups.

In general, multiple surveys can monitor not just what changes happen in your audience, but also how the audience changes. Ideally, you should run two surveys before the change and compare them to give you an idea of some of the natural variation in the way people respond to your survey (the natural bias in people's answers). Several surveys after the change can help you track how the changes progress. For example, running one survey a week after your change and then a second one several months later may tell you which changes were short term and which were more long term. Even a postsurvey a year after a presurvey is possible if the product does not change in a way significant to what you're testing.

When fielding multiple surveys, the most critical thing is to keep the surveys as similar as possible. Don't change the wording, the presentation, or the way that people are invited to take them. Analyze them the same way. Then compare the analyses with an eye for the element that you think changed between the two surveys. Say your changes were made to capture a different market—was your market in fact different? Was it different in the ways you had expected?

Again, the most important thing when analyzing the data from multiple surveys is to make sure that you have set out your questions in advance and that you've focused your whole survey effort on answering those questions. Otherwise, you risk snow blindness in the whiteout of data that surveys can generate.

This chapter merely scratches the surface of what surveys can do. The possible combinations of survey methods are limitless. When used carefully with supporting research, they can provide insight into who your audience really is and what they think.

Example: News Site Survey

This is a survey that was written to profile the users of a radio net-work's website and to find out the general categories of informa-tion that are driving people to go to the site. It was designed to reveal visitors' expectations in order to optimize the presentation of the content and to provide constraints for subsequent qualitative research. Secondary goals were to prioritize site functionality and to perform a basic analysis of the competitive landscape.

Question	Answers	Reason
1. How often do you listen to a news radio station? (Choose only one.)	○ More than once a week ○ Once a week ○ Once a month ○ Less than once a month ○ Never	For consistency with previous survey To verify news radio listenership
2. How often do you visit this website (Choose only one.)	○ This is my first time ○ Less than once a month ○ Once a month ○ Once a week ○ More than once a week	Comparison with previous surveys Cross-tab vs. functionality Cross-tab vs. reason for visit
3. Why are you visiting the site today? (Choose only one.)	○ Want to read news or information ○ Want to listen to a radio program ○ Conducting research ○ Looking to purchase a tape or transcript ○ Looking to purchase an item other than a tape or transcript ○ To see what is new on the site ○ Chat with other listeners ○ Communicate with staff and on-air personalities ○ Other (specify): _____	Find out general reason for visiting
4. If this is not your first time visiting the site, are these typical reasons for your arrival?	○ Yes ○ No ○ Not applicable (this is my first visit) ○ Not applicable	Cross-tab with reasons

Question	Answers	Reason
5. If you're looking to read news or information, what did you come here to find today? (Choose only one.)	○ Not looking for news ○ Current headlines ○ Information about a specific current news event ○ Information on a current news story heard on the radio ○ In-depth analysis of recent news events ○ Commentary or opinion ○ Newsmaker profile ○ In-depth research on a specific topic ○ Cultural or arts news coverage ○ Entertainment ○ A broadcast schedule ○ Information about a specific radio program ○ Other (specify): _____	If general reason is news- or information-related, find out more specific information about cause of visit
6. If you came to listen to a specific radio program on this site, please choose which one you came to hear from the list below.	○ [list of program names] ○ Not applicable (did not come to listen) ○ Other (specify): _____	To see which programs people are explicitly coming to see To see which programs appear in "Other"
7. Check which of the following topics you actively seek out information about regularly. (Check all that apply.)	☐ Politics ☐ Entertainment ☐ Sports ☐ Current events ☐ Business ☐ Science and technology ☐ Interesting people ☐ Local cultural events ☐ Local news ☐ In-depth reporting about your region ☐ Travel ☐ Fashion ☐ Other (specify): _____	To find out the general topics of interest

Question	Answers	Reason
8. Select any websites that you get news or information from at least once a week. (Check all that apply.)	☐ www.npr.org ☐ www.cnn.com ☐ www.bbc.co.uk ☐ www.nytimes.com ☐ www.news.com ☐ www.bloomberg.com ☐ news.yahoo.com ☐ www.msnbc.com ☐ www.ft.com ☐ www.wsj.com ☐ www.usatoday.com ☐ www.espn.com ☐ www.salon.com ☐ www.slate.com ☐ Other (specify): _____	Competitive analysis
9. How valuable have you found the following kinds of content when reading news online? [Formatted as a radio button grid with columns titled "not valuable," "somewhat valuable," and "extremely valuable"]	Maps showing specific locations mentioned in a news story Charts, tables, and graphs summarizing and illustrating information in a news story Photos displaying events described in news or feature stories Photo galleries that walk you through a story visually Video interviews with people mentioned in news or feature stories [etc.]	To get an idea of the desirability of different kinds of content offerings
10. Please rate the following site functions based on how often you think you would use them when visiting [site name]. [Formatted as a radio button grid with "never," "sometimes," and "often" buttons]	Lists of the top-10 stories read or listened to by [site name] users today, this week, or this year Lists of books related to a given story or topic Polls or surveys of [site name] readers Online chats with a reporter, host, or newsmaker Online discussions on a topic Lists of links to other sites relating to a given story The ability to email a story to a friend	To get an idea of the desirability of different kinds of site features
11. Please rate how important the following characteristics are in stories you read on [site name]. [Formatted as a radio button grid with "not important," "somewhat important," and "very important" buttons]	That they have the latest breaking information That they provide enough background information to help me understand what the news really means That the stories are original and the angles on common stories are unexpected	Help prioritize corporate values: timeliness, background detail, and original perspective.

Question	Answers	Reason
12. What is the resolution of the monitor you use to surf the web?	○ 1600 × 1200 ○ 1280 × 1024 ○ 1024 × 768 ○ 800 × 600 ○ 640 × 480 ○ Other ○ Don't know	
13. Do you own or regularly use a mobile device such as a touch screen smart phone or a tablet?	○ Yes ○ No ○ I don't know	
14. Which of the following describes how you usually connect to the Internet?	○ 28.8 Kbps modem ○ 56 Kbps modem ○ ISDN (128K) ○ DSL (128K+) ○ Cable modem ○ T1 or higher ○ Other ○ Don't know	
15. Are you male or female?	○ Male ○ Female	All demographics questions for advertising profiling to compare with previous survey research, both online and offline
16. What age group are you in?	○ Under 18 ○ 18–24 ○ 25–34 ○ 35–49 ○ 50–64 ○ 65+	
17. What is the highest level of education you've completed?	○ Grammar school ○ Some high school ○ High school graduate or equivalent ○ Some college ○ College graduate ○ Graduate/postgraduate degree	

CHAPTER 13

Global and Cross-Cultural Research

Many user research methods were originally directed toward a singular user and that person's experience with a product, service, or technology. They assumed some basic commonalities between the researcher and the research population, such as a shared language, or similar experiences with technology. So what happens when you're working with users from regions or cultures that are not your company's or your own?

Language is just the easiest difference to spot. When working with people from different regions from your own you may find unfamiliar aspirations and values, economic circumstances, family structures, social statuses, levels of literacy, available technical infrastructures, and expectations of physical safety or political stability. You will need to recognize these differences and determine if and how they affect people's experience with your product or service. You may need to consider how their experiences differ on several levels: as individuals, as members of a family or neighborhood, and even across an entire population. These are the kinds of questions that come up in global and cross-cultural research projects.

What Is Global and What Is Cross-Cultural?

The definition of "global" research is easy: it's research that takes you beyond your own national boundaries. But it's harder to define

385

what we mean by "cross-cultural." To start thinking about culture, we could do worse than Sir Edward Tylor's 1871 definition:

That complex whole which includes knowledge, belief, art, morals, law, custom, and any other capabilities and habits acquired by man as a member of society.

There are a couple of key points to make about this definition for the purposes of cross-cultural research for design. Cultures aren't personal or individual; they are shared by groups of people. But a shared culture doesn't mean that everyone has the same "capabilities and habits," or that everyone even agrees on who is in it. Different people can understand the boundaries of membership in their culture differently, and cultures can change over time. Consider U.S. culture. Many people would tell you that "freedom" is a central value in U.S. culture. At the same time, different people in America understand freedom quite differently and associate it with different objects and activities. At times, some Americans have decided that anyone with a different understanding of freedom was "un-American" even as those people identify themselves as highly patriotic Americans.

Talking about culture as "values" or "aspirations" can make it seem fuzzy and abstract, something that can't be understood by doing things like interviews and usability tests. But why not? Culture emerges from the meanings people associate with material objects. It becomes concrete and tangible when you observe what people actually say and do. For example, if you were researching how Americans view freedom, you might want to ask some Americans concrete questions about freedom, such as where they find freedom, how much of it they have relative to others, and how someone might gain or lose it.

Cross-cultural design research begins with the premise that if there are cultural differences between the creators of a product or service and its intended users, the users, *as a group*, are likely to understand the product or service in question differently than the creators. Keep in mind that while a research project can be global *and* cross-cultural, it's equally possible to have one without the other. Even if you are working within your own country, you may not need to travel far to encounter cultural differences that affect your research. Where we live and work in San Francisco, 45% of people speak a language other than English at home, suggesting that many are most comfortable speaking other languages. A little more than a third of the San Francisco population was born outside of the United States. (Both statistics are from the U.S. Census Bureau's 2010 American Community Survey.) Recent immigrants may still have much in common with friends and family in their birth countries; deeply rooted ethnic or religious communities may sustain practices over generations that differ from a regional or national majority culture.

On the other hand, you may do research involving users who live in different countries but do not have significant cultural differences that are relevant to your interests. If you are designing products for the financial industry, you may find that the concerns of bankers in New York and in London are more similar than not. Or—and this is more likely—other factors may be more important than cultural differences. Take a tourist hotel-booking service with a largely European user base, including Germans, Spaniards, and Italians. While the users obviously live in different places and have different native languages, it may be more important for the hotel-booking service to understand other differences among users: the kinds of amenities they expect when traveling, how far in advance they like to plan their holidays, whether they prefer quiet evenings or clubbing, and so on. Thus, cross-cultural research need not be global, and global research need not be cross-cultural.

About This Chapter

There is so much diversity and variation around the world, not to mention in your own backyard. Doing global and cross-cultural research means adapting methods you know to a very wide range of situations, and it's difficult to predict what challenges a given situation will produce and what adaptations you will have to make until you begin the project. This chapter will give you guidance about how to do that adaptation, whether your research is global, cross-cultural, or both.

This chapter follows a different pattern than many of the others in this book. In this chapter we're not describing a single technique, such as usability tests or site visits. Instead, we're offering some questions to consider and tips to make your work better when you're planning research that takes you outside of your national or cultural boundaries.

The website www.globaluserresearch.com offers a country-by-country guide to the user research conditions and practical considerations around the world.

Research Planning

Say you're planning your first study with users from a country or culture where your product or service is not available, or even a market that hasn't gotten much attention lately. The most important decisions you will make will occur during the initial planning stages, as you recognize what you know and don't know and set expectations with your stakeholders.

Check Your Assumptions

Take some time at the outset to identify and spell out what you expect to be different about the people you will be studying. How do the users you want to focus on compare with people in your region or culture who use the same type of product or service? Think about their language, income, education, technology savvy… or anything else that might matter to their user experience. Ask your team or stakeholders for their impressions, as well. For example, imagine you're based in North America, and you're planning to research potential users of digital picture frames in Brazil. You might come up with a list like this:

- They might have fewer computers per household.
- They might have started taking digital photos more recently than North American users, and so might not have as many photos stored.
- They might take more of their digital pictures with mobile phones, rather than digital cameras.
- They might have larger families.
- They might have closer relationships with grandparents, aunts, uncles, and cousins.
- They might spend more of their time outdoors or take more of their pictures outdoors.
- They may have a more positive view of our brand than customers in North America.

Are these things true? Maybe, maybe not, but you can probably fact-check at least some of them. For example, your company might have market research data about computer, mobile phone, and camera ownership in Brazil and how much is spent on consumer electronics. Similarly, you might be able to find demographic data that could tell you about family size and whether extended families live together, and talk to some Brazilian expatriates about whether the family relationships resemble their experiences. As you consider these questions, remember to ask about your target audience, which may be very different from (in this example) Brazilians in general.

Establish which perceived differences are supported by facts, previous research, or your company's prior experience with the target group. This exercise will help provide context for the research you are planning. As for the perceptions you and your team have that are not supported by any evidence, keep that list for later reference. As you design your study, you will want to make sure not to assume any of these things in the questions you ask.

"Beginner's Mind"

As you prepare for global or cross-cultural research, how can you make sure to ask questions that don't constrain the answers people can give? For IDEO, a design consultancy known for designing cross-culturally, the answer lies in approaching the environment as a "beginner." In its Human-Centered Design Toolkit, IDEO veterans explain, "Beginner's Mind is critical when entering a familiar environment without carrying assumptions with you that are based on prior experience. This is often very hard to do since we interpret the world based on our experience and what we think we know. This lens of personal experience can influence what we focus on and can make us unable to see important issues." Once you set aside assumptions, you may find you need to ask and answer very basic questions. Don't be afraid to admit ignorance of certain things, or to invite participants to correct you.

IDEO's toolkit includes several exercises you and your team can do before beginning research to help you practice seeing the world as a beginner and to understand when you are observing something and when you are interpreting it. You can download the toolkit for free at www.ideo.com/work/human-centered-design-toolkit/.

Focus Your Study

Insights are seldom about the place or the people you visit. The insights that have the greatest shelf life are the ones you have about your product, yourself, your assumptions.

– Patrick Larvie, Staff User Experience Researcher, Google

When you start planning your research, you may feel overwhelmed by all the things you don't yet know about your users. It may seem like you have more questions than you can possibly answer. Keep in mind that your primary goal is to understand the part of their lives that involves your product or service. You need to strike a balance between explaining aspects of your users' worlds that capture your attention and learning specific things about your users that your team will need to know to serve them better. Make a short list of questions that your study absolutely must address. Use them to set the parameters of the study and keep them in a location where they will be easy to refer to during the study, when many interesting differences may attract your attention.

To get you started, Table 13.1 lists some common objectives of companies conducting global and cross-cultural user research and an example of a research question that would support each objective.

Table 13.1 Common Objectives of Global or Cross-Cultural Research

Research Objective	Example Research Question
Explore opportunities in a new market.	How do Spanish-speaking Americans use the Internet for dating?
Compare users in multiple regional markets.	How do our mobile banking customers in different parts of Europe perceive the system's security?
Deepen or update understanding of current users in a specific region or culture.	How well do our stores in Shanghai meet the needs of office supply purchasers there?

Choose Your Approach: Travel, Remote Research, or Outsourcing

Whenever you do research with users who are different from the ones you know, you have gaps to bridge with those users. They may be distances you must travel, time zones to span, cultural gaps like language, or socioeconomic gaps such as differences in wealth that can profoundly influence users' attitudes. The greater those gaps, the more time, expense and complexity your research will involve. In bridging physical distances, you will need to decide the relative merits of traveling to do the research, conducting it remotely, or contracting it out to local user research providers. Then you will have to establish the relationships and teams you need to make it happen.

Global Research Rules of Thumb

Consider Travel if You…

…have the budget.
…need to build foundational knowledge.
…have access to local connections on the ground, or time to cultivate them.

Consider Remote Research if You…

…already have some foundational knowledge of this user population.
…know that your users have reliable access to the Internet.
…can also do in-person research periodically.

Consider Utilizing Local Research Providers if You…

…are doing an evaluative study that can be very well specified, such as a usability study.
…need the research to be conducted in person, *and*
…don't have budget for travel or time to prepare for travel. (If you can observe the study remotely, all the better.)

read the local newspapers. In global research, you may have many fewer initial assumptions to draw upon in finding appropriate participants, and checking them takes more work.

As a result, you may not be able to competently do the recruiting yourself—or even assess the quality of recruiting done on your behalf. There is substantial opportunity for professional recruiters to misunderstand your needs or even misrepresent the people they can recruit as people who are right for your research. This is why it's good to take advantage of the expertise of any local partners your company may have or draw upon market research studies about the regions you are interested in to inform recruiting criteria.

Recruiting, especially the kind you do yourself, often starts with reaching out to a social network. Chances are if you want to learn about your customers in a place where you have not lived or worked, you don't know lots of people in your target audience. Before beginning to recruit, talk to someone unaffiliated with the project who has spent a significant amount of time in your target region in the past five years. Get that person's take on where your target customers are and even whether they exist as you have defined them. As with research you do in your own country or culture, behavioral criteria should be considered before demographic ones. If the people you find in community X who use, say, online dating services don't resemble the segments in your market research, figure out why. Then choose participants who actually do online dating, not those who match the marketing segments.

Here's a thought-provoking experiment to get you started on global recruiting strategies: In your neighborhood or city, where/ how would you find someone who…

…talks on the telephone all day?

…loves Western classical music?

…carries a toolbox to work? Now try and answer the same questions for a country where you have never been.

Keep in mind that social networks such as Facebook that are used around the globe can be useful aids in finding people and confirming that people you have found have the characteristics you are looking for. Jan Chipchase, Executive Creative Director of Global Insights at frog design, has written on his blog,

> The ideal recruiting agency list-of-potential-participants contains hundreds of millions of entries and document every aspect of potential participant's lives—what they are doing, who they are doing it with, the causes they feel passionate about, the brands they connect with, the music they listen to, the places they go—and all updated in real time. Thanks to social networking sites like Weibo, Facebook, Orkut and Mixi this 'ideal list' already exists.

Chipchase describes his approach and offers advice to researchers doing their own global recruiting at http://janchipchase.com/2011/12/thenew-dawn/. Once you have found a few of the right people for your research, you can then expand your reach through the "snowball" method: asking your initial participants to refer others they know.

Field Interviews and Observation

It's easy to assume that "out there" everything is alien and different. More often, global research leads to a mix of impressions: some moments when you are surrounded by people and activities that seem foreign in every way, and other moments when what you observe feels surprisingly familiar.

Here's a story that illustrates some of those sharp transitions: Andrea was doing a user evaluation of educational software for grade-school children in a big city in India. As she drove to her test site, it because clear that the driver did not have a reliable map or detailed directions. Instead, he headed to the general neighborhood and, upon reaching a major intersection, began asking people where the building might be. Street maps and street signs, pieces of infrastructure that Andrea took for granted, did not exist or were not used. The navigation style used instead was like none she had ever seen in a city, which made the journey feel quite novel to Andrea. When she eventually got to the school, she conducted the testing with children in the target age group. Afterward, some younger kids wanted to try the computer game. Andrea had been told that none of the children at the school had computers at home, and the younger ones had barely ever touched a computer. But when they sat down to play, they did not seem disoriented at all. Instead, they picked up the mice, stared at the screen, and set about trying different ways to make the images on the screen change. As they played by themselves or together, there suddenly appeared to be very little difference between them and the American kids who had pilot tested the games in the United States.

Building Your Field Team

Your field research will be more fruitful if you conduct observations and interviews with people who currently live and work in the region or culture, or who have spent much of their lives there. Part of planning your field study should be contacting friends, colleagues, partners, agencies, and educational institutions in your destination region and asking for referrals to people who can join your research team and act as guides and interpreters. Ideally, they should also be able to help with routine field research tasks such as dealing with consent forms, audio and video recording, note taking, and transportation. If possible, don't commit to working with anyone specific until you have met in person and made sure you can operate well together.

Don't assume that the people available to work with will understand the goals of user research and how such research is done. If you find people with training in human-computer inter-action, the social sciences, or at least market research, you may be able to reference what they have learned; if not, you will need to explain in basic terms what you do and why your company is gathering this type of information, as well as what you need to learn from the current study.

Liaisons and Guides

When journalists report from a country or culture they don't know extremely well, they often employ "fixers": local people who know the environment, who can introduce the journalists to the people they want access to, and who can get things done with a mini-mum of trouble. While a user researcher is unlikely to need this help as urgently as a reporter on deadline, it can nonetheless make the difference between a successful round of field research and one compromised by logistical and interpersonal snafus.

The greater the cultural disparity between you and the research participants, the more helpful it is to have someone with you at the sessions who is known to the participants, or if not known, is perceived as a community member. Like translators, community liaisons need to speak the languages of the region fluently, but beyond that, they should be streetwise, insightful, flexible, and good negotiators. You may need different people for urban and rural areas or different subsets of the population, just as in San Francisco totally different people would be necessary to introduce us to members of a country club and a group of graffiti writers.

An established organization hosting you may be able to perform this function as well as an individual.

Translators and Moderators

In multilingual research, local language speakers may perform any of several related functions; it is up to you and the people you work with to decide how you will collaborate.

Translators tend to focus on listening as closely as possible to your research participants and translating their words accurately. Do not assume that your translator will attend to visual cues such as gestures or be able to interpret anything in the environment for you. This makes it especially important to take photos and video for later interpretation.

For some conversations, especially focus groups and usability tests, you may want to have a local language speaker act as a *moderator,* directly asking your questions and following up on the responses with questions of his or her own. If a larger team is a viable option, it's nice to have both a moderator and a translator to allow you to follow the discussion.

You may need to have one person focused on language and keeping the conversational exchange going, while another person, who may also be in charge of video and other functions, observes the interaction from the perspective of someone who understands local etiquette and nuances of body language and behavior, and notes their impressions for later review.

Research Assistants

In some research locations, you may be able to connect with students or others who are starting out in the field of user experience or the social sciences. Working with them can be great exchange of knowledge: They teach you about their region or culture and you teach them about user experience research and give them an opportunity to practice.

One potential pitfall is that someone starting out may be less understanding of the need to pursue research goals consistently and have a unified purpose on the team. They may change your protocol without telling you because they feel questions are unnecessary or irrelevant. Urge them to take ownership from the outset and give them an opportunity to give sincere feedback on the study design.

Building Trust

As in any user research, the quality of the information you gather depends largely on how much trust you can build with your participants, and that starts with creating trusting relationships among the research team members.

Field research in a new environment is almost always stressful, at least at the beginning. Unforeseen issues arise where improvisation is required. Transportation, space, or supplies you have arranged may fail to materialize; individuals at research sites may block access to the participants. Get a sense of which team members are best able to help with what, and give them some flexibility to improvise. This choice entails risk, but it can also help the team to bond.

In particular, seek advice and feedback on how to negotiate cultural mores in the community where you're working; this is an extension of the work you do to understand any new community you enter. Remember that differences may be greater in a country or culture that is unfamiliar to you. For example, in some places you may meet with resistance if you ask female participants to be interviewed by male researchers. Strive to meet participants on their terms and demonstrate respect for them and the rules they wish to observe.

At the same time, don't be the scientist in the white lab coat, treating people with research-session formality at all times. Elizabeth Churchill, a leading user experience researcher, tries to be accessible to participants outside the group setting during global field research. This basic openness can create opportunities for people to share things with you outside the formal context of the research. There have been times, Churchill says, when simply taking a bathroom break allowed "the ladies to tell me what was really going on."

Make the Most of Your Time on the Ground

Much of your time in the field will be spent in prearranged meetings with the users you are researching, but you are likely to learn an equal amount or more through experiences you have between sessions. You can maximize the value of your trip by noticing and reflecting on what is novel and strange to you, even when those things are as mundane as how people get around a city or how household chores are done.

Ame Elliott, a senior design researcher at the global consultancy IDEO, has developed specific tactics to "expand the footprint" of her one-on-one interactions with participants. In home interviews, she sometimes uses an artifact she sees in the home as the starting point of "a treasure hunt for examining the nearby environment." For example, she might ask a participant about the article of clothing they bought most recently, and then visit the store where they bought it. Elliott's approach and Churchill's are both ways of doing research beyond the study you are officially there to do, which helps you frame what you observe in the user study itself. For example, Andrea's research in India (described at the beginning of this section) primarily involved usability testing of a software game for groups of children. But it was by spending time with the children before and after the testing—playing games, watching classes in session, seeing them in groups outside the testing space—that Andrea was able to interpret their responses to the software.

Spending time on these things is generally more valuable than spending all your free time in activities that are primarily done by tourists to the region—unless, of course, your research objective is to understand the experience of tourism.

Global Research Ethics

Research ethics have three main components: fair compensation, informed consent, and respect for ownership of ideas. Doing research globally complicates all three and makes it necessary to rethink the approaches you would typically use.

Fair compensation means valuing the contribution research participants make and offering the right compensation in exchange. It can be difficult to figure out what is fair when you are working in an economy where wage structures and available work opportunities for people are different from the ones you are used to. You may think you can avoid the issue by erring on the side of overpayment, but this can create power imbalances and disrupt local economies in ways you didn't intend.

Informed consent means that participants understand what they are agreeing to share with you, what will happen to the information, and any consequences of participating. How well do you expect participants to understand what it means to have their image and voice recorded and used in product development? If they have never encountered product development as it is done in your industry and do not know anyone employed in product development, it may be difficult for them to be aware of any negative consequences. It becomes necessary to ask whether they are truly informed enough to consent, and how you can inform them. In a 2011 article called "Field Research in the Age of Data Servitude," Jan Chipchase, Executive Creative Director of Global Insights at frog design, describes giving participants control over which images of them are used. In his sessions, "the participant is handed the camera and shown how to move from photo to photo, shown how to delete a photo, and is asked to 'please delete any photos you don't like.' If the participant wants to delete all the photos, then frankly the team doesn't deserve to have them, but the reality is that most people delete a few where the split-second captures their worst side."

Respect for ownership of ideas means not claiming things you learn from someone else as your own ideas or your company's intellectual property. In cross-cultural research, you may learn a great deal that is new to you and offers dramatic new ways of approaching your company's challenges. Crediting the sources is only right, whether they are individuals or cultural groups. It may be difficult to devise and implement corporate policies that let you do so; begin with your research protocol itself. For example, Chipchase offers participants copies of the information they shared with him during the research, in an analog or digital format that is useful to them.

Global and Cross-Cultural Surveys

Surveys, diary instructions, and any written communication with global and cross-cultural research participants must be approached with extra care. Question wording is particularly important when surveys are intended for unfamiliar populations.

Work closely with your translator and provide the same detailed guidance about the participants and the focus of the research that you would give an interpreter who was helping you conduct interviews. In particular, review your survey text and any visual materials you are using to eliminate any conventions and cultural references that may not make sense to people outside your culture. Finally, be sure to pilot test your questionnaire or diary in each language you will be using, with native speakers of that language.

Research across Income Disparities: Special Challenges

In the developing world, there can be great opportunities and also especially deep cultural divides between participants and researchers.

The Elephant in the Room

The most unavoidable and pressing problems to anticipate are those relating to a wealth and status disparity between researchers and participants, especially American and European researchers and researchers from large international companies, and participants from less affluent regions. Participants may hope that their involvement will lead directly to more resources for them in the future. Depending on the project, those hopes may or may not be realistic; that's a difficult realization for both participants and researchers. Given widely shared hopes for the future, researchers may find themselves enmeshed in community politics surrounding access to those hoped-for rewards.

When introducing yourself and the research, make your role absolutely clear. If you cannot make the decision to allocate aid, hire people in the community, or get them an improved version of your product, do not represent that you can do these things. Make it clear that you are doing research, and that solutions are not yet on the table.

Tactical Challenges for Implementing Research Plans

- Varying literacy levels (both linguistic and technological) may require you to vary your procedures for recruitment, surveying, diary studies, and usability tests.
- Hardware/infrastructure constraints affect how you might deploy prototypes for usability tests.
- In some areas Research is more likely to occur in public places rather than private homes which attract the attention of many different people in the community, not just your target participants.

The field of information and communication technology for development (ICT4D) is engaged in developing best practices for these cases. Some great places to start in learning more are:

- Regina Scheyvens and Donovan Storey, eds. *Development Fieldwork: A Practical Guide*, Sage Publications, 2003
- IDEO Human Centered Design Toolkit, 2nd Edition www.ideo.com/work/human-centered-design-toolkit/

Analyzing the Data

When you return from travel or finish gathering data remotely, it can be easy to retreat back into the assumptions you made at home as you start analyzing the data. If at all possible, begin analysis while you are still in the field or otherwise in contact with your local team. When you return, you may need to take extra care in developing your analysis plan and schedule, to make sure you can involve the people who were there for the research and the people who are going to synthesize and present the research, even if those people are located in different countries and time zones.

Course Corrections

With any kind of global or cross-cultural research, you should be extra attentive to the possibility that your research protocol is not gathering the data you had hoped for. Spend at least part of each team debriefing session reflecting on your research methods and checking your learnings against your stated research goals. If the protocol comes up short, be open to ideas from your local collaborators on how to make changes so that you're answering the questions you need to answer.

Building Your Global Research Program

A global or cross-cultural research program should help your organization make useful distinctions, not just among individual users, but also among cultural and even national groups. This means you need to reexamine how you look at your users and research: There will be surprising differences and surprising similarities.

What happens when you have to maintain a product for some chunk of audience that's in another country—not just for a launch? The long-term solution may include managing international partners, contracting out individual studies, and making the best of brief visits.

Doing global research sustainably requires building trusted relationships. While short, immersive trips can be great for team building in your organization or reinvigorating the product development process, you are likely to find that your long-term research program matters most.

Getting good at global and cross-cultural user research is about constantly revising your assumptions. Get used to being wrong frequently, especially at the beginning, and see how quickly you can learn to change your methods in response to the conditions that emerge. Returning to the principle of Beginner's Mind, remember that beginners are often surprised. When you notice that users in a new region or culture surprise you a little less often, you will know you have learned a great deal.

CHAPTER 14

Others' Hard Work:
Published Information and Consultants

Not all research must be done from scratch. You can find out about important aspects of your audience without resorting to doing research from first principles. The judicious use of published information and consultants can save time, energy, and (occasionally) money when trying to know your audience and understand how they experience your product. It's even possible to get information that would not be feasible to collect on your own.

There are a number of reasons for going outside your company walls to acquire audience knowledge. Obviously, you can often save money and time by going to external sources if the information you're interested in is readily available, but it's not just economic reasons that justify outsourcing your research. By going outside your immediate development context, you can quickly acquire a high level of perspective that you probably wouldn't be able to recreate in-house. You probably don't have the resources to do a broad survey of all of your possible target audiences to find out whether they have the basic needs and meet the basic requirements to use your product, but a market research company does. And although it may involve some amount of interpretation and extrapolation, a perusal of high-level data may quickly focus your research by eliminating some obvious problems. Moreover, a different organization is likely to see things with a different perspective. Approaching the same audience with a different set of goals and assumptions produces results that are different from what you can collect. This can be invaluable in giving depth and understanding to your own results.

But this is not a trivial process. Finding trustworthy and appropriate information is hard, and interpreting it correctly is even harder. And consultants aren't the cavalry coming over the hill, either. For all of their value, their efforts need to be managed as carefully as you would manage your own research. External research is an important resource, but like all-powerful tools, it has to be used carefully.

Published Information

There are many kinds of published analysis for you to choose from. Even if something doesn't *exactly* apply to your problem, maybe it's useful enough for you to base a decision on. Maybe it gives you some information where to start looking for problems or who your audience isn't. Or maybe it just gives you a better perspective on how to approach your own research.

Keep in mind that published information is not the same as research done in-house. It's broader and shallower than the research that you would do, and it doesn't have the quality controls that you would put into your research. It may turn out to be more rigid than is necessary for your purposes or, alternatively, too unfocused. However, buying others' research is often much faster than doing it yourself. And so, in the long run, it can be cheaper.

Independent Analysis

The business model for most research companies is pretty simple: They do independent in-depth analysis on a specific topic or a specific industry, and then they sell reports to companies from the industry they just analyzed. These reports are not cheap, but they often represent a lot of comprehensive thinking by a group of industry experts (or, at least, research experts).

As an outgrowth of the marketing research industry, these companies tend to focus on the financial health of specific markets, industries, or companies. As part of this, however, they often research into the needs and desires of those markets' target audiences. Much of the knowledge necessary to sell to a target audience is the same as that which is necessary to give that audience a good experience, and such marketing-focused information can be immediately valuable when creating user personas or setting expectations for contextual inquiry.

Some companies specializing in this kind of research include:

- Forrester Research, www.forrester.com
- IDC, www.idc.com
- The Gartner Group, www.gartner.com
- eMarketer, www.emarketer.com
- ClickZ (a subsidiary of Incisive Media), www.clickz.com

Additionally, some other firms create research focused on evaluating the user experience presented by companies or industries rather than just their business metrics. These companies include:

- Nielsen Norman Group, www.nngroup.com
- User Interface Engineering, www.uie.com

Although these reports present a ready-made trove of potentially useful knowledge, it's important to read them closely. The researchers who write them will often not know the industry as well as insiders; they may misjudge the behaviors of users and the motivations of companies. A careful reading of the research methods is important.

Traffic/Demographics

By knowing who is using your competitors' products, how much they use them, and what they use them for, you can avoid your competitors' mistakes and capitalize on their strengths. Unfortunately, as great as it would be to have access to your competition's log files and survey data, this is rarely a legal option. Fortunately, services exist that collect some of these data independently, reporting the conglomerate information and selling access to specific slices of the data. By using these services' data and tools, it's possible to gain insight into the makeup and behavior of your competition's users.

Some companies that provide this kind of research include:

- ComScore, www.comscore.com
- Nielsen/Netratings (a subsidiary of AC Nielsen), www.netratings.com
- Hitwise (a subsidiary of Experian), www.hitwise.com

Interpreting these results and how they apply to your product is more difficult than reading an analyst's report, and the sheer amount of data received from one of these services can be daunting. There are typically two kinds of data in one of these reports: the participants' behavior, as it was tracked by the company, and the participants' profile, as it was reported to the company. Linking these produces a powerful set of measurements. For example, you can (hypothetically—not all services allow you to do this directly) get data about the most popular sites in a given market and then get a profile of the people who use those sites.

Of all the data that's possible to extract, often the most immediately interesting information is the demographic makeup of your competition (or of companies in a parallel industry) and their technological and Internet usage profile. You can immediately see how old, how tech-savvy, and how affluent their audience is (among many other variables). These are, of course, aspects that you probably considered when creating your own audience profile, but a set of independent data can confirm your assumptions or cast them in doubt.

Like all research, the process by which the data were collected needs to be carefully examined since that aspect is least under your control. Sometimes the data collection methods can introduce subtle biases, which need to be taken into account. For example, Comscore Media Metrix requires its participants to install a piece of software on their computer; the software tracks what sites they visit and when they visit them. Although they can get a mostly representative sample of users this way, this approach misses a key group of people: those who are unable to install this software on their work computers because it violates their company's software installation rules. This means that the data collected by the service skew toward home-based computers and companies with lax internal security standards. For many situations, this bias does not affect the applicability of the final data. But the data would be insufficiently representative for a business-to-business (B2B) sales site targeted toward Fortune 100 companies. It would be important to track B2B users at work, but it would be impossible under the management information system security rules of most of the target audience.

Marketing Research

As is obvious from many of these descriptions, the tools of marketing research can be used for user experience research. The marketing department of your company is interested in what will make people want to go to your site and use your product. The reasons that they will want to go to your site and will be able to use your product are directly related to the user experience.

Research marketing often can help in understanding your user population. Ask for any audience profiles or market segmentations that have been created. These can offer a high-level view of your users, often supported by quantitative data, that will help you define your users' likely interests and concerns.

Publications and Forums

Familiarizing yourself with the publications that cover and influence your field is probably a good first step in any kind of user research. Time spent at the library (or with a search engine) is rarely wasted and often reveals sources of information that would otherwise take a lot of work to replicate. Books and trade magazines are obvious sources, as well as blogs, podcasts, and especially RSS feeds. Subscribing to a handful of industry newsfeeds provides the media monitoring that the old newsclipping services used to, only for free. While industry-focused publications can be expensive, they are often accessible at your library.

White papers are essentially analyst reports, but from a biased source. They're often written to justify a particular company's perspective and explain their technology, but that doesn't mean that they're not useful. In defending their perspective, they often contain valuable information, though it should always be examined with attention to the bias inherent in its source.

For more links to directories, online magazines, blogs, and useful mailing lists, visit the book's website: www.mkp.com/observing-the-user-experience.

A number of user experience pundits, consultants, and groups publish blogs and online magazines, which offer advice not just in print form, but through podcasts and videos as well.

Finally, you can track breaking news, issues, and debates in your industry of interest by subscribing to email lists and joining industry-focused discussions on LinkedIn, Twitter, Quora, and other social networking sites.

Hiring Specialists

We're including consultants, contractors, and consulting agencies in our definition of specialist. Although a large consultancy (of the Accenture/KPMG/IBM Global Services model) works differently than a single contractor, their relationship to your product and your company is similar. They are called in to solve specific problems, and they work as an adjunct to your team, interacting when necessary, but keeping their responsibility to the one aspect of the development that they were hired to do. Your team's work may range all over the product as needs warrant it, but specialists will rarely leave their specialty to solve a problem they were not hired to solve.

There are times when resource constraints do not permit you to build the necessary expertise in-house to do something yourself. For nearly every task described in this book, from recruiting participants to competitive research to setting up video cameras, you can hire a professional to do it for you. In some cases, such as conducting global and cross-cultural research (Chapter 13), analyzing automatically gathered data (Chapter 16), and even moderating focus groups (Chapter 7), you may find that it is simply not worth your while to build up the necessary expertise. Global and cross-cultural research in particular can demand specialized language and cultural competencies that require local consultants. For a price, experts can immediately bring nearly any knowledge and experience that you need.

But working with a professional is not simply writing a check and forgetting about the task. To use specialists effectively, you need to hire them at the right time, with the proper set of expectations, and then carefully manage them.

Timing

A key to using specialists well is calling them in at the right moment. Often, consultants get the call to produce a perfect solution late in the game, after all in-house methods have failed and a deadline is approaching. More often than not, this is asking for a miracle. Unfortunately, despite the way some advertise themselves, consultants are not saints.

The work that hired specialists do is not all that different from what your in-house staff can do, and it needs to be scheduled just like in-house work. Actually, it needs even a little more time than what you give your in-house projects since the specialists will need to learn about your product and the task that's involved.

As consultants, we have been asked a number of times to "do a little user testing a couple weeks before launch." In response, we must tell the caller that this is not unlike looking up to see where the moon is after you've already launched the rocket. The kinds of results that testing a completed product will reveal may help with tiny course corrections, but no amount of testing and adjustments will help if the rocket was pointed in the wrong direction. This holds for any other kind of specialty.

In addition, consultants, as opposed to other kinds of specialists, need to be called in especially early. Technical specialists don't teach you; they do it for you. They don't know your business before they come in and, most likely, won't after they leave. Good consultants, on the other hand, absorb enough of your business to recommend solutions *and* strive to transfer some of their expertise to you. Good consultants will leave your company in a state where you won't have to go to them with the same problem again. Good technical specialists will do their job quickly and accurately, but if it has to be done again, you'll probably have to call them back in.

Fortunately, it's hard to call user researchers in too early, but it's still important to do the right research at the right time. As discussed in Part 1 of this book, a good iterative development process involves user input at nearly every iteration. The responsibility for picking what research is needed is as much the project developers' as it is the researchers'. For example, if a product's interaction is usability tested before the feature set has been defined, much of the information may go to waste since people's use of it will likely change based on the options available to them. Likewise, testing a product that's been built without first researching its audience's needs will result in a lot of unnecessary effort: If the product's audience has no interest in it, then they have little motivation to understand how it works or to use it in a realistic way.

Find a Specialist

For tasks with relatively straightforward needs, such as a single round of usability testing or some interviews to set feature priority, the procedure is similar to finding a carpenter for your house.

Write a description of your research needs and goals. What kind of research do you want to do? Why? How are you going to use the results? This is similar to how you would prepare for your own research, as described in Chapter 4.

Make a list of specialists to contact. Ask colleagues for recommendations or contact one of the usability professional organizations, all of which maintain lists of consultants and contractors. Some prominent organizations are the following:

- Usability Professionals' Association, www.upassoc.org
- Information Architecture Institute, iainstitute.org
- American Society for Information Science & Technology, especially their Information Architecture special interest group, www.asis.org
- Association for Computing Machinery's special interest group on computer human interaction (ACM SIGCHI), www.acm.org/sigchi/
- BayCHI, the San Francisco Bay Area's chapter of SIGCHI, maintains a list of consultants that includes people in many geographic areas, www.baychi.org/general/consultants.html
- The Interaction Design Association compiles resources for hiring user experience professionals at www.ixda.org/jobs/hiring

Check qualifications. The specific experience of the research companies should be investigated before you hire them. You probably don't want a carpenter who specializes in houses to make furniture or a furniture builder making a house. A user experience specialist may not have any experience doing marketing research even though the techniques are quite similar (and vice versa).

Get quotes and an explanation of philosophy and techniques. If possible, get a sample results document from all the consultants under consideration. Read the results for an explanation of techniques and look for a sensitivity to the needs of the product and the client.

Ask for references to several recent clients and follow up with the references. Inquire into the quality and timeliness of work, but also the quality of service. Did the consultant follow through on what was promised? Did they listen? Were they responsive?

The Casual Method: Email and Phone Call

Most user experience research and design work doesn't warrant a full, formal request for proposals (RFP). A simpler alternative is a short (several paragraph) email description of needs and problems, followed by a one- or two-hour conference call to delve into details. This procedure saves both parties time—neither a RFP document nor a detailed, formal RFP response need be written—and can focus quickly on the most relevant elements rather than trying to predict them ahead of time. Good consultants try to help clients understand and formulate their needs immediately rather than just responding to what they believe their needs to be. However, in situations where a project is huge and there are potentially many companies vying for it, a comprehensive RFP can be the best option.

The Formal Method: RFPs

For more complex tasks (large focus groups, surveys, multiple iterations with different techniques), the procedure is more like that of building a house from scratch. Because of the size of the tasks and their interrelationships, the process of finding the right group of specialists can get quite complex.

Write the RFP. An RFP is a description of your problem and a structured request for a solution. It's useful not just to set the parameters for evaluating a consultant's bid, but as the first step in managing and organizing a project. It sets out, in specific terms, what you believe your problems to be and what you want to gain from an outside solution.

Broadcast the RFP. You can send the RFP to certain consultants that you've first contacted, or you can post it to a larger group. Don't spam, but certain mailing lists and bulletin boards allow you to post such requests (ask the moderators of lists about their RFP posting policies).

Evaluate the responses. The consultants should respond quickly with specific solutions rather than sales pitches. Watch out for proposals that subcontract key work to another firm, if that's the case;

then evaluate the subcontractor with the same rigor as you evaluate the primary contractor.

The following is a sample RFP based on a template created by user experience consultant Janice Fraser, for a very large, long-term, multipart project. RFPs for smaller projects do not have to have all the sections and details of this one.

Request for Proposal

User Experience Research for a B2B Surplus Industrial Products Website
January 12, 2013
Responses due: February 12, 2013

Part 1: Project Summary

We represent one of the world's leading raw surplus materials trading websites, which is undergoing a system-wide redesign. We are committed to using the best practices of user-centered design as part of this redesign and on an ongoing basis thereafter. With this RFP we hope to find a vendor who can fulfill the full complement of user research needs the project requires.

This RFP will outline for you our vision for the project, our selection criteria, and our expectations for your response.

Background

Our company runs one of the world's largest online industrial raw materials trading services. With over a billion dollars in transactions in FY2012 and 30,000 active users, we are one of the most prominent surplus materials trading services in the world. Our users count on us for the livelihood of their business and entrust us to deliver. We continually strive to improve our service for the benefit of our users and for our profitability.

Project Description

In the interest of improving the user experience of our service, we have launched a major redesign program, creating the service from top to bottom with an eye on the needs of, and input from, our users.

The redesign will be done in a series of phases. Each phase will involve the reexamination of the current product and a refinement of the product vision for the next design. User experience research will be a major component of each phase, and each phase will contain a major research project that will be appropriate for the goals of that phase.

The project will take place Q2–Q4 2013.

Part 2: Elements of Your Proposal

We would like your proposal to be in a specific format, containing all the sections described below. You may add sections if you feel that these do not sufficiently address your core competencies.

Questions

We would like to understand how you are thinking about this project. Please use the information contained in this RFP to answer these questions.

One key to the success of this project will be to implement the users' needs as determined by the research, but those needs may not necessarily align with the business needs of the service. What process will you use to solve that challenge?

Another key to a successful product is the transfer of knowledge from the user research staff to the production staff. In your view, what are the chief barriers to transferring user knowledge within a company, and how would you address them?

What do you see as the most challenging barriers to the success of this project, and what should we do to ensure the best possible results?

Case Studies

Please present up to three case studies that highlight the strengths your company shows in managing projects such as the one described here. Present final deliverables and appropriate collateral.

Core Competencies

We seek a partner, or partners, that have demonstrated achievement in the following areas. Please give us specific examples, if possible, of your experience in these areas.

- Analysis of complex information research and purchasing tasks
- User experience-oriented focus groups
- User testing of websites
- Researching the needs of business website users, ideally large industrial and manufacturing users
- Understanding the needs of new or occasional users and frequent long-term users

Your Process with Deliverables

Please describe the process your company would use to accomplish this project. Include a description of research, spec development, production, integration, Q/A, and methods of building consensus and sign-off at each stage.

Schedule

The schedule for the entire project is 220 days. Please provide a specific development timeline for this project. Break down your process by deliverables, and be specific about the timing for each section.

Client's Role

Please describe what, if any, expectations you have or deliverables you will need from our company for the project. Describe what sorts of resources you are expecting at each phase, and who from our company you will want to meet with.

Your Team

Please describe the specific roles of the individuals who would be assigned to this project. How many individuals would you assign to the project? To the extent possible, provide background and contact information on the individuals who would be assigned to the account and describe their specific responsibilities. Please identify key projects that each member has worked on in this capacity. Please also indicate the percent of their time that would be allocated to this project.

Budget

Please provide us with a detailed budget proposal. You may present your budget in any format that is familiar to you, but do include cost per milestone, hourly cost per team member, and anticipated expenses.

Also include a description of how cost is typically communicated during the course of a project and how overages are managed and presented for approval.

References

Please provide us with names and contact information for three references from relevant recent projects that can comment on your services.

Process

We have invited several organizations to make a proposal on this project. Based on the quality and nature of those proposals, we will invite up to three companies to make presentations to us.

You will be given 1.5 hours to make your presentation to the management team and answer questions. Be prepared for detailed, specific review of budget and process. Please plan to bring the specific team members who will be assigned to this account, including the leads for project management, quantitative research, qualitative research, and analysis.

Set Expectations

Going into a relationship with a specialist, especially a consultant or a consulting company, requires setting appropriate expectations on both sides.

As a client, *you know your business better than they do.* If they knew what you know, they'd be your competitors. Even if you tell them everything that you know, you will still know your business better than they will. You have more experience and should frame what you expect specialists to do from that perspective. The role that they play is not as replacements, but as information sources and tools.

Some consultants are qualified to help you uncover problems and to create solutions to those problems. It's tempting (and may be advantageous) to get both services from a single source, but they require different capabilities and are best managed as separate pieces of consulting work. Scope the user research and the design as different projects and get separate proposals for each. Even if you end up working with one firm from start to finish, it will have been worth making sure they could meet your expectations throughout. And remember, consultants will happily give you what they believe is the best solution for a given problem, but it will still be coming from the perspective of someone who has limited experience with your business. The responsibility for taking their advice, understanding what it means in your situation, and applying it correctly is still yours.

Specialists provide perspective based on experience. Because of their experience, they know some general solutions that work better than others, and they can tailor those solutions to your problem. What they tell you may not match your perception of the world, but it's important to listen to them. Inside your development process, you come to conclusions based on a certain set of assumptions. No matter how honest and forthright you and your staff are, eventually you're all going to see the problems from much the same perspective, based on the same information. Outsiders come in with an entirely different set of assumptions and information, so their conclusions can be much different from yours. This does not mean that they are right and you are wrong, or vice versa, but the perspective they bring enriches yours. Allow them to ask fundamental questions and reintroduce topics that you may have already decided on.

One way to think about consultants is that they are people who know now what you will find out in two to three months if you don't hire them. That's it. Think of them as people who are a couple steps ahead of you, and by hiring them you are shaving a couple of months off your development schedule. A couple months of development time is really expensive, so bringing in specialists is generally worth the money. But what you're buying is time, not magic.

Guidelines for Managing Specialists

These expectations can be distilled into a series of guidelines for managing specialists.

Know what you want. If you familiarize yourself with the basic ideas and methods of the industry, you can be a much more informed consumer of consulting services. Calling a usability test a focus group is more than just a faux pas in a meeting with a consultant; it creates confusion as to the goals of the research and of the project as a whole. Once you know what's available, know what questions you want to get an answer to. Determining the goals of the research ahead of time based on the business needs of the company and the proposed product makes the results more meaningful and useful.

Schedule carefully. Research needs to address the needs of the company when it's delivered. When it comes too early, the project will likely have changed by the time it's needed. When it's too late, the time to fix the identified issues may have passed.

Provide lead time. As with any topic, the more preparation time the specialist has, the better the results are going to be. To recruit just the right audience may involve multiple iterations to get the screener right. To ask the right questions, the researcher needs to understand the research goals and your product. Analysis is always a time-consuming process, so the more time that is left for it, the better it's going to be. Consultants always benefit from an appropriate amount of lead time.

Be open to suggestions. Specialists may not know your business as well as you do. But if what they suggest challenges your assumptions about the product or its market, evaluate it—don't ignore it.

Observe the process. Although reports and presentations are valuable summaries, the amount of information that can be put in them is a small fraction of the knowledge that can be collected by directly observing the consultants' process. Whenever possible, have members of the development staff watch the research live. If direct observation is impossible (as in many studies with limited time, money, or other resources), ask for copies of the videos and notes and study them. Since you as the client are more familiar with the product and the problems it's trying to solve, you're likely to notice things that the consultant would not.

Get a presentation. It's tempting to get a consultant's written report and skip the presentation. After all, the thinking goes, the presentation consists of the consultant reading the report to us, which we can do on our own. A good presentation goes beyond that. It allows the consultant to prioritize and emphasize issues, elaborate on points, and answer questions.

Treat the consultants as a resource after the initial research is over. Once they've done the research, consultants have a level of expertise that should not be neglected. If you have questions about their work after they've completed it, don't hesitate to ask them about it (but pay them for their time!). Sometimes it's even valuable to keep consultants on retainer for a couple hours a month in between major research projects, bouncing ideas off them and clarifying observations. Over time, they may lose some objectivity, but they'll gain a deeper understanding and commitment to your product and its audience.

The relationship between a specialist and client can be a valuable one. When it works, both parties benefit and learn from each other, while making the development process a bit more efficient. When it doesn't, it can be broken off easily, and neither party is much the worse than before. In the long term, the most valuable aspect of reusing knowledge and experience is it makes the whole industry more efficient and gives everyone a reason to think about the things that really matter. Don't reinvent the wheel if you don't have to.

CHAPTER 15

Analyzing Qualitative Data

Research inevitably produces a lot of information: not just notes, but audio files, transcripts, sketches, and video. Add collages, maps, and other artifacts from interviews, and you're facing what we call "the wall of data."

Faced with that wall, it's easy to panic. Suddenly, the sheer amount of information isn't inspiring—it's terrifying. To scale that wall, you can't necessarily rely on the tools that helped so much in analyzing quantitative survey data. No, you're interested in rich accounts of people's behaviors, rationales, values, and personal characteristics. This kind of information is not particularly suited to statistical analysis. How to make sense of it all? Where to start?

This chapter will introduce some reliable techniques for drawing insights from qualitative—that is, nonnumerical—data. In doing so, we will lay out two sample processes: one "lightweight" and one "heavyweight." However, as will become clear, qualitative data analysis is an art and a craft. There is no one "right way" to do it, and your own projects will likely fall somewhere on a spectrum between the two extremes we present. The techniques you use will depend on the questions you need to answer, the constraints of schedule and budget, and your own skills and preferences.

Your goals, however, will remain the same: to find and confirm patterns within that data, interpret those patterns, and create analyses that inform action.

This Is Not a Fishing Trip

Luckily, you are not on a fishing expedition, and you are not flying blind. (How's *that* for mixed metaphors?) User research is applied research, which is to say that when you begin analysis you should already have a clear statement of the problem to solve and a specific list of questions to answer.

Those clear guidelines to what you need to get out of this process will shape your analysis. You can take them from any design briefs for your project, from a statement of work, from stakeholder interviews, or from talking with your team. Of course, guidelines aren't set in stone. You can and should negotiate with other stakeholders or revise your own understanding of the situation on your own. The point, however, is to start your research with at least a preliminary sense of what kind of reports or documents you'll be making at the end, and what kinds of information they should contain.

Then you can match analytical strategies to desired outcomes. For example, if you know you are building scenarios or informing the interaction flow of an application, you will probably want to focus on the sequence of tasks in an activity and what resources are required to complete that activity. If you know you are creating a touchpoint map for a service covering multiple locations, you will probably want to do a spatial analysis of where certain interactions with a service take place and what kinds of interfaces are used.

If you don't know what kind of outcomes your research will produce, read Chapter 17 before proceeding.

An Ideal Process for Qualitative Analysis

Later in this chapter, we'll present sample "lightweight" and "heavyweight" data analysis plans. For now, though, we'll simplify matters by describing the basic components of qualitative user research analysis in some detail. You don't have to follow these recommendations exactly—in fact, you'll probably always alter them—but it's useful to have some notion of what an ideal-world process would look like. If you're not sure how to climb your wall of data, you can start by adapting these components to your own schedule and needs.

Codes and Coding

Throughout this chapter we'll talk a lot about "codes." Despite what you may think, "coding" has nothing to do with programming software. A *code* is a descriptive word or short phrase that describes a piece of data. It's essentially a label. Codes can indicate the subject of a comment, the nature of the comment (a question, a feature request, etc.), its tone ("anger," "praise," etc.), its speaker, or whatever else makes sense for the analysis. Each code will likely describe multiple items, and the same item can have multiple codes. The end goal of coding is to categorize the data into code groups. Explaining the significance of the most important groups will form the backbone of your analysis.

Capture and Discuss Your Initial Insights

Data analysis starts immediately as we (naturally) try to identify patterns as soon as we have even a single unit of information. You may later decide that your first take on a person or situation is incorrect. But in order to do that, you have to have noted that observation in the first place! You should start analyzing your data during—not after—data collection so that the natural process becomes part of a planned approach.

As you take notes during a research activity, separate what you are seeing and hearing from your interpretations and analyses. You can do that by writing interpretations in a special place on the page, using a different color of pen, or bracketing them [like this] as you scribble. You don't want to confuse what you really did see and hear with your initial assumptions about what it means.

Develop a routine of capturing swift, gut-level observations as data come in. Discussing hypotheses early, while the data are fresh in your mind, will give you a head start and save you a lot of time. Whether working alone or with a partner, start noting initial analyses as soon as possible in your research encounter. That can mean making notes during the research activity, finding a quiet place to write down your thoughts when you have a break, or scheduling regular time to talk with other researchers.

This last activity, called "debriefing," is helpful even if you talk with team members who were not actually present at the research activity. Early discussions can prompt you to record concrete details, check your interpretations, question assumptions, and surface disagreements. Depending on your comfort level with this kind of research, your knowledge of the project subject area, and the progress of the project, debriefing may take as little as ten minutes or as long as an hour for each session.

These first-order, quick analyses help direct the data collection that happens later. If you wait until you have "everything in order" to begin noting any opinions or insights, you will likely have already forgotten many of your important initial thoughts—and you may not be conscious of how initial impressions shaped your perspective.

Prepare Your Data

You'll need to process your raw data before you can manipulate them. No one wants to read messy, handwritten notes, or view photographs on a digital camera screen, or watch hours of video when only 15 minutes is actually relevant. Getting your data into a manageable format for sharing and discussion is crucial.

For a list of online transcription services visit www.mkp.com/observing-the-user-experience

Transcription

Analysis often begins with transcription. The traditional method is to hire a transcription service. The service will provide a document containing every word every person said.

Transcription services vary in cost and expertise. Expect transcription to take at least a week, unless you are willing to pay for rush service. Noisy audio, more than two speakers, very technical terminology, and unfamiliar accents will also raise the price and lengthen the amount of time necessary.

You can transcribe your files yourself—and in fact, many academic social science researchers think doing so has benefits. However, expect to spend at least two hours of transcription per hour of recording. Transcripts can be unwieldy, and it's not unusual to get a 100-page transcript for a two-hour focus group.

The key to transcribing is capturing the meaning of people's words, so although you should aim for exact transcription, don't shy away from paraphrasing, dropping unnecessary words, or adding parenthetical expressions to provide context. However, always make it clear which words are yours and which are the participants'.

Even without formal transcription, review your audio and video files if you have any questions at all about your notes. Merely remembering a situation can miss subtle behaviors. Words can be misquoted. Researchers can fall into groupthink. Watching the original recordings can clarify ambiguities and reveal shades of meaning hidden when working from memory or notes alone. Review the files in order of presumed usefulness. As you watch, take more notes and revise the notes you have. Even if you are not transcribing word for word, note down especially compelling words and phrases.

Social science researchers working on long-term projects often use specialized qualitative data analysis software. This software is complex, and often expensive, but it does help make sense of very large data sets. For most user researcher projects, paper tools, a word processor, or simple spreadsheets work just fine. Visit www.mkp.com/ observing-the-user-experience for a list of quantitative data analysis resources.

Generally, that means:

- *Move photographs and video* from capture devices to file systems and label them with important information. Intial metadata might include: date and time of capture; participant name, pseudonym, or code; and perhaps researcher name.
- *Get audio and video transcribed* into text files. Messy handwritten notes should also be typed in.
- *Break up large chunks of data* into smaller units that can be recombined more easily. For example, you might copy each separate statement from an interview into a different row in a spreadsheet, or handwrite quotes and paraphrases onto Post-it notes. If you are doing remote interviews, you can save time by typing notes directly into a spreadsheet—but try to avoid doing so when the participant can see you, as it can seem impolite.

It can also be useful to keep photographs and brief summaries of participants' key characteristics posted on a wall near where you are working so that they are always in your mind.

Your end goal is to get all the relevant data—text, pictures, video, drawings, etc.—into a format that your team can work on together. Often, the best way to do that is by "making the data visual and physical," as Dan Saffer recommends in *Designing for Interaction*. That means organizing the data so the group can work on different clusters of data simultaneously, that anyone can easily make and break up groups of data, and work is preserved from session to session. Saffer recommends that you print out all interesting quotes and photographs on sticky notes so you can see all of them at once and move them around. For text analysis projects, shared spreadsheets with one quote per row will work fine, too.

Remember, preparing your data is also a form of analysis. You will never have the time, budget, or even necessity to transcribe every word and gesture from audio or video, or even every word from your notes. It is a filtering process. You are choosing to

Until you are sure you have a good handle on the direction of the project, it's a good idea to raise any questions with team members about data preparation choices as you go. That way, you can cooperatively decide on your priorities and make sure you check your choices against the research plan.

highlight some information and leave other information buried in your notes, or in video and audio files. Moreover, you will have to choose where, and how, to break up text into smaller pieces.

Find Patterns and Themes

Once you have prepared your data, you can look for patterns. In sections below, we will describe various tools and techniques more specifically. However, they all rely on the same basic principle: playing with different ways to categorize data until you are satisfied with how you can answer your research questions.

Like playing with your food, playing with your research data can feel messy and unpredictable. Nevertheless, following these steps will help you cope with even the highest mountain of data.

Sort the Data into Groups and Assign Codes

Categorizing and sorting data into groups is the first step in finding patterns in data. It typically involves both deductive—top-down—grouping, in which you use pre-predetermined categories to sort the data, and inductive—bottom-up—grouping, in which you immerse yourself in the data and allow them to suggest new groups to you.

Whether inductive or deductive, the goal of this grouping activity is to give each group a short, descriptive label, or code, that characterizes the group. A single item or group can have multiple codes.

To code a piece of data, start by examining it carefully.

For a photograph or other image, start by identifying the people, places, and things pictured in it. What is close together? What is far apart? What is publicly visible and easily accessible? What is hidden or hard to access? For example, Figure 15.3 shows an intermediate data analysis report for an observational study on working outside of offices.

Most of the data you will work with is likely some form of text. If it is a piece of text, read it carefully. What does it really mean in context of everything else the participant has told you? You might want to see if you can restate it in different words. Take a quote like this,

The tyranny of the urgent.

from a study of how people work when outside an office. The speaker, Kiran, is responding to a question asking why he works one day a week in a café near his house.

One obvious first category is "reasons to leave the office." But the phrase "tyranny of the urgent" is so vivid! It begs for a little more analysis. Clearly, Kiran feels in some way oppressed at the office. What does the "tyranny of the urgent" include? Well, earlier in the interview he complained about "distractions," and that his colleagues frequently visit his desk to ask him questions. Later in the interview, he says that it's not a problem for him to leave the office, because his firm only measures performance by results: "If you don't do your work, you're gone."

So, digging deeper, we could start to see this complaint as indicative of two properties of office work—interruptibility and obligation. Kiran feels obligated to respond to his colleague's interruptions, but he also knows that he needs to get his own work done in order to keep his job. So he leaves the office in order to manage access. After some analysis, this quote (and similar ones from other interviews) formed part of a coding structure in which managing interruptions was linked to leaving the office.

Over the course of coding, you will begin to identify various properties and dimensions (Strauss and Corbin, 1998) of the categories that the codes represent. For example, take the code "office." What makes an office an office? One property of the office as experienced by research participants, as Kiran's experience suggests, is interruptions. In turn, you find that interruptions vary along the dimension of time: "frequent," "occasional," and "rare." For this type of coding, it doesn't matter so much which of the specific workplaces in your study produce frequent or rare interruptions—what matters is how we can find comparative patterns. For example, are interruptions often cited as a reason to work at a café? Or do many people welcome interruptions and see them as a positive part of office work? Figure 15.1 illustrates how people can physically arrange pieces of data to represent those patterns.

Many, if not most, projects will start with a preexisting set of codes. These codes are based on the themes that you're trying to

Figure 15.1 A design team in the midst of data analysis at Adaptive Path, an interaction design consultancy. Each color of sticky note represents a different research participant. The team has clumped notes into large groups, and they are making patterns (labeled in red marker) within the themes.

follow or questions that you're trying to answer. That's why it's important to go into data analysis with a clear sense of your own desired outcomes.

For example, a common research goal is to identify and characterize different kinds of people who use a product or perform an activity. That goal often leads to the creation of *personas* (see Chapter 17). Here are some categories you can start with that may help you understand differences between people:?

- *Values.* People's value systems consist of likes, dislikes, beliefs, and the associations they make between these elements and the objects, people, and situations in their lives. What do people find of worth—not just in the product but in the activity that it supports? What are the criteria that they use when they decide whether they like or dislike something? How do their values interrelate?
- *Mental models.* Mental models, like metaphors, linguistically represent how we understand the world. Take George Lakoff and Mark Johnson's description of the "time is money" metaphor in their classic *Metaphors We Live By.* When talking

about time, English speakers will often an:
money—time is "made," "wasted," "spent
may be important for the maker of a piece
software to know since it may make the creation of an
mation architecture and the naming of interface elements
easier. Some people give software a personality and think of it,
in some sense, as a helper, friend, or confidant. Of course,
mental models have limits. Time can't really be "earned,"
except in prison, so that model should not be taken too
literally. Mental models are more detailed understandings of
how systems and institutions work. For example, people may
not realize that they can challenge an insurance claim adjuster's
estimate. Their mental model doesn't include the concept of
arbitration or second opinions.

- *Goals.* What do people want to get out the product or activity?
  How do they know when they have succeeded or failed?
- *Behaviors.* What actions do people regularly (or irregularly)
  perform? What are their stated goals in taking those actions?
  What triggers an action, and what is the usual result? Behaviors are one of the main building blocks of human-centered
  design. Whether you find moments of delight or pain points,
  understanding what people do, and the circumstances under
  which they do it, is an important starting point for design.
- *Role.* What function do they have in their organization, community, or household? In workplace studies, you may find it
  easier simply to start by sorting the data into roles, so that you
  look at all the salespeople together, all the tech support people
  together, etc. In families, you may want to compare parents and
  kids. However, you may find that there are relevant roles that are
  unofficial, or unstated, such as "cook," "peacemaker" or "home
  maintenance specialist." Those unofficial roles may be as important or more important than the official ones.
- *Skill level.* How do they define expertise? Is it different from
  how you or your clients would define expertise? How expert
  are they?
- *Preferred or alternative tools.* What means do they use to perform
  the activity or solve the problem? (This may be particularly
  useful for competitive analysis as well.)

Use demographic codes sparingly. It can be tempting to assume that characteristics like gender or age cause different responses to a product or service. But this assumption can come not from the data but from unconscious biases or stereotypes that you hold about different types of people. Sometimes, demographic coding can be useful—for example, if you are interested in how families shop for groceries. For that question, categorizing parents by age and number of children might be helpful. But in general, if your research does not specifically relate to demographic characteristics, avoid them in coding. They can be a waste of your time, and at worst will lead you to unsupported generalizations.

- *Pain points.* What difficulties do they face in using the product or performing the activity?
- *Demographics.* What stable personal characteristics do they share, such as gender, age, or income level?

If you want to understand people's priorities, you could have different codes for expressed preferences.

Another common goal is the decomposition of processes in an activity, leading to a process map or task analysis (see Chapter 17). In that case, your coding would focus less on personal characteristics and more on establishing the sequence of actions. For example:

- *Tasks.* What specific actions have to be successfully accomplished in order for the activity to proceed?

Then, for each task:

- *Resources.* What do people need to accomplish those tasks—whether tools, information, approval from others, etc.?
- *Mistakes/Corrections.* Are there errors, and if so, how do people recover from them?
- *Decision points.* When do choices need to be made between tasks?
- *Outcomes.* What are the possible outputs of the task?
- *Frequency.* How often does this task occur?
- *Importance.* How necessary is this task?
- *Risks.* What happens if there's failure along the way?
- *Purpose.* Why is this action here? How does it move the task toward its goal?
- *Cues.* What tells the person that it's time to perform this action?
- *Options.* What other actions are available at this point? How did this action get chosen?

In all cases, you can start your list of codes with the topics that drove the writing of the research plan, adding others that may have come up during debriefings and other meetings.

If you'd like to isolate the kinds of experiences people have in specific situations, you could code for different situations or experiences. Those situations or experiences will vary project by project.

For example, if your original goals were "to understand the mental models people use when researching insurance" and "to collect stories of how people's existing insurance failed them," and you observed that people felt intimidated by their insurance company, then your initial set of codes could include:

Bad Story: Episodes where the process of picking insurance or the process of filing an insurance claim has been difficult or frustrating. This can include mistaken expectations, disappointment, or even the insurer's outright failure to deliver on promises. If there are positive stories, these can be coded as "Good Story."

Intimidation: If the participant ever felt intimidated by his or her insurance company, scared by the process, or that the process was not under his or her control.

You could also work from the bottom up if you don't know where to start or have very broad questions about a location or an activity. In that case, you would group together items that seem like they belong together, and later work out the logic behind your groupings and give them more specific labels (see Figure 15.2). This activity is called *affinity clustering*.

However, analysis rarely starts with a genuinely blank slate, even if you are using affinity clustering. It's more likely that you have some organizational system at the back of your head that is prompting your choices. If you don't know where to begin, try beginning to organize your data following this simple system created by Christina Wasson and other researchers at the Doblin Group (see Chapter 9 for more on this organizational framework):

- **A**ctivities
- **E**nvironments
- **I**nteractions
- **O**bjects
- **U**sers

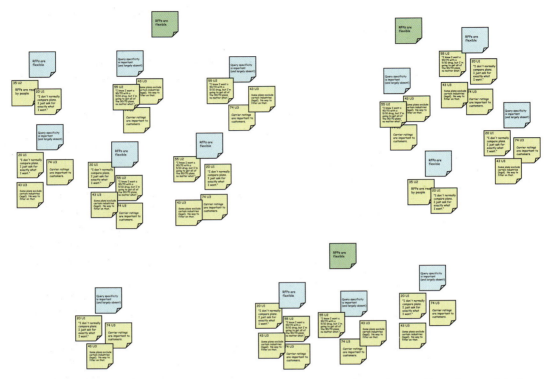

Figure 15.2 Use sticky notes to make different kinds of information visible from a distance. The yellow are data, the blue label single codes, and the green label groups of categories.

The results of following a basic scheme can generate a more project–specific set of codes for your actual interviews. For example, you might be designing a government service for issuing permits to street vendors. Through analyzing pilot interviews, you might discover that a street vending business involves activities such buying supplies, finding a spot, getting permission from the local authorities, cooking the food, managing money, etc. All of those could be used to prime your coding.

In any case, you will likely come up with ideas for new codes as you work. Feel free to include those in your analysis. If the initial codes you chose do not adequately describe the data, you should revisit them.

Here are some tips for getting the most useful
of the data.

- *Concentrate on the reasons people use* to explain what they do.
  Their actual actions are important, too, but the reasons behind
  them can be even more revealing.
- *Note people's terminology.* How does that terminology compare
  to how your clients or stakeholders describe the same situation? One of the most valuable outcomes of data analysis can
  be a better understanding of how to talk to people in their
  own preferred language.
- *Watch out for contradictions.* How people say they behave or
  what they say they want may not actually correspond to what
  they actually do or how they'll actually use a product.
- *Watch for situations where people change their mind.* Knowing that
  someone changed his or her mind can reveal a lot about what
  he or she values.
- *Look for stories about success or failure.* What tools or resources
  made the difference? More importantly, how do your participants themselves define what divides the two?
- *Treat words like "always" and "never" as red flags.* It's certainly
  possible that those statements are the final word. But it's
  equally possible that you can develop a more nuanced interpretation of the data by looking for examples that complicate
  those firm rules. Such rigid statements can mask more flexible
  options, responses, and workarounds in practice. You don't
  want to base design decisions on an illusory inflexibility.
- *Don't ignore personal judgments.* People often express belief systems
  through value judgments about other people and things. If a
  participant talks about a colleague who does not "respond to
  messages on time," the identity of that colleague isn't important.
  What's important is the importance placed on prompt
  responses—and how research participants define "prompt."

As you sort through your data, you will probably find some
photographs, video clips, quotations, or stories that seem particularly compelling or significant. Take note of them as you go. You
will want to have them handy later when you assemble your reports
(see Chapter 18 for more on reporting).

You will also probably begin to have a sense of the logic behind some of the groupings and the relationships between different groups. For example, does intimidation by the process of making an insurance claim relate to one's driving history? For the moment, don't get too focused on any of these ideas about the relationships between groups—what we might call tentative hypotheses. For now, your job is just to sort all the data. Write your ideas down, but just keep going with your overall sorting.

Coding Tools and Techniques

Before you start preparing your data, you will need to decide whether to start with the data on paper or in digital form. Both have advantages and disadvantages. In fact, for many projects you will want to move back and forth between the two in order to get the best of both worlds.

Coding with Paper

Many professional researchers transfer the snippets of data that seem most useful and relevant onto "stickies"—3M Post-it notes and their generic equivalents. Then the stickies are transferred to a wall or whiteboard, where they are physically moved into proximity with each other to make groups (see Figures 15.1, 15.2, and 15.11). The groups are then labeled with different colors or sizes of notes to make the difference between data and descriptive labels easily visible.

To code with sticky notes, begin by handwriting single quotes, paraphrases, or insights from the research onto the notes. Write the source of each quote on the note (you can use initials, or code numbers such as U01, U02, U10). You can also use different note colors to indicate the different participants, roles, or sites—but you may find that you run out of colors fast.

Get a group of people together in a room with a large open vertical space, such as a wall, a whiteboard, or a window (as in Figures 15.1 and 15.11). Add relevant stakeholders to the group such as developers or product managers if you can. By including these stakeholders in the analysis, you can build shared understandings and consensus during the process. You will likely need to ask people to block out a whole day, or more, for this activity—so you may not be able to achieve consistent participation from all the stakeholders. Aim for what is doable. This activity is best done with under ten people, especially if many of the people are unfamiliar with user experience research.

Ask everyone to start putting notes that belong together on the board in clusters. (You will likely need to kick off the process yourself, but once people see how simple it is they will likely join in.) As clusters form, give them labels written on notes of a different color, shape, or size. Tell the group to bring notes they are unsure about up for discussion.

As the number of clusters grows, you may see affinities between the clusters themselves. Move the groups together and label them with another size/shape/color of note. (It helps to have planned your labeling strategy ahead.) For example, in the car insurance research, a cluster titled "anger" and a cluster titled "disappointment" could be linked into a larger group called "negative reactions to disputes." Alternately, a single large cluster of notes should probably be broken down into smaller clusters, and with all the clusters relabeled in the right size/color/shape of note.

Sticky notes are, of course, not mandatory. But they are very convenient. The lightweight adhesive means that researchers can move the notes around easily. The small size forces writers to distill ideas and concepts down to a phrase or sentence. If stickies are not easily available, cut-up slips of paper with tape on them work almost as well.

Advantages. A three-week research project with more than ten participants can result in hundreds of snippets of data. Transforming those data into individual, tangible objects can help groups of people get a handle on the information they have and look for connections between the pieces. If you put the notes on a writeable surface, like a whiteboard, you can also use different colors of markers to indicate and label those connections, adding layers of meaning to your analysis. (See Figure 15.1 for an example of what this looks like in practice.)

As Dan Saffer writes, "The purpose of making everything visual and physical is to be able to draw connections across various pieces of data, and that can be hard to do unless you see the data, and can physically manipulate it." As well, writes Saffer, "Working while surrounded by images and quotes can lead to unexpected insights."

Spreading paper out on a wall makes it easier for different people to work on the data. Team members can work on different areas of simultaneously. It also helps people outside your team contribute to your work—from colleagues passing by who might have helpful ideas to external stakeholders who can get a better sense of the logic underlying your conclusions.

Disadvantages. You will need to get your digitized data onto those paper notes. You can use word processor templates to format text for printing to Post-its, but most often notes are handwritten—which is no small investment of time and effort. Nor can paper notes be easily shared—you will need to take high-resolution photographs of the final arrangement to archive them and share them online.

Rearranging them must also be done by hand. Unlike a spreadsheet, there are no cut-and-paste shortcuts. Once placed, large groups of stickies tend not to be moved until they are permanently removed to make more space. A sticky-based analysis can take over every available vertical surface like kudzu.

Digital

For many projects, especially with one or two researchers or solely text-based data, digital tools will speed up your process.

The simplest way to digitally sort data requires only a text editor. First, create a master document with all your codes. Then, go through the digitized transcripts/notes and cut and paste each statement under the code that best describes it. This case works much like the digital version of the Post-it notes—the codes serve as labels for groups of data snippets. If you do this with an online shared text editor, such as Google Docs, you can collaborate on the organizing the notes with colleagues working elsewhere.

Presentation software such as Keynote or PowerPoint is an easy way to collage text and images together (Figure 15.3). Each slide, or screen, represents a group. You can then print out the slides or project them in order to share them with a team.

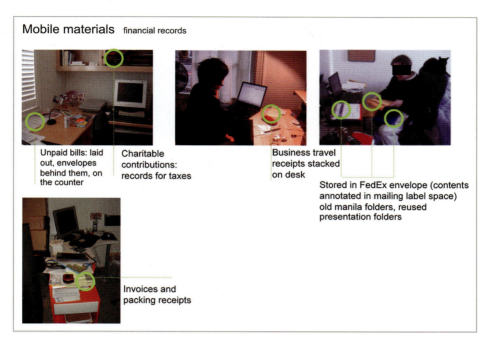

Figure 15.3 A PowerPoint slide showing images that have been clustered according their content. The cluster is labeled "financial records" and the green circles highlight why these images were organized together: they all show how people in the research study organize paper financial records when working outside the office.

However, you may want to have some more functionality for manipulating the data than text editors or presentation software possesses. As in card sorting, you may want to be able to see if the same snippet could belong to multiple groups, or perhaps be able to prioritize the most interesting quotes and observations.

That's where spreadsheets come in (see Figure 15.4). They can help you chop and recombine rows of data. Assign each snippet of data one row on the spreadsheet. The data go in the first column. Then, you fill the following columns with different codes—as many as you need. After that, you can use the spreadsheet functionality to sort rows by code, or you can manually move rows around to group them.

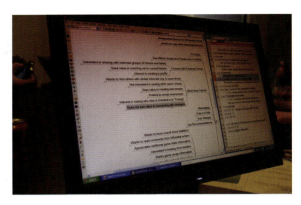

Figure 15.4 Qualitative analysis using a spreadsheet and diagramming software. The spreadsheet contains notes from the video, and the mind-mapping software organizes codes in families. In this case, a line of text from the video has been coded as "Does not see value in connecting with strangers," in the tentative code family "Meet new friends." Image courtesy of User Insight.

Advantages. Digital files are much quicker to manipulate and share than paper notes. They don't take up wall space, and you can quickly iterate on coding schemes.

Disadvantages. However, groups of two or more may find joint data analysis more difficult. Small computer screens do not leverage human peripheral vision and skill for visual pattern matching in the same way. However, some teams have recently started to solve this problem by projecting shared spreadsheets onto a wall. Each team member can edit the shared document, and the results are visible to everyone in the room.

Moreover, all the programs currently available have their disadvantages. It is difficult to work with photographs in a spreadsheet, but hard to draw connections between groups in presentation software.

At the time of writing this book, there are also numerous online "sticky note" applications that enable collaborative activities resembling those with Post-its. It's telling, though, that most design research companies tend not to use them, preferring the tactile qualities of paper. While there are promising experimental digital technologies for large touch screens, at the time of writing none of those technologies are available for commercial use.

Mixing Digital and Paper Coding

Most projects will utilize some combination of paper and digital tools. In order to free up wall space, you can take a high-resolution photograph of a wall of stickies, then type them into a spreadsheet. Alternately, typed quotations can be printed out onto stickies using a word processing template and printer-ready sticky pages for more convenient group work.

Revisit Your Codes and Groups

At this point, you will probably have lots of big groups of items. Now is the time to delve deeper into them and begin to look for internal petterns.

Maybe there are several clear subcategories; maybe the entire group consists of a time-based sequence of activities; maybe you can now identify some properties and dimensions. Some patterns will be expected and clear. Others will be surprising. There may be situations where you expected to find material to support an idea, but didn't. There may be extra items that, when you examine the groups more closely, don't fit where you thought.

Groups can be divided or combined. As with the case of the street vendor research, it may be appropriate to create several subgroups based on the properties and dimensions of each top-level code. But don't get overzealous. Although some social research studies are known to code hundreds of different kinds of events and utterances, you'll probably stick with under 50. Some related groups can probably be combined together, or at least moved in proximity so that you remember that they are related.

If a piece of data no longer fits in a group, move it somewhere more suitable. If the group itself no longer seems justified, break the group apart and redistribute the pieces into existing or new groups. Continue until you feel confident that your clusters show identifiable patterns, but don't get too obsessed about perfecting them. As Kim Goodwin writes in *Designing for the Digital Age*, "The diagram itself is not the point of the exercise; insight is".

Analysis can be contentious. Keeping distance between the analyst and the product is the key to a credible analysis. Even if you're deeply involved in the product, now is the time to take a neutral stance. Do not let expectations, hopes, or any conclusions you initially had affect your perception of the participants' statements and behavior.

Relate Groups into Frameworks

The ultimate purpose of the framing step is to reframe, to come up with a new story to tell about how the user might solve his or her problem or to come up with a new way of seeing the problem, which in turn will allow the team to come up with new solutions.

Sara L. Beckman and Michael Barry, in "Innovation as a Learning Process: Embedding Design Thinking"

Using your clusters to generate insights is not the final step of analysis. As Beckman and Barry imply, the goal of analysis is to see how those insights might create opportunities for change—to reframe how we see the world and our place in it.

The first step in reframing a situation is to relate the various groups and elements to each other—to understand the world as it is right now. There are a number of tools you can bring to bear on your grouped data, depending on what your questions are and what the data suggest to you. In fact, it's likely that you've been using some of these tools all along during coding in order to understand the internal logic of your code groups. Here's a short list of ways to make frameworks:

- *Taxonomies.* A taxonomy is a hierarchical organization. In this type of analysis, a taxonomy essentially brings together all your existing categories and subcategories. Taxonomies are especially useful in translating your analysis into frameworks useful for interface and information design. Card sorting (Chapter 8) is another way of making taxonomies. Taxonomies are often represented as branching tree diagrams, as seen in Figure 15.5.
- *Maps.* Placing data into spatial representations serves a variety of purposes. Designing mobile- or location-based services may involve where activities typically happen. For digital appliance design, for example, you may want to represent the location of important resources—such as power outlets. And product strategy decisions may rely on the emotional associations with familiar places. Figure 15.6 shows a typical customer's pathway through a café to help situate an educational display explaining the energy consumption of the various café appliances.

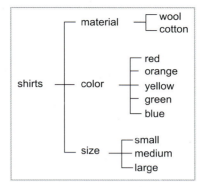

Figure 15.5 Example taxonomy diagram.

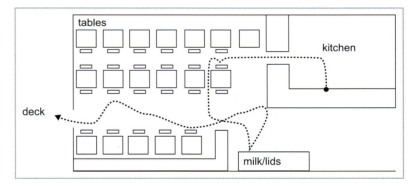

Figure 15.6 Example spatial map.

- *Timelines.* Chronological order is the basis for many research outcomes, such as day-in-the-life scenarios, task analysis, and process maps (see Chapter 17 for more on these). Timelines can help you track and present sequences of activities over a day, a month, or even decades. This is particularly important if you are interested in activities that follow cyclical schedules, such as annual tax preparation, or phenomena that change slowly, such as consumer attitudes towards recycling.

  Timelines can often immediately show you a number of interesting patterns that would be otherwise difficult to observe. For example, a diary study (Figure 15.7) could map the amount of times "advanced search options are mentioned" (one of the coding categories) against time in order to see whether people mention the advanced options more as they use the product.

- *Flowcharts.* Maybe the best way to describe a sequence of events isn't as a linear, chronological process. Maybe you have noticed that a process can go one way or another at an important decision points. You can capture that in a flowchart (Figure 15.8), a classic representation of branching action pathways used widely in engineering. The flowchart can help you work out different scenarios or use cases that the design of a system or service must take into account.

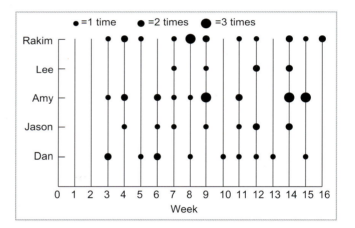

Figure 15.7 Example timeline.

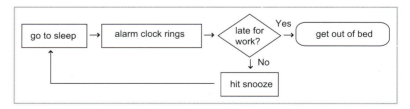

Figure 15.8 Example flowchart.

- *Spectrums.* You may have attitudes, behaviors, or values that seem in opposition. For example, perhaps insurance brokers intimidate some of the people in your study, while others treat insurance brokers as helpful assistants. Oppositions are rarely binary—that is, people rarely lie at the extremes. But two opposites create a spectrum along which people can vary. Naming the spectrum allows you to identify an important way in which people differ: attitude toward brokers. Typically, as in Figure 15.9, the spectrum is laid out horizontally, and each participant is given a specific point on the line.
- *Two-by-two matrixes.* A two-by-two matrix uses two spectrums as the axes for a grid (see Figure 15.10). Then research elements (people, objects, activities, products, etc.) can plotted on both. The resulting distribution of items around the four quadrants can tell you a lot. Is one quadrant overfull? One nearly empty? Does it seem like there is a relationship between an item's place on one axis and its place on the other? This can help you make comparisons between different categories or start thinking about cause-and-effect relationships. Sometimes, examples may fill all the quadrants of the matrix. Alternately, an empty space or an unusually crowded area in the matrix can prompt you to think more about the relationships between the axes.

The Importance of Stories

We will go into more detail on research outcomes in Chapter 17

As you work more and more with codes, you may find yourself losing sight of the people and stories who have motivated your work thus far. Making frameworks is, inevitably, a process of abstraction. But don't lose sight of the stories!

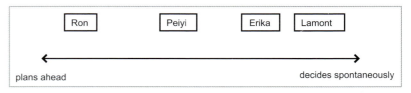

Figure 15.9 Example spectrum.

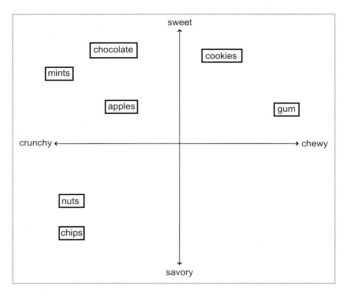

Figure 15.10 Example matrix.

In fact, a successful analysis has two parts: the framework, or model, and the representations of people and their behavior that support it. Without the stories and quotations as evidence, your framework will be less credible and less compelling. Without the framework, your stories and quotations may be compelling, but your audience may find it hard to draw out actionable recommendations.

Stories are a powerful way to understand the intricacies of people's experiences. They provide details about people's assumptions, the sequences in which they do things, how they solve problems (and what problems they have), and their opinions. Moreover, they can illuminate and clarify many choices in product development all at once.

Take Jim's story, from the same study of work outside the office.

When I first started freelancing, I worked from home and I had a desktop and I couldn't leave. I spent four or five months working with a company and I knew I had to be at my desk. They would call me, and I needed to be at home. I went nutty. You have to live in your house night and day for months on end. It's lonely.

For the report, this story could have been summarized as, "Jim works at cafés because he gets lonely at home." But that's a rather shallow description of a complex situation. After reading this story, however, you can imagine yourself in Jim's shoes—stuck at home, waiting for a phone call. You can empathize with his situation, and perhaps you might start thinking up ways to help Jim feel less lonely. Based on this story, you might also prioritize some of your product ideas over others. That's the role of stories—they prompt *informed* empathy and invention.

If you have been noting compelling stories and quotations along the way and keeping them linked back to your codes through documenting your analytic process, you will have a storehouse of examples—video, photographs, and quotations—to draw upon.

You will know you have completed research analysis when you can tell a compelling, relevant, evidence-based story to support each of your recommendations and conclusions. If you cannot, go back to the data and keep looking. If you can't find any story or quotation to support your recommendation, you may need to discard it as unsupported by your data. But more likely, there is a good story that you have simply overlooked.

Typical Analysis Plans

Many projects do not require and will not significantly benefit from the most rigorous analytic process possible. Your project will probably not require every component of the process we just described. Based on the amount of time and money available, your familiarity with the domain, and the stakes resting on the project's success, you will make choices that result in a more or less intensive analysis. There are many different possible configurations of techniques and timelines, but for the purposes of this book we'll outline two sample plans to give you a sense of the options available. The lightweight process, like that described below, will work fine for many projects. However, some projects, such as long-term strategic research or medical device design, may demand something resembling the heavyweight plan.

Figure 15.11 The results of data analysis. Two researchers initially transcribed interview notes to Post-its, one using pink and the other yellow. They then jointly clustered their notes, using blue Post-its for labels. The two researchers took two weeks to analyze 33 interviews. Image courtesy of the Centre for User Experience Research, KU Leuven (University of Leuven).

Lightweight Data Analysis

If you have short videos from a diary study, schedule time to review them and make summary notes during the collection period.

In lightweight data analysis, the notes taken during data collection (e.g., during/right after the interview, or as diary entries come in) are the main input to the analysis. You may go back to watch the video of someone especially interesting, or to verify or clarify an observation from the notes, but there is no time to review the recordings comprehensively.

In this case, make sure to take good notes at interviews. If you have the time, type up everything you think is interesting from those notes, or handwrite onto Post-its. If not, you will be working directly from your notes. If time is extra tight, skip the data preparation and coding stages. You will then draw conclusions based only on your notes, scribbled interpretations, and your discussions with team members.

For example, let's say you are helping a development team make a tiny, but high-quality, printer designed for people who work in cafés or other public places. Their schedule is tight: They need to select a single form factor from multiple concepts and they only have a week to do it.

First, you schedule three focus group series in one day, using a "friends and family" recruitment strategy to find people who work in cafés at least two days a week. On the day of the series, you set up a fake café table and chairs in a conference room to set the mood. The focus groups start with discussion about where and how the participants work, and then the participants physically demonstrate, using the café table and foam prototypes from the industrial designers, where and how they might set up the printers. At the end, participants fill out "debriefing sheets" ranking the prototypes and the features. Your assistant videotapes the sessions and takes photographs, along with detailed notes. On the drive home, you and your assistant note questions and conclusions from the groups.

Over the next week, you combine all the rankings into a unified set of recommendations for prototypes and features. You re-read your notes and discuss your conclusions with the rest of the team. Finally, you use quotations from the notes and photographs of the session to illustrate the final report that explains the results of the groups. You might try to turn the video into a highlights clip—but more likely you will only have time to paste a few stills into a presentation.

This is an extreme case of a lightweight analysis. You can complete a report this quickly because your questions are few and straightforward: provide guidance to select between concept designs.

In a lightweight process, by the time you start manipulating your data, you should already have an initial ordering scheme for the data and plans for making deliverables. For example, if you know that you will need to present compelling stories about user pain points, be on the lookout from the beginning for quotations, photographs, and video clips that will support that outcome.

A good rule of thumb for planning lightweight analysis is that two people can analyze and write the report for 8–10 interviews in two weeks.

When Do I Do It?

A lightweight process is appropriate when one or more of the following applies:

- The protocol remains uniform across most or all participants.
- The outcome is strongly structured, as with a prioritized feature list.
- The reporting format is predictable, as with a standard usability report.

Table 15.1 A Typical Lightweight Data Analysis Schedule

Timing	Activity
$t - 2$ weeks	Process notes and summaries. Begin data analysis.
$t - 1$ weeks	Finish analyzing data and make documentation.
t	Distribute documentation.

Heavyweight Data Analysis

Heavyweight data analysis follows the same basic steps, but in a more thorough way. Researchers take more time to prepare their data—including getting transcriptions—collaboratively code it, and revisit their conclusions before moving into frameworks.

A good rule of thumb for heavyweight analysis is that it will take four weeks for three researchers to thoroughly analyze and report the data from, for example, a diary study and onsite visit with 12–16 participants. In our experience, it is rare to have more than three researchers working on data analysis at a time, so consider these limits when budgeting and scheduling.

When Do I Do It?

As a rule of thumb you will likely need a more rigorous process if you have more participants than your team can easily name and describe off the top of their heads. You should also consider a more heavyweight process if you are analyzing more than three research activities simultaneously. For example, a study that involves an interview, a diary study, and then a follow-up home visit is a good candidate for a more organized and thorough approach. Open-ended questions with wide-ranging discussions, unfamiliar subject domains, cross-region, cross-cultural, and longitudinal comparisons—all of those should prompt you to invest more time and resources in analysis. Warning bells should also go off if you are trying to apply a lightweight process with the exact format of your final research deliverables still unsettled. If the final goal of the deliverables is in doubt, then a substantial amount of analytic work will likely go into settling it.

Table 15.2 A Typical Heavyweight Data Analysis Schedule

Timing	Activity
$t - 4$ weeks	Start preparing data as you research, if possible. Send off any recordings you have for transcription. Print out photos and post any maps/collages. Review videos and make notes on Post-its or digitize.
$t - 3$ weeks	Begin analysis in earnest. Start coding, sketching, and making notes. Start a rough draft of your deliverables, and start thinking about how your analysis will fit in.
$t - 1$ weeks	Complete results analysis. Complete deliverables.
t	Present and distribute documentation.

Conclusion

However intensive your process, you will know your analysis is complete when you feel that you are no longer consistently generating new ideas, insights, and questions. This is what many analysts call "saturation." Another signal is that you can tell coherent, compelling stories about the data. Of course, in most projects, you are likely to still want to do more analysis even as the project schedule forces you to deliver your final report!

And that's not a bad thing. Your report should accurately reflect what you saw but suggest new directions for more research or design. The process of making abstractions inevitably bleeds into the process of designing and delivering research outcomes. In the end, you don't just want to keep your insights to yourself—you also want to share them with other people and ask new questions to drive further research.

Does wooga's story illustrate that you don't need qualitative user research? As you might guess, we don't think so. Split testing and other automated methods are great for identifying problems to solve ("Users keep abandoning our game on the first level") and for evaluating proposed solutions ("Should we make it easier or add more monsters?"). But if you don't actually talk to users between those two steps, you will never understand why the problem occurred in the first place. (Maybe they just got confused and couldn't find the tutorial.) Not knowing this can lead your team down a development rabbit hole, where you test a bunch of different design changes and not one of them is a clear winner. It can also lead a team to optimize one small detail of the product at a time, while the overall user experience becomes less coherent and clear. The same thing can happen when a company relies exclusively on its customer support channel to understand users. The company learns specifically what problems people are having or what features they wish for, but not the underlying reasons.

It is likely that wooga could improve its games using metrics alone because its business thrived on novelty: users played a game until they got tired of it, and then moved on to others. Thus, wooga could experiment with various kinds of novelty to see which was most effective at keeping players engaged for a little while longer. But if you want to build a product or service that inspires long-term loyalty, that engages users more deeply over time, you need to gather usage data and customer feedback and conduct user research to learn *why* customers are doing what they're doing.

Unfortunately, this is not easy at many companies. Typically, one person or group collects and analyzes site usage metrics, other people support customers and collect their feedback, and yet others do user research. As a user researcher, it is your job to understand the metrics and feedback that are available to you, and then integrate that information into your research program. This chapter will explain how.

Usage Data

> It's like a finger pointing away to the moon. Don't concentrate on the finger, or you will miss all the heavenly glory.
> —Bruce Lee, *Enter the Dragon*

If you think back to the iterative development spiral discussed in Chapter 3, the beginning of the cycle was examination: defining problems with your product or service (or problems out in the world that could be solved by something new) and defining the group of people those problems affect. Usage data, also known as *metrics* or *analytics,* can provide detailed answers to these questions. Unlike all the other forms of user data described in this book, site metrics let you observe the behaviors of all of your users, not just a representative sample. That's a lot of data, of course, with more coming in every second. To keep from getting overwhelmed, you should begin by learning what measurements your company collects and which of these your stakeholders view as important. (In business-speak, the important ones are known as *key performance indicators,* or KPIs.)

Planning for Usage Data Analysis

When you talk to stakeholders during the planning phases of your research, be sure to ask some questions about usage data. Some important things to find out include the following:

- *What data are collected, for which parts of the user experience.*
  The most detailed data are likely to be available for websites, because there are lots of inexpensive and easy-to-use web analytics platforms. As of this writing, the best-known platform is the free service Google Analytics. Data are also commonly gathered for mobile apps, but they are typically less comprehensive. Beyond websites and apps, data collection varies widely. Some retailers have extensive purchase data for all their stores and may even know where in the stores people go. The makers of some media devices, such as gaming consoles, have installed telemetry in their devices that records who plays what and when and sends that information back to the company.

> If your product or service is not digital or not online, your best source of ongoing usage data is probably your customers' questions and feedback. See the "Customer Feedback" section later in this chapter for pointers on how to use that information.

- *Which measurements are critical for the organization and for specific stakeholders.* This will tell you something about the organization's mission. If the organization is a retailer, it will probably most care about sales figures. If it's a web publisher that makes

In addition to or instead of log file analysis, many websites and apps collect usage data through page-tagging and hosted analytics services such as Google Analytics (Figure 16.2.). When you sign up for one of these services, the service provides unique tracking codes that is included in the code of a web site's pages and in or in the code of an app. Whenever a user requests a page or performs an action tracked by one of these codes, a message is sent to the hosting service, which logs that action and saves the information on its servers. Page tagging has several advantages: It provides more accurate counts of page views and can record some user activity that log files can't capture, such as views of Flash movies and partial form completions. It also lets you get usage data easily if you don't have access to the server and its log files (for example, when the site is hosted on a server owned by another company).

Like log analysis software, page-tagging services provide charts, graphs, and other visualizations of your usage data to make them easier to understand and interpret. These services can also make it easy to conduct split testing on your site (see the next section).

Web Analytics Software and Services

This section assumes that your company has some technology in place for gathering and viewing usage data: log file analysis software, a page-tagging service, or both. If you don't, or your current technology isn't capturing enough of the data you need to measure, there are many choices available for adding analytics to your site or app, including quite a few free options (see Figure 16.2). Search the web for "web analytics software" to get a current list.

If your company does have an analytics platform but you're not sure what it offers, go through the tutorials provided with the software package or service and familiarize yourself with the data it gathers and how they are presented to you.

Figure 16.2 Google Analytics is a free web service that uses page-tagging technology to measure user activity on websites and mobile apps. Its default dashboard view displays a variety of frequently watched, site-wide metrics.

Types of Metrics

When you first look a web analytics dashboard, it is easy to be impressed by the statistics at your fingertips and the real-time view of your users' activities. The data are certainly interesting, but they are rarely useful out of the box. To make the best use of analytics data, it is necessary to compare the current data to what previously happened and to what you want to have happen.

Most websites and apps are designed to enable specific activities and experiences. Some might be fairly simple, such as watching, and perhaps rating, a video. Others can be complex and involve multiple steps, such as specifying, ordering, and paying for a custom-built bicycle and then finding a store where to pick it up. Chances are, the metrics of greatest interest are the ones that tell you how many users do these activities, how often, and how much revenue (or awareness, or some other payoff) you gain as a result.

lose consistency, overall because there is no unifying strategy. This is a problem that can't be diagnosed through measurement alone.

Laura Klein, principal of the user experience consultancy Users Know, has worked with many Internet startups and learned from experience not to "try to measure your way out of a problem," as she wrote in her 2011 case study, "UX, Design and Food on the Table." Klein notes that startups and other new ventures are especially prone to missing the mounting complexity of their products because they move fast and add features in rapid succession. One company she worked with, a menu planning service called Food on the Table, reached a frustrating point where "they would look at a metric, spot a problem, come up with an idea for how to fix it, release a change, and test it. But the needle wasn't moving."

After some quick general conversations with users, they realized that the new user activation process had become too complex, and users were "simply getting lost." Klein and the company stepped back and did some observations of users going through activation, making sure to cover all the variations that were being split tested at the time. (Since Food on the Table is a website, this could also be done very quickly using remote testing. See Chapter 11 for more on remote usability, such as described in Chapter 11.)

The tests revealed a number of technical problems that could be fixed right away, such as a page that was loading too slowly and causing users to make mistakes by clicking a button over and over. They also found some problems that needed to be fixed through a redesign. After some wireframing and prototype testing with users, they split tested the redesigned activation flow against the existing flow. Klein reports, "After running for about 6 weeks and a few thousand people, we had our statistically significant answer: a 77% increase in the number of new users who were making it all the way through activation." (The full case study can be found at www.startuplessonslearned.com/2011/01/case-study-ux-design-and-food-on-table.html.)

Collecting More Useful Metrics

In this section, we have discussed three main uses of usage metrics: locating suspected problems, evaluating a new design, and tracking progress toward broader business or organizational goals. As you work with usage data in any of these capacities, though, you should also ask yourself whether the analytics tools you use provide enough of the data you really need. For example, say you are working to increase the length of time users spend watching videos in your app, but you do not have access to data about when and how often they used video controls such as play and pause. Or imagine you want to determine how satisfied users are with a new feature of your website that lets users pick up their online purchases at a store, but your company isn't collecting data from the stores about how frequently they need to help customers using the service.

To a certain extent you can work around missing data, but if you can identify information that would provide valuable insight into improving the organization's performance, you should get involved in improving its data collection programs. This may mean working with a development team to add more measurement points to a web site, adopting new analytics tools, customizing reports that the tools generate, or even instituting new quantitative feedback mechanisms.

Collecting the right usage data is a critical part of being a user-centered organization. Cyd Harrell, VP of UX Research at the consultancy Bolt Peters, has found that "companies that have good analytics are especially able to act upon qualitative feedback." All told, the better you can articulate the benefits of better analytics, the more effective both your qualitative research and your data analysis will be.

Usage Data Ethics

People get the willies when you start talking about tracking them. This is natural. No one likes being followed, much less by salesmen or the boss. When people feel they're being followed, you lose their trust, and when you've lost their trust, you've lost their business.

Thus, it's critical to create and follow a strict user privacy policy and to tell your users that you're doing so. Here are some guidelines:

- *Keep confidentiality.* Never link people's identities to their behavior in a way that is not directly beneficial to them when prioritizing features, writing specifications, or comparing proposed solutions to a problem. At times like these, teams were unlikely to pull that rigorously researched, carefully-drafted research report off the shelf, re-read it, and figure out what it meant for them right now. Instead, the information should be such that key stakeholders could remember the key points from the research and put it to use.

To meet these needs, researchers developed different types of representations to supplement traditional written summaries, including personas, scenarios, task analysis diagrams, and experience models. Today, most research deliverables include both a written summary component, describing techniques and main findings, as well as one or more of these representations. Of course, you will likely always need to present a summary of your work, and sometimes a written report is sufficient on its own. This is typically the case for focused research, such as a usability study or a survey. This chapter will help you determine which, if any, of the most widely used types of research insight representations might make your insights easier to act on and more valuable to stakeholders.

*Chapter 18 describes how to organize these types of reports, as well as how to present research.
More information on all of these techniques, as well as links to more examples, are available on this book's website: www.mkp.com/observing-the-user-experience.*

Choosing the Right Deliverables

As we discussed in Chapter 4, when you make a research plan, you determine what questions your stakeholders need to answer and what research activities will best meet these needs. But it is equally important to specify what form the completed research will take. Research findings are essentially a story you tell about your users, their lives, and how your product or service may fit in. The "genre" of the story depends on what your stakeholders most need to know. It may be character-driven, all about *who* certain users are and what motivates them. Or it may be an action saga, with minimal description of the characters but lots of detailed play-by-play. The goal is for your team to remember the story, the problems or opportunities it reveals, and get to work addressing it.

Table 17.1 summarizes the major types of research deliverables and the questions they address most effectively.

Table 17.1 Selecting Appropriate Research Deliverable

Organizing Principle	Key Questions	
People who use (or could use) the product or service	Who are our users? How do different groups of people use our service? How do our customers differ from our competitors' customers? Which users can best help us grow the business? How might we build relationships with customers over time?	Personas
Situations in which the product or service is used	What are the most common reasons people use our product? Which features of our service do our users value most and least? When is our product most and least helpful to users?	Personas, scenarios
Activities people do that involve the product or service	What do users find difficult to do with our product and what is easy for them? Which features do they enjoy most and least? Do new and experienced users do certain things differently? What would users like to do with the product that they cannot do?	Scenarios, task analysis diagrams or process maps, usability evaluation (see Chapter 11)
Processes or systems that include the product or service	Aside from using our service, what else do people do to accomplish what our service helps them do? How do users integrate our product with other products they use for the same purpose or at the same time? What other products or services are required for ours to work?	Scenarios, process maps, experience models

Dan Brown's Communicating Design*: Developing Web Site Documentation for Design and Planning is an invaluable, easy-to-use guide to representing and sharing research insights. Though aimed at website development, it's applicable to many design domains.*

Representing People: Personas

What does your company most need to know about users themselves? In general, two lessons from research constantly need repeating: (1) the users you actually have are different from those you imagined having and (2) your users are not all the same. Personas, correctly developed and used, serve as ever-present reminders of those lessons. Personas are most valuable to have before you start developing anything: a product or service, a redesign, a new feature set, a new identity. They can also help in introducing an existing product or service to a new market.

Interaction designer Alan Cooper first popularized user personas for product design and development in his 1998 book on software design, *The Inmates are Running the Asylum*. As described in 2005 by designer Kim Goodwin, "A persona is a user archetype you can use to help guide decisions about product features, navigation, interactions, and even visual design." This "archetype" is not a real person, but a synthesis of facts and observations about real users that leads to a memorable character. By creating these characters and taking them through scenarios, you and your stakeholders can gain a sense of familiarity and empathy with your users.

Few companies these days develop anything without identifying a target market, and many also create market segmentations. But just because you can identify a market segment doesn't mean you know how to design for the people in it. Good design comes from understanding your users' behaviors. Personas, unlike market segment, represent goals and behavior patterns, not demographic attributes or job responsibilities.

Personas can assist design in serving as a shared reference point. Over time, they can even function as an efficient shorthand. Rather than describing a feature for "performance-focused, expert system administrators at large firms," you can say "it's for Leonard," and marketing, engineering, and design will know the qualities of these users and how they will use the feature. "Leonard" represents a shared understanding of a class of user experience issues that are important to the success of the product.

Opinions about the value of personas vary across the user experience community. Some practitioners and companies love them and put them at the center of their development process; others prefer to simply present stories of actual users. Many companies have successfully used personas to align the efforts of multiple departments around improving the user experience. However, the success of personas depends largely on how well their creators can ground them in data and integrate them into an organizational culture. You will know that your personas are effective if you hear stakeholders referring to them by name in the course of productive design and strategy discussions.

How to Do It

Research for Personas

Internal interviews. Begin by learning what your company knows and believes about its existing users and target audience by conducting a few short one-on-one interviews with stakeholders and experts. If your product has an established client base, talk to the people who work directly with it—salespeople, support staff, market researchers, technical sales consultants, trainers, and the like. If the company is trying to expand the audience for the product or enter a new market, talk with the people responsible for that effort. Interview these people about their personal experiences with users and customers, and also about meaningful ways in which users differ. What distinct types of users have they observed, if any? What impacts do they see various user types having on their work or on the business? (See Chapter 6 for more about interviewing.)

Research with participants. Most of the data you draw upon to create personas should come from qualitative research with individual users or potential users. Structure the interviews or field visits around people's entire experience with your product or service, not around specific tasks. In recruiting participants, you should represent the entire range of your target user base. While interviewing, keep a list of good quotations, problems, and anecdotes. (See Chapter 9 for more about field visits.)

Market research review. Sales and marketing often have detailed demographic profiles and market research that can give you big-picture breakdowns of your audience. If you have a market segmentation, especially one that draws upon usage data or other behavioral data, it's worth consulting. But don't just make personas that reinforce market segments. (See Chapter 14 for how to utilize existing sources of information about users.)

Usage data and customer feedback review. Consult customer forums or community sites (both those hosted by your company and others) and support systems for frequent user questions and problems, which can provide supporting data for making this information part of your personas. (See Chapter 16 for usage data and customer feedback.)

A First Pass: Provisional Personas

In some cases, such as a start-up venture, stakeholders want to start development before there is time to create fully researched personas. In this situation, consider creating *provisional personas*: draft versions meant to document the team's current assumptions about its audience.

Making provisional personas is a collective activity. Key members from each facet of the development of the product need to participate because everyone is going to bring different information and a different perspective to the persona. This method requires the participation of a good group moderator since it'll be important that everyone in the discussion has a chance to contribute. Be sure to include people with direct experience of the customers. Invite five to eight people. More than that, and meetings tend to get unwieldy; fewer, and the personas produced may not be useful to the whole team. The group should start by coming up with one or two primary personas as per the process outlined in this chapter, fleshing them out until they seem relatively complete. Add other personas built on attributes that haven't been used until everyone feels that all the important user groups have been described.

You may see conflicting personas emerging: sales may be selling to a group of people entirely different from those who contact support; market research may have constructed a persona different from the one business development is using. This is typical and fine. Capture all the personas, and don't get into fights about which one is more "right." The point of this is to make the group's assumptions explicit, so that you can start doing research to confirm or contradict them. Provisional personas are not a substitute for ones based on solid data.

Creating Personas

Analyze the Data

Start by extracting common threads from the information you have collected. What do the people have in common? Are there problems that seem to crop up frequently? Are there shared aspirations?

Then make a list of the important ways in which users vary. Some of these can be expressed as ranges: for example, users may range in their views of social media services from those who refuse to use them to those who are positively addicted. Other attributes are best defined as noncontinuous values. (See Chapter 15 for more on analyzing qualitative data and representing ranges.)

For example, there are many ways to characterize different groups of users of business analytics software. The authors of the "Leonard" persona chose three different attribute ranges that they believed most affected people's behavior with their product:

- Frequency of use
- Intensity of use
- Business size

You could express those in a diagram like the one shown in Figure 17.1.

Look for patterns in your interviews and usage data and consider what aspects of your users tend to drive their goals and needs. First, find attributes that matter to the selection and use of your product. Then identify those that distinguish different subsets of users from each other. This can be a tricky analysis, since there are

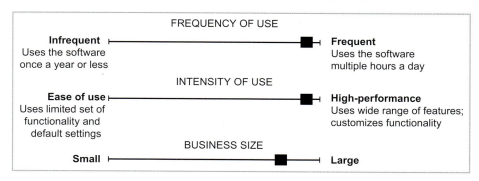

Figure 17.1 Expressing user attributes as ranges.

The Essential Persona Lifecycle, *by Tamara Adlin and John Pruitt, is an excellent in-depth guide to all aspects of creating and using personas.*

so many factors to keep in mind. It can help to brainstorm different points of variation in your data and list them on a whiteboard, so that you can see all of them at once.

At this point, you should begin to see relationships between different attributes and patterns in the way that different research participants exemplify them.

Prioritize Attributes and Patterns

From your data, you will likely see a number of patterns that could turn into personas. Adlin and Pruitt suggest this handy set of factors to help decide which attributes are most important to you:

- *Frequency of use.* The types of people who use your product more often should usually take precedence over those who use it only rarely.
- *Size of market.* How large are the groups of people represented by each pattern?
- *Historic or potential revenue.* How financially important are each of those groups?
- *Strategic importance.* Who are you trying to reach? Current customers? Your competitors' customers? Power users? Are you trying to move into a new market or make more of an existing audience?
- *"The magic question."* As Adlin and Pruitt ask, who does your team need to make "ridiculously happy" for the product to be considered a success?

If you have the time, review these factors with stakeholder experts outside of the research team. If you don't have the time, use market research reviews and usage data reports to guide an initial cut.

Define Your Personas

Once you've decided which attributes to include and how each attribute varies across your user population, it's time to draw upon the personal details and anecdotes you observed in your research to synthesize realistic people from the clusters of attributes. Don't be afraid to go with your gut in creating the personas and telling their stories. Later on, you can share the personas with customer-facing people in your organization and tweak them based on the feedback you receive.

In some cases, adding details is as straightforward as creating a specific "fact" that falls within an attribute range you've defined. So, for example:

40-something
Female
Married, with children
Small business manager

becomes

Doris Washington
45 years old
Married to Steve
Has two kids: Greg, 17, and André, 13
Manages three convenience stores

Don't create wacky idiosyncrasies. Strong features tend to distract from the important attributes. So if the base audience is typical teenagers, don't make your persona an Olympic-class ice skater. If there are attributes that all personas have in equal measure, you don't need to describe them in each persona. You need enough detail for realistic, memorable personas, but don't load them up with information that isn't relevant.

Flesh out the rest of the attributes, using materials gathered from your interviews. In this example, you may decide to base Doris on someone you met who works for someone else, is confident in her knowledge of her domain, and has direct (though not ultimate) responsibility for her business. You may want to write a little story about it, incorporating details drawn from similar users.

The stores are all owned by Sammy, whom she's been working for since she was in her late 20s. Over the years, she's gone from working as a clerk to being Sammy's most trusted employee, to the point that they both agree that she knows how the stores run better than he does.

- Income and purchasing power. If your product is for personal use, what is your users' household income? What economic possibilities and constraints do they face as individuals and as within families? If for business use, what is the company's purchasing power? What are the constraints on their industry?
- Location. Are your users urban, suburban, or rural? Do they come from certain regions, a certain country, or are they spread out all over the world?
- Company size. If your product or service is for a business, how big is the company? How much money does it make? Where does it operate?

Technological

Whether your product or service is online or delivered solely in the physical world, certain devices, networks, and other technologies likely play a role in the user's experience. For each important technology, consider:

- Hardware ownership and access. Do they own the equipment or device? Is it their personal equipment or is it shared? Is it owned by their employer? How much control over hardware do they have?
- Connectivity. What connections do they have to the Internet or other data and communications services? How do they connect, and how often? How expensive is it to transmit data?
- Experience. How have they been using any relevant technologies? How comfortable are they with them? What experiences might have shaped your users' attitudes toward them?

Environment

The environment in which people use your product can affect the way that they perceive it. The complexity of your description will depend on the nature of your product, but you should always have some description of where people will use it.

- Use location. Do they use your product or service at home? At work? While moving about in a city? While traveling or commuting?
- Use time. Are they going to be using the product during work or during their off hours? Will they be using it first thing in the morning, when they've just returned from the opera, or after the day's last milking?
- Tool context. What other things do they use or do at the same time as they're using your product? How important are their tools? How does your product fit in with them? How often are they interrupted while using it? Who uses it with them?
- Competition. What products or services are competing for your users' attention? What is the nature of the competition? What benefits do competing products offer?

Lifestyle/Psychographic

Besides the way they use your product, people have interests, ideas, and values. When creating a persona, consider the lives of your users outside the immediate sphere of use, and define who they are as people, not just as customers or clients.

- Cultural. Particularly in global or cross-cultural research (see Chapter 13), you can't assume that your research stakeholders share users' languages, religious commitments, definitions of emotional and physical health, family responsibilities, etc. This can be a significant problem when those cultural practices strongly influence the use of the product. If you suspect that your stakeholders do not share these values and practices, personas can help you weave them into product development decisions.
- Values and attitudes. What do your customers value as individuals? What is important in their lives? Thrift? Speed? Fun? Comfort? What has their experience been with services like yours?
- Media. How do they learn about new products, services, and ideas? What magazines do they read? What TV programs do they watch? What websites do they go to most often?

- Activities. What else do your users do in their lives? What are their important commitments? What do they most enjoy doing?

Roles

People play different roles in life, and they interact with other people playing roles. The informal roles people play are often more important than their official titles or listed responsibilities.

- Titles. Even if the people involved don't have official titles, they will likely have some specific name for what they do—such as "teacher," "parent," "fan." What are the official titles of groups or people involved, if anything—and what do they call themselves?
- Responsibilities. What are job responsibilities of each group? What do they get rewarded for (both formally and informally)? How?
- Training. How did they learn to use the product? Did they educate themselves or receive training? Where and how does continuing learning take place, if at all?
- Power. What is their responsibility for the product? Do they choose it, or are they assigned to it? Do they pay for it, or does someone else sign the checks? What happens if something goes wrong?
- Relationships. Whom do they consult when making a choice? Whom do they work with? What will those people need?

Using Personas

The process of creating personas can be useful by itself. It creates a set of documents that communicate a shared understanding of users, their perspectives, and their problems. However, to get the full benefit from the process, the personas need to remain in use. They should be documented, shared, updated, and used in everyday product development.

Prioritize

Not all personas are equally important, so the group should prioritize them. Business needs may dictate the prioritization, in which case the priorities will resemble the target market order. It can also be dictated by the needs of design. An audience may be important for the success of the product, but its needs may not be as pressing as those of another group. By focusing on the needs of the more challenging group, you're satisfying both their needs and those of the larger market. Porsche's auto design philosophy, for example, is to surpass the expectations of luxury performance car geeks. Since most of the people who buy Porsches aren't luxury performance car geeks, this ensures that most of us will be really impressed and satisfied if we buy a Porsche, and the auto geeks, whose opinions are important for Porsche's public image, keep recommending the cars.

For the banking example, this means that the needs of someone like Doris, who has three busy stores to run, will probably subsume the needs of Clarence, who has only one. Clarence may have other niche needs, but most of the same functionality that works for Doris will also serve him well. It may be that there are more Clarences out there than Dorises, so Clarence may be the target market for sales and marketing. But for the purposes of design, serving Doris's needs satisfies them both.

From a development perspective, prioritizing also creates a consistent way of deciding between competing solutions. When you have two ways of resolving a problem, always choosing the one that favors your primary persona ensures coherency.

Document

Teaching the whole team about the personas and how to use them is the best way to ensure that the work remains useful in the long run. Not all the people using a persona will have been part of the group that developed it, and even those who were will need reminders.

Persona creation may produce large, involved character studies, but the final product should be short, easily readable, and focused on the specific needs of the project. Since a persona is a concise communication tool, you should first determine the audience for your personas so that you can present them appropriately. Different groups have different needs: identity design deals with branding, engineering with technical constraints, business development with partnerships and competitors, and interaction design with the functionality and organization of features. The document you create must reflect the needs and concerns of its audience.

A basic persona contains the following elements:

- The name of the persona
- A description of the persona's needs and aspirations for the product or service
- The persona's immediate goals in using that product or service
- His or her abilities and experience
- His or her perspective on the task and the product

A portrait is the final element. An image that represents a real person adds a human touch to the persona and makes it seem more "real" than a textual description. The process of finding just the right picture can crystallize many of the decisions that you've made. Moreover, picking a picture is fun and can be a good way to wrap up a long brainstorming session.

Find a source of stock photos (you can get one from a stock photo website such as Gettyimages.com). Walk through them together until you find one that says "Doris!" and then make that the face of Doris.

Share

The most challenging part of sharing personas is communicating them in a succinct yet useful way.

Summarize the personas in an easily usable form. Design firm Hot Studio creates a one-page "snapshot" version of their personas, which they laminate and give to everyone on the development team. That way the personas remain easily available. The lamination makes them more durable, easier to find in a stack of papers, and less likely to get thrown out by accident. It's also easy to turn those snapshots into large posters for the office.

An introduction meeting is a good second step. Describe the creation process to the whole team when you introduce the

Images can be emotionally charged and highly controversial. Consider whether an image might trigger negative reactions before getting too invested in any one image.

Never use pictures or names of people you know when creating a persona. Or, for that matter, never base a persona on someone you know personally. It's distracting and restrictive when it's time to change the persona ("But my friend Charlie doesn't *own* a car!").

personas. Explaining the reasoning behind this specific set of personas and walking through the key characteristics of each persona will make them more credible and reinforce their function as useful abstractions. Then leave the physical documentation behind after the meeting as a reference.

Many product teams create posters with the picture and key attributes of the user and tack them to walls. Others give the personas their own cube, where everything that relates to a persona (and consequently to the project) is displayed. This reinforces that there are real people who depend on you every day.

A persona keeper position can be useful for centralizing the information. This person is present during the persona creation process and is responsible for keeping them updated. He or she also serves as a resource for interpreting personas to the development team ("What would Jeff think about a mobile download option?").

Develop with Personas

It's easy to go through the process of developing a set of personas and then never use them again. In order for the personas to remain useful, they need to be actively used. Most immediately, they can serve as bases for recruiting screeners (though they're too specific to use entirely: you generally want more variety than a roomful of Leonards). More important, you should encourage the development staff to talk using personas during meetings and to think about how features work for the various personas.

One of the easiest ways to get people thinking in terms of personas is to use the persona names in your documentation and specs. For example, when describing a new feature, discuss how it would help Jeff or Doris and how you think they would approach it.

Use personas to evaluate your competitors. Use a competitor's product and try to determine which persona it's creating for. Try to identify how your personas would use it. Whom would the sites be attractive to? Why? Where do they succeed? Where do they fail?

In the future, he and Keith would like to expand KJ Build to include several permanent employees and be able to build two houses at once, each supervising a job site.

Tasks

Both Jeff and KJ Build have accounts with Great Lakes Bank, and Jeff uses Great Lakes' website to check on his personal account and pay bills.

His typical tasks include:

- Paying salaries to contractors
- Paying for materials
- Collecting income from clients, often in installments
- At tax time, collecting all of his invoices and expenditures to give to the accountant
- Keeping track of deductible expenses
- Paying various small-business fees (licenses, bonds, etc.)
- Paying business taxes (for both Ann Arbor and Dexter, Michigan)

He often uses credit cards for short-term revolving credit.

Current Problems

Money comes in "feast or famine" waves to KJ, occasionally causing cash flow problems, as materials and hourly subcontractors have to be paid before KJ receives the final contract payment.

Sometimes Jeff has to let the bills pile up because he's too busy working on the houses, and this further complicates the payment process.

It takes a lot of time to organize all the paperwork for tax time.

When a client is late with a payment, some credit card and utility bills don't get paid.

Desires

Would like to be able to pay his materials and subcontractor bills more easily and keep track of which contracts are outstanding.

Wants to reduce the amount of paper (and numbers) he needs to keep track of.

Would like to be able to share financial information more easily with Keith.

Would like to better predict upcoming cash shortfalls.

Values

Prefers to work with small family-run businesses like his rather than giant conglomerates. He is worried about how giant companies, especially Facebook, use personal information.

Persona *Non Grata?*

Personas, though a popular research deliverable, are controversial.

On one side: enthusiasts. For enthusiasts, personas are indispensable. They help teams conceptualize differences between user groups and prioritize the development of functionality for each group. They underwrite empathy-driven design. They are vivid illustrations of research insights that might otherwise languish in unread reports. They are a simple way to unify teams.

On the other side: the doubters. For doubters, personas are unhelpful. They promise to bring nuance, but actually oversimplify complex behaviors into worn clichés. They encourage design teams to make decisions based on personal interpretations of fictional characters, rather than just asking real users. Often, design teams forget about personas after an initial flurry of interest.

We don't take a stand in this fight. But we do believe that personas are tricky to get right and that many well-intentioned attempts at using personas fall short. Here are some tips for avoiding common pitfalls and making the most of personas.

Build Characters, Not Stereotypes

While personas are fictional characters, they should be sympathetic enough to unite a team in designing for them. Associating your personas with clichés and stereotypes undercuts this function.

For example, it may seem like a good idea to give your personas catchy names like "Jeff Toolbelt" or "Dutiful Doris." It's true that these types of names *are* evocative and memorable. But they also invoke people's preexisting associations with certain phrases and images. Since you're not a mind reader, you can't predict what those associations will be. For all you know, the associations might be negative, disrupting any empathy you are trying to build. And worse, since people will have different associations, your catchy names might actually create disagreement instead of unifying people.

In the same way, try to find photographs that look like ordinary people going about their lives, not models in generic stock-photo poses. It's better to use an illustration than a photograph that looks fake. That's why we gave Jeff and Doris names that sound like real people and gave Jeff a photograph that looks like a snapshot taken by a friend.

Connect Personas to Action

One reason teams abandon personas is because they don't necessarily trigger immediate design responses. "It's too bad that Jeff lets the bills pile up," your clients might say. "But what are we supposed to do about it?"

An easy first step is to rewrite your personas around needs. Instead of phrasing your story as "Jeff is late paying his bills," write: "Jeff needs help paying his bills on time."

A second step is to use personas to guide team design brainstorms. How many ideas can you come up with to help Jeff pay his bills using your product or service?

Finally, you can link together personas with design scenarios to start organizing and prioritizing that brainstormed functionality. Figure 17.11 shows how a combination of a persona, design scenario, and task analysis can ground feature development in a representation of current needs and behavior. However, be careful not to introduce design requirements or proposed functionality into the persona itself. The purpose of the persona is to inspire multiple design concepts, not document one or two.

Don't Let Personas Stand Alone

One of the difficulties with personas is that they represent individual people. That works great if the individual portrait really is the best way to understand a situation. But design projects are often more complicated than that, especially if you are addressing long-term processes or products used across complex organizations (e.g., a hospital records system).

Projects need multiple perspectives and personas are insufficient by themselves to convey a range of design insights. Personas should be used alongside scenarios, experience models, task analyses, and traditional written reports, not instead of them.

In the end, personas are a convenient, data-driven composites of factors that need to be taken into account when developing a product, and personifying a set of ideas and values is an old technique for communicating complex sets of ideas. Tapping into people's ability to remember stories goes all the way back to the morals taught by Aesop and legends passed on over the campfire. By creating a cast of characters and engaging them in a representative set of stories, you create not only an effective tool for communicating an understanding of the audience, but one that helps you reach that understanding in the first place.

Representing Situations: Scenarios

Humans are wired to think and communicate through stories and to understand the world as interpersonal relationships tied together in a narrative. *Scenarios* are stories that describe how a person behaves or thinks about an activity or a situation. They explain what the person is doing along with his or her motivations, expectations, and attitudes. They even sketch in some details of time and place. Like all stories, scenarios have specific settings and characters, as well as plots with distinct beginnings, middles, and ends.

As stories, scenarios communicate the subtleties of using your product, helping stakeholders see the product in context of people's lives. A table of statistics or an abstract description would not reveal relationships nearly as well.

When to Use Scenarios

Different types of scenarios are used throughout design projects to describe current as well as future interactions between people, products, and services. Scenarios describing the current state of affairs are often called *context* or *problem* scenarios, since they are intended to show how the status quo could be improved. Those that envision proposals for change are called *design* scenarios.

Context scenarios are most actively used in the early stages of design. Each context scenario takes the perspective of one type of user. By vividly illustrating problems or gaps in existing practices, they prompt teams to imagine possible solutions. Later on, they are often paired with design scenarios to demonstrate how a design response might improve upon the current state of affairs.

Design scenarios come into play throughout design and development. In early brainstorming, design scenarios can trigger discussion and feedback about possible concepts. With early concepts in hand, design scenarios can help teams work through their possible implications. Early design scenarios can also serve as interview prompts to elicit feedback from potential users. Later, when concepts are more refined, design scenarios help unite teams. They guide consistent feature implementation and help resolve differences through providing a shared vision for the project direction.

How to Make Scenarios

Scenarios are created by storytelling, either with personas you created or by drawing directly from stories you heard in your research.

Decide What Stories to Tell

If you had all the time in the world, you could turn every story about how someone could use your product into a scenario. But you don't have unlimited time, and your research clients certainly don't have unlimited attention. To make scenarios useful, you must pare down a large collection of stories to only the most relevant.

Scenarios are based on goals and the activities that people take to achieve them. If you have existing personas, you will likely have already established those goals and activities. These will form the

If you've worked in software development, you may be familiar with use cases. *Use cases are also stories about system interactions. Use cases focus on how systems function in response to user action. Scenarios focus on how users experience that functionality. In practice, the two can blur together, especially in Agile software development. The job of a researcher, however, is to keep the focus on human experiences, no matter what you call the output.*

basis for scenarios. If you are not using personas, return to your research analysis and list the most pressing goals for each target audience. Walk through all the ways your research shows that people are meeting—or trying to meet—those needs and goals. As you go, take good notes on the stories you're using—you'll need them to support your scenario writing later.

Our process for deciding which activities to include in scenarios follows that of Alan Cooper in *The Inmates Are Running the Asylum*. For each major goal of research participants or personas:

- Which of these activities are *most frequently* taken to achieve it?
- Which of these activities, though perhaps not frequent, are *necessary* to achieve it?
- Which frequent and/or necessary activities take place as part of *a single sequence*?

After this, you will likely have clusters of frequent and necessary activities that support each critical goal and take place together. Those clusters of activities form the basis of scenarios. (This may be a good time to use some of the analysis techniques described in Chapter 15.)

For example, one of Doris the store manager's goals is "keeping track of each store's performance." That includes the daily activity of "making a report," which in itself requires:

- Logging into the website
- Copying the day's totals into a spreadsheet
- Totaling the daily and weekly performance
- Comparing each store's performance to last year

With this set of activities in hand, we can write a short scenario called "Generate a report."

Writing a Scenario

Now that you have pared down your collection of scenarios to a short list, go back to your research plan and consider *how* to tell stories about how people use your product or service. Scenarios are based on people's perspectives. Anything that the user does not perceive should not be part of a scenario, especially a context scenario. Scenarios are not meant to list every possible interaction. To inform design work, they just have to describe the most important user actions and system responses at a fairly high level.

With your list of activities and goals in hand, return to situations you recall from your encounters with potential users. If you are using personas, imagine how they would react to them. How would Doris handle that situation? What would she do? How would she think about it? How would Jeff, the building contractor, handle it? Also consider how people's goals, needs, and desires might *change* through interaction with a product or service. If you are not using personas, look to the reactions of your different participants.

Introduce constraints one at a time and see how the story changes. Say that Doris can't get the day's totals automatically input into the site. What will she do? What would happen if she couldn't get them into her spreadsheet? When will she stop using the product because it's too cumbersome or too complicated? Role play with the persona to determine which values drive Doris's decision making and what is most important to her.

If you are deeply engaged with the lives of your participants, you should be able to imagine alternate constraints, settings, and tools. While telling these stories, note any major departures from the stories you gathered in research. At some point, you will need to validate any assumptions you've made by walking through the resulting problem scenarios with users. That way, you can be sure that any stories you have invented describe things they would actually do.

A typical context scenario often has a "day in the life" feel, describing a series of tasks over the course of a few hours or a day. A context scenario should situate those activities within the flow and rhythms of life, explaining how people engage with a product or service in relation to other concerns. It shouldn't feel abstract or cold; instead, it should feel organically driven by people's values and experiences. Here's a brief version of a "Generate a report" scenario written for Doris, the accountant:

Scenarios should stay high-level and not dwell on interface elements or system implementation. It's more important to illustrate the whole arc of a story than to explain everything. In a problem

Introducing imagined elements that could alter the way the story plays out is the beginning of moving the scenario from context to design. Depending on your goals for the project, you may want to avoid proposing specific design solutions.

At 5 PM Doris goes home. She makes dinner and eats with Steve and the kids before touching her computer. While she cares about her job, her family is her first priority. As is her routine, she sits down to do the books at 8 PM. She checks the day's register totals online, then runs the day's totals through a spreadsheet to see how each of the stores is doing. Then she calculates their performance over the week and compares it to the same time last year. She chooses the "quick report" option and sends the result to Sammy. She knows that he's not going to read it, but she also knows that he wants to see it in his inbox every morning. At 8:20, she's finished her report with just enough time to watch her favorite television show with Steve before going to bed.

Design Scenarios

Design scenarios attempt to envision a technical solution without worrying about the specifics. They gloss over many details in order to evoke the feeling of how a technology could change the world. It's doubtful many people are ever going to watch TV on their all-digital kitchen counter top, as they do in many design scenario visions, but that image evokes the idea that displays could be anywhere, which is what the scenario makers are trying to do. If you are working with a design scenario, try to create the ideal outcome for each of your personas. In a perfect world, how would everything work for them? In what situations would your service anticipate their wishes? How would it help them make decisions? Aside from the persona, what other people would play roles in the story? What other tools or services might be involved? What would be the best outcome If you're stuck, pretend that there are no technical or financial constraints. As Alan Cooper suggests, "Pretend it's magic."

Scenario Checklist

Here's a useful list of scenario components drawn from the work of computer scientist John Carroll. If you're having trouble writing a scenario, use these components to get you started. If you've finished a writing a scenario, check it against this list to see if you're missing anything.

Actors. Who is involved? Scenarios and personas are often written from the perspective of individual people. But actors can also include groups and organizations.

Setting. What is the context? This usually means the physical environment. Depending on the subject matter, it could also include the time of day and the date. It might also include past events if they're important to the situation. Doris's scenario might look very different if the company was facing a tax audit.

Actions. What is the observable behavior of the actors? How do they affect the world around them?

Events. What happens in response to actions? What are the reactions of other people, organizations, products, services, etc.?

Evaluation. How do actors interpret the events? How do they make decisions, and what rationales do they offer for their reactions? Scenarios are accounts of goal-directed activity, so you need to have some description of actor's goals. But you shouldn't neglect other factors that might affect action, such as aspirations, past experiences, and values. In this case, it's important to know that Doris really wants to spend her evenings with her family, not fiddling with spreadsheets. As well, people don't always act logically. Scenarios should account for irrational and even self-defeating decisions if the research warrants it.

Plot. How does the sequence of actions and events add up to a specific outcome? How do the actors expect the situation to play out? How do actors know when they have achieved their goals—or not? Do they get what they want? Doris gets a happy ending—she finishes her report in time to spend time with her husband. We can imagine a less happy story in which she struggles with the spreadsheet program and/or doesn't have enough information to complete her task. As a result, she doesn't achieve what she wants. She either does not finish the report or has less time with her family that evening.

scenario, this means avoiding the kind of specificity more usually found in a task analysis (see the next section); in a design scenario, this means avoiding fussy technical details. Scenarios, especially context scenarios, should spark the imagination, not end discussion.

Communicating Scenarios

The easiest and fastest way to communicate context scenarios is in writing, just as we did with the scenario we wrote for Doris. And

Communicating design scenarios often requires more investment in illustrating the product or service in question, since the role of a design scenario is to make the case for certain design decisions.

much of the time, text—accompanied by a few images of important people (such as Doris) and important places (such as her home office)—is all you need, especially for early problem scenarios. If you need to get more specific, the easiest solution is to take or find photographs that represent key moments in the scenario, then use phrases from the scenario text as captions.

Using Scenarios

Walk through your scenarios with the team to identify pain points in your current customer experience or potential difficulties with a new feature or flow you are designing. If walking through a scenario prompts a proposal for a solution, write a new scenario that describes what happens with the proposed solution in place.

Representing Activities and Processes

Designing tools often means understanding not just people's goals, but more specifically the *exact* steps they take to accomplish them. How critical is a task to accomplishing the goal? How often is it performed? What is the order of actions? What are the tools involved? Where do problems typically occur? Where is there flexibility in the process? What decisions must be made, and who makes them? What kinds of resources, informational and otherwise, do people need and use at various points in the process?

One way to answer these questions is by doing a *task analysis*. Task analysis answers those questions by breaking down a single activity into a structured sequence of steps. Early on in a design process, the results should make it clear where current tools do not support—or poorly support—important steps to accomplish people's goals. Later, the results can help develop and prioritize the features and content your product will provide to support those processes. There are many different outcomes for task analyses. We'll talk about one of the most common: flowcharts.

But task analyses detail activities from the perspective of one user. What if you need to map an activity holistically, from the perspective of an organization trying to support it? You would need to follow not just the actions taken by one person, but also the actions of all the other actors in the situation, some unknown to the user. The swimlane diagram is one of the most common ways to map processes that may involve many different actors, and we'll describe the construction of swimlane diagrams below.

How to Do It: Task Analysis

Personas portray characters, and scenarios tell stories. In contrast, a task analysis details *sequences* of actions taken by an individual person. After outlining how to adapt qualitative research methods such as interviews and field visits for this technique, we'll discuss three different ways to communicate the results: the *diagram*, the *grid*, and the *alignment diagram*.

When Task Analysis Is Appropriate

Traditional task analysis is best used when you already know what problem you're trying to solve but you don't know how people are solving it right now. It can help diagnose potential usability pain points, establish system dependencies, or identify new product development opportunities in areas where people lack the tools they need to accomplish their goals. Task analysis is also best used for goal-directed, well-bounded procedures, such as buying furniture. Activities with no clear criteria for success and no defined sequences of steps are not likely to be amenable to decomposition. Doing a task analysis of falling in love, for example, would get you no usable data (and miss the point, besides).

Task analysis generally falls in the examination phase of a spiral development process or the requirements gathering phase of a waterfall process. It requires that you know what the task is and, roughly, who your audience is. Although task analysis can be done when there's already a solution of some sort under consideration, teams should ideally complete task analysis before investing a lot of design and development effort. Knowing exactly how a task is accomplished is likely to revise your initial assumptions about features and functionality—and undoing decisions made on the basis of those assumptions can be expensive.

So if you've already decided that you're going to be selling furniture online, but you haven't yet built the ordering system, now would be a good time to do a task analysis of how shoppers pick out a sofa. Where a persona system might portray the different kinds of shoppers and the company's sales support staff, and scenarios might examine how and where shoppers consider a sofa purchase, the task analysis would concentrate solely on the steps they take to pick out and pay for a sofa.

How to Do It

Like the other research outcomes, a task analysis typically relies on qualitative methods such as interviews and field visits. However, the usefulness of any task analysis depends on carefully targeting research activities and questions.

For people who like precision, task analysis can be tempting, perhaps too tempting. You can break any task into infinitely small pieces, spending enormous amounts of your time and your clients' time in the process. Using stakeholder interviews (described in Chapter 4), decide how detailed your task analysis needs to be to support the needs of design and development through the next major product development cycle. It can be helpful to create a template or example ahead of time to help you figure out when you've provided enough detail. *Then stop.*

Studying Tasks

Task analysis usually involves a combination of interviews and observation at field sites. Interviews alone can lend themselves to retrospective mythmaking—participants will want to tell you how the task is *supposed* to be done, how they think it *ought* to be done... anything but how they *actually* do their job. It goes without saying that interviewing managers about how employees do their jobs is also not likely to give you accurate information about the resources people need, the troubles they encounter, and the reasoning behind their decisions. And it is that very information, of course, that makes for a truly useful task analysis.

However, participant observation (see Chapter 9) and interviews can give you deep insights into how people actually accomplish their goals and where they fall short. Depending on the job at hand, use the apprentice model to ask questions during the activity. Alternately, if questions are not appropriate during the task, you can schedule interviews for right afterward. However, retrospective interviews, for all the reasons mentioned above, are not as desirable.

Questions at these interviews should be geared toward understanding how the participant performs the task at hand.

- What do they see as the options at any given point?
- What are the tools available? What tools are needed but *not* available?
- How do they choose one over the other?
- Where do they change their minds?
- How variable is the process?
- Where do they make mistakes? What are common mistakes?
- What causes the mistakes, and how are they corrected?
- What are the inputs to the process? The outputs?
- What is the frequency and importance of the tasks they perform?
- What are the risks of failure?

Here's a snippet of the notes from a session observing an interior designer picking out a sofa (for an online furniture-buying tool).

"I get out my catalogs. I go to [manufacturer A] first, unless it's for a waiting room, then I go to [manufacturer B]. I have a big shelf of catalogs. Recently, I've been getting on the Internet, but I get better results on the catalogs. Hard to find things. Each website is so different, it takes time to find your way through the website."

Gets four catalogs: A, B, C, D. Gets the [B] catalog. Looks in index for "couch," flips to couch section.

"I usually find a couple of options and weigh cost, availability, delivery, if there's something similar I've seen. You can't tell color from pictures, and they're often slow about getting fabric swatches. I talk to sales reps on the phone and try to get as complete a picture as I can. Some of the companies we don't do so much business with will come in, and also try to sell me other stuff."

Marks several sofas with small notes, in preparation to call the manufacturer about fabric/color availability.

"I know I can get this one pretty fast since I've gotten a couple before, but I'm not sure if they can offer it in the fabric we want. I'll make a note to ask about it. Sometimes they can make it out of a different fabric even if they don't officially offer it in that, but it depends."

"I total it all up. This is what we need, and this is what it w cost, and this how long it'll take to get it made, assuming they have the fabric in stock. I'll fill out purchase requisitions, going through the catalog and picking out the options I want. I put together a description for the client. Project explanation, list of things to buy, schedules, and so on. I may not have time to explain it all to the client, so I have to make sure the write up is clear enough."

"Different vendors offer different warranties. I don't shop for warranties, though, I shop for matches and manufacturing time. Cost is important, too, but once the client has signed off on a budget, that limits your options right there."

Prepares to call vendor.

Analyzing the Data

Once you've gotten some data, the next step is analysis. The two main ways to understand tasks—*task decomposition* and *hierarchical task analysis* (HTA)—are complementary, so you will likely do a little of both. The former describes the inputs, outputs, and triggers for the actions in a task, while the latter arranges the actions into a coherent flow.

Break the Task Apart (Task Decomposition)

Task decomposition is the process of breaking the task into its component actions. This is easier said than done. If someone is operating a control panel with a bunch of buttons and dials, then every time he or she presses a button or reads a dial, it's an action. But when that same person is shopping for a new car, the decomposition is more difficult since the steps taken—the choices, the capitulations, the comparisons—aren't nearly as obvious. In such situations, encourage the participant to speak all of his or her thoughts aloud and prompt him or her for explanations of specific actions.

Keep the end goal in mind. This will help you pick out the most relevant aspects of each action. If you have a specific tool or solution in mind, you can emphasize one or the other in your decomposition. Sometimes you can work backward from the solution you have in mind to the problem people are facing to see if one matches the other.

Describe each action (see Table 17.3). There are lots of ways to scribe actions, but some common ones include:

> *Purpose.* Why is this action here? How does it move the task toward its goal?
> *Triggers.* What tells the person that it's time to perform this action?

- *Resources.* What objects does the action operate on? What resources (tools, information, people) are required?
- *Method.* What is the action?
- *Options.* What other actions are available at this point? How did this action get chosen?

While you're describing the actions, do some error projection. Ask what would happen if the action weren't done or if there were an error. If there are enough actions with interesting error conditions or if the consequences of errors are particularly serious, you can even make errors a separate category you use to describe each action.

For each action, provide answers in as many of these categories as you can. Often the process of describing an action will create questions and inspire new interpretation, so it can be useful to walk through the decomposition a couple of times to make sure that it's consistent and thorough.

Table 17.3 Excerpt from decomposition of furniture-buying

Action Name	Purpose	Cues	Objects	Method	Options
List requirements	Clarify choice categories		Word template: size (h, w, l), color, budget, style notes	Talk to client	
Get available catalogs	List available options		Catalogs, requirements list	Compare options in catalogs with requirements	
Set order for catalog perusal	Start with best known/best chance manufacturers	Knowledge of vendor's options	Catalogs, requirements list	Flip through catalogs, comparing options with requirements	Go to A first, unless designing a waiting room, then B
Mark items in catalog	Get primary candidates		Catalogs, requirements list	Visual inspection and comparison to list	

Table 17.3 Excerpt from decomposition of furniture-buying—cont'd

Action Name	Purpose	Cues	Objects	Method	Options
Mark items that need follow-up	Separate items for further investigation	When it's not clear whether all options are available for a specific item	Catalogs, marked items	Visual inspection and comparison to list	
Investigate marked items	Complete list of available options based on requirements	List of items for further investigation	Catalogs, list of items needing follow-up	Call reps and wait for responses if necessary	
Total options	Make final list for client	All follow-up is completed	Completed options template, budget template, requirements list	Fill out budget template with options and costs	

Resource or time constraints can make it impractical to do this level of task decomposition. In those situations, you can use a more informal version of this process. Instead of going all the way to the atomic task and filling out all the facets, concentrate on larger ideas and use only the facets that you think are most important. After several interviews, you may be able to list basic tasks and tentatively order them into a sequence. As you interview more people, move the pieces of paper to fit your new information. This process is not as thorough, but it is a lot faster.

Prepare for decomposition by determining the categories that are likely going to be useful ahead of time and then creating spreadsheets that you fill out as you observe. That way, you know what information you have about each action and what else you need. However, in situations where there are many actions in every task or steps come fast and furious, this technique can be pretty daunting. In such situations, it may be better to use the spreadsheet to determine useful categories for note taking, then fill in the spreadsheet later from your notes.

Put It Back Together (Hierarchical Task Analysis)

"Hierarchical task analysis" sounds impressive, doesn't it? Actually, it's just a fancy way of saying "one thing leads to another." An HTA maps out the relationships between steps by putting them into groups, then indicating how the individual steps and groups are connected. The final result often resembles a flowchart. It will detail the sequence of goals, the choices that are made, and the consequences of actions.

It's possible to do this kind of analysis quickly as part of a debriefing session after a research activity. Standing in front of an erasable surface, start talking through what you saw people doing, sketching goals as boxes and the relationships between them as directional arrows (see Figure 17.3).

1. Start with a goal. This can be the person's ultimate goal ("Furnish the house"), but abstract end goals often require analysis that's too involved for straightforward task analysis. You may want to start with something very concrete ("Get list of available couches") and work down from there.
2. Determine the subgoals for that goal. Subgoals are all the things that have to happen before the main goal can be met. For example, if your goal is to get a list of available couches, you may need to get a list of couches from the catalogs and a list of couches that are not listed (or unavailable) from furniture company representatives. You should rarely have more than three or four subgoals for every goal. If you do, you may want to create a couple of intermediate goals that will subsume several of the intermediate tasks.
3. Determine how those actions have to be arranged and create a plan for how they flow together. This includes determining which ones must follow which others, which are optional, which can be swapped out for each other, and so forth. When goals don't have a natural flow, pick one that seems to work and adjust it later if it turns out to be awkward.
4. Repeat the decomposition with each goal and subgoal until you are down to individual actions.

When you're doing HTA more formally, the procedure is nearly identical, except that you should base it directly on evidence from your data analysis using a form of bottom–up affinity clustering (see Chapter 15 for mote).

1. Start by ordering and clustering actions into groups that are all associated with the same result. Actions that occur in parallel are optional or are alternatives for each other and should be labeled as such.
2. Label the clusters with the results. These are the subgoals.
3. Order and cluster the subgoals in terms of what ends *they* achieve.

4. Label these clusters. These are the goals.
5. Repeat until all the actions have been clustered and all the clusters have been ordered and labeled.
6. Create a diagram by organizing the subgoal clusters underneath the goal clusters and linking these with arrows that show how goals are related to their subgoals.

The end result will be a diagram in the familiar "boxes and arrows" style, where a single goal has been turned into a goal tree, with all the subcomponents of every goal beneath it and linked to it, creating a procedure for accomplishing that goal (Figure 17.3).

The order in which these two techniques are used depends on your needs. If you're mostly interested in how the components of a task fit together (for example, if you're looking for where a tool can optimize a task's speed), then start with HTA and flesh out key details with decomposition. If you're interested in making a tool that fits with existing practice, then start with decomposition as a way to understand inputs and outputs, and then quickly sketch out the progress of the task in hierarchical form.

Representing Tasks

Task analysis can be time consuming, but it can be extremely effective at disentangling complex interactions as a way to develop roadmaps for design. It reveals not just breakdowns, inefficiencies, and redundancies, but also opportunities. That's a lot of information produced by a single method. None of the following representations will communicate everything about your analysis; in order to support design and strategic decision making you may need to use more than one to get different findings across.

Flowchart Diagrams

Flowchart-style "boxes and arrows" diagrams (see Figure 17.3) work especially well as overviews of complex activities with multiple decision points and outcomes. Visually emphasizing steps that are difficult, lead to failure, or provoke mistakes can help target action at trouble spots while contextualizing the problems' origins and consequences.

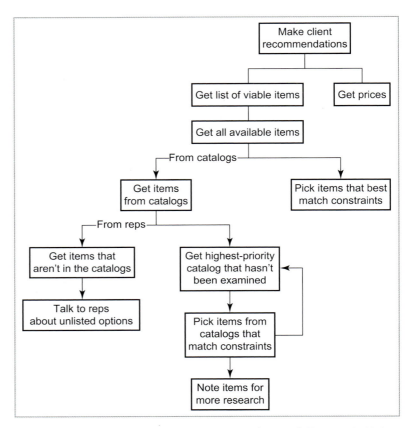

Figure 17.3 Excerpt of sofa-buying analysis diagram (segment). Flowchart highlights relationship of goals to activities.

Checking Your Logic

Flowchart–style task analyses need to follow a rigorous internal logic. If one step does not logically lead to another, or the chart is missing a crucial intermediate step, the analysis can fall apart. There are two ways to check for completeness.

The easiest way, of course, is to ask! Walk through the flow–chart with a few people who know the task to make sure that it matches their experience and that the sequences, tasks, and goals are familiar to them from their experience.

The second way is a little more complex, but doesn't require the effort of tracking down participants. It involves testing the internal logic yourself. For each box on your diagram, ask yourself whether:

- The boxes in the chain *above* a given box in the hierarchy answer the question "Why do I _____?" where _____ is what's written in the box. Using the example in Figure 17.3, when asking, "Why do I talk to reps about unlisted options?" the diagram answers, "Because you need to know what items are available that aren't in the catalog so that you can make a complete list of all available items to make a list of viable options for the client recommendation."
- Boxes below a given box answer the question, "How do I _____?" Asking the question, "How do I get items from a catalog?" is answered by, "Find the highest priority catalog that hasn't been examined and pick items from it while noting down which ones require more research."

The process is a little finicky, but if you can answer *both* of the above questions for every box, and you don't come up with any more boxes, you can be reasonably sure your diagram is complete.

See B. Kirwan and L. K. Ainsworth's *A Guide to Task Analysis* for more information on this technique.

Grids

Flowchart-style diagrams are good at giving an overview of a task. But the format makes it difficult to include any explanation of each individual step beyond its name and outcome. Important dimensions such as a task's purpose, cues, and objects can get lost.

Enter the *task analysis grid*, first introduced by designer Todd Zaki Warfel. Grids emphasize the linear nature of tasks by representing each step as a box on a horizontal line. Below each step, however, there is now a stack of information about its purpose, triggers, resources, etc. Figure 17.4 shows the analysis of sofa-buying represented as a grid.

Because they contain so much detail, grids work best as large paper printouts or projections. That way, groups of people can see and discuss the details and the big picture at the same time.

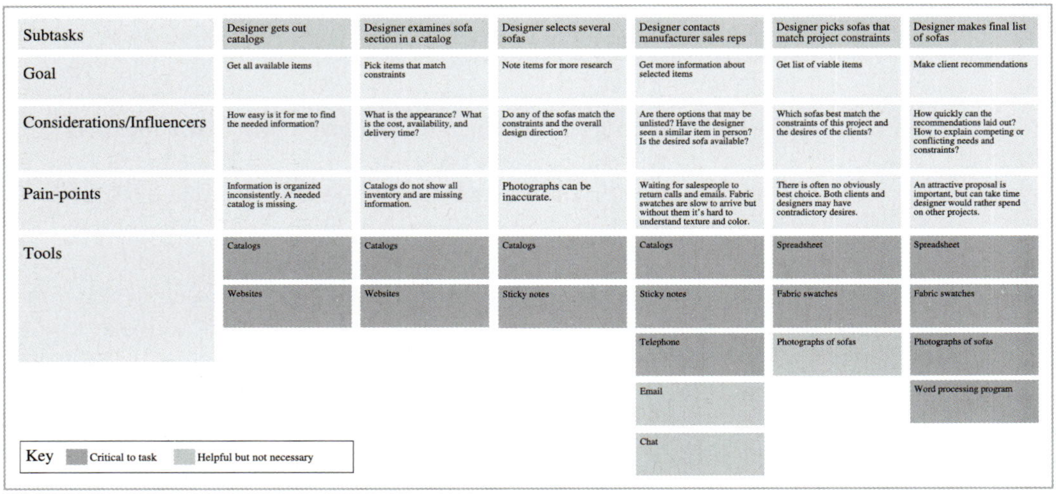

Subtasks	Designer gets out catalogs	Designer examines sofa section in a catalog	Designer selects several sofas	Designer contacts manufacturer sales reps	Designer picks sofas that match project constraints	Designer makes final list of sofas
Goal	Get all available items	Pick items that match constraints	Note items for more research	Get more information about selected items	Get list of viable items	Make client recommendations
Considerations/Influencers	How easy is it for me to find the needed information?	What is the appearance? What is the cost, availability, and delivery time?	Do any of the sofas match the constraints and the overall design direction?	Are there options that may be unlisted? Have the designer seen a similar item in person? Is the desired sofa available?	Which sofas best match the constraints of this project and the desires of the clients?	How quickly can the recommendations laid out? How to explain competing or conflicting needs and constraints?
Pain-points	Information is organized inconsistently. A needed catalog is missing.	Catalogs do not show all inventory and are missing information.	Photographs can be inaccurate.	Waiting for salespeople to return calls and emails. Fabric swatches are slow to arrive but without them it's hard to understand texture and color.	There is often no obviously best choice. Both clients and designers may have contradictory desires.	An attractive proposal is important, but can take time designer would rather spend on other projects.
Tools	Catalogs	Catalogs	Catalogs	Catalogs	Spreadsheet	Spreadsheet
	Websites	Websites	Sticky notes	Sticky notes	Fabric swatches	Fabric swatches
				Telephone	Photographs of sofas	Photographs of sofas
				Email		Word processing program
				Chat		

Key ▮ Critical to task ▮ Helpful but not necessary

Figure 17.4 Simple grid for sofa-buying analysis highlights the relationship between tools and goals.

Towers

Towers, first proposed by interaction design consultant Indi Young, visually resemble grids. However, unlike grids, they do not necessarily represent linear steps in a process. Towers, instead, represent different *options* for action along the way and how people *feel* about them. They are what user experience designers James Kalbach and Paul Kahn call *alignment diagrams*—tools for seeing the intersection between what people want to do and the resources available to them (Figure 17.5).

In a tower diagram, each major section represents a high-level goal, laid out in chronological order from left to right. Thick vertical lines divide the goals. Within those major sections are towers of boxes, which represent conceptual groups of tasks. There's a horizontal line below the towers of tasks that represents the line between the user's experience and the tools, content, or features that support it. Each tool, content, or feature gets a box of its own.

Towers make gaps or negative experiences in tools (as for a workflow), content (as for a website), and functionality (for software) immediately visible. Towers can include many different people's or groups' attitudes toward an activity. Unlike scenarios, they do not necessarily take a single perspective. While new features can be added below towers with gaps, Young suggests that the first step

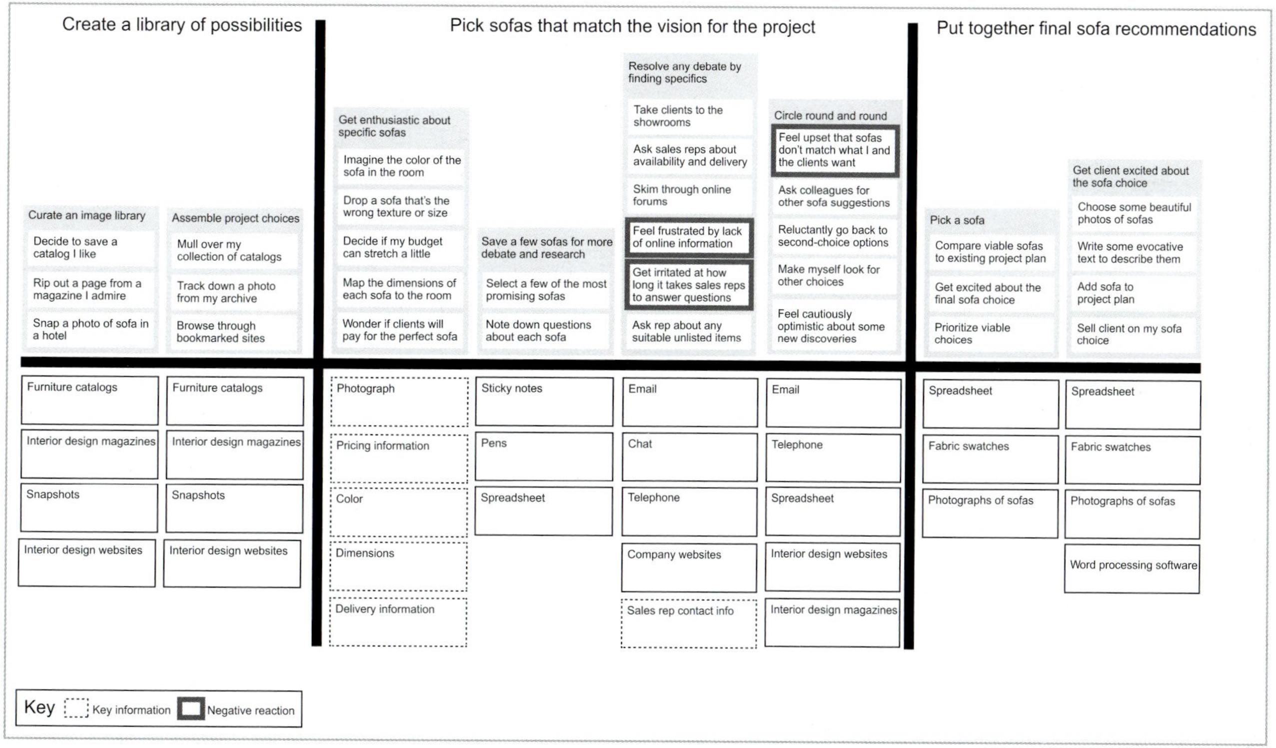

Figure 17.5 Towers representation for the sofa-buying analysis highlights pain points and key website content.

Tower-style representations began with Young's work on "mental models." See her book on the subject, Mental Models, for a more complete presentation of how to make and use these diagrams.

is to concentrate on goals: "Don't think about solving the problem; think about representing *what people are trying to accomplish* at each step." In order to make sure that the towers represent people's experience of an activity, Young advises using participants' own vocabulary. "It's not supposed to be clinical," she says.

Because they list every different option in the same task, tower-style representations tend to sprawl horizontally. When presenting a tower-style representation, it can help to print it out as several landscape-oriented pages taped together to form a long banner.

Mapping Processes

Task analysis typically follows individuals. If you are surveying activities that involve multiple people, systems, or businesses, process mapping is a better choice.

Process maps result from applying the task analysis approach to an entire business or organization. It's essentially a combination of several high-level task analyses. Unlike scenarios and task analyses, process maps incorporate not just the experience of a user but also the system activities and business processes necessary to support it. Process mapping has come to prominence in support of service design for activities such as banking that rely on multiple *touchpoints*, or opportunities for use. Checking one's bank balance on a mobile phone, for example, depends on the interaction of multiple components: interaction with a phone interface, authentication, the formation of a secure connection with the bank's server, and the retrieval of account information. From the user's perspective, this is as simple as selecting "see balance" and reading some numbers a few seconds later. From the bank's perspective, even retrieving a few numbers is the result of complex, interlocked processes.

The most well-known form of process map is a *swimlane diagram*. A swimlane diagram does just what you think: it visually distinguishes the tasks required of different actors by dividing them into separate "lanes." An actor, in this case, might be a person, an organization, a piece of software, a device—anything that is responsible for part of the activity that the diagram represents. Swimlanes resemble task analysis flowcharts—they visually represent decision points in sequences of tasks. However, unlike task analysis flowcharts, they emphasize how different actors must cooperate to accomplish a process. As such, they represent processes and tools—such as querying inventory management software—that may be invisible to the user or customer. This can be useful in demonstrating how business processes may be responsible for a poor user experience. For example, a swimlane diagram (Figure 17.6) for the sofa-buying analysis illustrates why sales reps might seem irritatingly slow in responding to questions: they may need information from a furniture product line specialist, who may be busy or slow in responding herself.

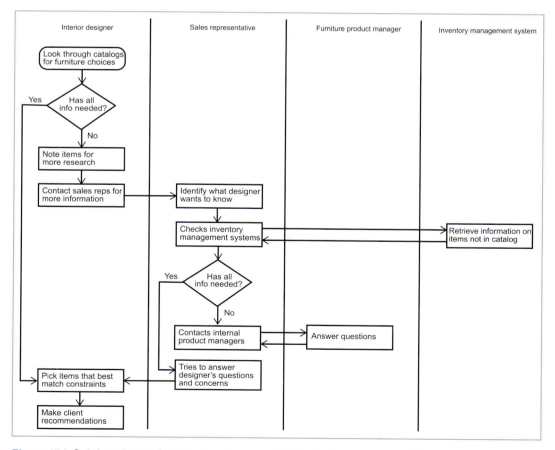

Figure 17.6 Swimlane diagram for the sofa-buying analysis highlights the work done by different actors.

Representing Systems: Experience Models

Sometimes the most important things your research uncovers are too complex to explain in a single story, or for that matter, in words alone. Say you want to present your findings about how several large organizations do business together, how a group of friends shares pictures and videos over time, or what happens during a shopping trip as a shopper moves through a store, looking at products and interacting with people and information systems. This is when you need to draw upon your information design skills (or those of a collaborator) and create an experience model.

By "experience model," we mean a diagrammatic presentation of *relationships* between people, organizations, product attributes, places, etc. Experience models, unlike scenarios or personas, aren't narratives. They're maps—either of the current experience or of a proposed improvement. Unlike personas, scenarios, and task analyses, experience models have no set format. They can organize relationships by spatial location, chronological order, cause-and-effect outcomes, affinity, or hierarchy. What defines an experience model is simply a focus on abstracting and simplifying the ways in which a group of people perceive the world.

Remember this principle: A map is not the territory. Your goal is to simplify your representation so that the features of greatest interest are most visible. Think of natural resource maps, the kind that global companies make to identify areas for profitable exploration. Ask yourself where the gold (that is, the design opportunity) lies for your organization. Then make a map that effectively marks that spot.

The spatial "customer journey" examples in Figures 17.7–17.10 were created by Lextant, a design research and user experience design firm. They demonstrate the advantages of creating an experience model: They let you organize and share rich research findings with a broad range of stakeholders, including the ones who will never read a long report or attend a two-hour presentation. They also give everyone a visual, memorable way to understand how a user's world works, so that they can apply their understanding when making everyday decisions about the product or service.

There are many possible approaches to experience modeling; a complete how-to is beyond the scope of this book. Dan Brown's Communicating Design *is a great introduction to the art.*

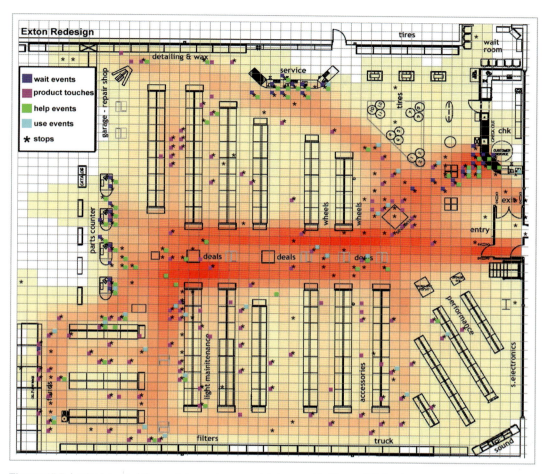

Figure 17.7 Lextant created the spatial experience models here and in Figure 17.8 for the Pep Boys Automotive store chain to visualize what researchers found when they observed customers shopping in a Pep Boys store with a new floor plan. This figure maps a composite "customer journey," showing where key events in the customers' shopping trips occurred. The findings demonstrated that Pep Boys' new store design and layout did not support certain customer goals and needs.

Making Experience Models

To make a model, you will need to take text and images from your research and synthesize them into a diagram. Because experience models can include so many different kinds of representations, there are no hard and fast rules for what should go into one.

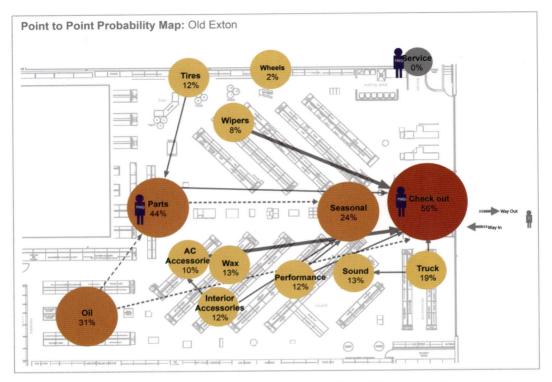

Figure 17.8 Lextant created the spatial experience models here and in Figure 17.7 for the Pep Boys Automotive store chain to visualize what researchers found when they observed customers shopping in a Pep Boys store with a new floor plan. This figure plots the most frequently taken paths throughout the store, showing the sequences and probability of a customer stop at each area.

Experience models are among the most demanding research outcomes because they require so much visual creativity.

Research Required for Experience Models

Typically, the type of research needed to build a robust experience model is qualitative research that captures multiple aspects of a user experience, such as physical and digital, short- and long-term, or the perspectives of different people on organizations. This information may be gathered through site visits (see Chapter 9) or in-depth interviews with many diverse participants (see Chapter 6). During

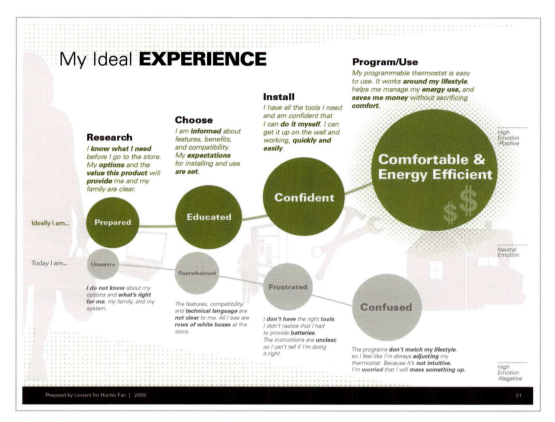

Figure 17.9 In this experience model, created for Hunter Fans, Lextant's researchers wanted to show the discrepancies between users' ideal experience of choosing and installing a home heating system and the experiences they had recently had. The diagram highlights the critical steps in the process; each step is annotated with a description of the user mindset researchers observed (below) and the way users wanted to feel (above).

quantitative and qualitative analysis (discussed in Chapters 12 and 15), you may have already found some relationships in the data. Those relationships are a good starting point as you begin to sketch.

Starting to Draw

Who doesn't get intimidated by a blank page? We certainly do. It helps to think of drawing as a way to work out your ideas, not just as a way to document finished ones. Despite what you may believe, no one ever works out an experience model fully before

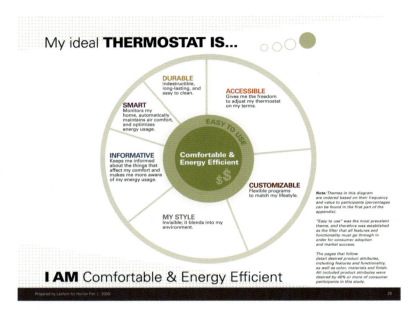

Figure 17.10 This model combines qualitative and quantitative data to show the ideal outcome of the activities in Figure 17.9, according to the same group of users. Each segment of the circle represents a theme expressed by users, with segment placement based on the percentage of users mentioning it and the level of importance they assigned to it. Since "Easy to Use" was the most prevalent theme, it is portrayed as a filter to be applied to all thermostat features.

drawing it. The process of drawing seems to be integral to thinking itself. The faster you get drawing, the faster you'll be thinking. So, to begin:

1. Get out the pencil and paper. You can move to a computer later. But starting with paper-based sketching can help you think creatively instead of accepting the default choices provided by your software.
2. List the main elements in the model. You will probably add and remove elements as you draw. But you can get a good sense of the scope of your model from an initial set of labels. Plus, doing something simple helps make that blank page less intimidating.

3. Take an item from that list, and write its name down on the page. Dan Roam calls this the "draw a circle and give it a name" step.

4. What other items on your list are related to the first one? Write down the name of another list item somewhere else on the page.

5. Next, sketch the relationship between your first and second items. Maybe there is an arrow going from one to the other, indicating causation. Maybe they should be overlapping circles, indicating shared attributes. Maybe they are both points on a spectrum. Chapter 15 presents many examples of conceptual relationships that you can draw from. Repeat the process until you have a diagram that makes sense. If you want, you can now take the diagram into a software program of your choice.

6. Now, get some feedback from someone you trust. Is the diagram telling the story of the data effectively? Have you missed anything important to the project? Integrate that feedback, and share again. Now do it again. And again. Making diagrams is an iterative process.

7. When you've got something you think is relatively solid, start experimenting! Start moving components around. Does repositioning change how you see the concepts? Try out a different organizing principle. If you have been working with circles, go for a quadrant system. You may find that different formats highlight different stories about the data.

8. Refine for effective communication. Just as you edit your text for sharing, edit your diagrams. Less, as they say, is more. Limit your use of different colors and typefaces. Remove any elements that are redundant or unnecessary to your main point. And, paradoxically, add more text. Don't assume that the point of your diagram is obvious. The Hunter Fan examples (Figures 17.9 and 17.10) use bold, single-word labels— but back them up with explanations in smaller type. As Dan Brown reminds us, "Label, label, label."

For more helpful tips on drawing and thinking, check out Dan Roam's Unfolding the Napkin: Solving Complex Problems.

Using Experience Models

Like personas, experience models are most useful when they are broadly shared, widely visible, and updated or replaced as projects and objectives change. But experience models can be trickier to share than task analyses, personas, and scenarios. Research stakeholders who are unfamiliar with how to interpret them may find dealing with the abstract concepts less engaging than hearing the stories in personas and scenarios.

Your experience model is more likely to influence design work if you introduce it to your clients in person, walking through it section by section. In that meeting:

- Explain how you made the model and describe the research findings it represents.
- Moderate a team discussion of the problems, gaps, and opportunities depicted in the model.
- Post a poster of your experience model in your team's work area. Consider creating "insets" or partial views of the model that you can use to guide design discussions that focus on certain aspects of the customer experience.

Putting It All Together

You don't have to keep the separate types of representations separate. Some of the most useful kinds of diagrams and models bring them together.

For example, take grids. Todd Zaki Warfel uses a grid format to ground feature prioritization in personas, scenarios, and task analysis (Figure 17.11). The persona forms the anchor for the entire grid, justifying its relevance. Each step in the task analysis forms one column along the top row of the grid. The scenario text, in the row below, explains and motivates each step. There are separate rows for pain points and motivations. Each set of proposed functionality (at the bottom, colored to indicate priority) is linked to research insights. What Zaki Warfel delivers to the client is not just one representation, but a mutually reinforcing set of research insights that convincingly underpins design proposals.

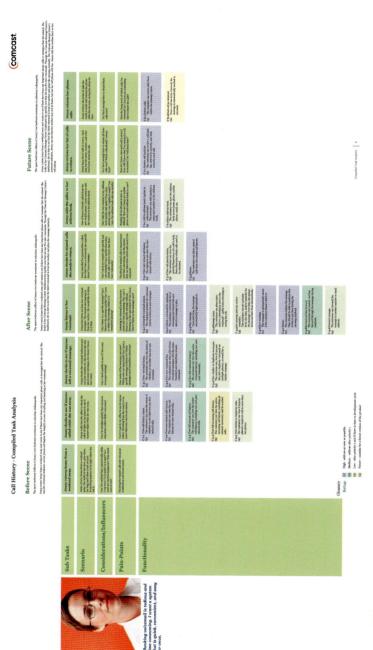

Figure 17.11 Scenario-based task analysis grid. Image courtesy of Todd Zaki Warfel. You can download this grid for your own use at http://zakiwarfel.com/dl/TaskGrid_Sample.pdf.

A Final Warning

One common mistake in research planning is to treat a research diagram or model as an end, not a means. People may come to you and ask for personas or for scenarios without having a real sense of how they will use them. Or perhaps you have just gotten used to delivering task analyses, because "that's how we always do it." Don't give in! As Dan Brown cautions in *Communicating Web Design*, "Choose activities for your project based on their ability to take you closer to an objective, not because you want to make a particular kind of output." Your job as a researcher is not just to deliver "as promised." It's also to negotiate with stakeholders when you believe that their business goals will be better served by a different kind of research outcome.

Similarly, the job of a researcher is not just to hand off a document and head home. The final goal of research is *action*, not awed contemplation of the brilliance of your insights. In the next chapter, we'll look at techniques for reporting that help move research deliverables into design processes.

CHAPTER 18
Reports, Presentations, and Workshops

Reports are the product of research. Like any product, they need to be useful to their audience in order to be successful. A good results report should consist of more than just a list of a product's problems; it should enable the development team to make changes to the product and avoid similar problems in the future. Structuring the presentation of results—in effect, designing their delivery—is one of the most important steps to making research useful, since the best research is useless if it's misunderstood or ignored.

The audience's needs determine the best way to present a given piece of research. It could be a simple email message or an elaborate 100-page report. It could be a phone call or a daylong presentation with highlight videos. It could be a bug database. Fortunately, the process is the same regardless of the complexity of the final product. In fact, much of the advice in this chapter is not unique to user experience research. It's true about nearly any business-oriented presentation. Whether it's a song-and-dance number or a short chant the steps to make it are pretty much identical. What varies is how long each step takes.

In the previous section, we talked about different kinds of diagrams and models that one might use to crystallize research insights. This chapter addresses how to structure and present the reports that contain them. Because written reports and in-person presentations are the two most prevalent methods of reporting results, this chapter will primarily focus on them. However, most of the ideas here can apply to any delivery medium.

Informal Reporting

Often, reporting doesn't involve a formal report. Simple projects, such as "guerilla" usability tests, can result in an email summary or a quick "stand-up" report in a status meeting. Email and verbal summaries are also useful for interim updates (usually weekly) over the course of the project. These "highlights" updates simplify the basic report structure into a few key points:

- What you did to generate the results
- The most important results
- Any upcoming research activities

The primary goal of these informal reports is to get research findings quickly to people making decisions. An important secondary goal, however, is to get research clients engaged with the process of research so that they are able to influence the research direction and feel more invested in the results.

Another way to keep your research clients involved in the research is to maintain an online repository of data and findings, such as a blog or a wiki. Instead of circulating as email, they remain on a central site. Stakeholders can comment directly on each interim post, keeping the discussion neatly archived and easy to find.

In reporting usability findings, you may find that a photograph or a screenshot tells the story of the results faster and with less ambiguity than words. Annotate photographs and screenshots with circles and arrows to indicate specific problems or successes.

Teams must make a commitment to maintaining and visiting online repositories in order to get value from them. There's no point to posting reports to a blog if no one ever reads it, and stakeholders will quickly stop visiting if new content rarely arrives. To make an online repository useful, contribute frequently and send emails reminding research stakeholders to visit.

Preparing and Presenting Formal Reports

However, a user research report is different from informational reports such as annual reports or white papers. Its main purpose is to help your stakeholders make decisions about their product or service: what needs fixing, what to add, what kind of product or service to build in the first place. It should address each of the key questions that motivated the research, and emphasize the findings that most urgently demand action.

User research reports tend to follow one of three genres:

- *Usability reports* document specific problems or successes in existing product interfaces.

- *Documentaries* present an overall portrait of how people use products and services. While acknowledging the complexity of experience, they focus attention on a few key observations to support strategic thinking.
- *Design springboards* lay out opportunities for product innovation. Less tightly focused than usability reports, but more tuned to concrete action than documentaries, springboards inspire design exploration around specific questions, audiences, or activities.

To choose between those genres, ask your stakeholders how they will use this research. What benefit do they expect to get from it?

Formal reports are not the only way your research can affect an organization, project, or service. Informal reports, as well as workshops and other forms of "socializing" the research, are also important. But by and large, many organizations insist upon reports as an *official* research output. They are, for many organizations, the main way that research findings circulate in organizations and have long-lasting effects. For many organizations a long, polished report demonstrates the rigor of your approach and the value of your contribution. Some research stakeholders *need* a long report to feel that your conclusions are justified and that the money and time spent on research was worth it. Even if you suspect that a workshop or other collaborative event will get your research more personal engagement from stakeholders, a formal report can still be a Big Deal.

Preparation

Preparing a report is different than analyzing the data. You should have the content of the report mostly complete before report writing begins. It can help to consider the format of the report beforehand, but you need to have the content in place before putting too much effort into figuring out how to present it.

Know Your Audience

An audience profile helps to establish what to present and how to present it. This doesn't have to be a formal profiling process, but establishing several things about the audience helps write a report that makes sense and that people want to use. Here are several questions to ask:

- *Who is getting the report?* The composition of the report's audience will change its emphasis. CEOs will certainly need a shorter and more high-level report than the QA team. If one specific person has the power or influence to determine what gets done with the findings, take his or her needs into account.
- *What are their goals?* How are they going to use the information? Sometimes all they need is a list of problems to fix. In other cases, the audience may need the research to help them justify more resources. Goals can change quickly in some organizations, which is why you should check with your stakeholders while preparing the report.
- *What do they know?* What's the level of technical sophistication in the group? This applies not just to any technology under consideration but also the methods you are employing. If they've never been involved in user experience research, you may need to explain the reasoning behind your methods. *Remember that your research is likely just one of many forms of evidence they rely on*. For example, you may be presenting the results of a usability test. If you're talking to product managers, chances are they spend lots of time looking at usage data. If you present a finding that contradicts what they might conclude from usage data, you need to be ready to defend that finding and explain why it is valid or significant.
- *What do they need to know?* What decisions do they need to make, and how will your findings help them? The primary purpose of the report is to answer the study's initial questions, but other information may be important. Research may have shifted the project's focus or revealed a secondary class of information. If it's important to the project, you need to communicate it. For example, when doing a contextual inquiry series for a web development guide for kids, it became apparent that the parents' level of technical sophistication wasn't much greater than that of the kids. This insight was outside the original research focus on the kids, but it was valuable to know.

- *What are they expecting?* Anticipating the audience's reactions to the information in a report helps you structure an effective presentation. If the VP of Product Development believes that the product is basically ready to launch, she will expect a list of quick fixes. When user testing reveals systemic problems, the evidence backing up the resulting report must be watertight and the unexpected revelations phrased diplomatically. In fact, successfully presenting any conclusions that violate research stakeholders' current beliefs requires strong, believable evidence. However, if the findings mostly echo the team's current beliefs, any differences in your report will need less justification.

Know Your Process

Even the most extensive and rigorous research has limitations. When considering how to present findings, keep them in mind. Acknowledging any limitations in your knowledge helps the audience understand the results, believe in them, and act on the recommendations.

If parts of your audience will have very different needs, experience, and expectations—for example, you have to deliver information to nontechnical executives and the core programming staff—consider making different reports and separating the presentations. That way, parts of the audience won't feel either lost or patronized, and the presenters will have to field fewer questions.

- *What are the data collection problems?* Mention any limitations and potential distortions in the data collection methods upfront ("We were only able to speak to one of the two user audiences"), but justify your choices ("We chose to focus on one user group because we believe that, given our limited resources, they will give us the best feedback"). If you recognize potential flaws, address them before your audience members bring them up.
- *What are the limitations of the analysis?* There are many ways to analyze a given data set. Your analysis will only use a few. Acknowledge the strengths and limitations of the chosen analysis method. For example, although tabulating survey results is fast and easy, it may not reveal as much as cross-tabulating the results of several of the variables. But cross-tabulation is trickier and requires more responses to be valid.
- *Where is the bias?* The recruiting process, the participants' perspective, the research conditions, the analyst's experience— each can subtly skew the information collection process.

Pretending that these sources of bias do not matter will only undermine your conclusions. Identifying and minimizing sources of bias will only strengthen the credibility of your analysis.

Creating Formal Reports

In some cases, such as a simple usability study, it may be clear what actions should result. In others, your stakeholders will need to talk through the research together and come up with different ideas to address the challenges you have identified. In the former case, you can use your report structure as the basis for your presentation. In the latter case, it can be helpful to hold an interactive workshop as a follow-up to the presentation. In this kind of presentation, you define goals (perhaps with the help of a leading stakeholder) and use research findings to help generate potential responses. Ideally, you should have worked out which type of presentation will be needed at the start of the project, but if not, communicate as soon as you know and negotiate the right presentation.

Pick a Format

Before writing the report, discuss the format with its audience. Different organizations and industries will have different expectations for the report format. Some organizations demand a paper report with illustrations and a fancy cover, with a secondary presentation file. Others expect comprehensive slideware files that support in-person presentations, and that stakeholders will later share with others in the organization, or excerpt for their own presentations. Increasingly, short video files function as accompanying "illustrations" to slideware reports or even serve as standalone documentation.

With a general format chosen, arrange the findings to suit the audience. "Nice-to-know" information is included only in the most complete version of the report; "should know" is in the general report, while "must know" is the kind of stuff that's put in email to the project lead when time is critical. Pull quotations or video clips to support or elaborate on the findings.

Some stakeholders, especially small companies and teams, prefer to keep reporting simple rather than generate multiple documents that developers must review and reference. For small, focused studies where time is short, consider presenting results by walking the team through your report. Make this easier by including links to supporting material in the body of the document in the executive summary. You could also create the report in the form of a slide deck with the "must-know" material up front and the complete, detailed findings tucked away in an appendix. For the presentation, use your presentation software's "hide" feature to hide the detailed slides while keeping them available to address specific questions that come up.

Basic Research Report Organization

The following structure applies to all of the user research report models. See Chapter 11 for a more detailed example of a usability report.

Executive Summary

The executive summary tells the whole story in broad strokes (Figure 18.1). It begins with a brief statement of the most important observation and then gives a short summary of any other findings. If the reader only gets through the first paragraph, what would you want understood?

Procedure

The next section in the report summarizes the main research activities. In a slide presentation, this section may be compressed to one or two slides, as in Figure 18.2 and Figure 18.3. A long-form text document may include much more detailed explanation, as in the following examples from a usability report. These provide complete background on the research methods. They describe how the

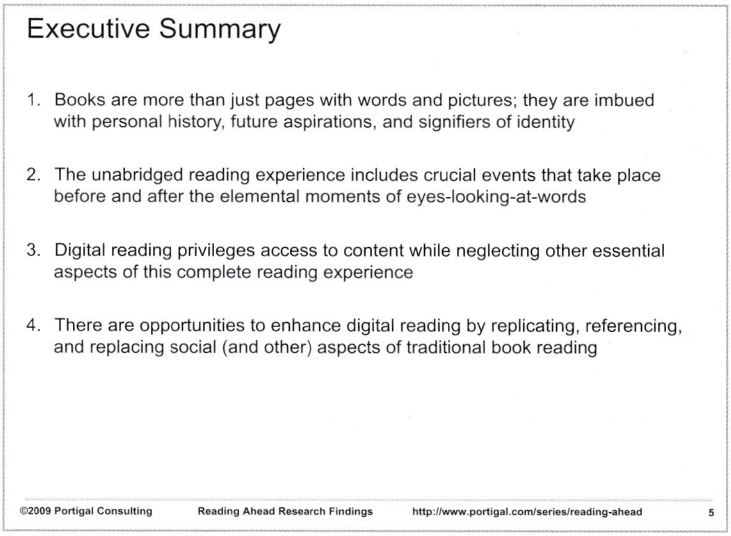

Figure 18.1 An executive summary slide from *Reading Ahead,* a strategic research project on the future of books and reading by Portigal Consulting. The entire presentation is available at www.portigal.com/series/reading-ahead/.

Project Overview

- Objective: Explore the evolution of reading and books and develop product, service, and business opportunities

- Recruited 6 active readers (3 books, 3 Kindle) in the San Francisco Bay Area

- Photo-diaries: self-documentation of reading and environments

- In-depth contextual interviews (with participatory design component)

- Synthesis into findings, recommendations, and opportunities (this document!)

- **Ongoing:** dialog with different audiences

©2009 Portigal Consulting   Reading Ahead Research Findings   http://www.portigal.com/series/reading-ahead   11

Figure 18.2 Procedures slide in the *Reading Ahead* presentation.

team recruited participants, collected and analyzed the data, and where the limits of this type of research lie.

- *Recruiting.* How did you define a profile for participants? How did you find people to participate? What criteria did you use?

> We invited six people with electronic greeting card experience to evaluate the Webcard interface and comment on a prototype of Gift Bucks. They were selected from Webcard's user lists based on their recent usage of the site (they had to have used it in the past month), their online shopping activity (they had to have bought a present in the last two months), and their availability to come into the Webcard offices during working hours on January 20th and 21st.

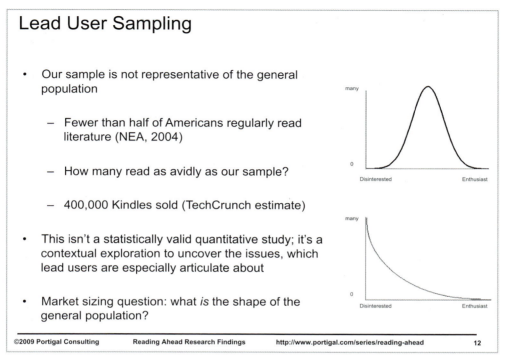

Figure 18.3 Limits slide in the *Reading Ahead* presentation.

- *Data collection.* What research techniques did you use? Where did they take place? How long did they take? How many participants did they involve? What kinds of questions did you ask, or tasks did you have them perform? How did you document the activities (video recording, notes, etc.)? If you used any standard metrics, such as error rates or time to task completion, this is the place to explain them.

Each 90-minute interview began with a series of questions about the evaluators' web usage, their experiences with online shopping, and their experiences with online greeting services. The moderator then showed them the current Webcard site and asked for their immediate impressions as they moved through it. After looking at it for a few minutes, the moderator asked them to search for an Easter greeting card for a friend. After several minutes of searching the moderator asked them to return to the main page and go through the interface thoroughly, discussing every element on the front door and most of the catalog and personalization page elements. Their next task was to find a card with a picture of San Francisco. After spending several minutes on this task, they were shown a prototype of the card personalization interface with Gift Bucks attached and asked to discuss the new interface elements found therein.

The moderator concluded the interviews with an exercise to help the evaluators summarize their views of the product and brainstorm on additional features.

- *Analysis.* What kinds of tools or methods did you use to analyze the data?

All of the interviews were video recorded. The recordings were examined in detail for trends in participants' behaviors, beliefs, and statements. Partial transcripts were made of interesting and/or illustrative quotations. The observations were then organized and grouped. These groups provided the material from which more general trends were distilled.

- *Limits.* Are there any important qualifications to make about your procedures? Did any recruiting decisions introduce systematic bias? Are there any questions your data cannot answer? Don't hide any concerns, but instead explain why they exist, and any efforts you have taken to mitigate problems. In the case of the *Reading Ahead* project (Figure 18.3), the authors use illustrations to explain the limits of lead user sampling for their study and why they adopted the technique.

If the audience is well versed in the relevant techniques, you may only need to sketch them in a couple of short sentences or bullet points. If your audience is unfamiliar with user research or with the technique you used, a more thorough description (such as the ones above) might be appropriate. In any case, paragraphs of text are more suited to a multipage written report; avoid too much text in slides.

Remember, your audience will be more interested in the results than the methods. A photograph of a usability test in progress, the video recording setup for an interview, or a wall covered in sticky notes can convey your methods faster and more vividly than pages of text. Add appendices to the back of the report for important details such as the discussion guide, the in-depth recruiting strategy, or explanations of statistical analysis choices.

Participant Profiles

Describing participants reinforces the reality of the research to people who did not observe it and provides context for interpreting their statements. Although everyone knows that research participants are real people, details bring home the participants' perspectives, their differences, and—most importantly—the authenticity of their experience. There should at least be a table summarizing how the participants fit the recruiting profile, or there can be a more extensive description with a photograph, as in Figure 18.4.

To protect your participants' privacy and confidentiality, be extremely careful when revealing any personal information—especially names—in a report. When recruiting people from the general public who will likely never participate in research about this product again, it's usually okay to use their first names in the report. However, when reporting on people who are in-house (or who are friends and family of people in-house), it's often safest to remove all identifying information. Rename participants as "P1," "P2," etc.

> Likewise, be wary when creating highlight videos with people who viewers may recognize. If someone is likely to be recognized, they should generally not be shown and a transcript of their comments be used instead.

Main Themes

After establishing the context, present your observations as directly and succinctly as possible, avoiding jargon (Figure 18.5). Whether reporting on a usability test, a diary study, or an in-home visit, each theme or observation will have three main components:

1. A brief descriptive label
2. A slightly longer summary (if needed)
3. Supporting evidence (photographs, videos, statistics, or quotations)

Erica

- **Erica** is 28 and lives by herself in an apartment in San Francisco
- She described growing up without a lot of money but in a house where there were "walls of bookshelves"
- She had been planning to open a cookbook store, until the recent economic slump. She's working now as an office manager at a software startup and regrouping
- Erica talked about buying certain books just because she likes them as objects: *"I love books. I almost like books more than reading."*

©2009 Portigal Consulting   Reading Ahead Research Findings   http://www.portigal.com/series/reading-ahead   16

Figure 18.4 A participant profile from the *Reading Ahead* presentation.

If the report covers multiple research activities, you will need to include multiple procedure/profile sections. However, it is up to you whether to combine findings from all the activities into a single thematic group or to present by activity.

Research Outcomes

Targeted recommendations may appear next to specific findings, as in usability reports. However, broader recommendations that emerge from several different themes can appear in their own section at the end (as in Figure 18.6). This can include models and diagrams such as personas, scenarios, and experience models.

Conclusions

You may not need a conclusion if you have a research outcomes section. However, a conclusion can be a good place to discuss the larger issues raised by the research or future work. It should help the audience pull back from the details and understand the product and research process as a whole. In a longer written report, it can help the audience move from specific fixes or recommendations to strategic implications, as in the following example:

Books enable *unplugging*

- For some people books are a refuge: a way to unplug and get away from the ubiquity of computers, screens, and digital information

- In contrast to the scanning and multi-tasking typical of computer use, books afford a slower, more focused experience

- *Erica: "I have a very hard time reading…sustaining it without doing something else. It's a problem I recognize and have been trying to break. I could be sitting on the couch and feel this need to check my email"*

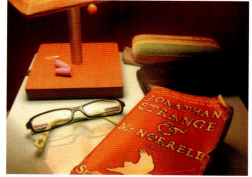

Erica's bedside table

©2009 Portigal Consulting   Reading Ahead Research Findings   http://www.portigal.com/series/reading-ahead   54

Figure 18.5 Thematic finding slide from the *Reading Ahead* presentation.

Conclusion

The Webcard service is considered useful and generally well done by its audience.

Although people's inability to find specific cards was ameliorated by their light attachment to any given card, this does not eliminate the problems with the search functionality and the information structure. As people's performance in the task to find a San Francisco-themed card shows, whole sections of the site are inaccessible because of an information structure that doesn't match people's expectations.

We recommend using card sorting and observational methods to research users' expectations and "natural" organizational schemes and simplifying the search process by using a full-text search interface and carefully chosen keywords.

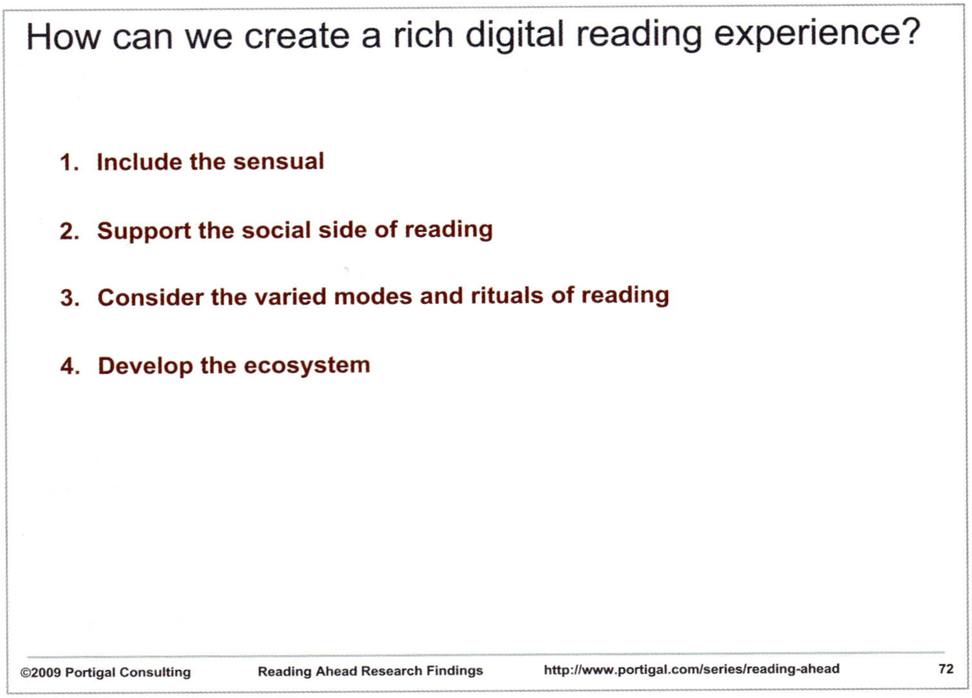

How can we create a rich digital reading experience?

1. **Include the sensual**

2. **Support the social side of reading**

3. **Consider the varied modes and rituals of reading**

4. **Develop the ecosystem**

©2009 Portigal Consulting   Reading Ahead Research Findings   http://www.portigal.com/series/reading-ahead   72

Figure 18.6 Overview slide for design strategy recommendations in the *Reading Ahead* presentation.

Appendices

If you have additional information that is of value to your stake-holders but unrelated to the main points of the report, put it in an appendix at the end. It is tempting to include every scrap of information that you've collected in the presentation, just in case it'll be of use to the readers, but don't inundate the audience.

"Newspaper Style"
Regardless of the format, structure all reports like newspaper stories. News journalists assume that some people will only have time to read the first couple of paragraphs, some will read a page or two, some will skim the whole thing, and some will closely read every word. Each of these audiences needs to be satisfied by the report's contents.

In classic newspaper style, the first sentence tells the most important fact ("The stock market rose dramatically today in spite of signs of weak consumer confidence," for example). The first paragraph tells the basic facts, the next couple of paragraphs elaborate on several key elements mentioned in the first paragraph, and the rest of the story provides background, finishing with a historical summary of the story.

Thus, when writing a report, never "save the best for last." Save the least important for last.

Testing Reports

As with any product, test reports before launching them. Maybe the development staff wants screenshots with problem areas explicitly marked. Maybe they would like the problems broken out by department or by user market. Maybe they need a different emphasis for the report to be useful at all.

Show a couple of people from the reports' audience a "beta" version of the report. A 10- to 15-minute conversation after they've had a day or two to look at the report reveals a lot about how well it addresses the audience's needs. Does it cover the topics that they had expected? Does it prioritize the results appropriately? Do they expect other staff members to have any issues with it?

The Presentation

When you gathered research questions in the planning phase, you documented what mattered to whom. Now you have the opportunity to show that you have addressed everyone's questions. Don't be afraid to customize a presentation for specific people. People in different functional roles within an organization will have different goals, concerns, and requirements for user research.

In general, when presenting to a specialized audience, lead with the overall "must know" information, but spend most of your time on issues specific to the group. If the findings suggest a problem with something that this group feels they "own" (such as system performance for engineers or messaging for marketers), leave time for discussion directly following your presentation of this issue: They will ask you lots of questions and will want to start hashing out the issue among themselves.

However, presentations are more than just readings of the report. The way results are presented is nearly as important as the report that summarizes them, and maybe more important. The complexity of a product's user experience is often difficult to understand from a description, and functionality details are often easier to explain with a demonstration than with a text description.

We cannot do justice to the art of creating and delivering effective presentations in this book. From high school speech classes to motivational executive speeches, there is a lot of presentation advice in the world. That said, a couple of points are particularly appropriate to user research presentations:

- *Prepare your audience.* Before talking about specifics, put the audience into a mindset that helps them value your contribution. Remind them why this research was undertaken, that is, the area in which they want to improve or the question they are trying to answer. Then show *how* your findings address these issues and questions. If you present to this audience infrequently or they are inexperienced with user research, you may want to explain how certain methods work, and why they are credible.
- *Pick your themes and supporting evidence carefully.* What do you have really great, compelling evidence for? What will be new or unexpected? Imagine asking your audience to guess the answer to one of your research questions. Would they guess correctly? Sometimes when user research is presented, the results make so much "common sense" that stakeholders can come to believe they are not learning anything new. The right themes, illustrated by real examples, can shed new light and keep the audience's attention.
- *Use real examples.* Showing beats out telling. The closer the audience gets to seeing the exact behavior or attitude, the better. A video of several people saying the same thing or making the same mistake over and over is much more effective than a written description. When that's not possible,

a quick demo of the problem using the actual product is also effective. If a demo isn't possible, then try a description using actual participant names and quotations. For example, "Jim spent three minutes examining the home page before he gave up and said that there must not be a search interface. When it was pointed out to him, he spent another minute apologizing for being 'so stupid,' despite the moderator's statements that it wasn't his fault." Any such description or demo, however, should not last more than a minute or two.

- *Emphasize users' perspectives.* Whenever people start creating solutions, or even when they try to understand the nature of problems, they naturally begin with their own perspective. Since developers are almost never the same people as end users, this can lead to erroneous or distorted conclusions. Use quotes and other evidence to demonstrate differences between the user's perspective and that of the team, such as the users' own statements about their goals for the product or pictures of where and how they typically use it.

- *Use professional terminology sparingly,* and only after defining it. When people hear a lot of words they don't understand, they can feel out of touch or patronized (or both). Sometimes, however, it's useful for the audience to know a term for a technical concept because it's important in understanding the report. A single sentence defining information architecture as "the discipline of categorizing and organizing information in a way that makes sense to a given audience" can make it much more palatable. In addition, know your audience's terminology and highlight differences between their definition and that used in the report. A group of radio editors, for example, used the word "headline" to refer to the title of an important breaking news story, while the designers used it to refer to a text presentation style. Before researchers realized the terminology difference, they couldn't figure out why both groups found the research findings confusing.

- *Use numbers carefully.* Humans have a tendency to see numbers as objective and absolute, even when told they're not. Numbers, histograms, and pie charts look good, but you should avoid them unless backed by sufficient data. Don't hide the fact that your results come from a small number of users. For example, report that "four out of six users" did something, rather than "most." Ask yourself: does the statistic genuinely clarify your observation, or just make it seem more authoritative? If it's the latter, restate it or skip it.

- *Leave one-third of your time for questions.* If a presentation ends early and there are no questions, no one will complain. But they will get upset if they have questions and no time to ask them. Anticipating what an audience is going to ask and producing "canned" answers can save you trouble. Along with the findings themselves, be prepared to answer questions about the research design and how the user research findings relate to other information about customer experience, such as usage data, market research, and industry reports.

Using Video

Video highlights can be useful for reports. For usability research, they detail the mechanics of how people use the product and demonstrate the severity of problems. For task analysis, video clips can illustrate unexpected details of an important process. And for field visits, video clips provide a sense of the atmosphere that it's hard to convey any other way. People who couldn't make it to the presentation can easily review and share videos online.

Some tips for making video clips that people want to watch and share:

- *Label each segment* with a succinct description of the point you want to make. For example, a usability report might include the label: "Problems finding a search box." Never assume that your video evidence will be self-evident. If there are key phrases you want your audience to notice, you can add that text to the video as well.
- *Make video clips short,* and use video selectively. Video demands a lot of attention and can't be skimmed like text. You don't want to bore or distract people from the point you're trying to make. Break up video clips for each main point into separate files so that people only need to watch

what interests them. Keep the files under three minutes long unless absolutely necessary.

- And, most importantly, *tell a story.* Even when illustrating a single problem or type of action, you can give your clips a sense of narrative through sequencing and titles. For example, let's say one of your participants struggled for five minutes to complete a task in a usability test before giving up. You want to highlight his difficulties—but five minutes of video is too long. Instead, you select three significant moments: the initial optimism and first difficulty; annoyance at about two minutes in; then the final capitulation at five minutes. You string the segments together, labeling each with the time. The final video clip is less than a minute long, but effectively conveys five minutes of growing frustration.

Most user research reports don't require complicated, high-end video editing software. All you need is a lightweight application that allows you to cut clips, sequence them, and overlay some titles at key points. There are many such programs available for free or little cost, often bundled with new computers, such as Mac's iMovie or Windows Movie Maker.

You will need a way to share your video clips with your research stakeholders. If you are creating slides, embed links to video into the presentation (as in Figure 18.2) so that they are easily accessible during the presentation. Sharing video clips online is a little more difficult. There are many free services for sharing video, but you will need to make sure that your clients are comfortable with having their business information stored on a commercial service. You will also need to make sure you can limit access to the videos as needed while still making it easy for research stakeholders to view them.

Common Problems in Presenting Research

Researchers often face very similar unproductive or negative reactions to presentations. As the presenter, if you haven't anticipated these reactions, you can find yourself stammering and hedging uncomfortably. Happily, a little advance preparation will reduce a lot of the on-the-spot consternation.

- *"This is not statistically significant!"* Often heard when presenting qualitative results from focus groups, usability tests, or interviews. It's true, these research methods do not usually produce statistically significant results...but that's not their purpose. The goal of qualitative research is to uncover likely problems or design opportunities, understand their causes, and explain them credibly. It's not about conclusively establishing the precise frequency of problems within the population at large. Another way to counter this objection is by showing that different kinds of research—say usability tests and log file analysis—provide different insights into the same behavior. Taken together, these research techniques are more useful than just a "statistically significant" method alone.

- *Triggering internal conflicts.* Sometimes, user research reveals more about the company than about the users. For example, consider a car company website. The online sales group wants to increase the company's direct sales effort, while the dealer support group wants to appease car dealers' fears of competition from manufacturer direct sales. Designers compromise by dividing the interface between direct sales and dealers, but the split interface confuses usability test participants. In that situation, even mentioning the confusion may provoke heated debate. If you don't work for the company, it's best to stay out of the fight in order to serve as an impartial resource to both camps. If you're part of the company, it's especially important to defend the impartiality of the research lest you be seen as partisan. Defend your findings and clarify the facts of your research, but let the two groups decide their implications.

- *"This user is stupid."* This belief comes in a variety of flavors: "This user is unsophisticated," "Well, this person doesn't have the right amount of experience," etc. It is of course possible that one of your participants was unusually slow to grasp a concept—but if your findings come from careful analysis, they will rest on evidence from multiple participants. And if you recruited correctly, the participants will have fit the team's stated target audience profile. Remind your audience that they agreed to the target audience profile at the beginning of the project and point out that all the participants fit the target audience profile. The team must respect participants' responses as those of legitimate members of the target audience, or the team needs to explicitly redefine their target audience.

- *"Participant X is not our market."* Similarly, if the target audience was rigorously defined at the start of the research and the recruiting followed that definition, then Participant X is a member of the target audience. If an audience member feels otherwise, then ask for specific reasons. Statements like "Participant X just doesn't seem like our kind of customer" are a good opportunity to explore how actual participants matching the target audience might differ from the imagined "our kind of customer."

- *"User X did Y; therefore, everyone must do Y"* (often followed by a variation of "Told you so!"). This is overgeneralization. As Carolyn Snyder, principal at Snyder Consulting, says, "From one data point, you can extrapolate in any direction." One user's behavior (or even several users' behavior) could be interesting and could point to a potential problem. *But it does not represent the experiences of the population at large.* A single data point cannot resolve an internal debate about the prevalence of a certain phenomenon (but it may be a good starting point for a future project).

- *"They all hated the green, so we need to make it all white, like Amazon."* People, especially solution-oriented people, often tend to assume that addressing a simple complaint solves the underlying problem. Treat the disease, not the symptom. Steer discussions away from too-early solutions in order to explore underlying issues.

- *Stealth problems.* Some problematic aspects of users' experience are invisible to both users and developers because they are so fundamental to the product. Take the experience of a for-profit website intended to streamline the process of donating money to nonprofit organizations. Research participants universally disliked having a for-profit company make money from their charitable giving. That rejection haunted every usability evaluation, even though participants rarely mentioned it explicitly. Nevertheless, any readability or navigation problems paled in comparison to participants' distaste for the company's entire

Workshops often involve an idea generation technique called brainstorming. Design firm IDEO's Human Centered Design Toolkit is one good source for brainstorming instructions and suggestions. It's available at www.ideo.com/ work/human-centered-design-toolkit/.

At least some of the attendees should have specific skills that support each activity. If you want to produce concept sketches, some of your attendees should know how to draw. If you want to generate insights for business strategy, you need some planners. If the workshop should solve specific product problems, you need at least some people with in-depth knowledge of the product. And if you put workshop participants into small groups, each group should have at least one expert. Don't do an activity that makes everyone in the room feel unqualified.

pursuing. One way to do this is to include prioritization exercises.

- *Document your results.* Documentation will of course be useful if your company decides to build any of the concepts produced in the workshop. Even if that doesn't happen, people who didn't attend will want to know the outcomes. Photograph not just the final results (sketches, whiteboard drawings, lists, etc.) but also people in action.

Common Interpretation Session Activities

The basic structure of almost all research-driven workshops is simple: A presentation of research findings kicks off a working session in which stakeholders come up with ideas to address the issues documented in the research and then sketch or prototype those ideas. Then the group categorizes or prioritizes those ideas. The possible variations are infinite. The idea is to choreograph your attendee's path from user needs and problems to ideas and solutions. Here are a number of ideas to start you thinking about your own workshops.

Presentation Styles

Rather than give a lecture-style presentation, share your findings with a workshop group in a more immersive way. You might do this by putting posters on the wall that show your procedures and findings, and letting the group literally walk through the study. Alternatively, you might tell stories about users' interactions and experiences that illustrate your findings.

More ambitiously, you might convey your findings more experientially. You can ask attendees to handle objects or listen to sound recordings from site visits. You can design games or playful activities related to the research topic that elicit feelings of joy or frustration similar to those felt by participants. You can even arrange furniture to mimic the configuration of critical spaces—such as workplaces or bedrooms—in order to demonstrate very cramped or very spacious settings of use.

Identify Business Implications of Research Insights

After the presentation of your research, split people into small groups. If you have personas, assign one persona to each group. If you are working with a thematically organized report, have each group take a theme or an opportunity. Then ask them to list as many ways they can imagine in which supporting that persona's needs, or filling each gap, or exploiting each opportunity might change how they do business.

Once ideas have started to fly, it's time to record them for communication to others. Your method of doing this will depend on the business you are in, the participants involved, and their comfort with "hands-on" work. You can list them, draw them, or even plan to act them out. Then each group presents their ideas to all the workshop participants.

Cultivate Empathy

There are many ways to help workshop attendees identify with the experiences of customers or users. Personas (discussed in Chapter 17) are a very popular way to create sympathetic research representations. But personas on their own do not guarantee emotional connections. Splitting workshop participants into small groups and then having the groups brainstorm ways to support the needs of each persona is one common way to engage research stakeholders with the needs of customers.

You can induce empathy more directly by creating activities for research stakeholders that allow them to feel something like the physical sensations research participants experience. This is particularly useful when the target audience faces physical hurdles that the development team does not. Invite the team to use their product while wearing clothing or tools that are characteristic of users' jobs or life conditions (e.g., a cane, high-heeled shoes, a low-end phone from two years ago, or a giant book-filled backpack). You can even rent fake "pregnancy bellies" or hire facilitators who specialize in simulating the physical effects of partial blindness and reduced dexterity. *Feeling* difficulty reading or walking can be more effective in building empathy than a thousand quotations or photographs.

One way to encourage creativity is to turn your session into a game. Put people into teams. Limit how much time they have. Give them an extreme scenario and ask them to respond. Award prizes to the team that comes up with the most ideas, or the wildest ideas.

Ways to Collaboratively Solve Problems

In order to move teams from research to action, most interpretation sessions will have some problem-solving components. The question is how to most effectively use your insights as a springboard for productive discussions. We've already discussed how to use personas as springboards—but you certainly don't need personas to start talking about solutions. Usability evaluations lend themselves most directly to solution-oriented discussions: you've already presented the most important problems and perhaps even made some initial recommendations for solutions. Andrea has helped teams make progress in as little as an hour—15 minutes to present high level usability findings and 45 minutes to talk, sketch, and brainstorm solutions.

Don't expect these workshops to produce definitive solutions or huge breakthroughs, and make sure that attendees don't expect that either. Instead, aim to help people come up with fresh ideas about the problems or opportunities in the research.

Extending the Reach of Research

What happens after the presentation? The need for the research doesn't go away after you leave the room. Some researchers work permanently with product teams, which gives them more opportunities to keep the insights alive. But many others work as consultants—either in detached research groups within an organization or as external consultants. In either case, researchers have fewer opportunities to support decision making.

Here are three strategies for providing ongoing support, even when you can't be physically present:

- *Augment your deliverables.* Stuffing every last bit of data into your main reports will overwhelm your audience. But leaving behind a little extra information can help answer later questions. Often, reports include protocol details in appendices. But you can also hand over project archives: transcripts of interviews and all the raw data from interviews, video, and photographs (with the permission of your participants, of course!).
- *Encourage research ownership.* Help your clients feel comfortable putting the research findings to work on their own. You can

do this throughout the process by involving them in research and analysis activities. If it's not obvious how the research findings lead to action, consider arranging a workshop to help them get started.

- *Follow up.* Check back with your research clients periodically about how they're using (or not using) the information. That way, you can answer nagging questions, get a sense of any potential future projects, and learn how your research is helping—or what you could do differently next time.

Conclusion

Understanding the desires and expectations of the presentation audience is not very different from understanding the needs of a product's audience. The media are different, but the issues are the same. In general, the best strategy to overcome people's doubts and answer their questions is to understand them, anticipate their needs, and work with them to find solutions.

Sometimes, this can be in the form of expectation setting, but mostly it's in preparation. Knowing your audience's agendas and questions is more than just good showmanship—it's critical to moving research findings from optional information to indispensable tool.

CHAPTER 19

Creating a User-Centered Corporate Culture

Throughout this book we have argued that observing and engaging with your users are essential to making a popular, compelling, and profitable product or service. But let's face it: User research is just one of many, many inputs that shape what an organization makes and does. How much does it currently matter to your company? That's a question you should try to answer honestly. We have tried to show how to do the best possible research and how to deliver it most effectively; the remaining challenge is to make your organization into one that values high-quality research, and where critical decisions are made based on what that research reveals. This goes beyond what you, or even your team, can do all on your own. It's a matter of corporate culture.

A user-centered development process often demands that developers shift perspectives and spend time walking in their users' shoes. This fundamental shift takes time and happens differently in different organizations. The International Standards Organization has defined several levels of organizational "usability maturity": At the lowest level, the company does not recognize it might have any problem with usability, while at the highest level, user-centered design is "embedded in...development strategy to ensure usability." Most companies, of course, fall somewhere in between.

With examples of companies succeeding through design and user focus in front of them, many organizations delcare that they value user-centered design and user research. A CEO might express this in terms of a core company value, or point to another company to emulate, such as the LEGO Group or Zappos. But organizations still find it difficult in practice to prioritize research when they need to ship a product on schedule or to spend money on user experience research that could be used to advertise or market the product. Rather than make the case anew for each project, we recommend that you focus on changing the development process to make user research and design an expected step, and give the people who do research and design a clear place at the table in decision making.

Work with the Current Process

When you begin each research project, you ideally go through a planning and definition process, as we describe in Chapter 4, when you get some context on the product or service your research is about. Why is it being developed? What does it do? You meet the stakeholders and sponsors who care about it and understand their priorities and success criteria for it.

If you continue to work with the same organization across projects (whether as a consultant or in-house), you have the opportunity to learn these things about the organization itself. When you take time to do this "internal discovery," you learn how employees want development to work, how it *actually* works, and how you can help it work better.

You also get better at identifying key stakeholders for any given research project: those who are clearly interested, who *should* be interested, those who oppose it, and those who are likely to help it succeed. They may be people who are already on your team, or they may be in adjacent departments. They may be top executives, opinionated engineers, or the salespeople who must represent your product to customers.

Even if a high-up executive wants the whole company to be user-centered tomorrow, speedy transitions are almost impossible. These practices stabilize in one project and one team at a time. In the same way, taking methods onboard wholesale almost never works either, because organizations have different expectations, resources, and relationships. Instead, making user research work for your company means trying something, observing the impact, reflecting on how it could work better next time, and doing it again.

Start Small and Scale Up

Starting small often works best. If they fail, small projects are not seen as severe setbacks. When they succeed, they can be used as leverage for larger projects. Moreover, they educate everyone in the methods, goals, and expectations of user experience research and user-centered design.

How small is small? Initial targets should be short-term, doable, and straightforward. The ideal project revises or adds a feature with few dependencies, so that changes are achievable in a short time frame and the impact is easy to observe. For example, if you were working on a website, a good first project might be to investigate the usability of an underperforming registration experience and identify changes that might increase the number or rate of sign-ups. If there isn't a small project readily available, you might choose a project on which you can start early, integrating user research from day one into an initiative that is separate enough from the rest of the company's efforts that you have license to do things a different way. Finally, you might start at the grassroots level, getting one small team to adopt user-centered processes in a way that can serve as an example for others.

John Shiple, former director of user experience for BigStep.com, suggests building user experience research into website home page redesigns. Home pages and landing pages are redesigned on a regular basis and they serve as entryways and billboards for the company. They are important parts of the user experience, but their design often affects presentation more than functionality, so unsuccessful designs can be rolled back easily. This gives their redesign scope and importance but without the weight of core functionality redesign.

Prepare for Failure

Prepare to stumble as you start bringing user-focused techniques in-house. You may do the wrong research at the wrong time with the wrong part of the product. You may ask all the wrong questions in all the wrong ways. You may be asked to do something that's inappropriate, but you have to do it anyway. The research results may be useless to the development staff, or they may completely ignore it. Management may ask for hard numbers that are impossible to produce.

This is one of the reasons to start small. This is also an occasion to be philosophical. Bad research happens to everyone, but every piece of user research, no matter how flawed, provides insight, even if it's only into how to structure the research better next time. Recognizing failure greatly reduces the likelihood of such failure in the future. Set appropriate expectations for yourself and for those who may be receiving the results, use problems to make further plans, get feedback from your interview subjects, and examine how well the research is going even as it's still underway.

Involve Stakeholders

A heuristic evaluation—or, thoughtful criticism—often does not convince partners that such and such sucks. A live event—with donuts—behind one-way glass can. That's sad, but true.
—Dave Hendry, Assistant Professor, University of Washington Information School

Making people observe and participate in research is one of the most effective ways to sell them on its value and effectiveness. Observing users failing to use a product is an incredibly powerful experience. It communicates to the observers that their perspective may be entirely unlike the way their users think.

The development team and key stakeholders need to be involved in research, but in different ways.

The Stakeholders

Those who make decisions about a product need to see the value of research firsthand. The best way to accomplish that is to make them watch it happen. They don't have to actively participate, but if they can be in the same room (or observing remotely) while people struggle, then listen to the discussions that these struggles inspire in the development team, they are much more likely to support such efforts in the future.

The Development Team

Those who are directly involved need to see the research process and its results. For them, involvement in the research should include direct participation in developing the research goals, creating research prototypes, and analyzing the results. Once they've participated, they are much more apt to appreciate the process and to integrate it into their future plans.

Including everyone in every bit of research is often difficult, however, and developers need to be directed toward research that will be most meaningful for them. For example, people from marketing and business development are more likely to be interested in ideas that speak to broad, strategic issues with the product. These are often embodied in focus groups or contextual research studies and less so in usability tests. Technical writers and trainers benefit from knowing which concepts people want explained better, issues that are revealed during task analysis or usability testing interviews. Engineering and interaction design absolutely need to be included in usability testing, but participating in field visits may not be as immediately useful to them (that said, these two groups should probably be in as much research as possible, since they are in the best position to apply bottom-to-top knowledge of the user experience).

Respect your development team. Just as there's a tendency in developers to write off users who don't understand their software as "stupid," there's a tendency in user experience researchers to write off developers who don't understand user-centered design processes as "stupid" or at least "clueless." Take an active part in development, explain processes, and listen for suggestions. If a development team seems clueless at first, it's surprising how quickly they appear to wise up when engaged as partners in a research project.

Interaction designer Jeff Veen described the reaction he got from one company's staff to the idea of user research. "To the engineers, usability was a set of handcuffs that I was distributing; to the designers, it was marketing." Jeff's solution was to turn research into an event. He made it clear that something special was happening to the company and to the developers: that management was listening to them and really looking carefully at their product. He first arranged for the delivery schedule to be loosened, giving the developers more breathing room and alleviating their apprehension that this process was going to add extra work that they wouldn't be able to do. Then he invited all of them to watch the usability research in a comfortable space, with all meals included. As they all watched the interviews together, Jeff analyzed the test for them, emphasizing the importance of certain behaviors and putting the others in context. He also encouraged the developers to discuss the product. After a while, they noticed that they were debating functionality in terms of specific users and their statements, rather than first principles or opinions.

Make Research Visible

Don't wait until the end of a study to share your findings. Report as you go, enlisting your stakeholders to help you communicate if necessary. Create deliverables that are visually and conceptually engaging and that can be shared easily, even among people who did not attend the research and presentations. Of course, if you have involved the team and shared short interim updates, both the findings and your process will be all the more accessible.

When you have research findings, put them in front of people. For example, if you once had ten minutes with a VP, request a similar amount of time after every piece of research on a regular basis, presenting the highlights of the research once a month. Even though she may not be interested in the specifics of each research project, the stream of interesting tidbits of information will be a useful reminder of the process and its value. Schedule lunchtime seminars on user-centered design and invite people in from outside your company to talk about successful projects. Buy some pizza. Having an outside voice discussing situations similar to those your group is encountering can be quite convincing.

You might also look for opportunities to share your work outside the company. Demonstrating your successes (with company permission, of course) can enhance the company's prestige in their industry and may attract new customers.

Measure Your Impact

Don't just use metrics in your research. Remember to measure the effectiveness of your research program as a whole. In an ideal world, your products and processes will be so improved that it's unnecessary to convince anyone that user research and user-centered design are valuable, but in most cases you will need to be able to demonstrate the effectiveness of these practices. Even when everyone notices improvements, organizations need some measurement to determine just how much change has occurred and to set goals for the future. See Chapter 16 for how to identify the product metrics the company currently cares about, and consider looking beyond those, to metrics that speak to the company's operations.

Pricing Usability

The ideas in this section are heavily influenced by Cost Justifying Usability, *edited by Randolph G. Bias and Deborah Mayhew. It is a much more thorough and subtle presentation of the issues involved in pricing user experience changes than can be included here.*

Using metrics to calculate return on investment (ROI) is very convincing, but notoriously difficult. Many factors simultaneously affect the financial success of a product, so it's often impossible to tease out the effects of user experience changes from the accumulated effects of other changes.

That said, a solid case for bottom-line financial benefits is the most convincing argument for implementing and continuing a user-centered design process. On the web this is somewhat easier than for consumer electronics, for example, where many changes may happen simultaneously with the release of a new version of a product. E-commerce sites have it the easiest. Their metrics are quickly convertible to revenue:

- *Visitor-to-buyer conversion* directly measures how many visitors eventually purchase something (where "eventually" may mean within three months of their first visit, or some such time window).
- *Basket size* is the size of the average lump purchase.
- *Basket abandonment* is a measure of how many people started the purchasing process and never completed it. Multiplied by basket size, this produces a measure of lost revenue.

Each of these measures is a reasonably straightforward way of showing that changes to the site have made it more or less profitable.

Other kinds of services, for example, those who sell advertising or disseminate information to employees, require different measures. Since salaried staff answer customer support calls and email, reducing the number of support calls and email can translate to direct savings in terms of staff reduction. However, support is a relatively minor cost. Reducing it generally increases the bottom line insignificantly. What's important is to find ways of measuring increases in revenue because a product was developed in a user-centered way.

For example, take the redesign of a news website to make it easier to find content. The average clickstream grows from 1.2 pages to 1.5 pages, which represents a 25% increase in page views, which translates to a proportional increase in advertising revenue. Seems pretty cut and dried. But say a marketing campaign launches at the same time. Both the usability and marketing groups can claim that their effort was responsible for the increased revenue. To justify the user experience perspective and separate it from marketing, estimate the impact of usability and its ROI. This creates a formula that can spark a discussion about the relative effects of advertising and usability, but at least the discussion can be on a (relatively) even plane.

Here's an example of how the argument for the ROI of user experience versus marketing might go.

Recently, our site underwent a redesign that resulted in increased page views and advertising revenue. This came at the same time as a marketing campaign encouraging people to visit the site.

Our site analytics tell us that the average length of a session was 1.2 pages for the 8-week period before the redesign. This means that people were primarily looking at the home page, with roughly 20% of the people looking at two or more pages (very few people looked at more than four).

Usability testing showed that users had a lot of trouble finding content that was not on the home page. One of the goals of the redesign was to enable them to find such content more easily.

For the 4 weeks after the redesign, the average clickstream was 1.5 pages, a 25% increase in per-session pages and pageviews. The marketing campaign certainly contributed to this increase, but how much was due to increased usability of the site? If we suppose that 30% of the increase was due to the greater ease with which people could find content, this implies that 7.5% of the increase in pageviews is a direct result of a more usable site.

Using the average number of monthly pageviews from the past year (1.5 million) and our standard revenue share per click of $0.02, this implies a monthly increase in revenue of $1125. If the marketing effort was responsible for getting people to the site, but the new design was responsible for all the additional clicks, the added accessibility would have been responsible for $3750.00 of the increase in monthly revenue.

However, deep use of the site is different than just visiting the front door and has an additional effect on revenue. The revenue per click for subsections is $0.016. At 30% effectiveness, this would imply an increase of $1800 in revenue per month, $21,600 per year, or roughly 10% of all revenue.

Our costs consisted of 60 hours of personnel time at approximately $75/hour, or $4500 plus $500 in incentive and equipment fees. Thus, the total cost to the company was approximately $5000. When compared to the annual return this represents a 270% to 330% return on investment at the end of the first year.

In some cases the ROI may be purely internal. If good user research streamlines the development process by reducing the need for postlaunch revisions, it could actually be creating considerable savings to the company that does not affect direct revenue. Comparing the cost of revisions or delays in a development cycle that used user-centered techniques to one that did not could yield to a useful measurement of "internal ROI."

Build Long-Term Value

You need to be stubborn, committed, and shrewd, but know when to back off and when to barge into the senior VP's office.
—Chauncey Wilson, senior user experience researcher

As you do more research projects, look for ways to leverage and demonstrate the value of accumulated research. As the expert on your research "body of knowledge" and on the users themselves, you can add value by answering questions that come up on a day-to-day basis and by preventing the reintroduction of problems identified in previous research. Sometimes, the response to research will be lukewarm. Reports can sit unread on managers' desks or be discounted by engineers who see insufficient scientific rigor in them. In these situations, continuing the research is especially important, showing that results are real, valuable, and consistent.

What If It's Just Too Difficult?

None of this stuff is easy, but what if the entrenched corporate culture just resists your efforts to integrate user research? What do you do then?

First, identify the nature of the resistance. Resistance comes in two primary forms: momentum and hostility.

People fall into old habits easily. User-centered design takes time, energy, and commitment. Doing things "the old way" is almost always going to be easier and may seem like a more efficient way of doing things. "Well, if we just did this the old way, we could do it in three weeks. You want us to do a month of research first? That'll just make us miss our deadline even more!" Using near-term efficiency as a pretext for rejecting long-term thinking will lead to more inefficiency over time. Gut-level decisions made in the "old school" fashion are much more likely to ultimately create more work in fixing avoidable mistakes.

The way to counter momentum is to build speed in a different direction. As described above, a slow introduction of user experience research techniques can be effective when coupled with an internal "marketing campaign" documenting the process's effects on the product and the company. Likewise, an executive commitment to revamping the whole development process can be effective, although it requires more resources and commitment than some companies are willing to expend. Large changes in direction can't happen overnight, though: They take time and a commitment to incremental advances.

Hostility is more difficult to resolve. In certain cases, developers find users threatening. They call users "lusers," describe the process of making usable products as making them "idiot proof," and approach their users' demands or misunderstandings with derision. Such statements betray an attitude toward the product that's somewhere between arrogance and insecurity. Unfortunately, when hostility is especially irrational and obstinate there's little that can be done except to focus your efforts on the more rational stakeholders on the team.

However, direct exposure to users can help convince the doubtful. At first, seeing users fail at something can confirm the doubter's

Avoid research paralysis. When user-centered processes start becoming popular and the development team has bought into them, there's a tendency to want to make all changes based on user research. This is an admirable ideal, but it's generally impractical and can cause development to grind to a halt.

Don't get distracted by research and forget the product. It's okay to make decisions without first asking people. Just don't make all your decisions that way.

worst fears: that people are profoundly different and alien. The experience can feel really uncomfortable, but it brings home many of the core ideas. Extended exposure almost always reveals that a products' users aren't idiots. They just see the world differently from the developers, and their problems and concerns may be easier to alleviate than the developers think. In some ways an aggressive challenge can allow for a more radical, more rapid change in mindset than a program of slow subterfuge. Sometimes, that challenge doesn't work. But there's no way to discover whether the hostility can be resolved without addressing it through a simple, small project.

Following and Leading

As new product development becomes globalized, companies used to leading on technology find that they have an ever-shorter window to establish market presence before their innovative new product or service becomes a low-price commodity. Increasingly, companies like these are turning to user experience as a proven differentiator. There are examples of companies in every sector that have successfully used user experience research and design to create profitable products they would not have developed otherwise. And simply put, the best way to learn what "great" really means is to learn it from users.

One of Google's first principles is "Follow the users and all else will follow." But as you incorporate research-driven, user-centered design, something unexpected happens. You begin to know your users so well that you can sometimes anticipate what they might want. By understanding how they act and how they think about the problems you are trying to help them solve, you can get a feel for what they will adopt and what they won't. Knowing that you can count on users' feedback, help, and collaboration allows you to experiment with bolder ideas, consider a wider range of solutions, or take risks more confidently than you might otherwise. When user experience is truly part of your corporate DNA, you can be a leading company in every sense.

References

References used in multiple chapters are in the General References section; otherwise, you will find references divided by chapter.

General References
Goodwin, K. (2009). *Designing for the Digital Age: How to Create Human-Centered Products and Services*. New York, NY: John Wiley and Sons.
Wasson, C. (2000). Ethnography in the field of design. *Human Organization*, 59(4), 377–388.

1. Introduction
British Design Council. (n.d). Eleven Lessons: Managing Design at LEGO. Retrieved from http://www.designcouncil.org.uk/Case-studies/LEGO/.
Greene, J. (2010). *Design Is How It Works: How the Smartest Companies Turn Products into Icons*. New York, NY: Portfolio Hardcover.
Janssen, H. (2009, Feb. 23). Social Media Helps Lego Connect with Users. *Ericsson Telecom Report*. Retrieved from Internet Archive website: http://web.archive.org/web/20101006225654/http://www.ericsson.com/ericsson/corpinfo/publications/telecomreport/archive/2009/social-media/article1.shtml.
Koetzier, W. (2009). *Innovation: A Priority for Growth in the Aftermath of the Downturn*. Retrieved from Accenture website: http://www.accenture.com/us-en/Pages/insight-innovation-priority-growth-aftermath-downturn-summary.aspx.
McKee, J. (2009). *Diving into LEGO's Strategy Behind Connecting Their Amazing Network of Fans*. [Video] Retrieved from http://vimeo.com/11937815.
Wieners, B. (2011, Dec. 14). Lego Is for Girls, *Businessweek*. Retrieved from. http://www.businessweek.com/magazine/lego-is-for-girls-12142011.html.

3. Balancing Needs through Iterative Development
Boehm, B. (1988). A spiral model of software development and enhancement. *Computer*, 21(5), 61–72. doi:10.1109/2.59.
Norman, D. (2002). *The Design of Everyday Things*. New York, NY: Basic Books.
Sinha, R. (2005, April 3). Open Source Usability: The Birth of a Movement. [Blog post] Retrieved from http://rashmisinha.com/2005/04/03/open-source-usability-the-birth-of-a-movement/.

4. Research Planning

Ries, E., & Blank, S. (2009). The Lean Startup: Low Burn by Design Not Crisis. [Video] Retrieved from http://www.slideshare.net/startuplessonslearned/lean-startup-presentation-to-maples-investments-by-steve-blank-and-eric-ries-presentation.

5. Competitive Research

Goto, K., & Cotler, E. (2003). *Web ReDesign 2.0: Workflow That Works* (2nd ed.). Berkeley, CA: New Riders.

Hawley, M. (n.d.). A Visual Approach to Competitive Reviews. Retrieved from Mad*Pow website: http://madpow.com/Insights/WhitePapers/A-Visual-Approach-to-Competitive-Reviews.aspx.

6. Universal Tools: Recruiting and Interviewing

Bottomore, T. B., & Rubel, M. (Eds.). (1956). *Karl Marx: Selected Writings in Sociology and Social Philosophy*. New York: McGraw-Hill.

7. Focus Groups

Greenbaum, T. (1998). *The Handbook for Focus Group Research* (2nd ed.). Thousand Oaks, CA: Sage Publications.

Krueger, R. A. (1988). *Focus Groups: A Practical Guide for Applied Research* (3rd ed.). Thousand Oaks, CA: Sage Publications.

Morgan, D. L. (1996). *Focus Groups as Qualitative Research* (2nd ed.). Qualitative Research Methods Series 16, Thousand Oaks, CA: Sage Publications.

8. More Than Words: Object-Based Techniques

Adams, P. (2007). Communication Mapping: Understanding Anyone's Social Network in 60 Minutes. In *Proceedings of the 2007 Conference on Designing for User eXperiences*. Chicago, Illinois, USA: DUX 2007. doi:10.1145/1389908.1389918.

Adams, P. (2010). *The Real Life Social Network v2*. [Presentation] Retrieved from http://www.slideshare.net/padday/the-real-life-social-network-v2.

Brewer, W. F., & Nakamura, G.V. (1984). *The Nature and Function of Schemas (Center for the Study of Reading Technical Report 325)*. Available at the University of Illinois website: http://www.ideals.illinois.edu/handle/2142/17542.

Hasbrouck, J. (2007, Feb.). Mapping the Digital Home: Making Cultural Sense of Domestic Space and Place. *Intel Technology Journal*. Retrieved from http://www.intel.com/technology/itj/2007/v11i1/s1-mapping/1-sidebar.htm.

Sanders, E. (2000). Generative Tools for Co Designing. In S. A.R. Scrivener, L. J. Ball, & A. Woodcock (Eds.), *Collaborative Design*. London, UK: Springer-Verlag. Retrieved from http://www.maketools.com/articles-papers/GenerativeToolsforCoDesiging_Sanders_00.pdf.

Sleeswijk Visser, F., Stappers, P. J., van der Lugt, R., & Sanders, E. B.N. (2005). Contextmapping: Experiences from practice. *CoDesign*, 1(2), 119–149. Retrieved from http://www.maketools.com/articles-papers/Contextmapping_SleeswijkVisseretal_05.pdf.

Spenser, D. (2010). *Card Sorting: Designing Usable Categories*. New York, NY: Rosenfeld Media.

Stappers, P. J., Sleeswijk Visser, F., & Keller, I. (2003). Mapping the Experiential Context of Product Use: Generative Techniques Beyond Questions and Observations. 6th Asian Design Conference, Tsukuba: Asian Society for Science of Design. doi: 10.1.1.111.195.

9. Field Visits: Learning from Observation

Agar, M. H. (1996). *The Professional Stranger: An Informal Introduction to Ethnography* (2nd ed.). New York, NY: Academic Press.

Bean, J. (2008). *Beyond Walking With Video: Co-Creating Representation*. In Ethnographic Praxis in Industry Conference Proceedings, 104–115. doi: 10.1111/j.1559-8918.2008.tb00099.x.

Beyer, H., & Holtzblatt, K. (1998). *Contextual Design: Defining Customer-Centered Systems*. Waltham, MA: Morgan Kaufmann.

ElBoghdady, D. (2002, Feb. 24). Naked Truth Meets Market Research. *The Washington Post*, H1, H4–H5.

Ikeya, N., Vinkhuyzen, E., Whalen, J., & Yamauchi, Y. (2007). Teaching organizational ethnography. In *Ethnographic Praxis in Industry Conference Proceedings*, 270–282. doi: 10.1111/j.1559-8918.2007.tb00082.x

Jordan, B., & Dalal, B. (2006). Persuasive encounters: Ethnography in the corporation. *Field Methods*, 18(4), 359–381.

Reichenbach, L., & Wesolkowska, M. (2008). All That Is Seen and Unseen: The Physical Environment as Informant. In *Ethnographic Praxis in Industry Conference Proceedings*, 160–174. doi: 10.1111/j.1559-8918.2008.tb00103.x

schraefel, m. c., et al. (2004). Making tea: Iterative design through analogy. In *Proceedings of Designing Interactive Systems: Processes, Practices, Methods, and Techniques*, 49–58. New York, NY, USA: ACM. doi: 10.1145/1013115.1013124.

10. Diary Studies

Arbitron. 2007). *The Arbitron Radio Listening Diary*. Retrieved from http://www.arbitron.com/diary/home.htm.

Bolger, N., Davis, A., & Rafaeli, E. (2003). Diary methods: Capturing life as it is lived. *Annual Review of Psychology*, 54(1), 579–616.

Carter, S., & Mankoff, J. (2005). When Participants Do the Capturing: The Role of Media in Diary Studies. In *Proceedings of the SIGCHI Conference on Human Factors in Computing Systems*, 899–908. New York, NY, USA: ACM. doi: 10.1145/1054972.1055098.

Gaver, B., Dunne, T., & Pacenti, E. (1999). Design: Cultural probes. *interactions*, 6(1), 21–29. doi: 10.1145/291224.291235.

Khalil, C. (2009). *The new digital ethnographer's toolkit: Capturing a participant's lifestream*. [Video] Retrieved from http://www.slideshare.net/chris_khalil/the-new-digital-ethnographers-toolkit-capturing-a-participants-lifestream.

Reiman, J. (1993). The Diary Study: A Workplace-Oriented Research Tool to Guide Laboratory Efforts. In *Proceedings of the INTERACT '93 and CHI '93 Conference on Human Factors in Computing Systems*, 321–326. New York, NY, USA: ACM. doi: 10.1145/169059.169255.

11. Usability Tests

Nielsen, J. (1994). *Guerrilla HCI: Using Discount Usability Engineering to Penetrate the Intimidation Barrier.* Available from Jakob Nielsen's website: www.useit.com/papers/guerrilla_hci.html.

Nielsen, J. (1994). *Usability Engineering.* San Francisco, CA: Morgan Kaufmann.

Nielsen, J., & Pernice, K. (2009). Eyetracking Methodology: 65 Guidelines for How to Conduct and Evaluate Usability Studies Using Eyetracking. Available from Jakob Nielsen's website: http://www.useit.com/eyetracking/methodology/.

Lindgaard, G., & Chattratichart, J. (2007). Usability Testing: What Have We Overlooked? In *Proceedings of the SIGCHI Conference on Human Factors in Computing Systems,* 1415–1424. New York, NY, USA: ACM Press. doi: 10.1145/1240624.1240839.

Rubin, J. (1994). *Handbook of Usability Testing.* New York, NY: John Wiley & Sons.

12. Surveys

Babbie, E. R. (1990). *Survey Research Methods* (2nd ed.). Belmont, CA: Wadsworth Publishing.

Dillman, D. A. (1999). *Mail and Internet Surveys* (2nd ed.). New York, NY: John Wiley & Sons.

Grossnickle, J., & Raskin, O. (2000). *The Handbook of Online Marketing Research.* New York, NY: McGraw-Hill.

Hargittai, E. (2005). Survey measures of web-oriented digital literacy. *Soc. Sci. Comput. Rev.*, 23(3), 371–379. doi: 10.1177/0894439305275911.

Kirk, R. E. (1998). *Statistics: An Introduction.* Belmont, CA: Wadsworth Publishing.

Moore, D. S. (2001). *Statistics: Concepts and Controversies* (5th ed.). New York, NY: W.H. Freeman.

Rosenthal, R., & Rosnow, R. L. (1991). *Essentials of Behavioral Research: Methods and Data Analysis* (2nd ed.). New York, NY: McGraw-Hill.

Tufte, E. (2001). *The Visual Display of Quantitative Information.* Cheshire, CT: Graphics Press.

13. Global and Cross-Cultural Research

Chipchase, J. (2011, Dec. 18). Connections. Connectors. [Blog post] Retrieved from Future Perfect blog: http://janchipchase.com/2011/12/thenew-dawn/.

Chipchase, J. (2011, June 28). Field Research in the Age of Data Servitude. [Blog post] Retrieved from Future Perfect blog: http://janchipchase.com/2011/06/field-research-in-the-age-of-data-servitude/.

Churchill, E., Dray, S., Elliott, A., Larvie, P., & Siegel, D. (2010). Addressing Challenges in Doing International Field Research. In *Extended of the Proceedings of the SIGCHI Conference on Human Factors in Computing Systems,* 3127–3130. New York, NY, USA: ACM. doi: 10.1145/1753846.1753932.

Scheyvens, R., & Storey, D. (2003). *Development Fieldwork: A Practical Guide.* Thousand Oaks, CA: Sage Publications.

Tylor, E. (2010). (1871). *Primitive Culture.* (Vol. 1). Cambridge, UK: Cambridge University Press.

United States Census Bureau. (2012). *State and County Quickfacts: San Francisco County, California.* Retrieved from http://quickfacts.census.gov/qfd/states/06/06075.html.

Vattuone, M. (2011, Aug. 17). A Native Language Approach. [Blog post] Retrieved from Bolt Peters website: http://boltpeters.com/blog/a-native-language-approach/.

15. Analyzing Qualitative Data

Beckman, S. L., & Barry, M. (2007). Innovation as a learning process: Embedding design thinking. *California Management Review,* 50(1), 25–56.

Saffer, D. (2009). *Designing for Interaction: Creating Innovative Applications and Devices* (2nd ed.). Berkeley, CA: New Riders.

Sharp, H., Rogers, Y., & Preece, J. (2007). *Interaction Design: Beyond Human-Computer Interaction* (2nd ed.). New York, NY: John Wiley and Sons.

Strauss, A., & Corbin, J. M. (1998). *Basics of Qualitative Research: Techniques and Procedures for Developing Grounded Theory* (2nd ed.). Thousand Oaks, CA: Sage Publications.

Lakoff, G., & Johnson, M. (2003). *Metaphors We Live By* (2nd ed.). Chicago, IL: University of Chicago Press.

16. Automatically Gathered Information: Usage Data and Customer Feedback

Cheshire, T. (2012, Jan. 5). Test. Test. Test: How wooga Turned the Games Business into a Science. *Wired UK.* Retrieved from: http://www.wired.co.uk/magazine/archive/2012/01/features/test-test-test.

Elms, T. (1999). A Web Statistics Primer. Retrieved from the Internet Archive: http://web.archive.org/web/200012160545/http://builder.cnet.com/Servers/Statistics/.

Klein, L. Ries, E. (2011, Jan. 18). UX, Design and Food on the Table. [Blog post]. Retrieved from Startup Lessons Learned website: http://www.startuplessons learned/2011/01/case-study-ux-design-and-food-on-table-html.

Muller, T. (2011, Feb. 17). Giant Steps Are What You Take, Walking in Your Customers' Shoes. [Blog post]. Retrieved from Get Satisfaction Social Studies website: http://blog.getsatisfaction.com/2011/02/17/giant-steps-are-what-you-take-walking-in-your-customers-shoes/.

17. Research into Action: Representing Insights

Adlin, T., & Pruitt, J. (2010). *The Essential Persona Lifecycle: Your Guide to Building and Using Personas.* Waltham, MA: Morgan Kaufman.

Carroll, J. (2003). *Making Use: Scenario-Based Design of Human-Computer Interactions.* Cambridge, MA: The MIT Press.

Cooper, A. (1999). *The Inmates Are Running the Asylum.* Indianapolis, IN: SAMS.

Cooper, A., Reimann, R., & Cronin, D. (2007). *About Face 3: The Essentials of Interaction Design.* New York, NY: John Wiley.

Goodwin, K. (2005, Jan. 13). Perfecting Your Personas. Retrieved from User Interface Engineering website: http://www.uie.com/articles/perfecting_personas/.

Kalbach, J., & Kahn, P. (2011). Locating Value with Alignment Diagrams. *Parsons Journal for Information Mapping* 3(2). Available from http://piim.newschool.ed u/journal/issues/2011/02/.

Kirwan, B., & Ainsworth, L. K. (1992). *A Guide to Task Analysis*. London, UK: Taylor and Francis.

Roam, D. (2009). *Unfolding the Napkin: Solving Complex Problems*. New York, NY: Portfolio.

Young, I. (2008). *Mental Models: Aligning Design Strategy with Human Behavior*. New York, NY: Rosenfeld Media.

18. Creating a User-Centered Corporate Culture

Bias, R. B., & Mayhew, D. (Eds.). (1994). *Cost Justifying Usability: An Update for the Internet Age* (2nd ed.). Waltham, MA: Morgan Kaufman.

Index

Note: Page numbers with "f" denote figures; "t" tables; "b" boxes.